Shojo Beat

The Story of SAIUNKOKU

Art by
Kairi Yura

Story by
Sai Yukino

Volume 1
Contents

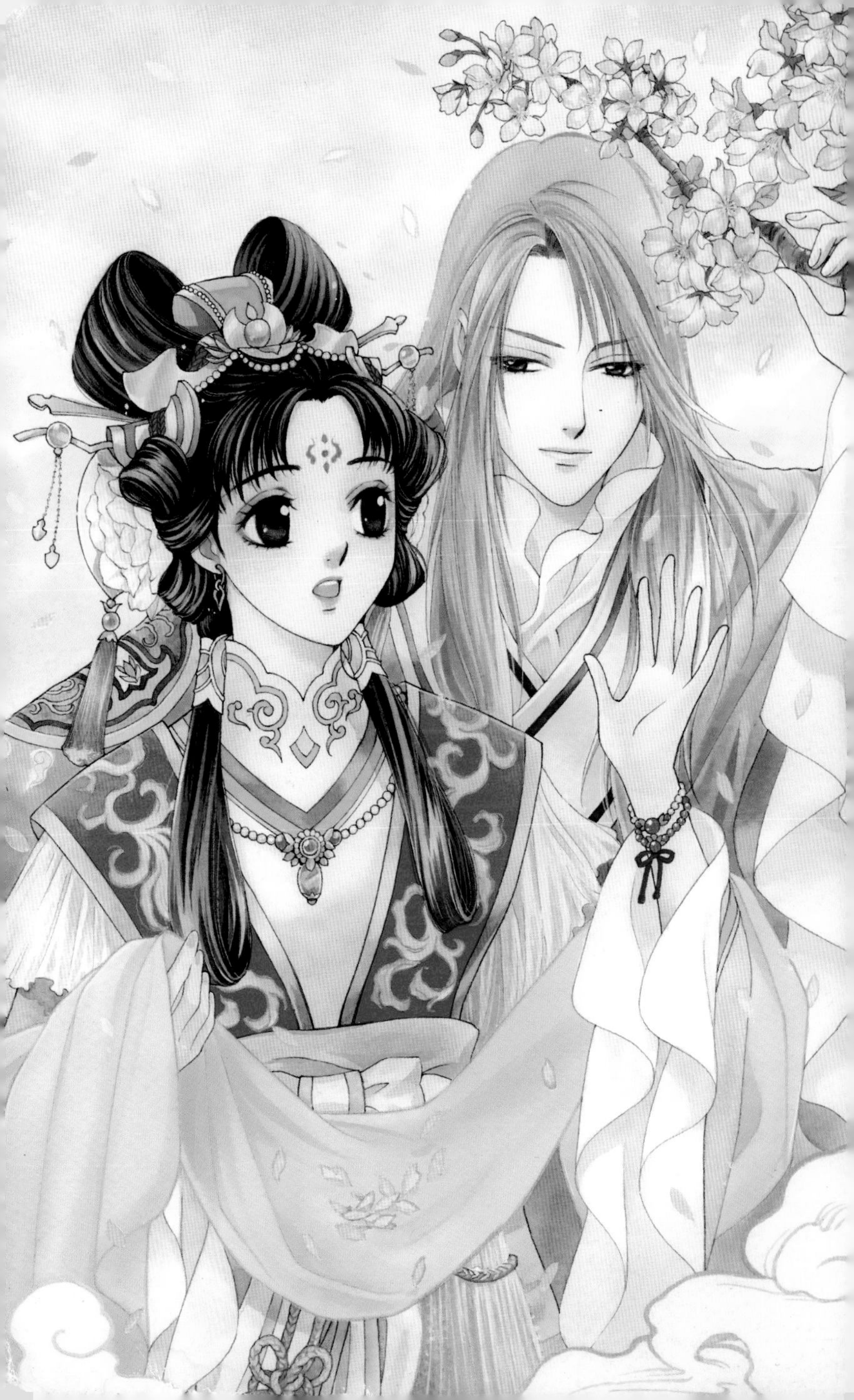

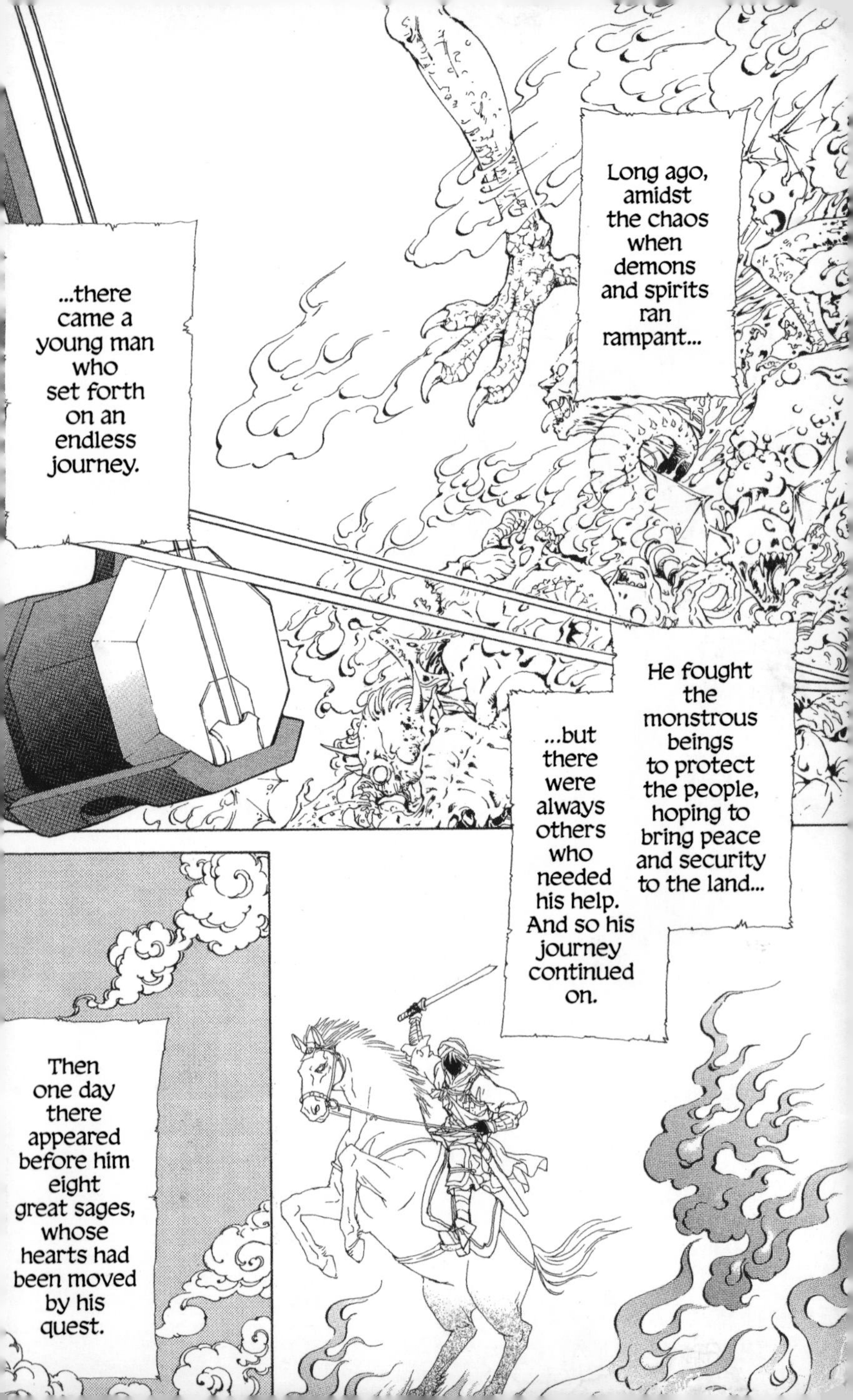
Long ago, amidst the chaos when demons and spirits ran rampant...
...there came a young man who set forth on an endless journey.
He fought the monstrous beings to protect the people, hoping to bring peace and security to the land...
...but there were always others who needed his help. And so his journey continued on.
Then one day there appeared before him eight great sages, whose hearts had been moved by his quest.

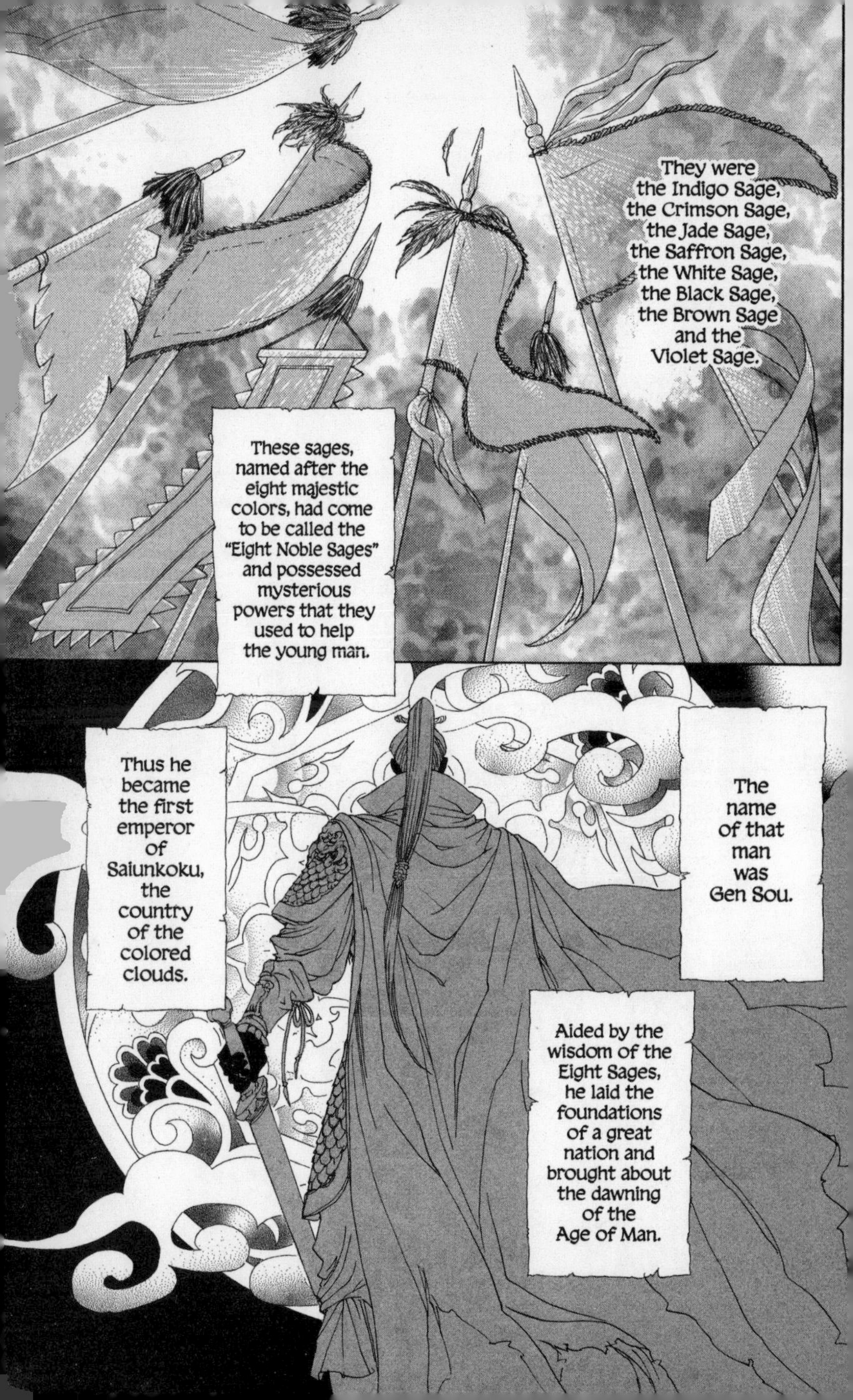
They were the Indigo Sage, the Crimson Sage, the Jade Sage, the Saffron Sage, the White Sage, the Black Sage, the Brown Sage and the Violet Sage.
These sages, named after the eight majestic colors, had come to be called the "Eight Noble Sages" and possessed mysterious powers that they used to help the young man.
The name of that man was Gen Sou.
Thus he became the first emperor of Saiunkoku, the country of the colored clouds.
Aided by the wisdom of the Eight Sages, he laid the foundations of a great nation and brought about the dawning of the Age of Man.

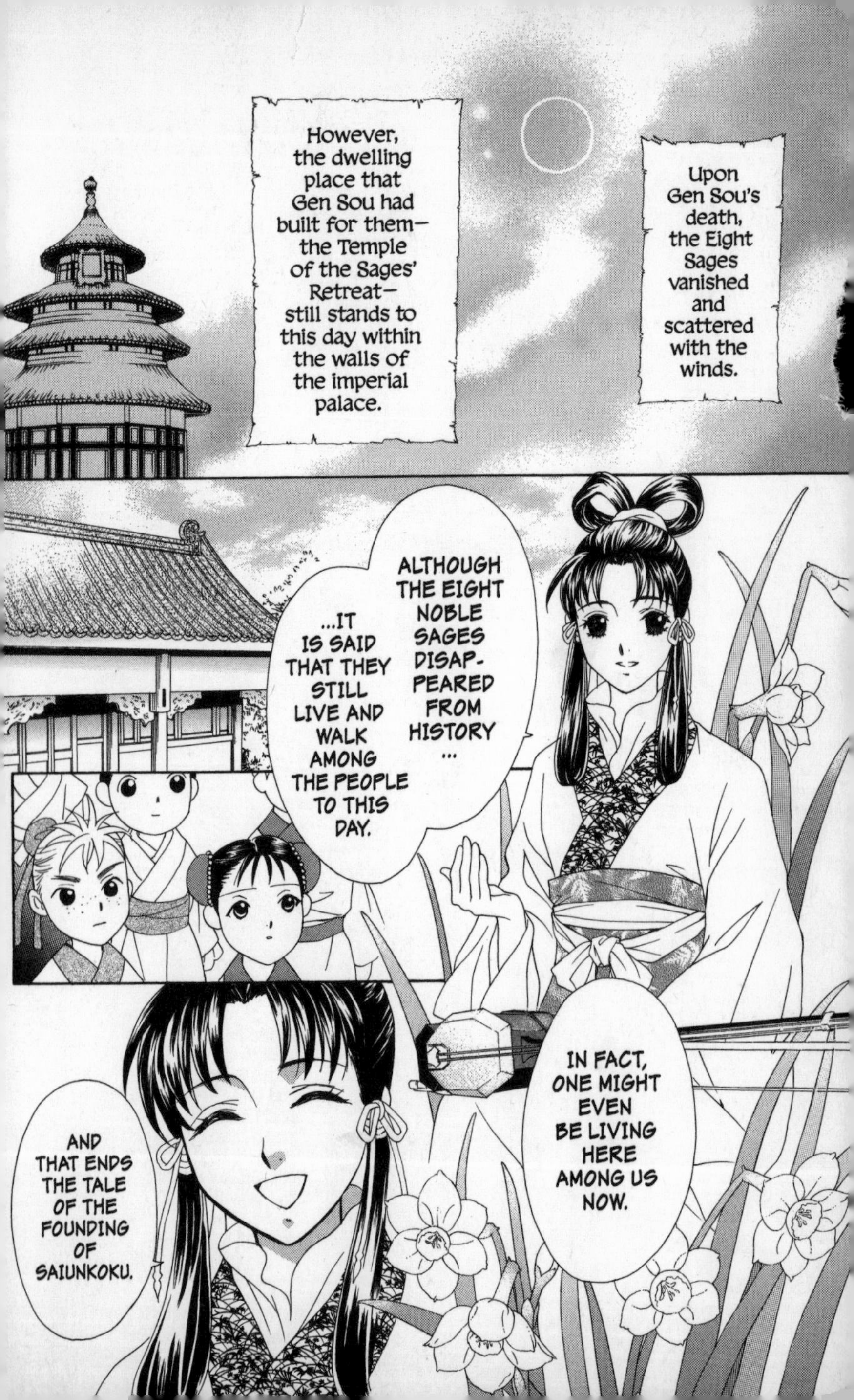
Upon Gen Sou's death, the Eight Sages vanished and scattered with the winds.
However, the dwelling place that Gen Sou had built for them—the Temple of the Sages' Retreat—still stands to this day within the walls of the imperial palace.
ALTHOUGH THE EIGHT NOBLE SAGES DISAP-PEARED FROM HISTORY...
...IT IS SAID THAT THEY STILL LIVE AND WALK AMONG THE PEOPLE TO THIS DAY.
IN FACT, ONE MIGHT EVEN BE LIVING HERE AMONG US NOW.
AND THAT ENDS THE TALE OF THE FOUNDING OF SAIUNKOKU.

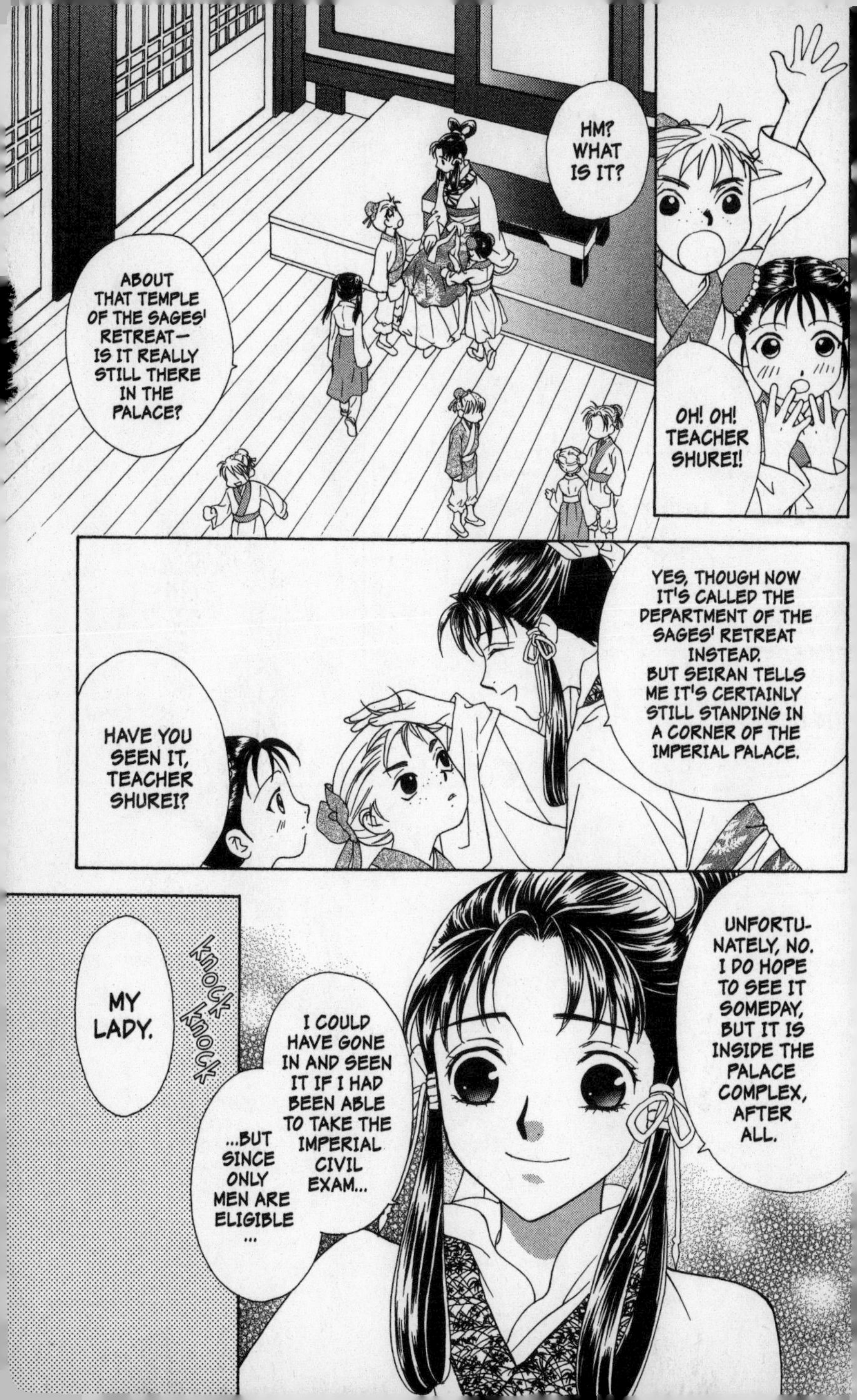
OH! OH! TEACHER SHUREI!
HM? WHAT IS IT?
ABOUT THAT TEMPLE OF THE SAGES' RETREAT—IS IT REALLY STILL THERE IN THE PALACE?
YES, THOUGH NOW IT'S CALLED THE DEPARTMENT OF THE SAGES' RETREAT INSTEAD. BUT SEIRAN TELLS ME IT'S CERTAINLY STILL STANDING IN A CORNER OF THE IMPERIAL PALACE.
HAVE YOU SEEN IT, TEACHER SHUREI?
UNFORTUNATELY, NO. I DO HOPE TO SEE IT SOMEDAY, BUT IT IS INSIDE THE PALACE COMPLEX, AFTER ALL.
I COULD HAVE GONE IN AND SEEN IT IF I HAD BEEN ABLE TO TAKE THE IMPERIAL CIVIL EXAM...
...BUT SINCE ONLY MEN ARE ELIGIBLE...
KNOCK KNOCK
MY LADY.

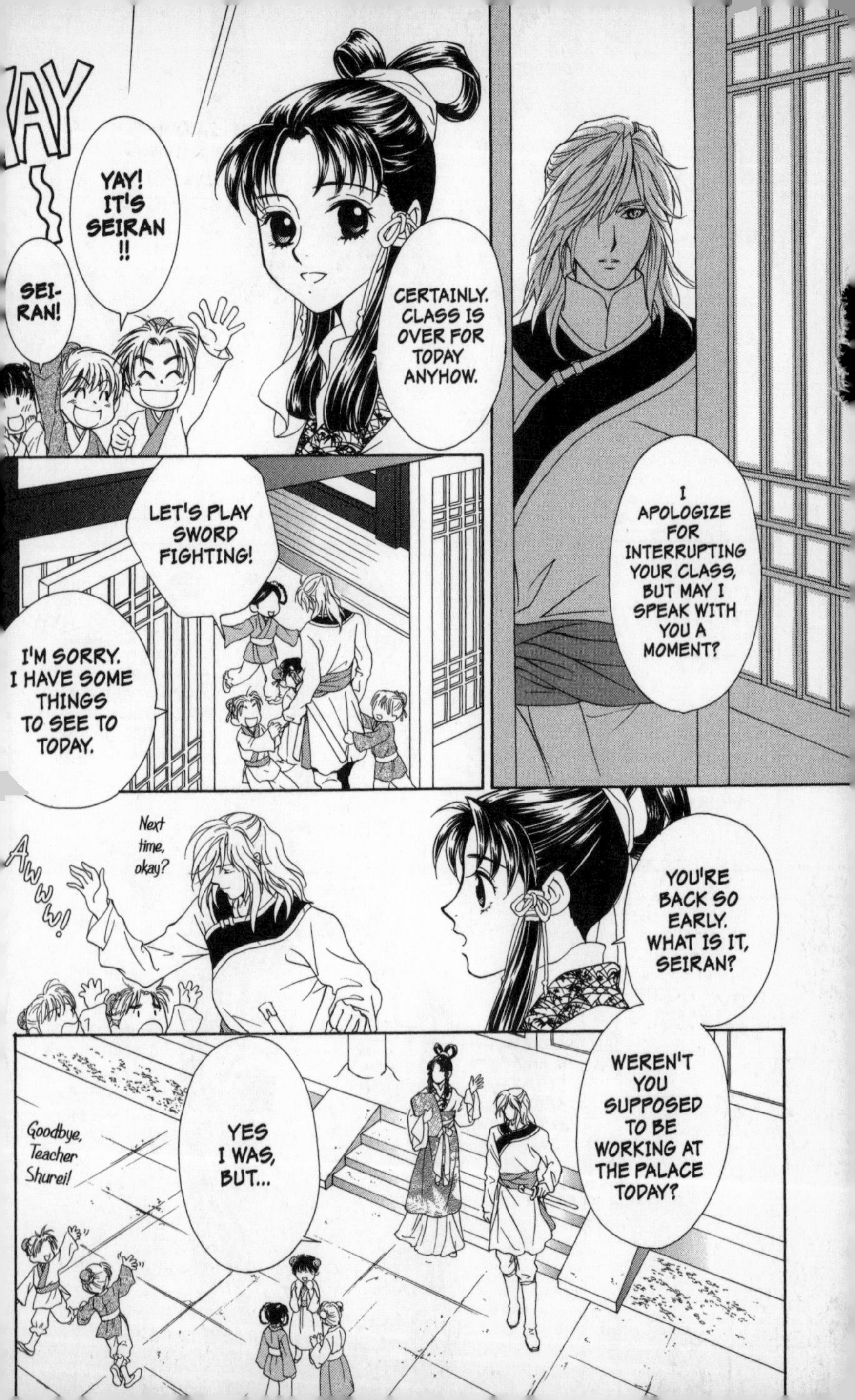
I APOLOGIZE FOR INTERRUPTING YOUR CLASS, BUT MAY I SPEAK WITH YOU A MOMENT?
CERTAINLY. CLASS IS OVER FOR TODAY ANYHOW.
AY
YAY! IT'S SEIRAN !!
SEI-RAN!
LET'S PLAY SWORD FIGHTING!
I'M SORRY. I HAVE SOME THINGS TO SEE TO TODAY.
YOU'RE BACK SO EARLY. WHAT IS IT, SEIRAN?
Next time, okay?
Awww!
WEREN'T YOU SUPPOSED TO BE WORKING AT THE PALACE TODAY?
YES I WAS, BUT...
Goodbye, Teacher Shurei!

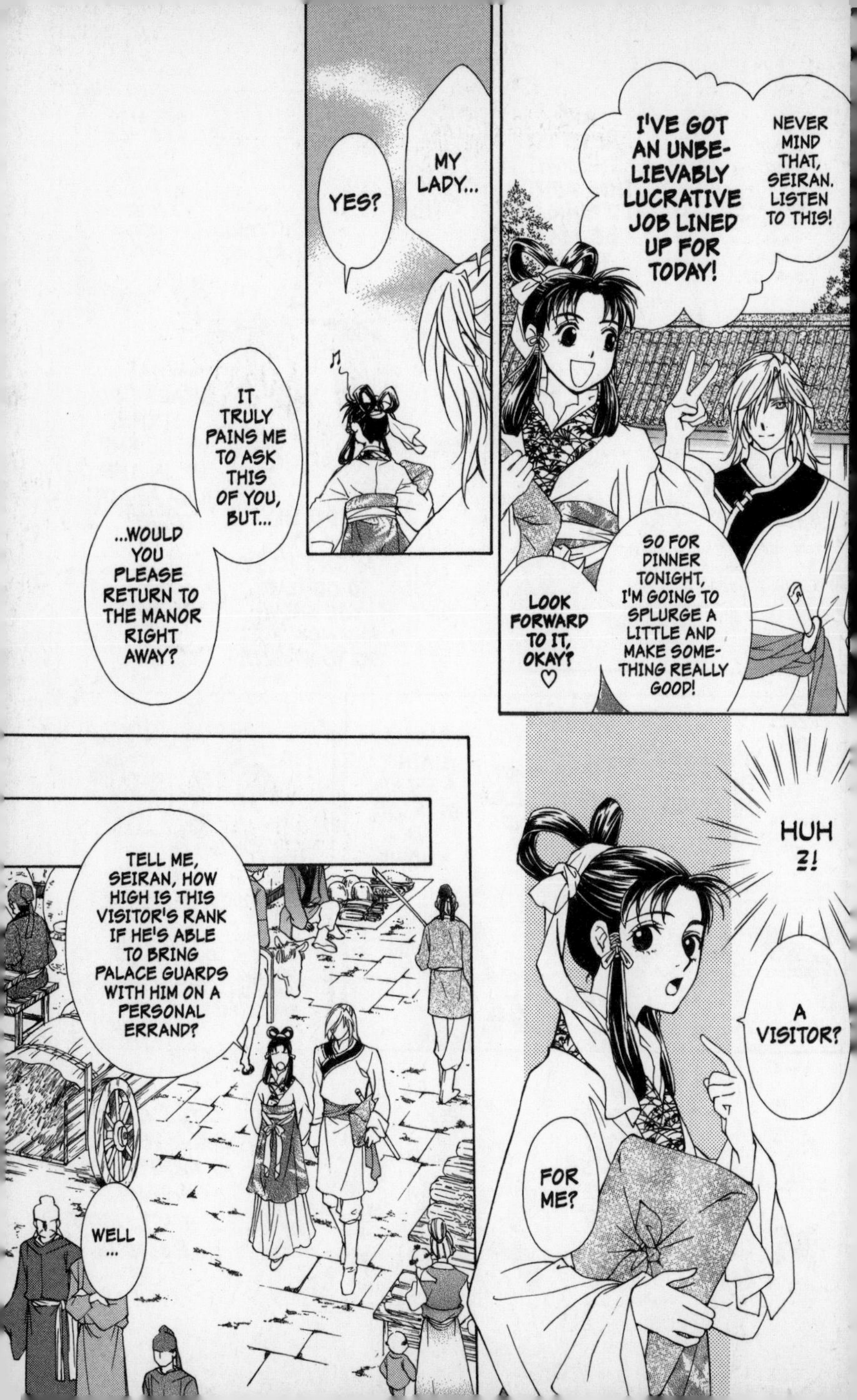
NEVER MIND THAT, SEIRAN. LISTEN TO THIS!
I'VE GOT AN UNBE-LIEVABLY LUCRATIVE JOB LINED UP FOR TODAY!
SO FOR DINNER TONIGHT, I'M GOING TO SPLURGE A LITTLE AND MAKE SOME-THING REALLY GOOD!
LOOK FORWARD TO IT, OKAY? ♡
MY LADY...
YES?
IT TRULY PAINS ME TO ASK THIS OF YOU, BUT...
...WOULD YOU PLEASE RETURN TO THE MANOR RIGHT AWAY?
HUH ?!
A VISITOR?
FOR ME?
TELL ME, SEIRAN, HOW HIGH IS THIS VISITOR'S RANK IF HE'S ABLE TO BRING PALACE GUARDS WITH HIM ON A PERSONAL ERRAND?
WELL ...

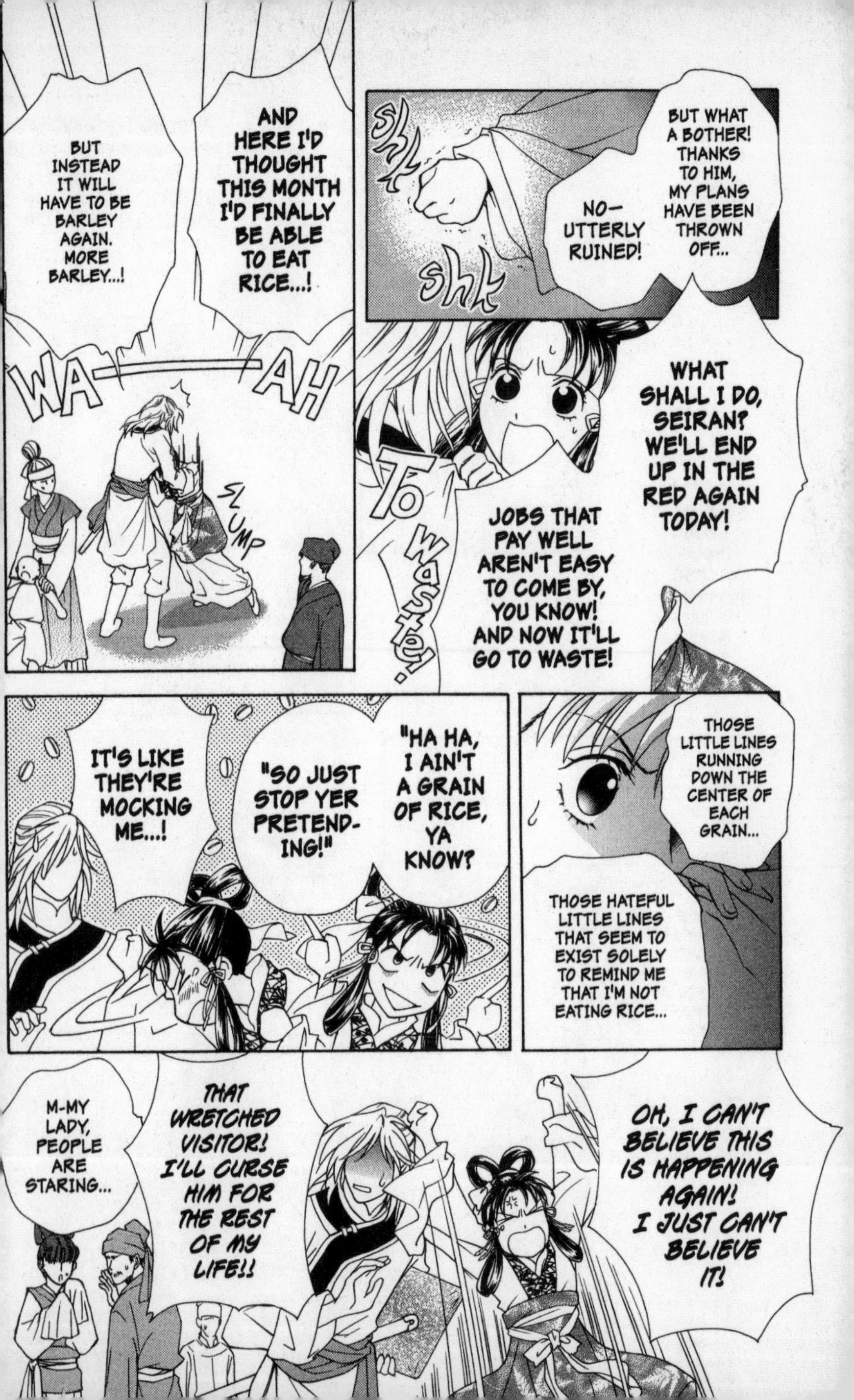
BUT WHAT A BOTHER! THANKS TO HIM, MY PLANS HAVE BEEN THROWN OFF...
NO— UTTERLY RUINED!
shk
shk
WHAT SHALL I DO, SEIRAN? WE'LL END UP IN THE RED AGAIN TODAY!
JOBS THAT PAY WELL AREN'T EASY TO COME BY, YOU KNOW! AND NOW IT'LL GO TO WASTE!
To waste!
AND HERE I'D THOUGHT THIS MONTH I'D FINALLY BE ABLE TO EAT RICE...!
BUT INSTEAD IT WILL HAVE TO BE BARLEY AGAIN. MORE BARLEY...!
WA——AH
SLUMP
THOSE LITTLE LINES RUNNING DOWN THE CENTER OF EACH GRAIN...
THOSE HATEFUL LITTLE LINES THAT SEEM TO EXIST SOLELY TO REMIND ME THAT I'M NOT EATING RICE...
"HA HA, I AIN'T A GRAIN OF RICE, YA KNOW?
"SO JUST STOP YER PRETEND-ING!"
IT'S LIKE THEY'RE MOCKING ME...!
OH, I CAN'T BELIEVE THIS IS HAPPENING AGAIN! I JUST CAN'T BELIEVE IT!
THAT WRETCHED VISITOR! I'LL CURSE HIM FOR THE REST OF MY LIFE!!
M-MY LADY, PEOPLE ARE STARING...

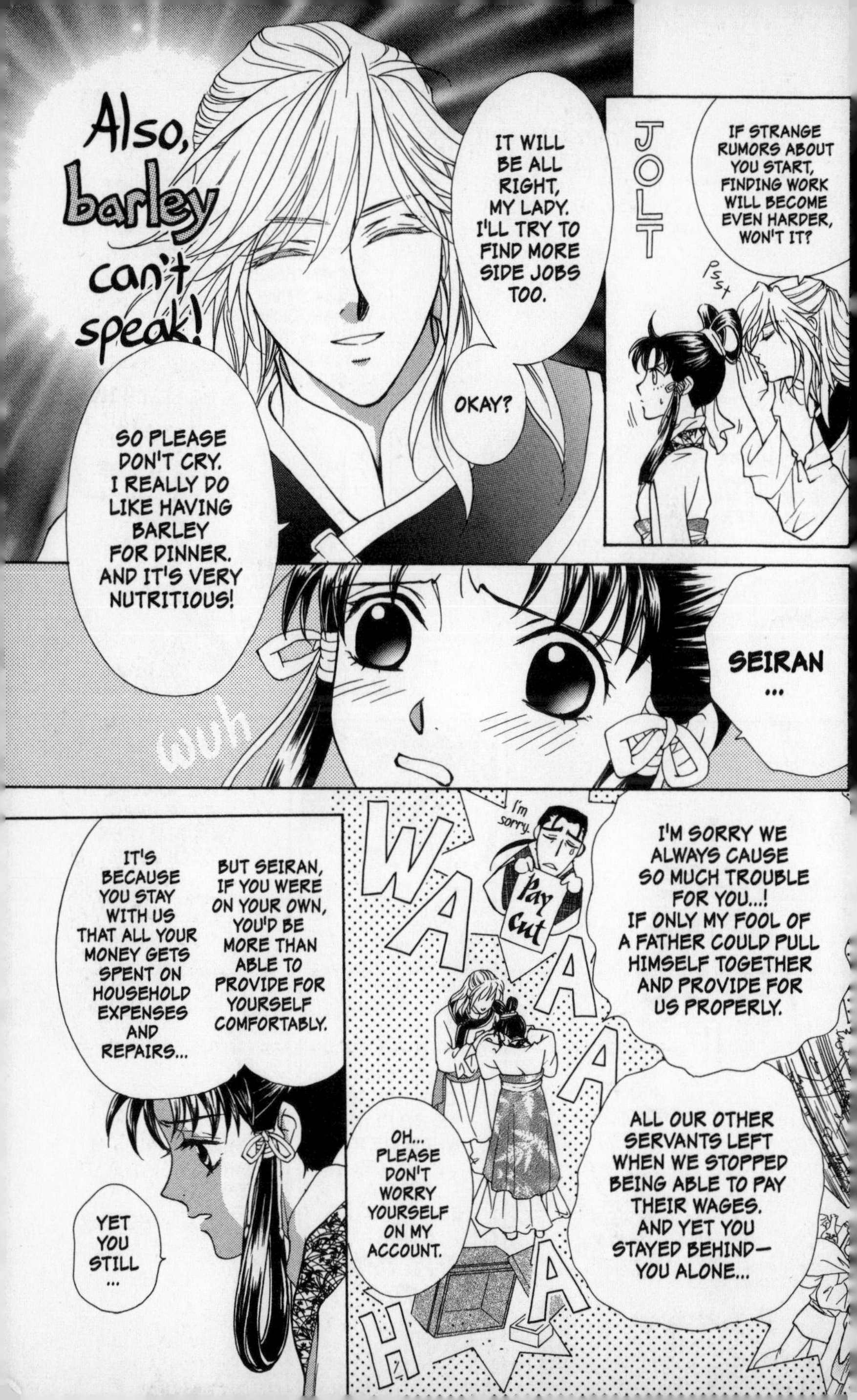
IF STRANGE RUMORS ABOUT YOU START, FINDING WORK WILL BECOME EVEN HARDER, WON'T IT?
JOLT
Psst
IT WILL BE ALL RIGHT, MY LADY. I'LL TRY TO FIND MORE SIDE JOBS TOO.
OKAY?
Also, barley can't speak!
SO PLEASE DON'T CRY. I REALLY DO LIKE HAVING BARLEY FOR DINNER. AND IT'S VERY NUTRITIOUS!
SEIRAN ...
wuh
I'M SORRY WE ALWAYS CAUSE SO MUCH TROUBLE FOR YOU...! IF ONLY MY FOOL OF A FATHER COULD PULL HIMSELF TOGETHER AND PROVIDE FOR US PROPERLY.
I'm sorry.
Pay cut
WAAAAAH
ALL OUR OTHER SERVANTS LEFT WHEN WE STOPPED BEING ABLE TO PAY THEIR WAGES. AND YET YOU STAYED BEHIND— YOU ALONE...
OH... PLEASE DON'T WORRY YOURSELF ON MY ACCOUNT.
BUT SEIRAN, IF YOU WERE ON YOUR OWN, YOU'D BE MORE THAN ABLE TO PROVIDE FOR YOURSELF COMFORTABLY.
IT'S BECAUSE YOU STAY WITH US THAT ALL YOUR MONEY GETS SPENT ON HOUSEHOLD EXPENSES AND REPAIRS...
YET YOU STILL ...

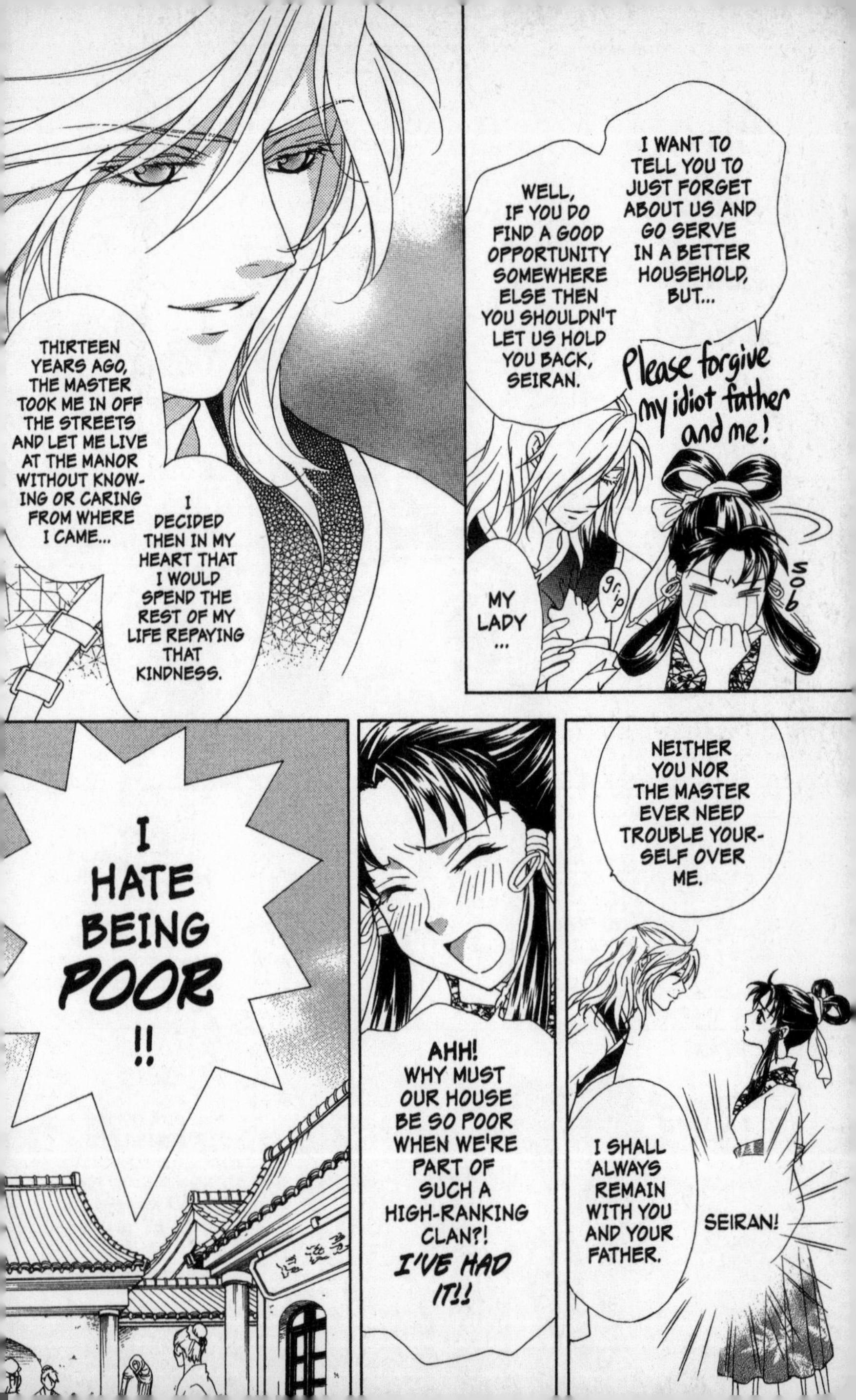

I WANT TO TELL YOU TO JUST FORGET ABOUT US AND GO SERVE IN A BETTER HOUSEHOLD, BUT...
WELL, IF YOU DO FIND A GOOD OPPORTUNITY SOMEWHERE ELSE THEN YOU SHOULDN'T LET US HOLD YOU BACK, SEIRAN.
Please forgive my idiot father and me!
sob
grip
MY LADY ...
THIRTEEN YEARS AGO, THE MASTER TOOK ME IN OFF THE STREETS AND LET ME LIVE AT THE MANOR WITHOUT KNOWING OR CARING FROM WHERE I CAME...
I DECIDED THEN IN MY HEART THAT I WOULD SPEND THE REST OF MY LIFE REPAYING THAT KINDNESS.
NEITHER YOU NOR THE MASTER EVER NEED TROUBLE YOURSELF OVER ME.
I SHALL ALWAYS REMAIN WITH YOU AND YOUR FATHER.
SEIRAN!
AHH! WHY MUST OUR HOUSE BE SO POOR WHEN WE'RE PART OF SUCH A HIGH-RANKING CLAN?! I'VE HAD IT!!
I HATE BEING POOR!!

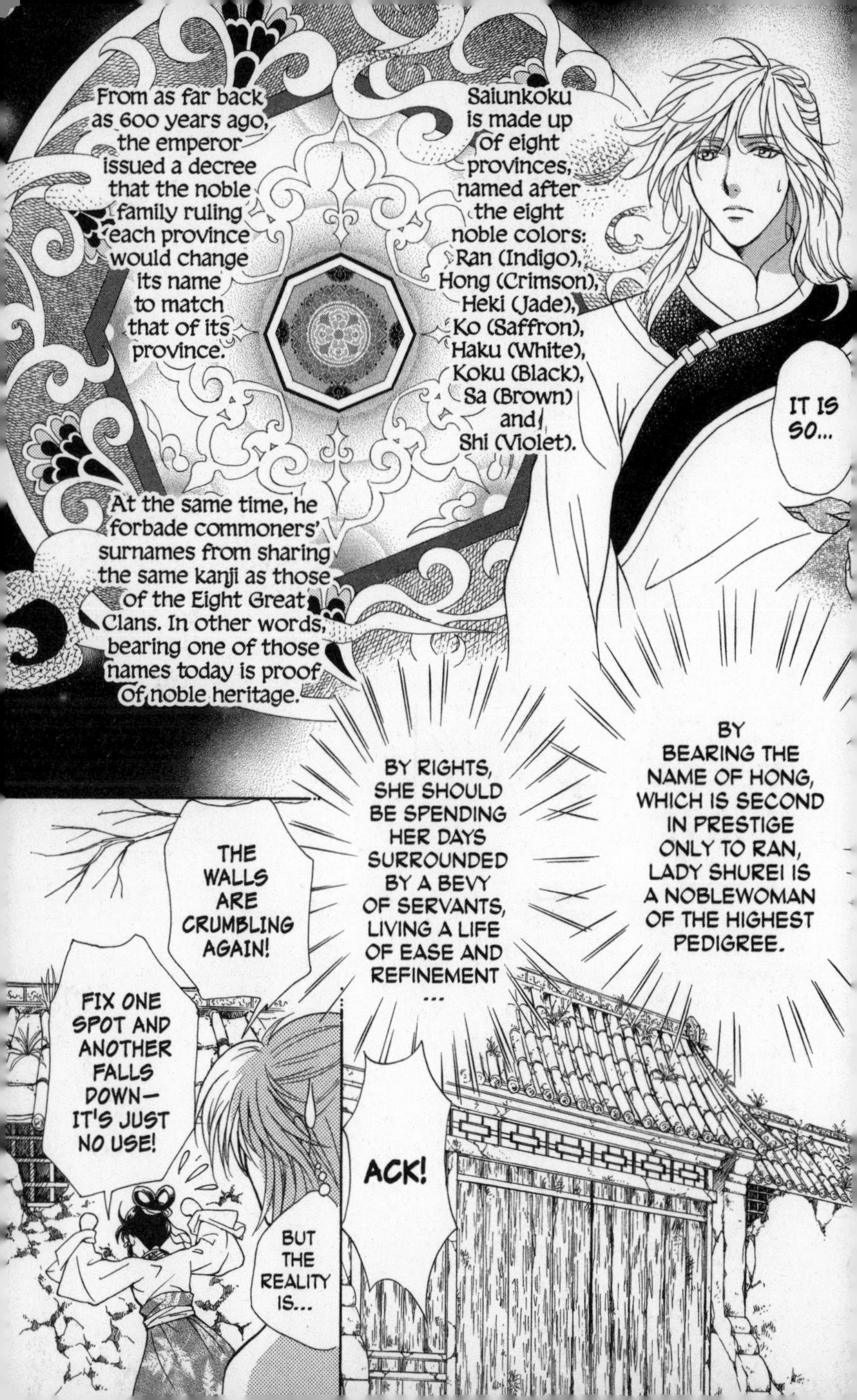

Saiunkoku is made up of eight provinces, named after the eight noble colors: Ran (Indigo), Hong (Crimson), Heki (Jade), Ko (Saffron), Haku (White), Koku (Black), Sa (Brown) and Shi (Violet).
From as far back as 600 years ago, the emperor issued a decree that the noble family ruling each province would change its name to match that of its province.
At the same time, he forbade commoners' surnames from sharing the same kanji as those of the Eight Great Clans. In other words, bearing one of those names today is proof of noble heritage.
IT IS SO...
BY BEARING THE NAME OF HONG, WHICH IS SECOND IN PRESTIGE ONLY TO RAN, LADY SHUREI IS A NOBLEWOMAN OF THE HIGHEST PEDIGREE.
BY RIGHTS, SHE SHOULD BE SPENDING HER DAYS SURROUNDED BY A BEVY OF SERVANTS, LIVING A LIFE OF EASE AND REFINEMENT ...
BUT THE REALITY IS...
ACK!
THE WALLS ARE CRUMBLING AGAIN!
FIX ONE SPOT AND ANOTHER FALLS DOWN— IT'S JUST NO USE!

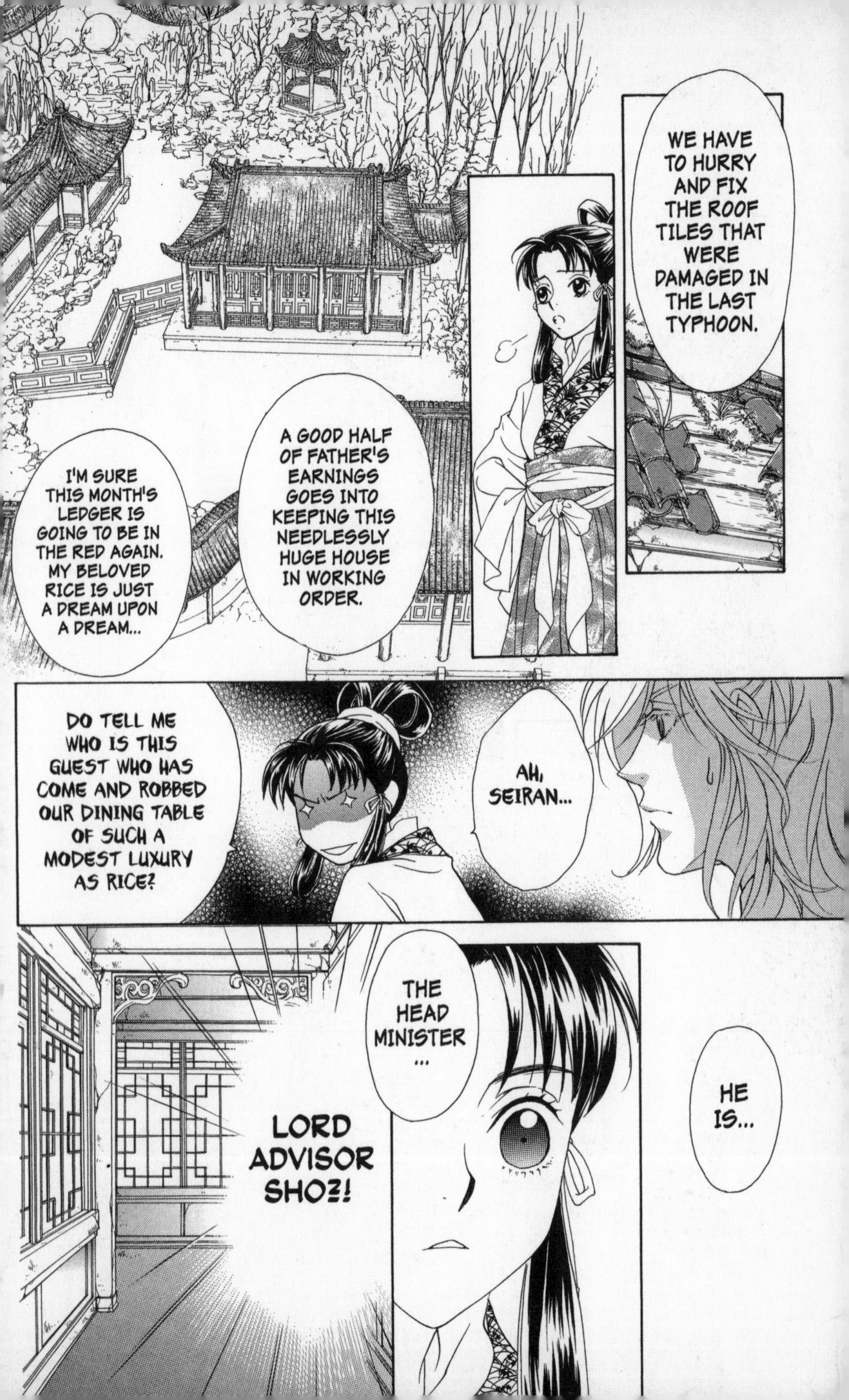
WE HAVE TO HURRY AND FIX THE ROOF TILES THAT WERE DAMAGED IN THE LAST TYPHOON.
A GOOD HALF OF FATHER'S EARNINGS GOES INTO KEEPING THIS NEEDLESSLY HUGE HOUSE IN WORKING ORDER.
I'M SURE THIS MONTH'S LEDGER IS GOING TO BE IN THE RED AGAIN. MY BELOVED RICE IS JUST A DREAM UPON A DREAM...
AH, SEIRAN...
DO TELL ME WHO IS THIS GUEST WHO HAS COME AND ROBBED OUR DINING TABLE OF SUCH A MODEST LUXURY AS RICE?
HE IS...
THE HEAD MINISTER...
LORD ADVISOR SHO?!

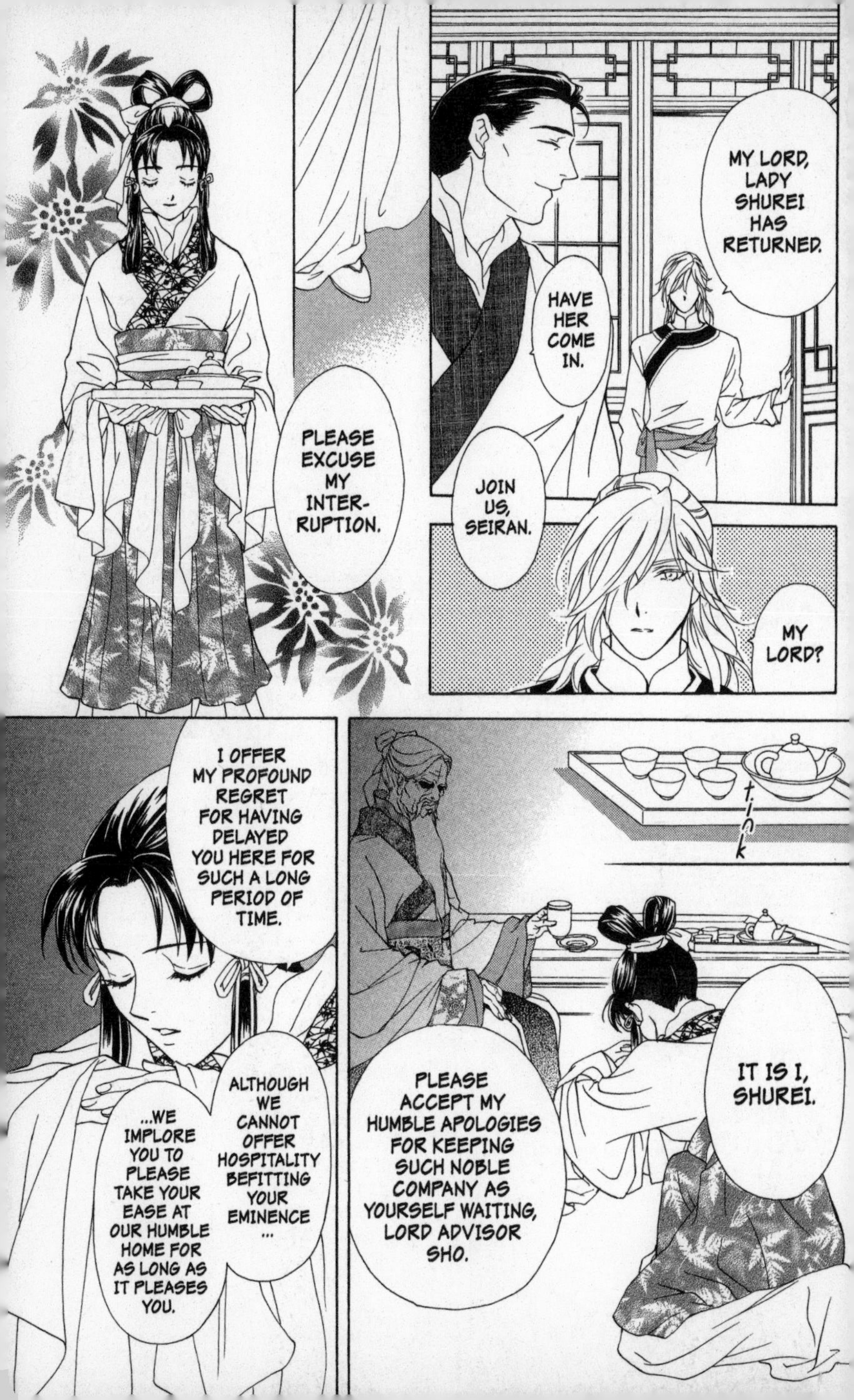
MY LORD, LADY SHUREI HAS RETURNED.
HAVE HER COME IN.
JOIN US, SEIRAN.
MY LORD?
PLEASE EXCUSE MY INTER-RUPTION.
tink
IT IS I, SHUREI.
PLEASE ACCEPT MY HUMBLE APOLOGIES FOR KEEPING SUCH NOBLE COMPANY AS YOURSELF WAITING, LORD ADVISOR SHO.
I OFFER MY PROFOUND REGRET FOR HAVING DELAYED YOU HERE FOR SUCH A LONG PERIOD OF TIME.
ALTHOUGH WE CANNOT OFFER HOSPITALITY BEFITTING YOUR EMINENCE ...
...WE IMPLORE YOU TO PLEASE TAKE YOUR EASE AT OUR HUMBLE HOME FOR AS LONG AS IT PLEASES YOU.

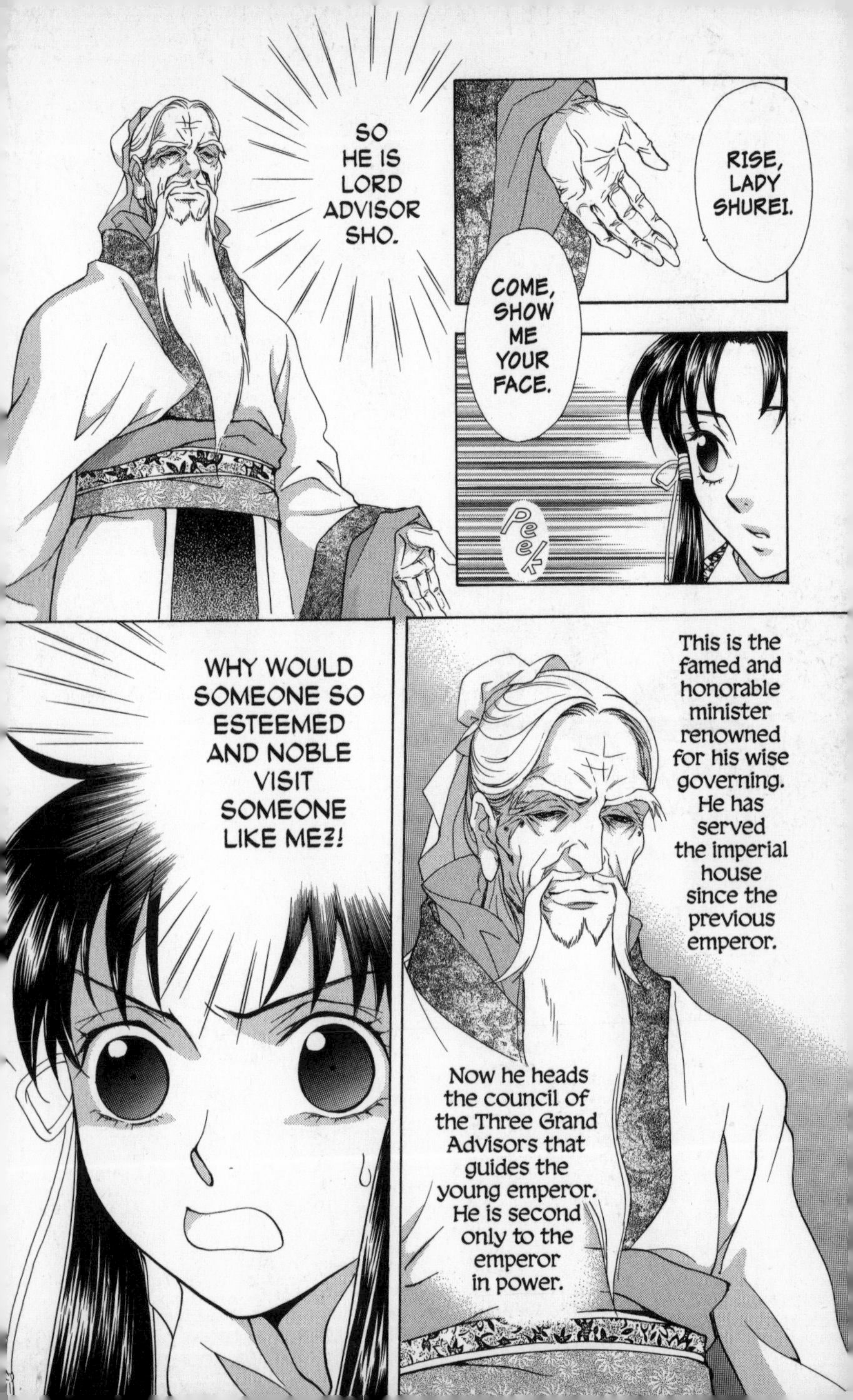
RISE, LADY SHUREI.
COME, SHOW ME YOUR FACE.
Peek
SO HE IS LORD ADVISOR SHO.
This is the famed and honorable minister renowned for his wise governing. He has served the imperial house since the previous emperor.
Now he heads the council of the Three Grand Advisors that guides the young emperor. He is second only to the emperor in power.
WHY WOULD SOMEONE SO ESTEEMED AND NOBLE VISIT SOMEONE LIKE ME⁈

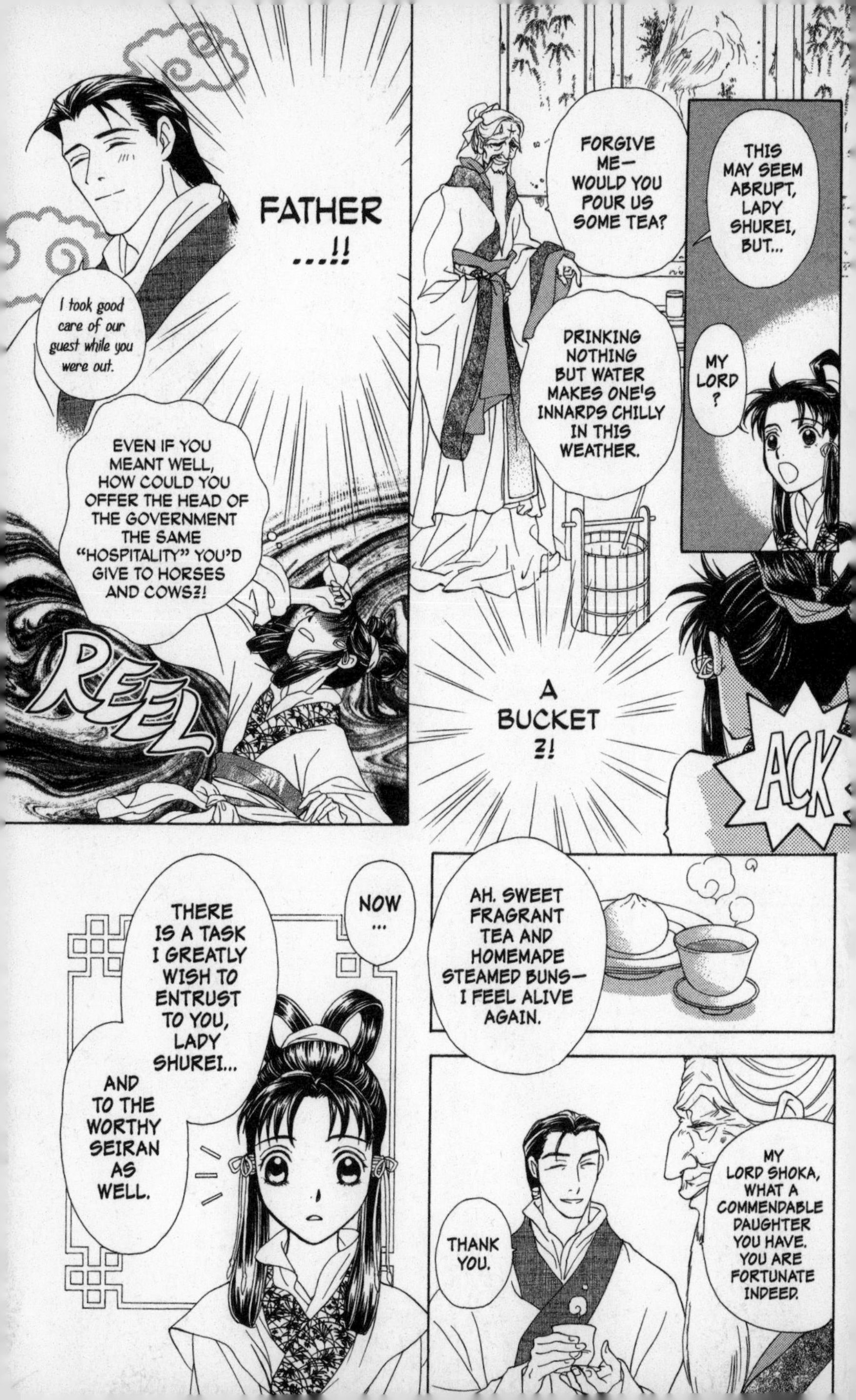
THIS MAY SEEM ABRUPT, LADY SHUREI, BUT...
MY LORD?
FORGIVE ME— WOULD YOU POUR US SOME TEA?
DRINKING NOTHING BUT WATER MAKES ONE'S INNARDS CHILLY IN THIS WEATHER.
A BUCKET?!
ACK
FATHER...!!
I took good care of our guest while you were out.
EVEN IF YOU MEANT WELL, HOW COULD YOU OFFER THE HEAD OF THE GOVERNMENT THE SAME "HOSPITALITY" YOU'D GIVE TO HORSES AND COWS?!
REEL
AH. SWEET FRAGRANT TEA AND HOMEMADE STEAMED BUNS— I FEEL ALIVE AGAIN.
MY LORD SHOKA, WHAT A COMMENDABLE DAUGHTER YOU HAVE. YOU ARE FORTUNATE INDEED.
THANK YOU.
NOW...
THERE IS A TASK I GREATLY WISH TO ENTRUST TO YOU, LADY SHUREI...
AND TO THE WORTHY SEIRAN AS WELL.

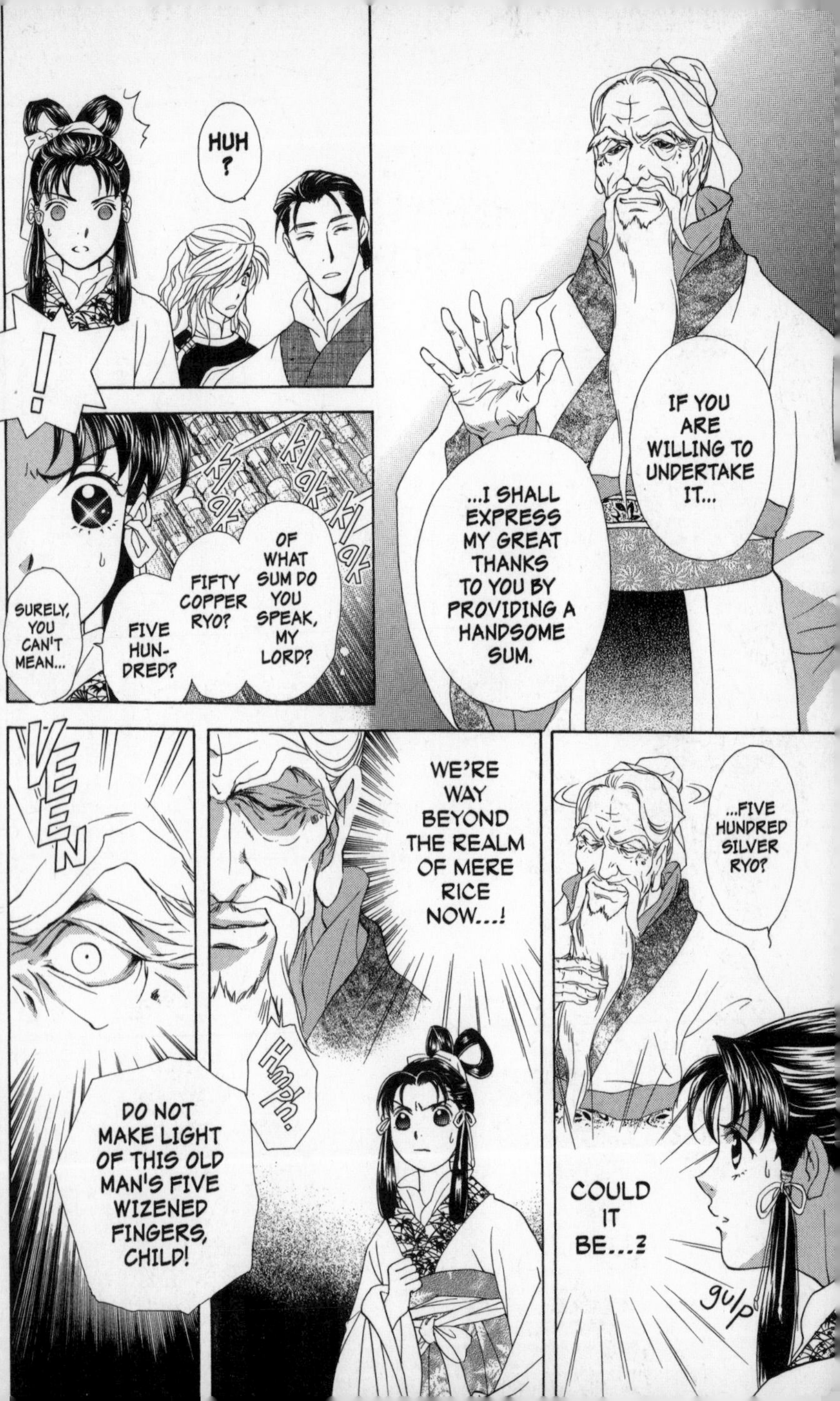
IF YOU ARE WILLING TO UNDERTAKE IT...
...I SHALL EXPRESS MY GREAT THANKS TO YOU BY PROVIDING A HANDSOME SUM.
HUH?
!
klak klak klak
OF WHAT SUM DO YOU SPEAK, MY LORD?
FIFTY COPPER RYO?
FIVE HUNDRED?
SURELY, YOU CAN'T MEAN...
...FIVE HUNDRED SILVER RYO?
COULD IT BE...?
gulp
WE'RE WAY BEYOND THE REALM OF MERE RICE NOW...!
Hmph.
VEEN
DO NOT MAKE LIGHT OF THIS OLD MAN'S FIVE WIZENED FINGERS, CHILD!

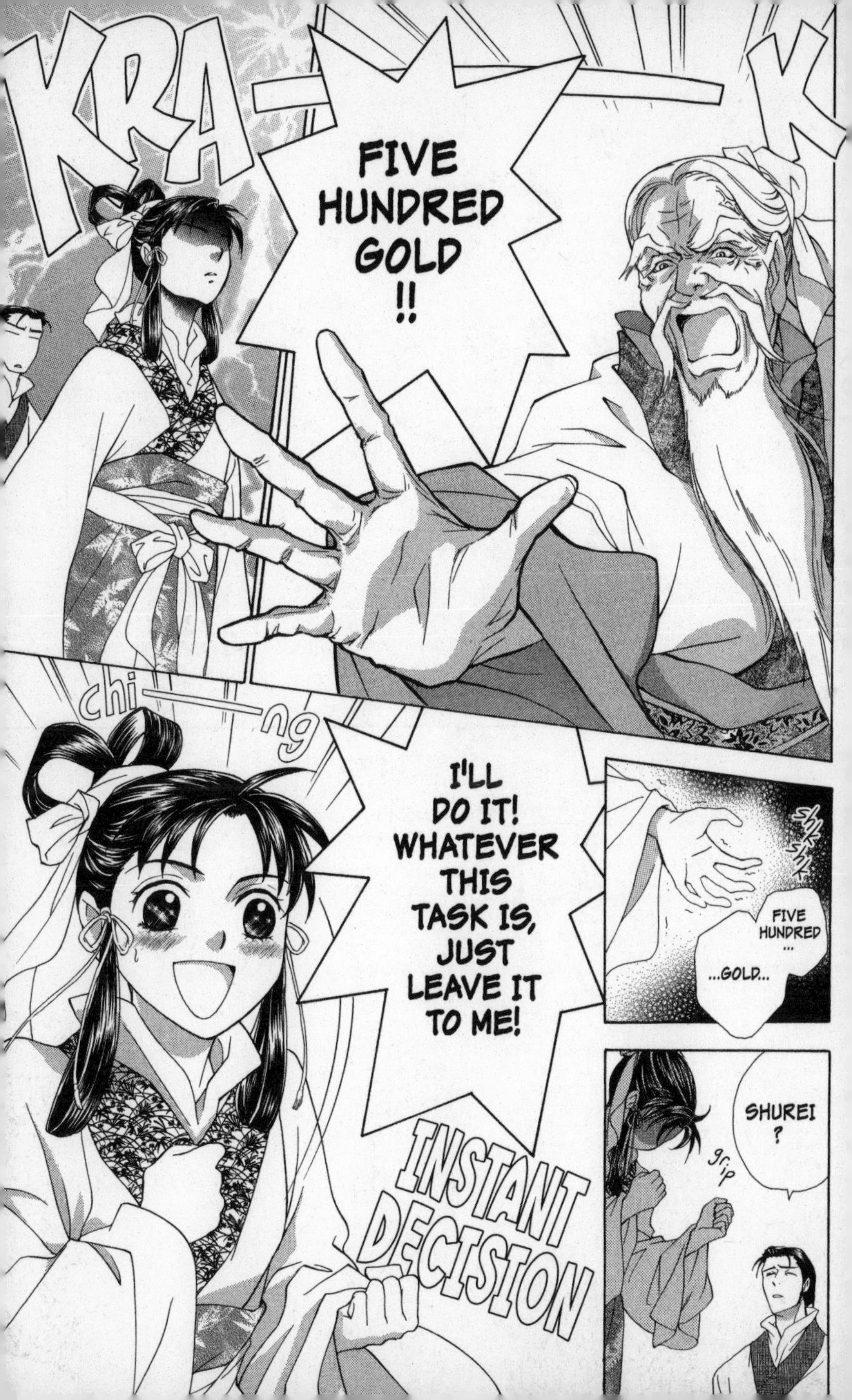
KRA-K
FIVE HUNDRED GOLD !!
shk shk
FIVE HUNDRED ...
...GOLD...
grip
SHUREI ?
chi-ng
I'LL DO IT! WHATEVER THIS TASK IS, JUST LEAVE IT TO ME!
INSTANT DECISION

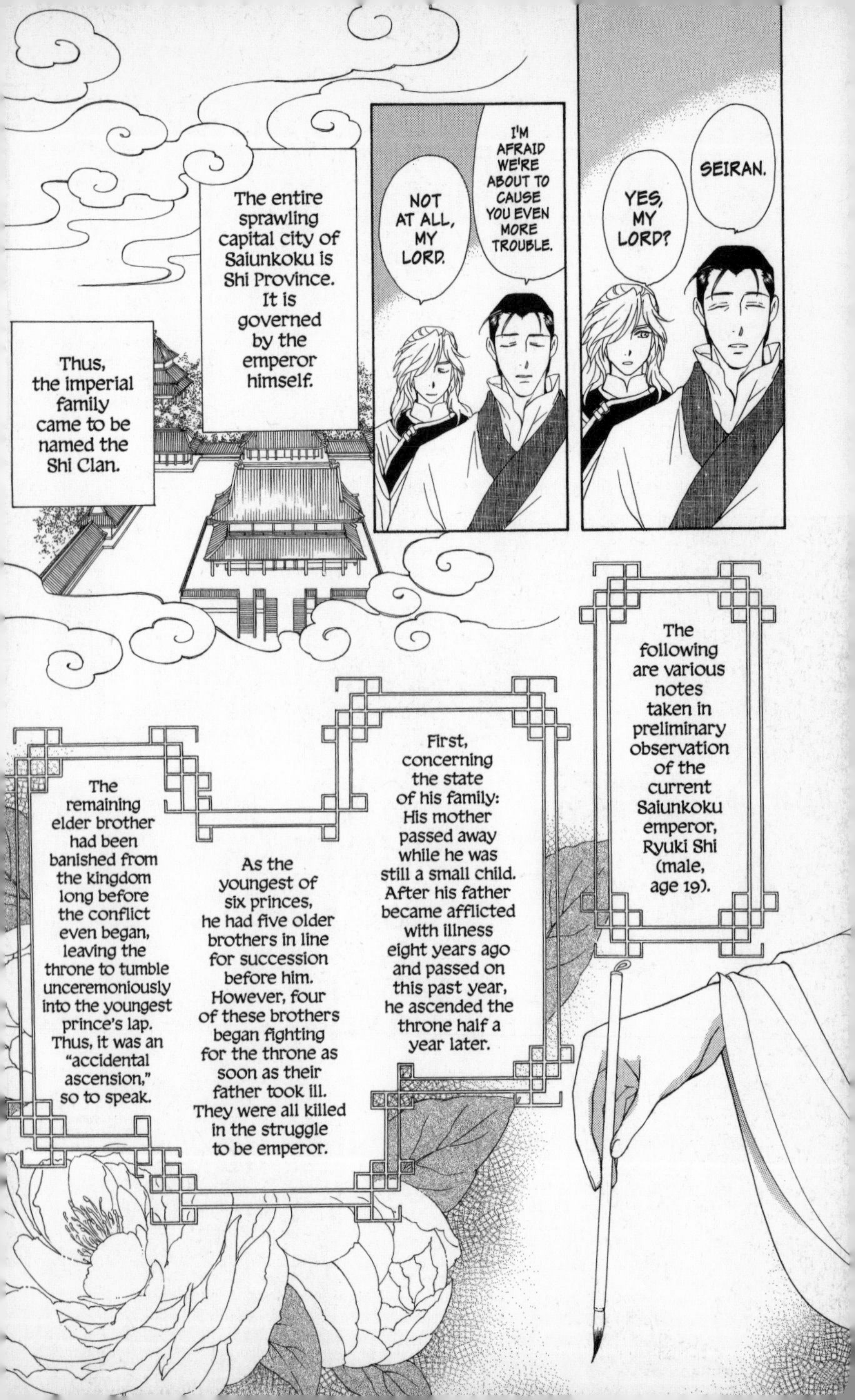
SEIRAN.
YES, MY LORD?
I'M AFRAID WE'RE ABOUT TO CAUSE YOU EVEN MORE TROUBLE.
NOT AT ALL, MY LORD.
The entire sprawling capital city of Saiunkoku is Shi Province. It is governed by the emperor himself.
Thus, the imperial family came to be named the Shi Clan.
The following are various notes taken in preliminary observation of the current Saiunkoku emperor, Ryuki Shi (male, age 19).
First, concerning the state of his family: His mother passed away while he was still a small child. After his father became afflicted with illness eight years ago and passed on this past year, he ascended the throne half a year later.
As the youngest of six princes, he had five older brothers in line for succession before him. However, four of these brothers began fighting for the throne as soon as their father took ill. They were all killed in the struggle to be emperor.
The remaining elder brother had been banished from the kingdom long before the conflict even began, leaving the throne to tumble unceremoniously into the youngest prince's lap. Thus, it was an "accidental ascension," so to speak.

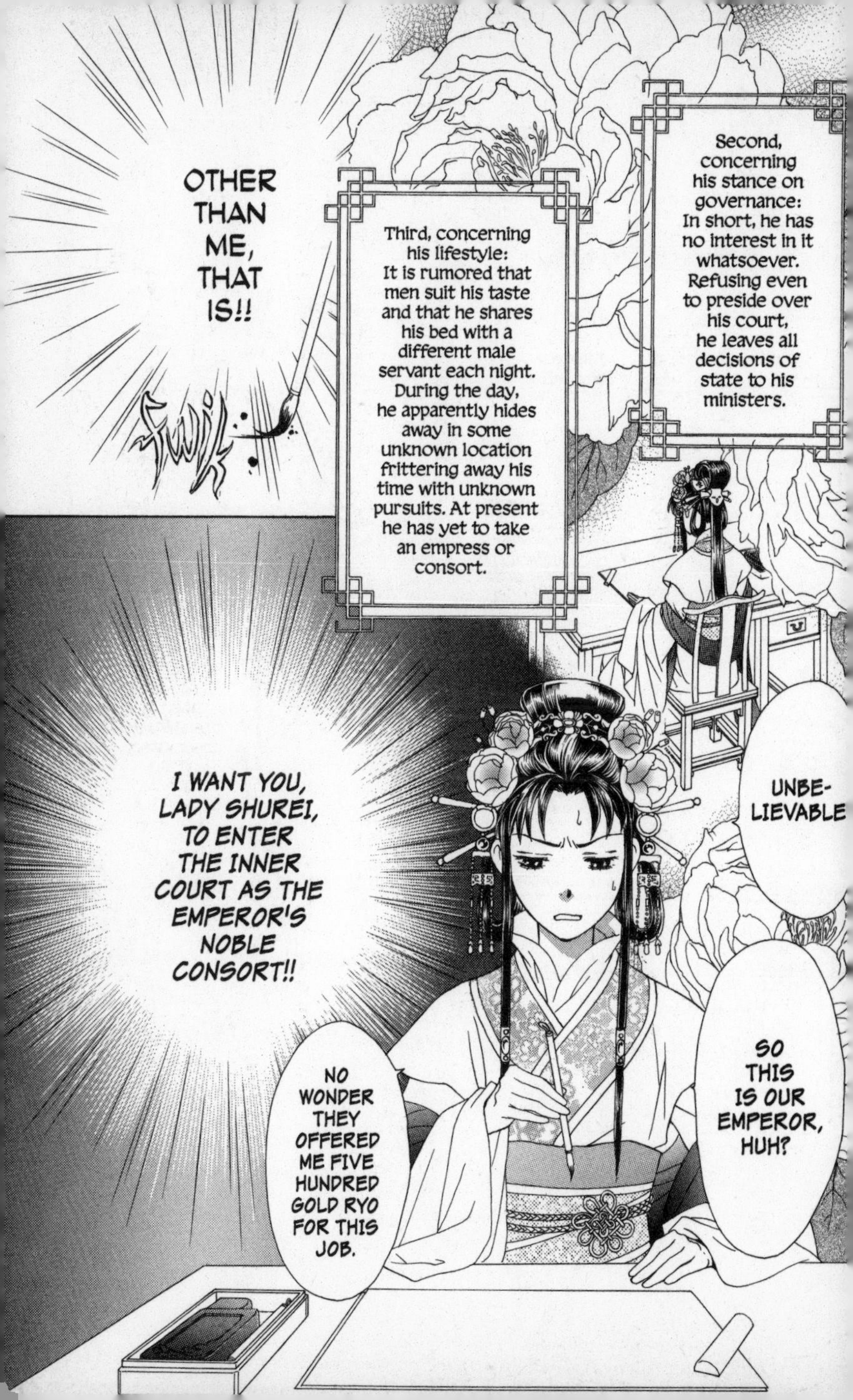

Second, concerning his stance on governance: In short, he has no interest in it whatsoever. Refusing even to preside over his court, he leaves all decisions of state to his ministers.
Third, concerning his lifestyle: It is rumored that men suit his taste and that he shares his bed with a different male servant each night. During the day, he apparently hides away in some unknown location frittering away his time with unknown pursuits. At present he has yet to take an empress or consort.
OTHER THAN ME, THAT IS!!
fwip
UNBE-LIEVABLE
SO THIS IS OUR EMPEROR, HUH?
NO WONDER THEY OFFERED ME FIVE HUNDRED GOLD RYO FOR THIS JOB.
I WANT YOU, LADY SHUREI, TO ENTER THE INNER COURT AS THE EMPEROR'S NOBLE CONSORT!!

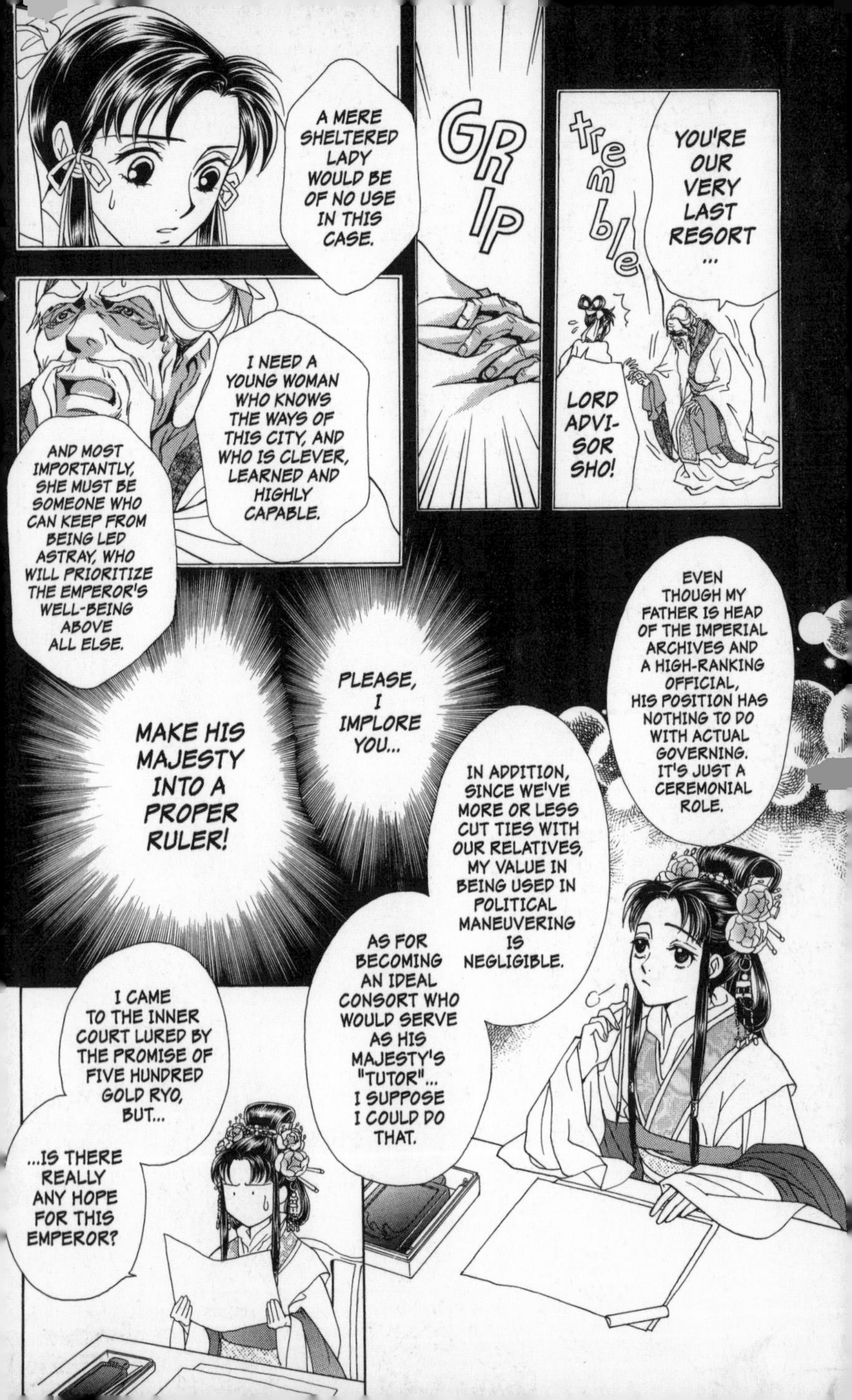
tremble
YOU'RE OUR VERY LAST RESORT ...
LORD ADVISOR SHO!
GRIP
A MERE SHELTERED LADY WOULD BE OF NO USE IN THIS CASE.
I NEED A YOUNG WOMAN WHO KNOWS THE WAYS OF THIS CITY, AND WHO IS CLEVER, LEARNED AND HIGHLY CAPABLE.
AND MOST IMPORTANTLY, SHE MUST BE SOMEONE WHO CAN KEEP FROM BEING LED ASTRAY, WHO WILL PRIORITIZE THE EMPEROR'S WELL-BEING ABOVE ALL ELSE.
PLEASE, I IMPLORE YOU...
MAKE HIS MAJESTY INTO A PROPER RULER!
EVEN THOUGH MY FATHER IS HEAD OF THE IMPERIAL ARCHIVES AND A HIGH-RANKING OFFICIAL, HIS POSITION HAS NOTHING TO DO WITH ACTUAL GOVERNING. IT'S JUST A CEREMONIAL ROLE.
IN ADDITION, SINCE WE'VE MORE OR LESS CUT TIES WITH OUR RELATIVES, MY VALUE IN BEING USED IN POLITICAL MANEUVERING IS NEGLIGIBLE.
AS FOR BECOMING AN IDEAL CONSORT WHO WOULD SERVE AS HIS MAJESTY'S "TUTOR"... I SUPPOSE I COULD DO THAT.
I CAME TO THE INNER COURT LURED BY THE PROMISE OF FIVE HUNDRED GOLD RYO, BUT...
...IS THERE REALLY ANY HOPE FOR THIS EMPEROR?

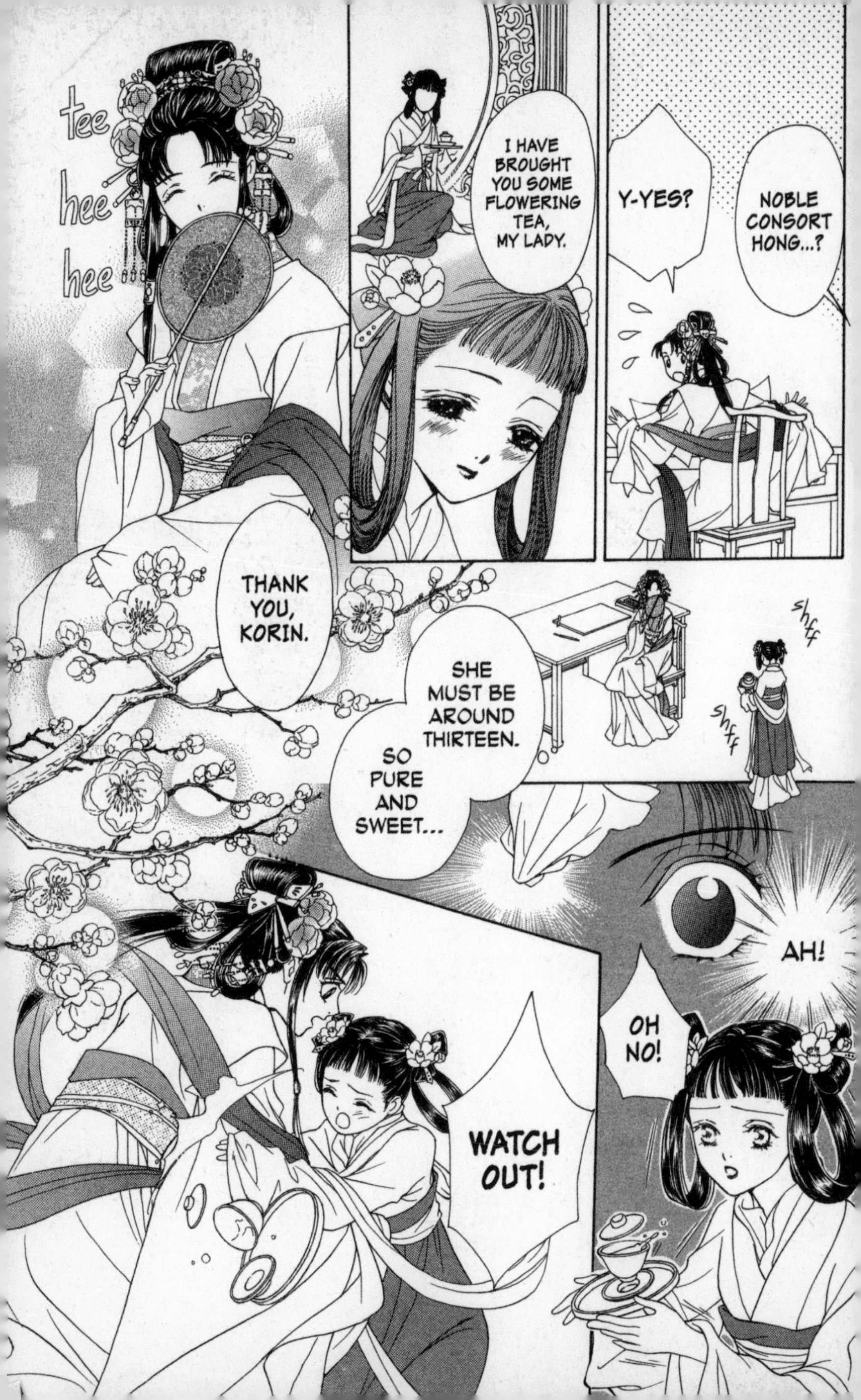
NOBLE CONSORT HONG...?
Y-YES?
I HAVE BROUGHT YOU SOME FLOWERING TEA, MY LADY.
tee hee hee
THANK YOU, KORIN.
shff shff
SHE MUST BE AROUND THIRTEEN.
SO PURE AND SWEET...
AH!
OH NO!
WATCH OUT!

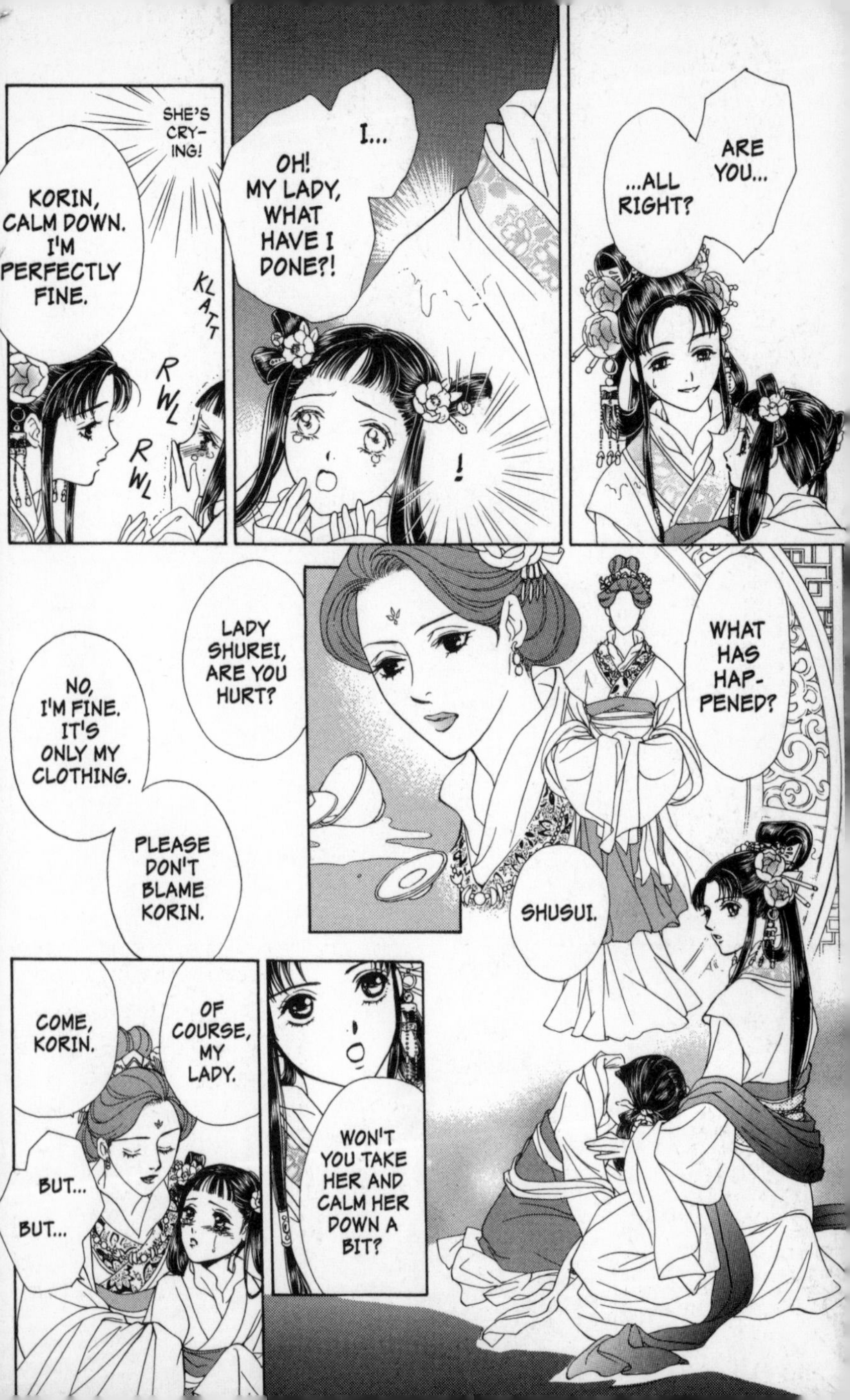

ARE YOU...
...ALL RIGHT?
I...
OH! MY LADY, WHAT HAVE I DONE?!
!
SHE'S CRY-ING!
KORIN, CALM DOWN. I'M PERFECTLY FINE.
KLATT
RWL
RWL
WHAT HAS HAP-PENED?
SHUSUI.
LADY SHUREI, ARE YOU HURT?
NO, I'M FINE. IT'S ONLY MY CLOTHING.
PLEASE DON'T BLAME KORIN.
WON'T YOU TAKE HER AND CALM HER DOWN A BIT?
OF COURSE, MY LADY.
COME, KORIN.
BUT...
BUT...

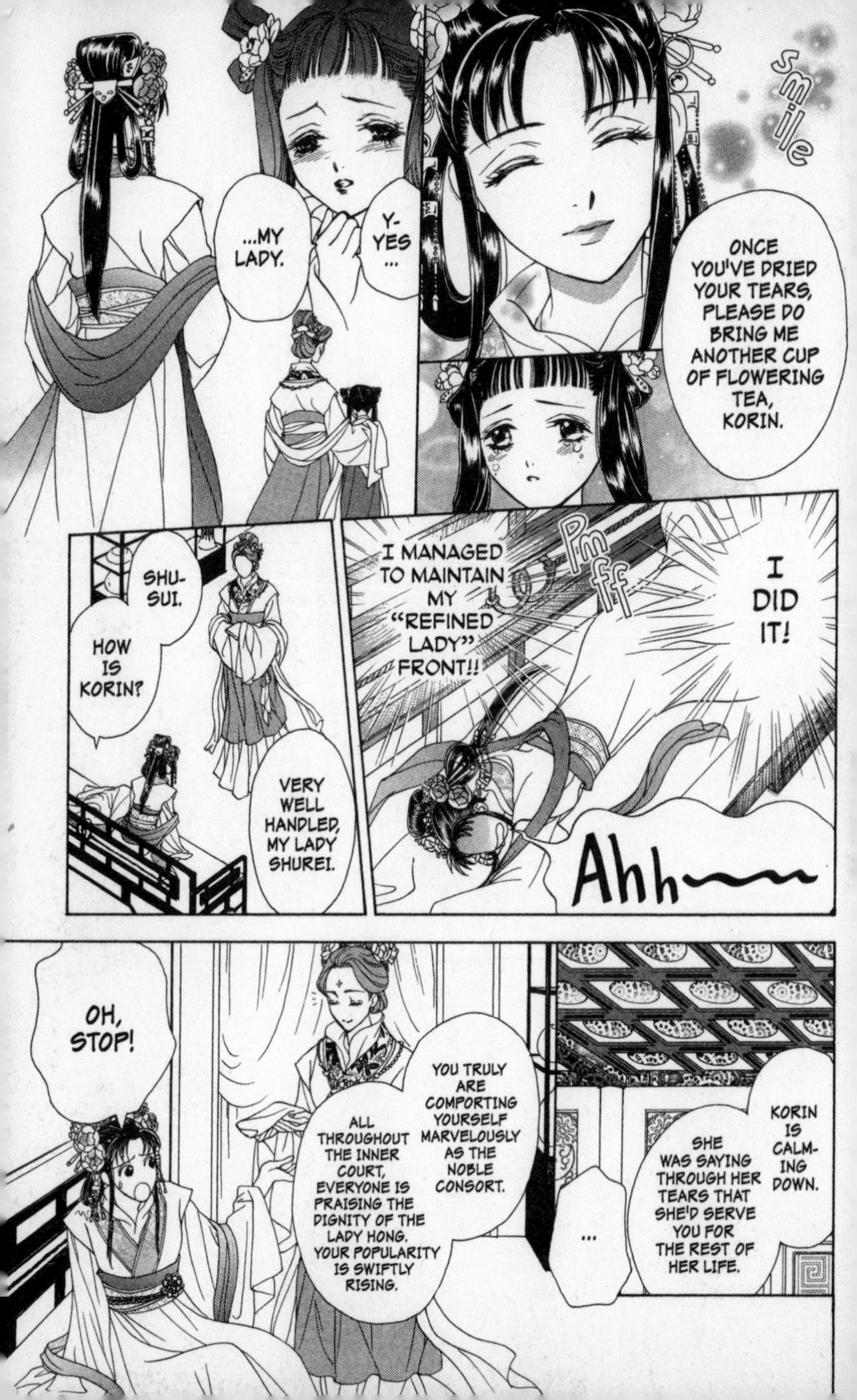
smile
ONCE YOU'VE DRIED YOUR TEARS, PLEASE DO BRING ME ANOTHER CUP OF FLOWERING TEA, KORIN.
Y-YES...
...MY LADY.
I DID IT!
Pmff
I MANAGED TO MAINTAIN MY "REFINED LADY" FRONT!!
Ahh~~
SHU-SUI.
HOW IS KORIN?
VERY WELL HANDLED, MY LADY SHUREI.
KORIN IS CALMING DOWN.
SHE WAS SAYING THROUGH HER TEARS THAT SHE'D SERVE YOU FOR THE REST OF HER LIFE.
...
YOU TRULY ARE COMPORTING YOURSELF MARVELOUSLY AS THE NOBLE CONSORT.
ALL THROUGHOUT THE INNER COURT, EVERYONE IS PRAISING THE DIGNITY OF THE LADY HONG. YOUR POPULARITY IS SWIFTLY RISING.
OH, STOP!

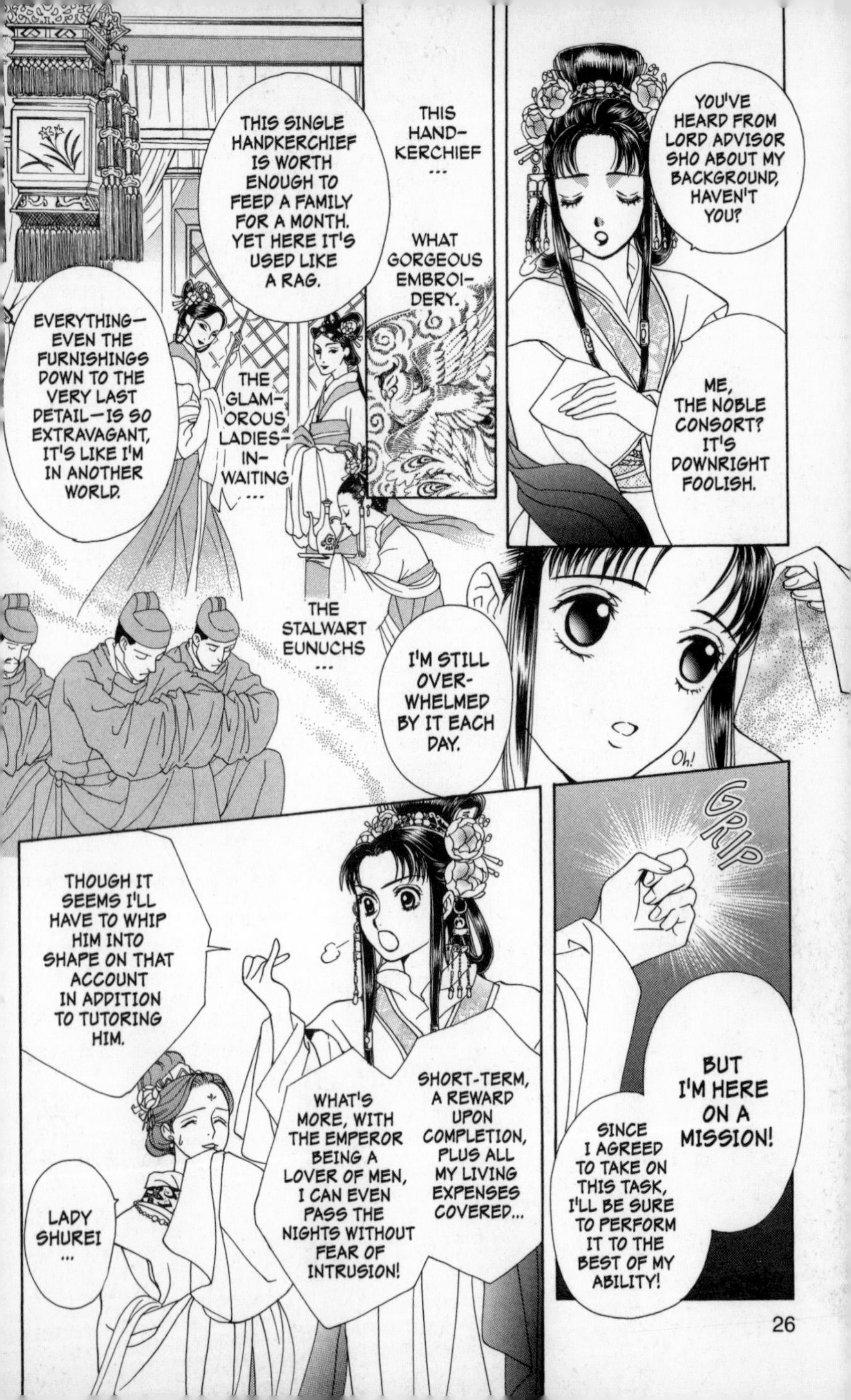
YOU'VE HEARD FROM LORD ADVISOR SHO ABOUT MY BACKGROUND, HAVEN'T YOU?
ME, THE NOBLE CONSORT? IT'S DOWNRIGHT FOOLISH.
THIS HAND-KERCHIEF...
WHAT GORGEOUS EMBROI-DERY.
THIS SINGLE HANDKERCHIEF IS WORTH ENOUGH TO FEED A FAMILY FOR A MONTH. YET HERE IT'S USED LIKE A RAG.
THE GLAM-OROUS LADIES-IN-WAITING...
THE STALWART EUNUCHS...
EVERYTHING—EVEN THE FURNISHINGS DOWN TO THE VERY LAST DETAIL—IS SO EXTRAVAGANT, IT'S LIKE I'M IN ANOTHER WORLD.
Oh!
I'M STILL OVER-WHELMED BY IT EACH DAY.
GRIP
BUT I'M HERE ON A MISSION!
SINCE I AGREED TO TAKE ON THIS TASK, I'LL BE SURE TO PERFORM IT TO THE BEST OF MY ABILITY!
SHORT-TERM, A REWARD UPON COMPLETION, PLUS ALL MY LIVING EXPENSES COVERED...
WHAT'S MORE, WITH THE EMPEROR BEING A LOVER OF MEN, I CAN EVEN PASS THE NIGHTS WITHOUT FEAR OF INTRUSION!
THOUGH IT SEEMS I'LL HAVE TO WHIP HIM INTO SHAPE ON THAT ACCOUNT IN ADDITION TO TUTORING HIM.
LADY SHUREI...

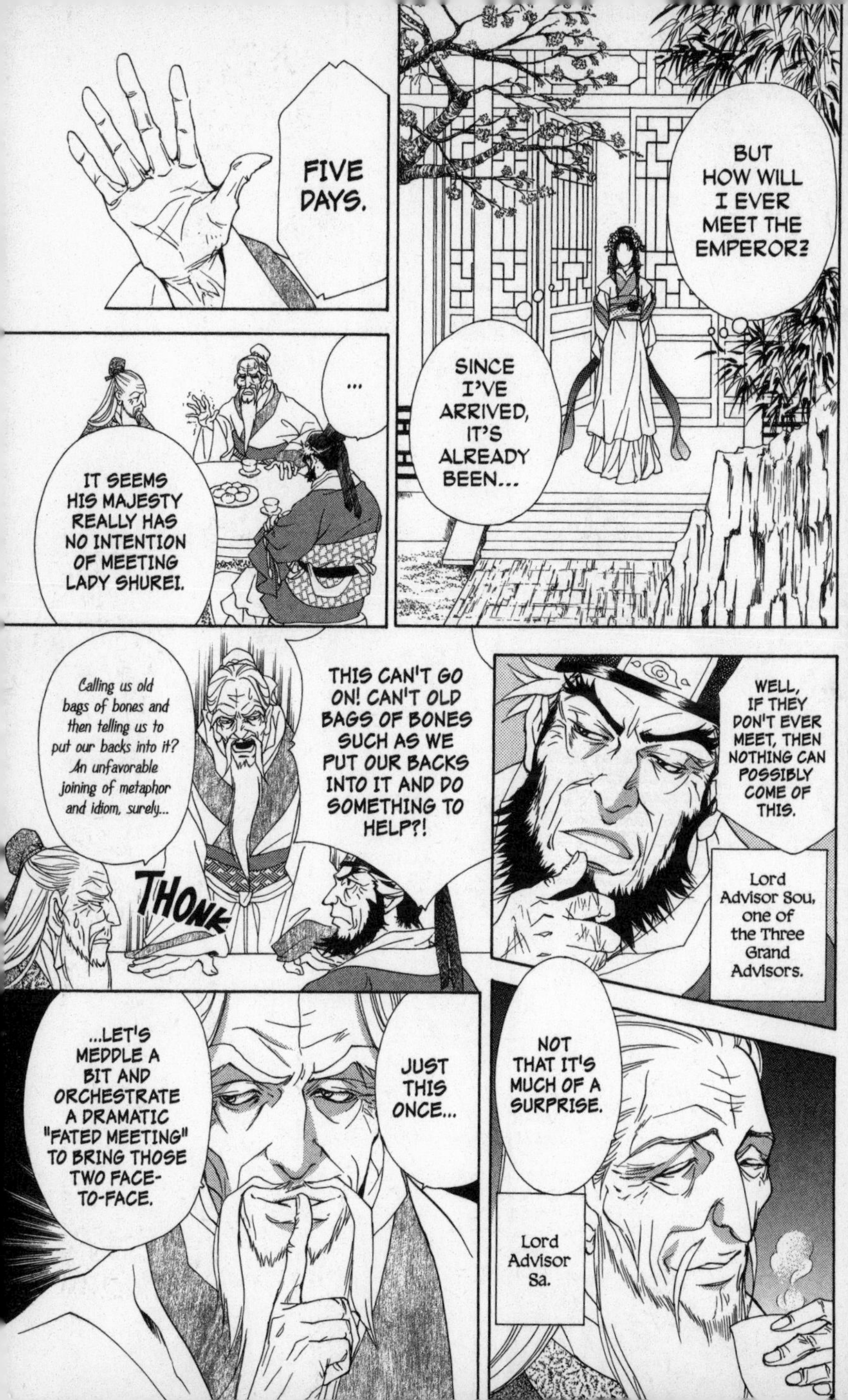
BUT HOW WILL I EVER MEET THE EMPEROR?
SINCE I'VE ARRIVED, IT'S ALREADY BEEN...
FIVE DAYS.
...
IT SEEMS HIS MAJESTY REALLY HAS NO INTENTION OF MEETING LADY SHUREI.
WELL, IF THEY DON'T EVER MEET, THEN NOTHING CAN POSSIBLY COME OF THIS.
Lord Advisor Sou, one of the Three Grand Advisors.
THIS CAN'T GO ON! CAN'T OLD BAGS OF BONES SUCH AS WE PUT OUR BACKS INTO IT AND DO SOMETHING TO HELP?!
Calling us old bags of bones and then telling us to put our backs into it? An unfavorable joining of metaphor and idiom, surely...
THONK
NOT THAT IT'S MUCH OF A SURPRISE.
Lord Advisor Sa.
JUST THIS ONCE...
...LET'S MEDDLE A BIT AND ORCHESTRATE A DRAMATIC "FATED MEETING" TO BRING THOSE TWO FACE-TO-FACE.

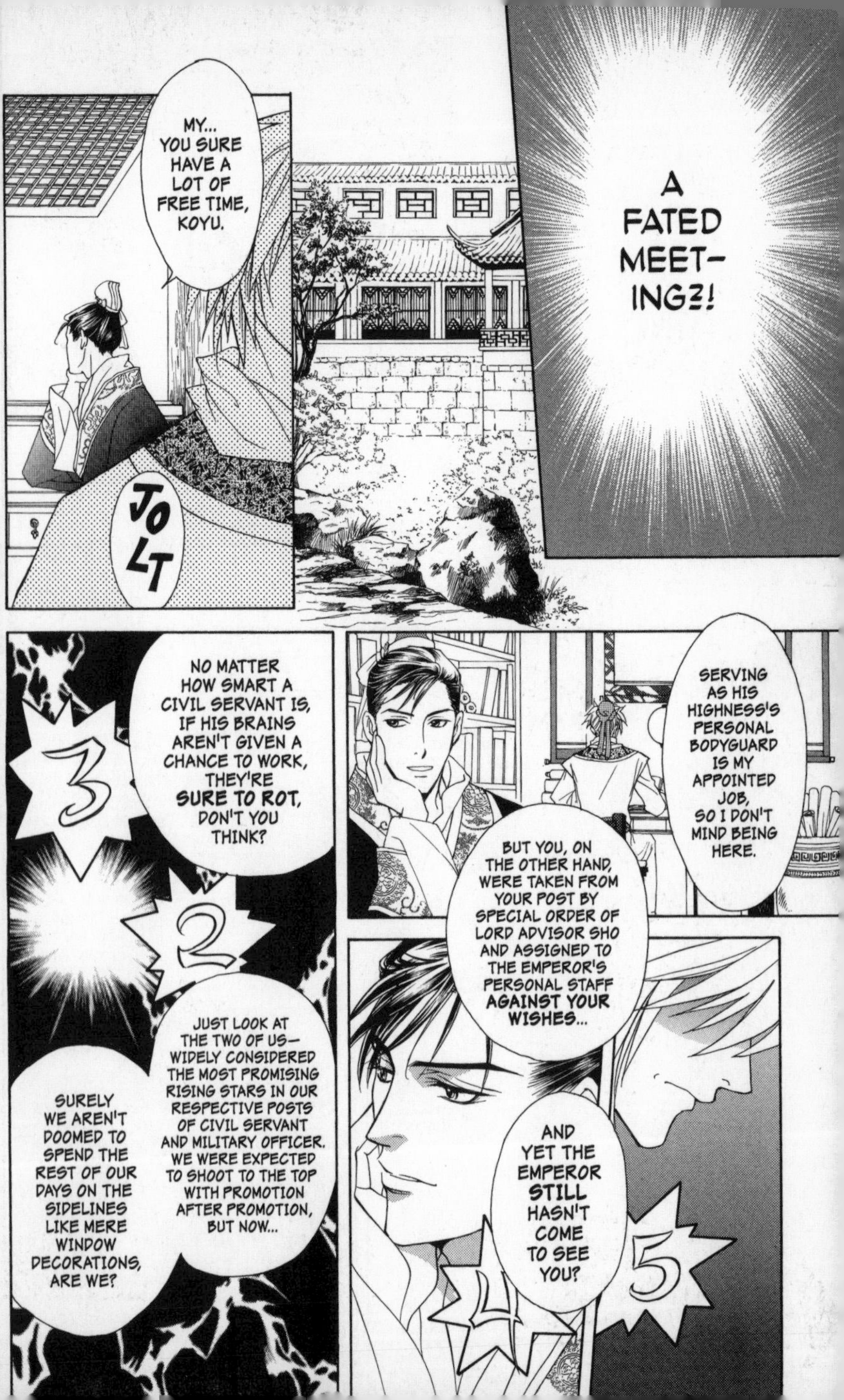
A FATED MEET-ING?!
MY... YOU SURE HAVE A LOT OF FREE TIME, KOYU.
JOLT
SERVING AS HIS HIGHNESS'S PERSONAL BODYGUARD IS MY APPOINTED JOB, SO I DON'T MIND BEING HERE.
BUT YOU, ON THE OTHER HAND, WERE TAKEN FROM YOUR POST BY SPECIAL ORDER OF LORD ADVISOR SHO AND ASSIGNED TO THE EMPEROR'S PERSONAL STAFF AGAINST YOUR WISHES...
AND YET THE EMPEROR STILL HASN'T COME TO SEE YOU?
5
4
NO MATTER HOW SMART A CIVIL SERVANT IS, IF HIS BRAINS AREN'T GIVEN A CHANCE TO WORK, THEY'RE SURE TO ROT, DON'T YOU THINK?
3
2
JUST LOOK AT THE TWO OF US— WIDELY CONSIDERED THE MOST PROMISING RISING STARS IN OUR RESPECTIVE POSTS OF CIVIL SERVANT AND MILITARY OFFICER. WE WERE EXPECTED TO SHOOT TO THE TOP WITH PROMOTION AFTER PROMOTION, BUT NOW...
SURELY WE AREN'T DOOMED TO SPEND THE REST OF OUR DAYS ON THE SIDELINES LIKE MERE WINDOW DECORATIONS, ARE WE?

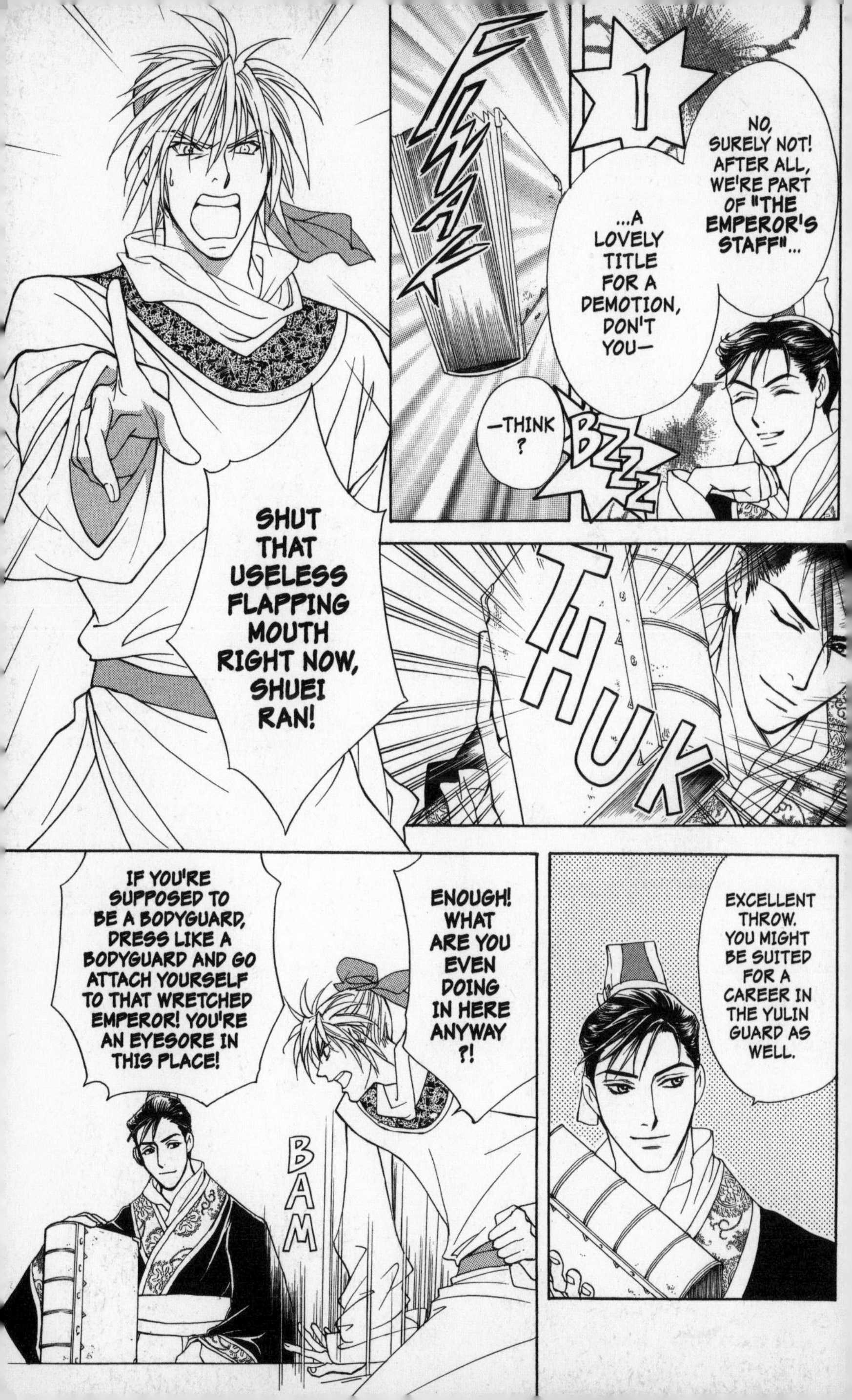
1
NO, SURELY NOT! AFTER ALL, WE'RE PART OF "THE EMPEROR'S STAFF"...
...A LOVELY TITLE FOR A DEMOTION, DON'T YOU—
—THINK?
BZZZ
FWAAK
THUK
SHUT THAT USELESS FLAPPING MOUTH RIGHT NOW, SHUEI RAN!
EXCELLENT THROW. YOU MIGHT BE SUITED FOR A CAREER IN THE YULIN GUARD AS WELL.
ENOUGH! WHAT ARE YOU EVEN DOING IN HERE ANYWAY?!
IF YOU'RE SUPPOSED TO BE A BODYGUARD, DRESS LIKE A BODYGUARD AND GO ATTACH YOURSELF TO THAT WRETCHED EMPEROR! YOU'RE AN EYESORE IN THIS PLACE!
BAM

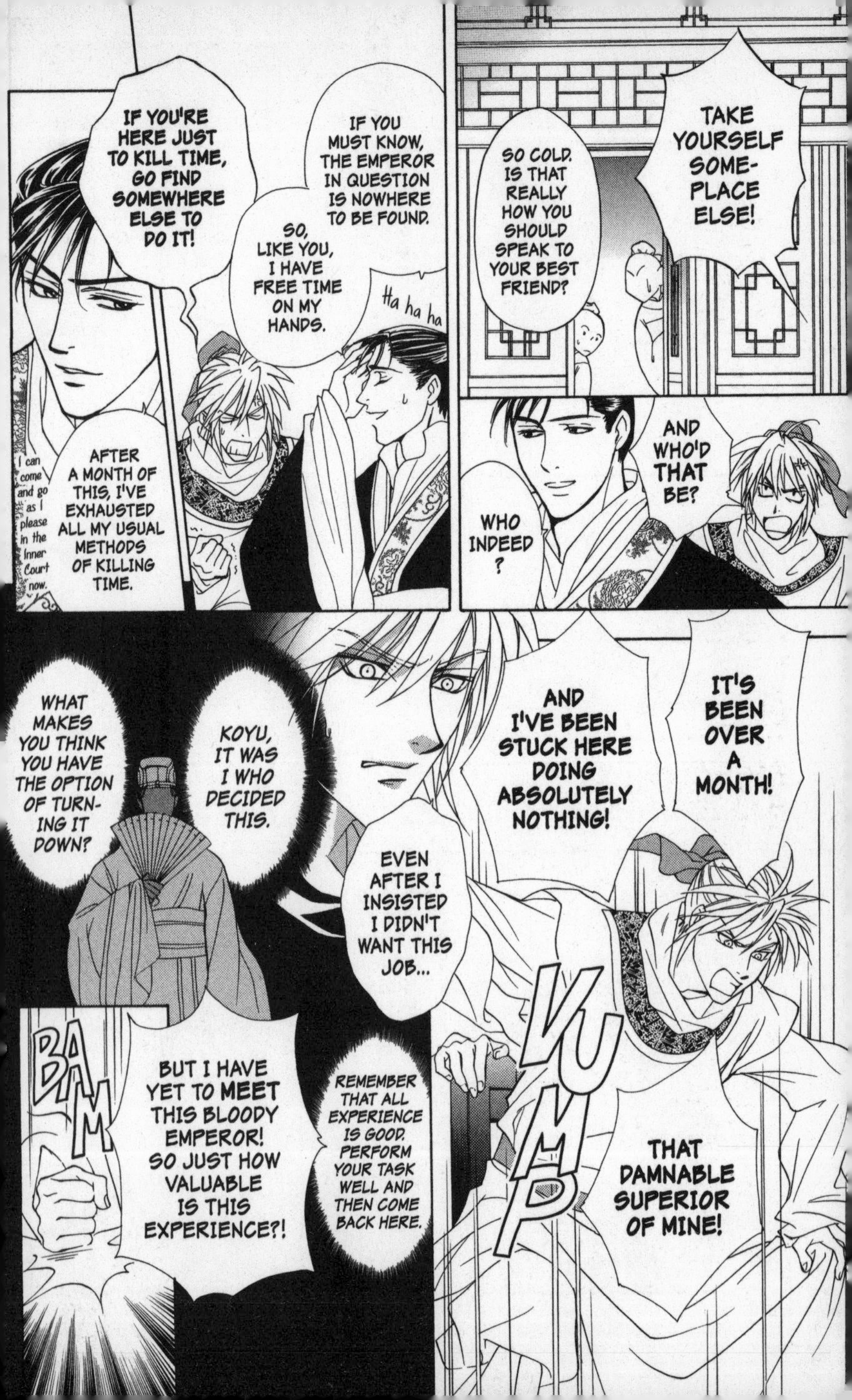
TAKE YOURSELF SOME-PLACE ELSE!
SO COLD. IS THAT REALLY HOW YOU SHOULD SPEAK TO YOUR BEST FRIEND?
AND WHO'D THAT BE?
WHO INDEED?
IF YOU'RE HERE JUST TO KILL TIME, GO FIND SOMEWHERE ELSE TO DO IT!
IF YOU MUST KNOW, THE EMPEROR IN QUESTION IS NOWHERE TO BE FOUND.
SO, LIKE YOU, I HAVE FREE TIME ON MY HANDS.
Ha ha ha
AFTER A MONTH OF THIS, I'VE EXHAUSTED ALL MY USUAL METHODS OF KILLING TIME.
I can come and go as I please in the Inner Court now.
IT'S BEEN OVER A MONTH!
AND I'VE BEEN STUCK HERE DOING ABSOLUTELY NOTHING!
EVEN AFTER I INSISTED I DIDN'T WANT THIS JOB...
KOYU, IT WAS I WHO DECIDED THIS.
WHAT MAKES YOU THINK YOU HAVE THE OPTION OF TURN-ING IT DOWN?
THAT DAMNABLE SUPERIOR OF MINE!
VUMP
REMEMBER THAT ALL EXPERIENCE IS GOOD. PERFORM YOUR TASK WELL AND THEN COME BACK HERE.
BUT I HAVE YET TO MEET THIS BLOODY EMPEROR! SO JUST HOW VALUABLE IS THIS EXPERIENCE?!
BAM

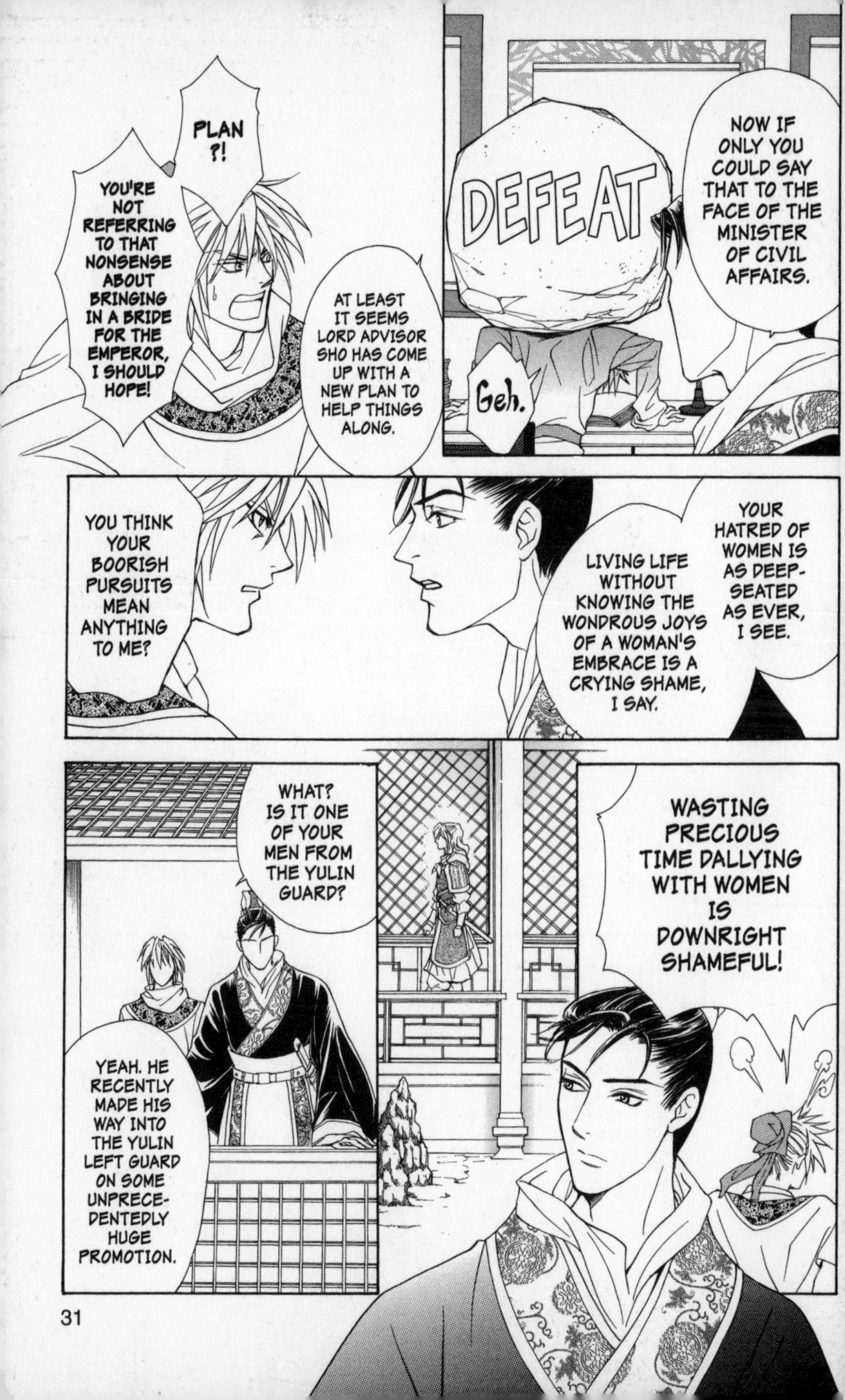
NOW IF ONLY YOU COULD SAY THAT TO THE FACE OF THE MINISTER OF CIVIL AFFAIRS.
DEFEAT
Geh.
AT LEAST IT SEEMS LORD ADVISOR SHO HAS COME UP WITH A NEW PLAN TO HELP THINGS ALONG.
PLAN ?!
YOU'RE NOT REFERRING TO THAT NONSENSE ABOUT BRINGING IN A BRIDE FOR THE EMPEROR, I SHOULD HOPE!
YOUR HATRED OF WOMEN IS AS DEEP-SEATED AS EVER, I SEE.
LIVING LIFE WITHOUT KNOWING THE WONDROUS JOYS OF A WOMAN'S EMBRACE IS A CRYING SHAME, I SAY.
YOU THINK YOUR BOORISH PURSUITS MEAN ANYTHING TO ME?
WASTING PRECIOUS TIME DALLYING WITH WOMEN IS DOWNRIGHT SHAMEFUL!
WHAT? IS IT ONE OF YOUR MEN FROM THE YULIN GUARD?
YEAH. HE RECENTLY MADE HIS WAY INTO THE YULIN LEFT GUARD ON SOME UNPRECE-DENTEDLY HUGE PROMOTION.

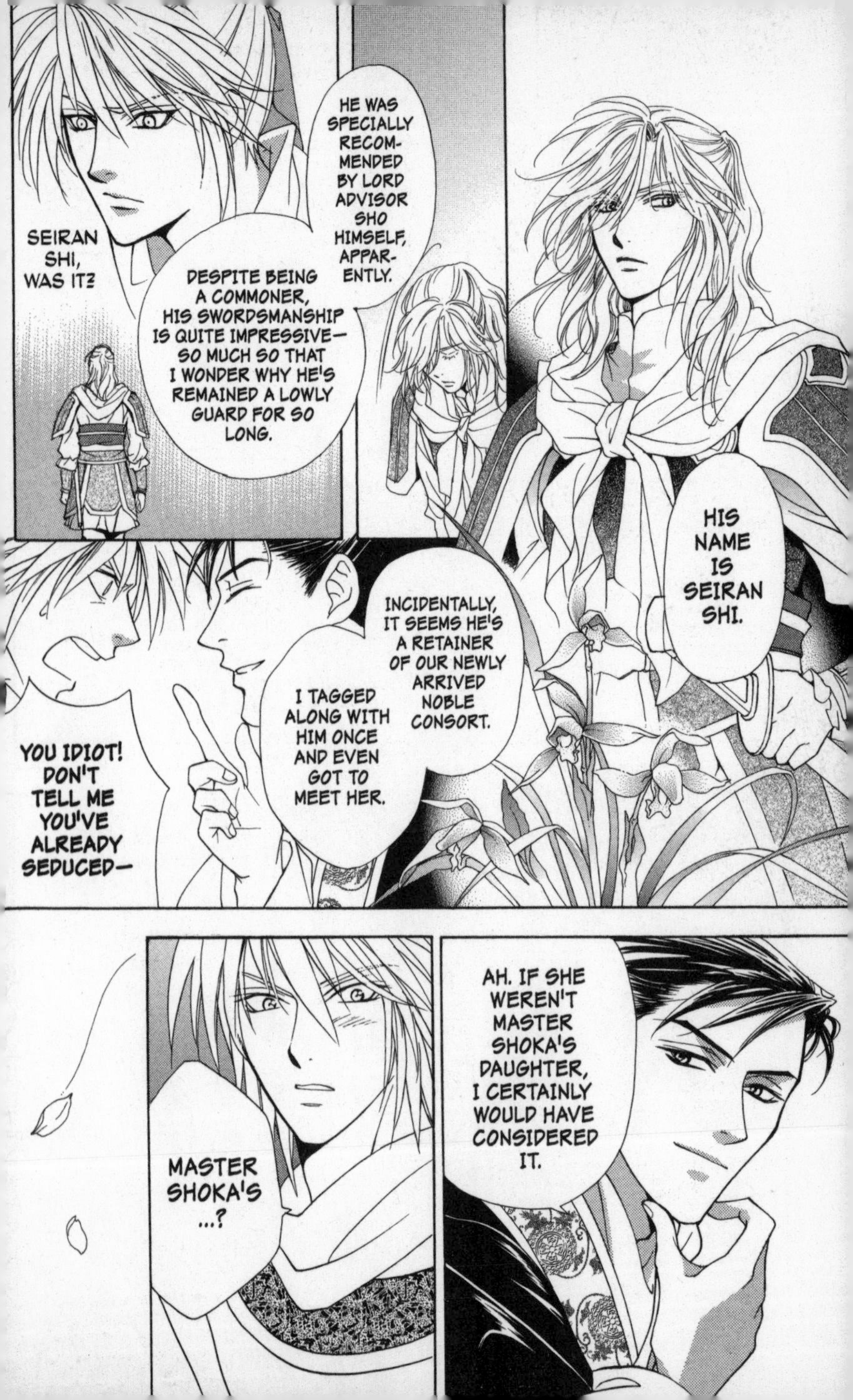
HIS NAME IS SEIRAN SHI.
SEIRAN SHI, WAS IT?
HE WAS SPECIALLY RECOMMENDED BY LORD ADVISOR SHO HIMSELF, APPARENTLY.
DESPITE BEING A COMMONER, HIS SWORDSMANSHIP IS QUITE IMPRESSIVE—SO MUCH SO THAT I WONDER WHY HE'S REMAINED A LOWLY GUARD FOR SO LONG.
INCIDENTALLY, IT SEEMS HE'S A RETAINER OF OUR NEWLY ARRIVED NOBLE CONSORT.
I TAGGED ALONG WITH HIM ONCE AND EVEN GOT TO MEET HER.
YOU IDIOT! DON'T TELL ME YOU'VE ALREADY SEDUCED—
AH. IF SHE WEREN'T MASTER SHOKA'S DAUGHTER, I CERTAINLY WOULD HAVE CONSIDERED IT.
MASTER SHOKA'S ...?

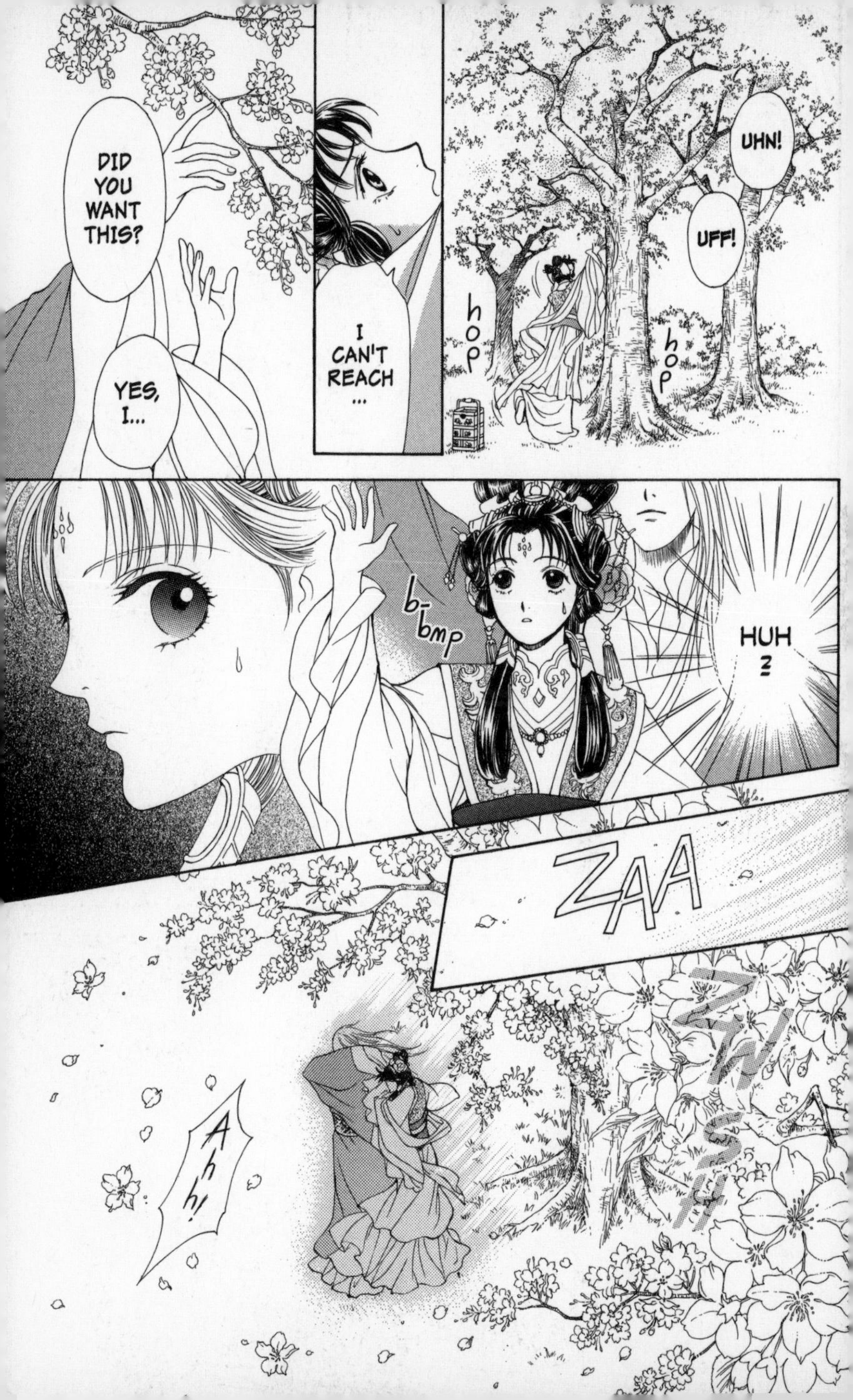
hop
hop
UHN!
UFF!
I CAN'T REACH ...
DID YOU WANT THIS?
YES, I...
HUH?
b-bmp
ZAA
SWISH
Ahh!

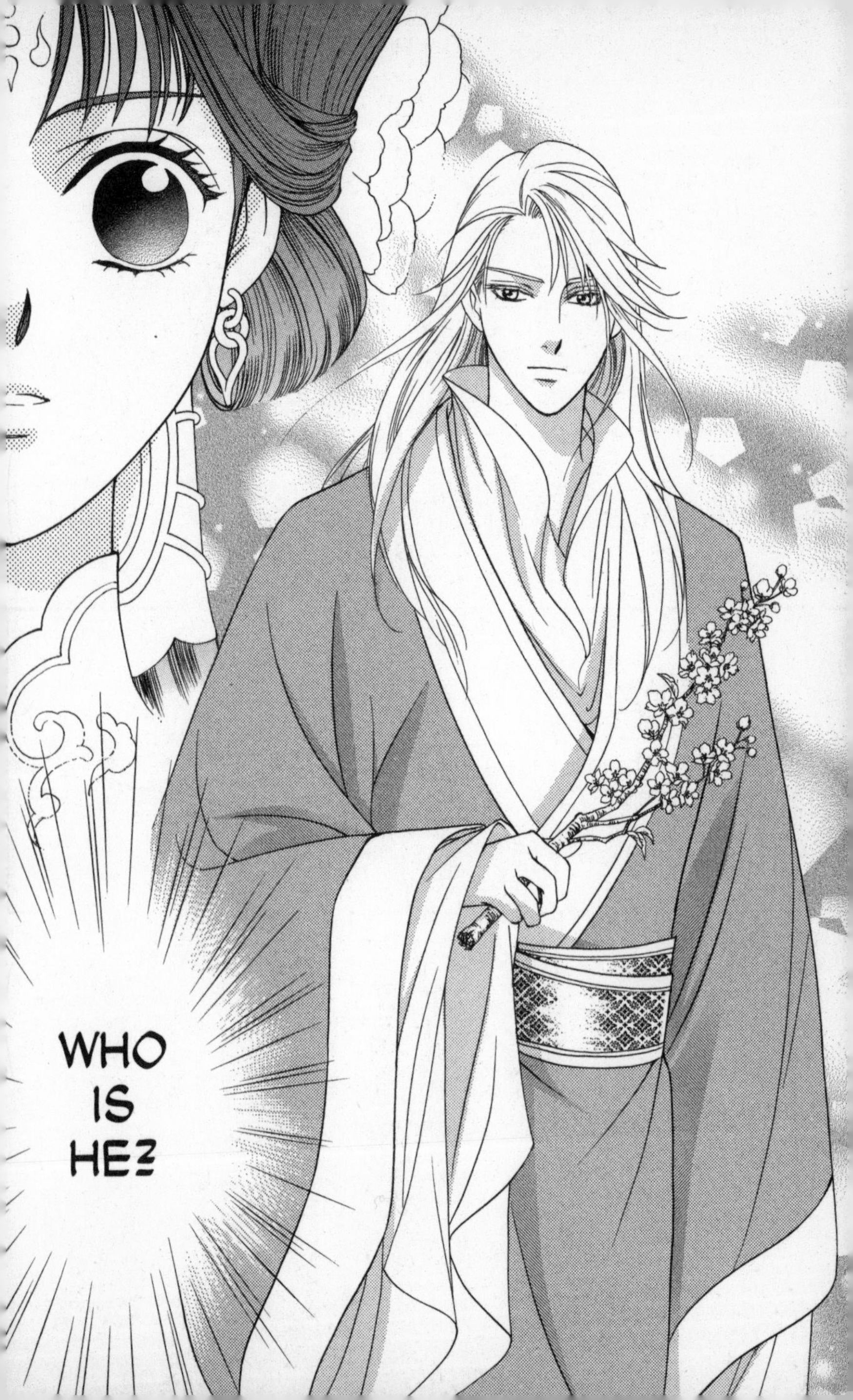
WHO IS HE?

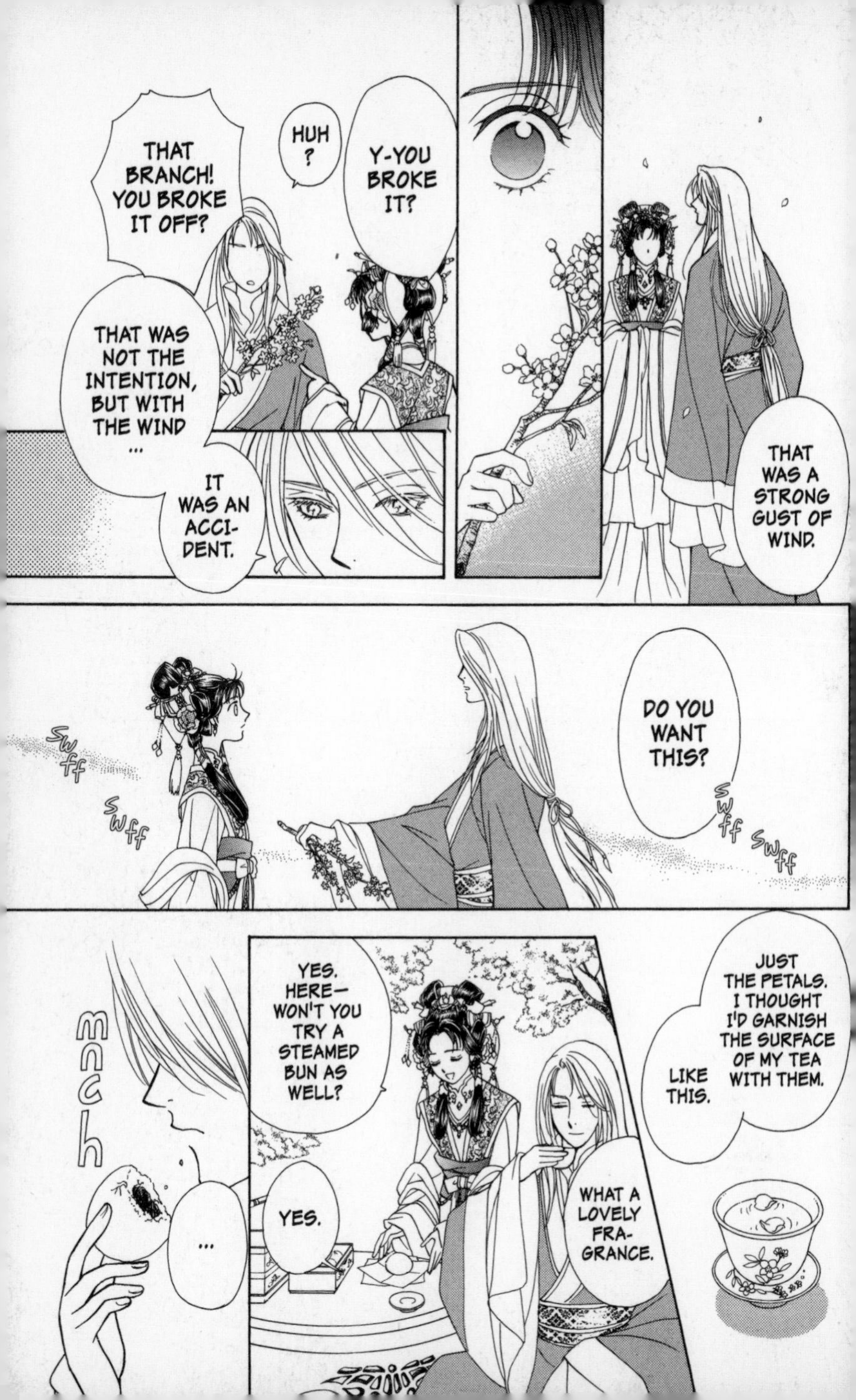
THAT WAS A STRONG GUST OF WIND.
Y-YOU BROKE IT?
HUH?
THAT BRANCH! YOU BROKE IT OFF?
THAT WAS NOT THE INTENTION, BUT WITH THE WIND ...
IT WAS AN ACCI-DENT.
DO YOU WANT THIS?
SWFF SWFF
SWFF
SWFF
JUST THE PETALS. I THOUGHT I'D GARNISH THE SURFACE OF MY TEA WITH THEM.
LIKE THIS.
WHAT A LOVELY FRA-GRANCE.
YES. HERE— WON'T YOU TRY A STEAMED BUN AS WELL?
YES.
mnch
...

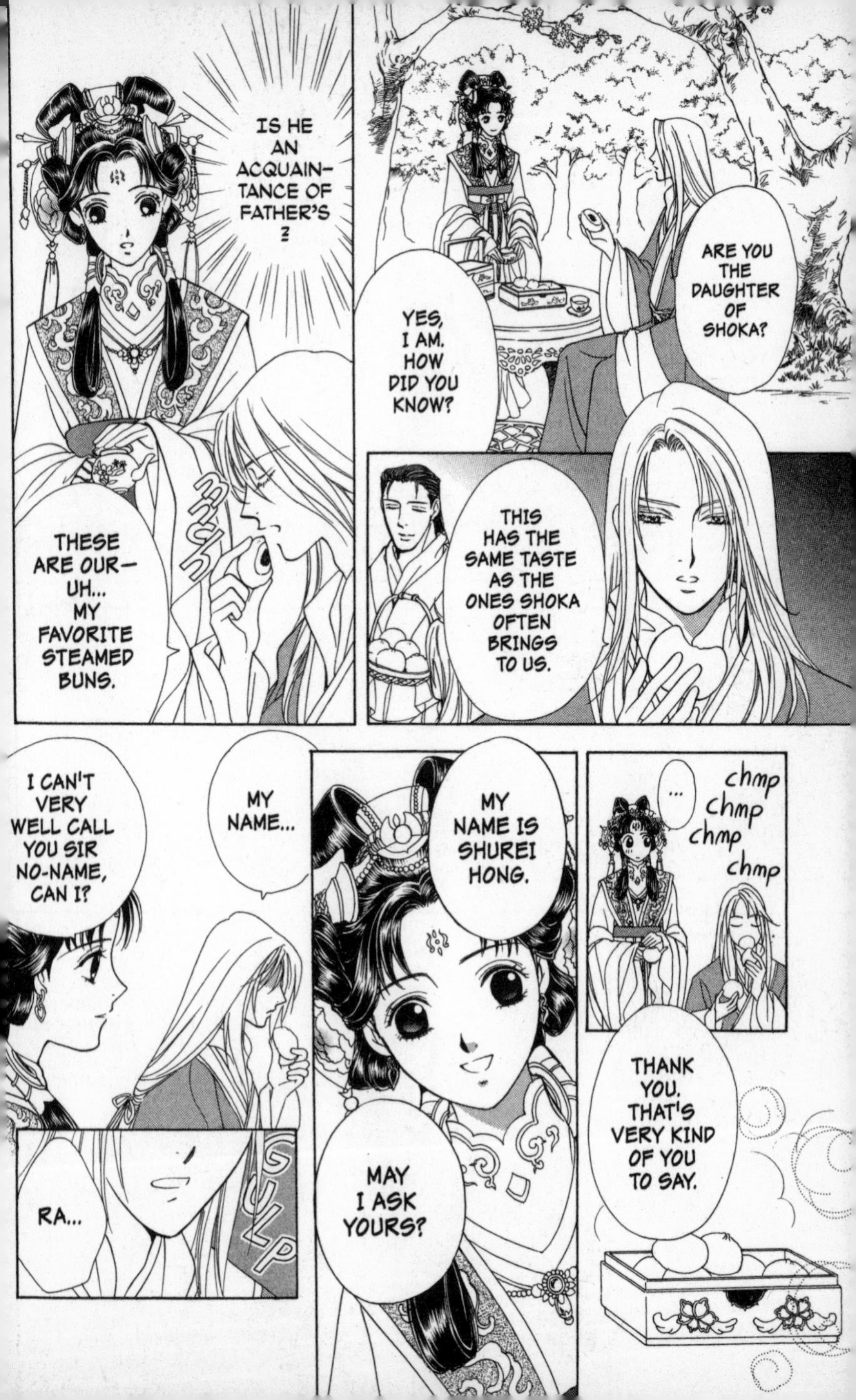
ARE YOU THE DAUGHTER OF SHOKA?
YES, I AM. HOW DID YOU KNOW?
THIS HAS THE SAME TASTE AS THE ONES SHOKA OFTEN BRINGS TO US.
IS HE AN ACQUAINTANCE OF FATHER'S?
munch
THESE ARE OUR— UH... MY FAVORITE STEAMED BUNS.
...
chmp chmp chmp chmp
THANK YOU. THAT'S VERY KIND OF YOU TO SAY.
MY NAME IS SHUREI HONG.
MAY I ASK YOURS?
MY NAME...
I CAN'T VERY WELL CALL YOU SIR NO-NAME, CAN I?
GULP
RA...

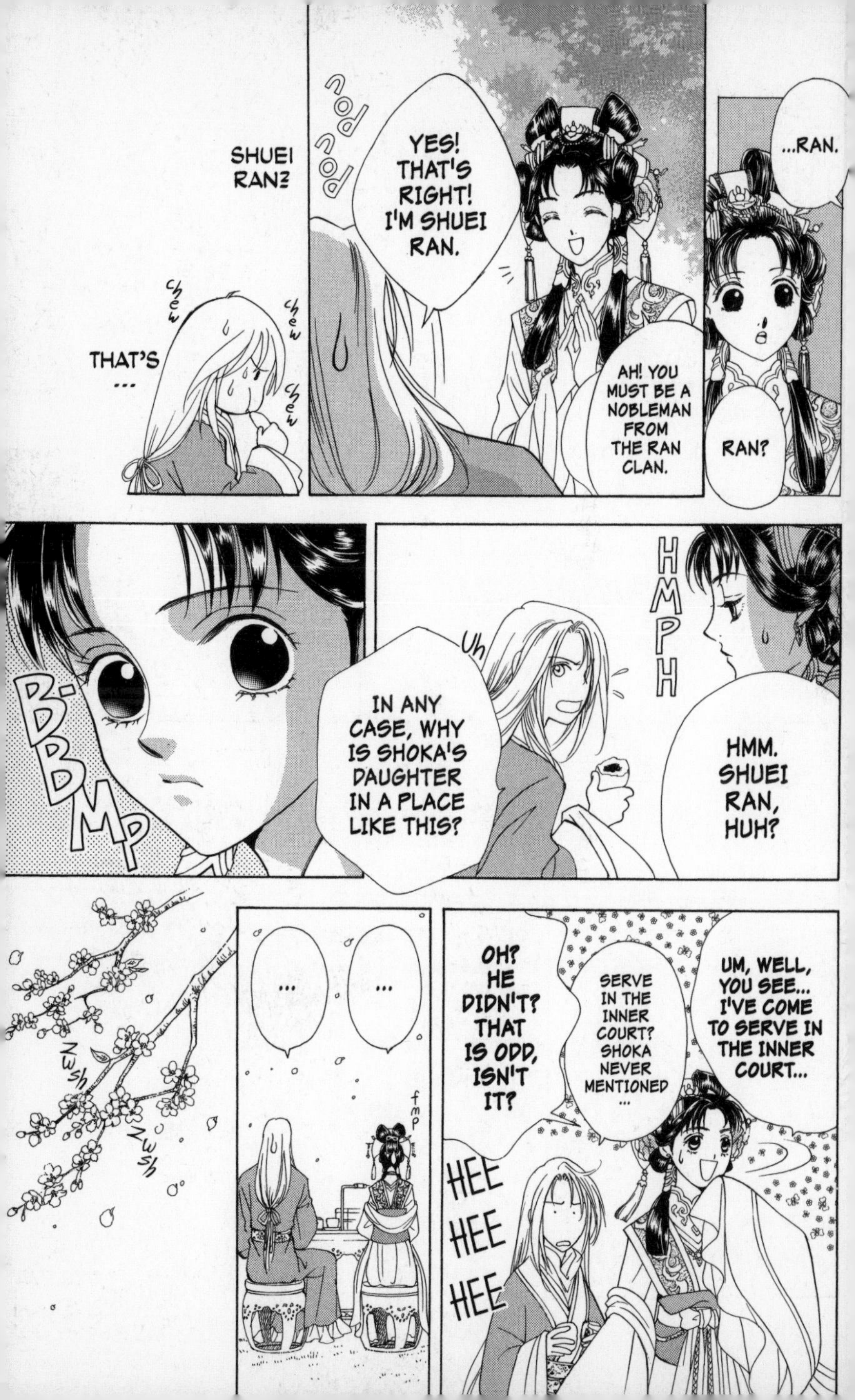

RAN?
...RAN.
AH! YOU MUST BE A NOBLEMAN FROM THE RAN CLAN.
YES! THAT'S RIGHT! I'M SHUEI RAN.
PO PO PO
SHUEI RAN?
chew chew chew
THAT'S ...
HMM. SHUEI RAN, HUH?
HMPH
Uh
IN ANY CASE, WHY IS SHOKA'S DAUGHTER IN A PLACE LIKE THIS?
B-BMP
UM, WELL, YOU SEE... I'VE COME TO SERVE IN THE INNER COURT...
SERVE IN THE INNER COURT? SHOKA NEVER MENTIONED ...
OH? HE DIDN'T? THAT IS ODD, ISN'T IT?
HEE HEE HEE
...
...
fmp
ZWSH
ZWSH

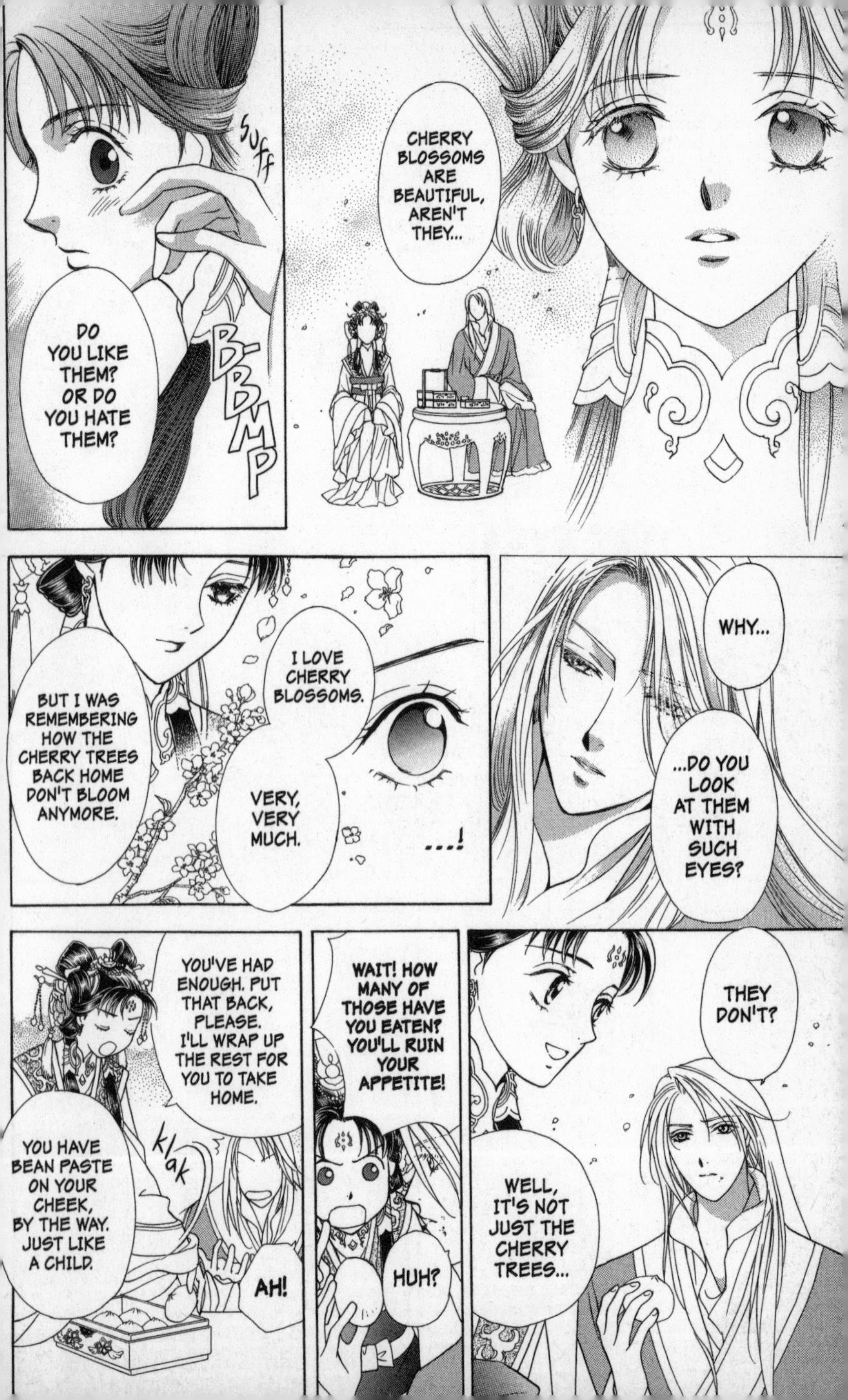
CHERRY BLOSSOMS ARE BEAUTIFUL, AREN'T THEY...
suff
DO YOU LIKE THEM? OR DO YOU HATE THEM?
B-BUMP
WHY...
...DO YOU LOOK AT THEM WITH SUCH EYES?
I LOVE CHERRY BLOSSOMS.
VERY, VERY MUCH.
...!
BUT I WAS REMEMBERING HOW THE CHERRY TREES BACK HOME DON'T BLOOM ANYMORE.
THEY DON'T?
WELL, IT'S NOT JUST THE CHERRY TREES...
WAIT! HOW MANY OF THOSE HAVE YOU EATEN? YOU'LL RUIN YOUR APPETITE!
HUH?
YOU'VE HAD ENOUGH. PUT THAT BACK, PLEASE. I'LL WRAP UP THE REST FOR YOU TO TAKE HOME.
klak
AH!
YOU HAVE BEAN PASTE ON YOUR CHEEK, BY THE WAY. JUST LIKE A CHILD.

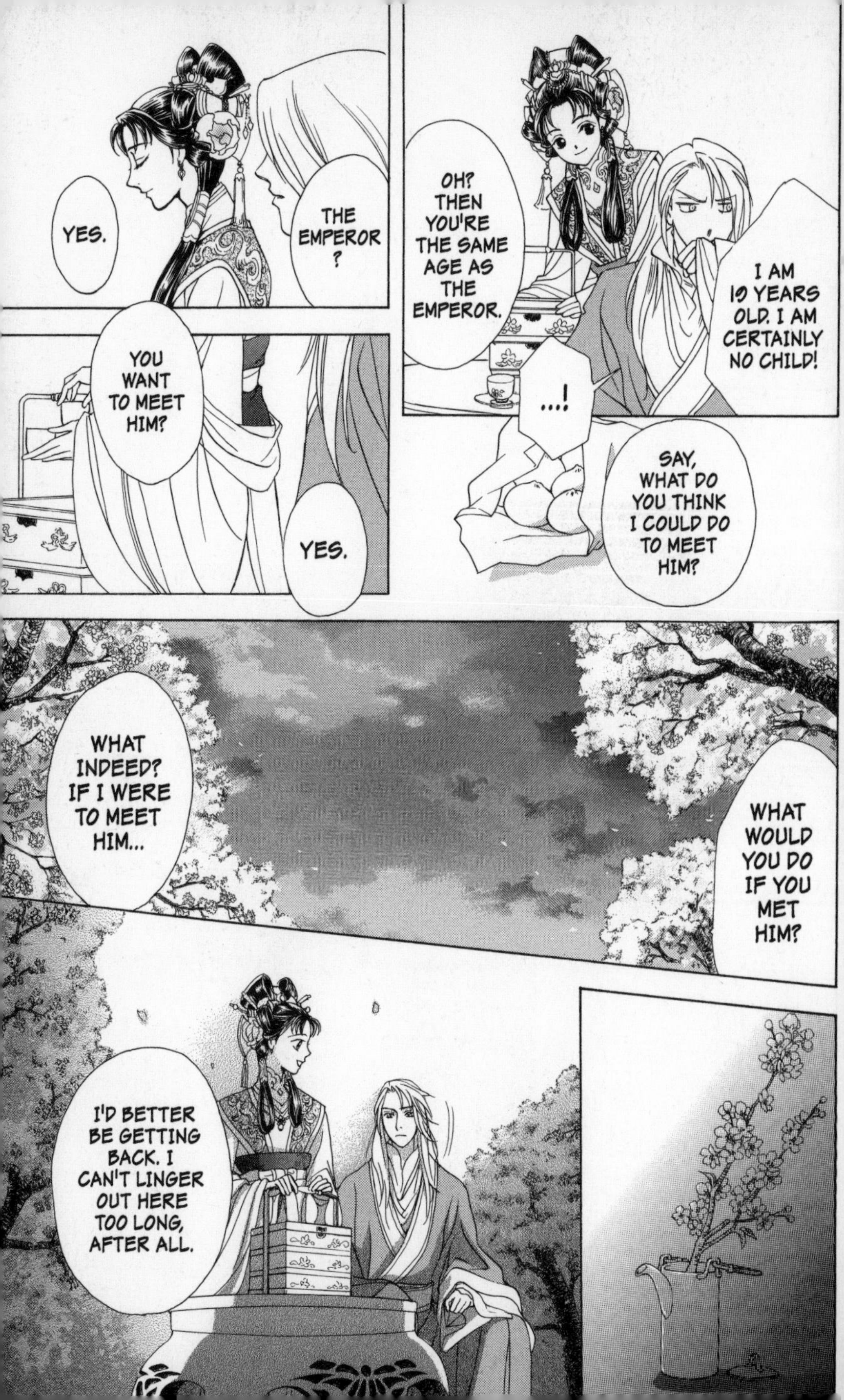
I AM 19 YEARS OLD. I AM CERTAINLY NO CHILD!
OH? THEN YOU'RE THE SAME AGE AS THE EMPEROR.
...!
SAY, WHAT DO YOU THINK I COULD DO TO MEET HIM?
THE EMPEROR?
YES.
YOU WANT TO MEET HIM?
YES.
WHAT WOULD YOU DO IF YOU MET HIM?
WHAT INDEED? IF I WERE TO MEET HIM...
I'D BETTER BE GETTING BACK. I CAN'T LINGER OUT HERE TOO LONG, AFTER ALL.

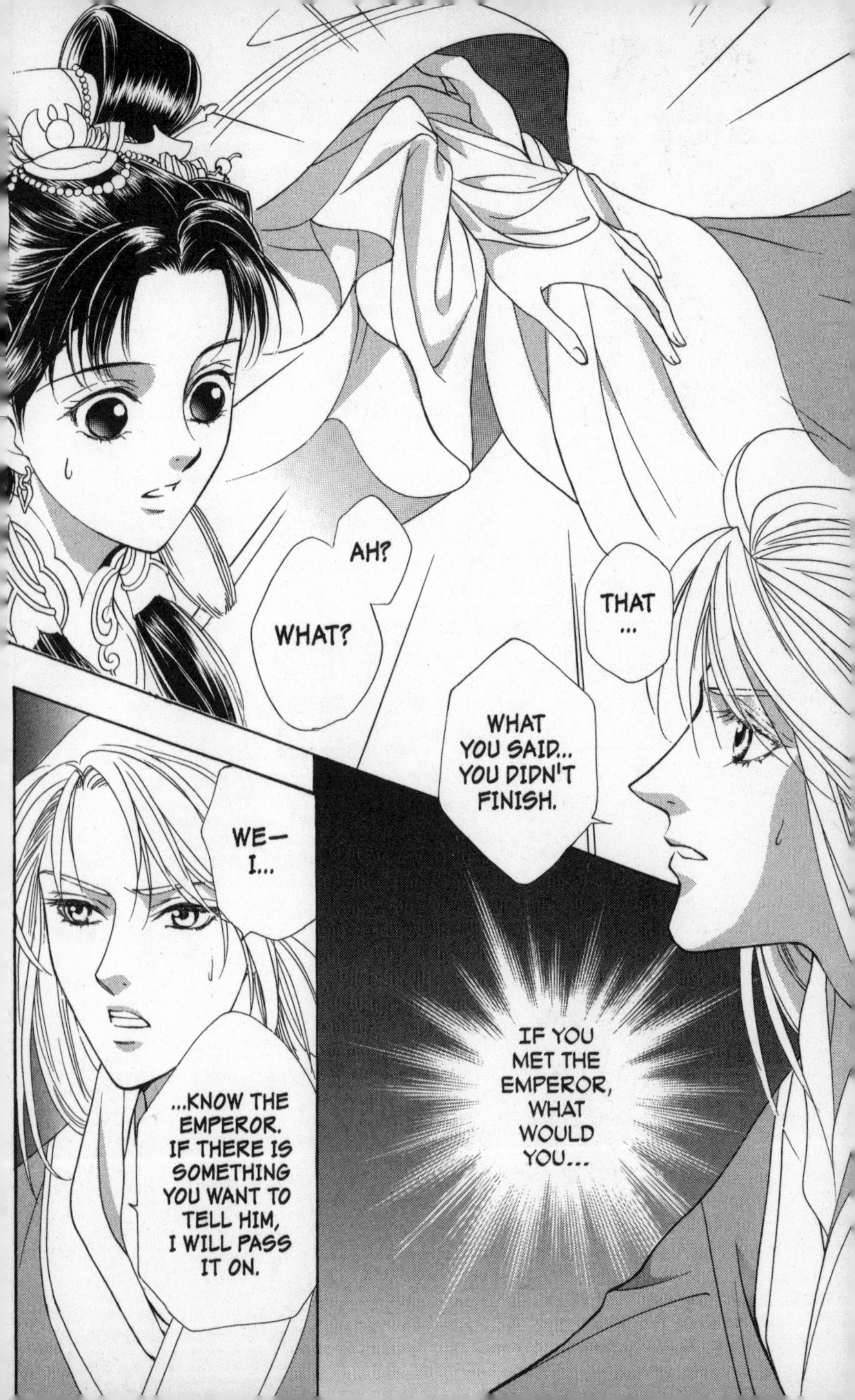
AH?
WHAT?
THAT...
WHAT YOU SAID... YOU DIDN'T FINISH.
IF YOU MET THE EMPEROR, WHAT WOULD YOU...
WE— I...
...KNOW THE EMPEROR. IF THERE IS SOMETHING YOU WANT TO TELL HIM, I WILL PASS IT ON.

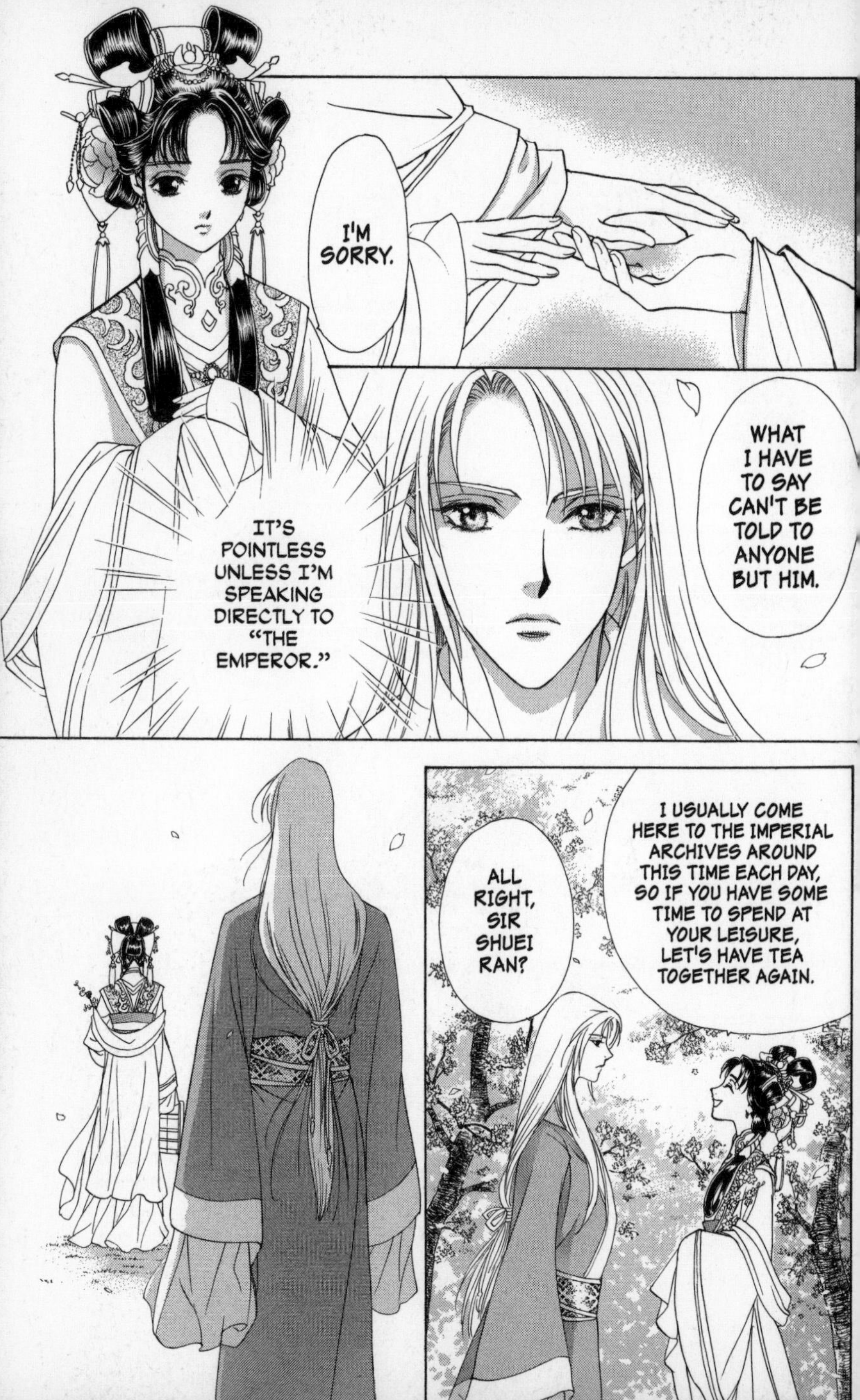
I'M SORRY.
WHAT I HAVE TO SAY CAN'T BE TOLD TO ANYONE BUT HIM.
IT'S POINTLESS UNLESS I'M SPEAKING DIRECTLY TO "THE EMPEROR."
I USUALLY COME HERE TO THE IMPERIAL ARCHIVES AROUND THIS TIME EACH DAY, SO IF YOU HAVE SOME TIME TO SPEND AT YOUR LEISURE, LET'S HAVE TEA TOGETHER AGAIN.
ALL RIGHT, SIR SHUEI RAN?

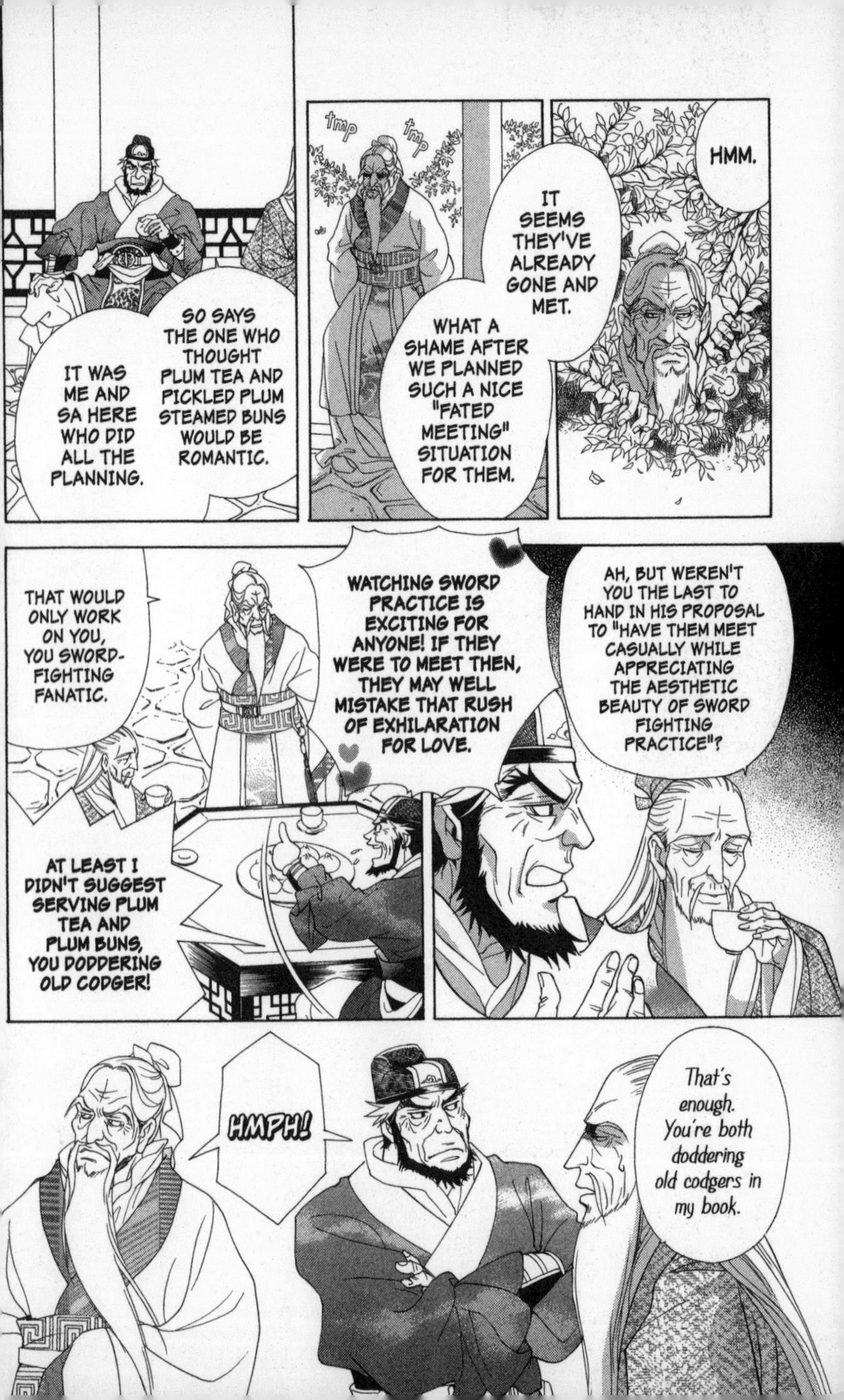
HMM.
IT SEEMS THEY'VE ALREADY GONE AND MET.
WHAT A SHAME AFTER WE PLANNED SUCH A NICE "FATED MEETING" SITUATION FOR THEM.
tmp
tmp
SO SAYS THE ONE WHO THOUGHT PLUM TEA AND PICKLED PLUM STEAMED BUNS WOULD BE ROMANTIC.
IT WAS ME AND SA HERE WHO DID ALL THE PLANNING.
AH, BUT WEREN'T YOU THE LAST TO HAND IN HIS PROPOSAL TO "HAVE THEM MEET CASUALLY WHILE APPRECIATING THE AESTHETIC BEAUTY OF SWORD FIGHTING PRACTICE"?
WATCHING SWORD PRACTICE IS EXCITING FOR ANYONE! IF THEY WERE TO MEET THEN, THEY MAY WELL MISTAKE THAT RUSH OF EXHILARATION FOR LOVE.
THAT WOULD ONLY WORK ON YOU, YOU SWORD-FIGHTING FANATIC.
AT LEAST I DIDN'T SUGGEST SERVING PLUM TEA AND PLUM BUNS, YOU DODDERING OLD CODGER!
That's enough. You're both doddering old codgers in my book.
HMPH!

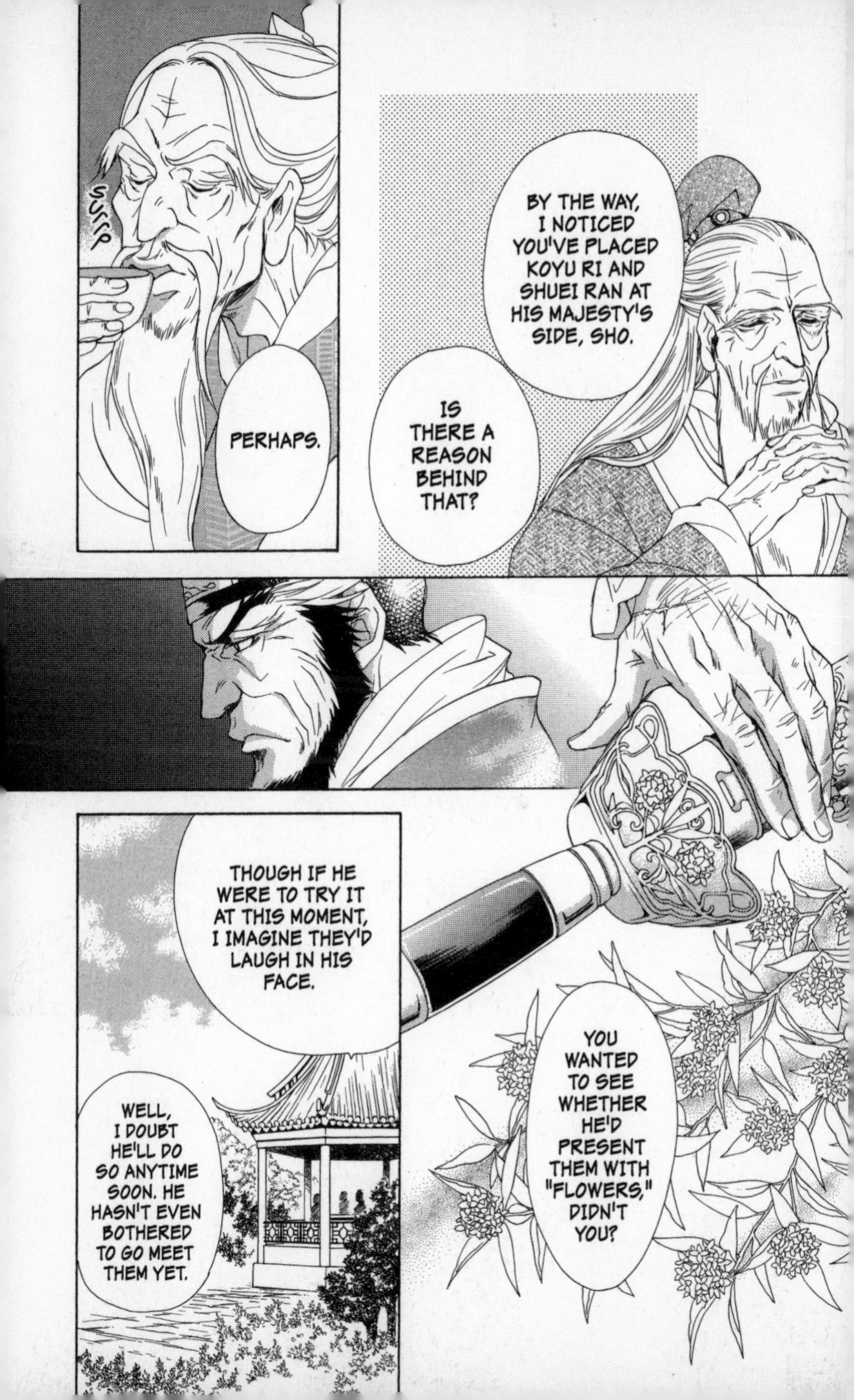
BY THE WAY, I NOTICED YOU'VE PLACED KOYU RI AND SHUEI RAN AT HIS MAJESTY'S SIDE, SHO.
IS THERE A REASON BEHIND THAT?
SURRP
PERHAPS.
YOU WANTED TO SEE WHETHER HE'D PRESENT THEM WITH "FLOWERS," DIDN'T YOU?
WELL, I DOUBT HE'LL DO SO ANYTIME SOON. HE HASN'T EVEN BOTHERED TO GO MEET THEM YET.
THOUGH IF HE WERE TO TRY IT AT THIS MOMENT, I IMAGINE THEY'D LAUGH IN HIS FACE.

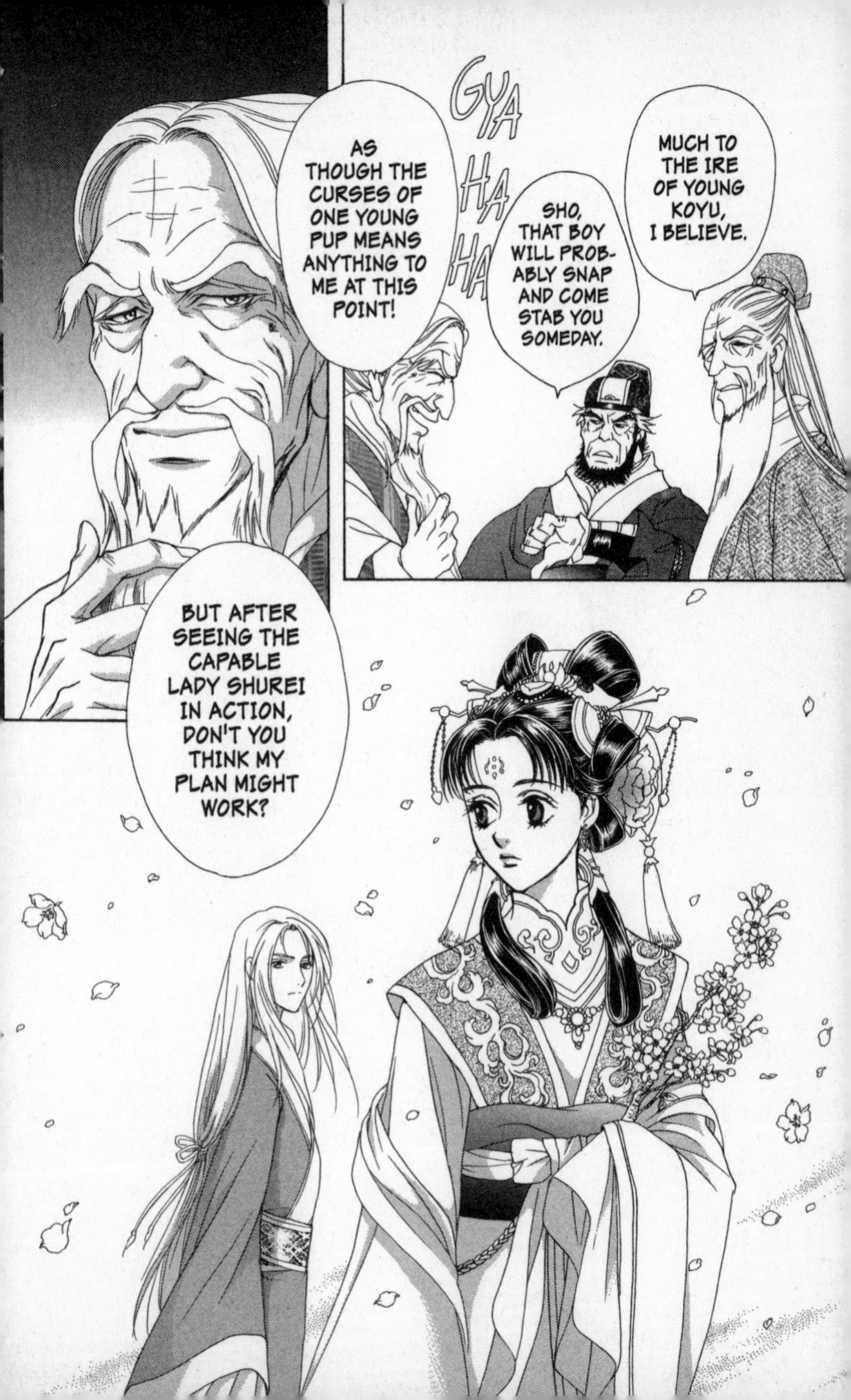
MUCH TO THE IRE OF YOUNG KOYU, I BELIEVE.
SHO, THAT BOY WILL PROB-ABLY SNAP AND COME STAB YOU SOMEDAY.
GYA HA HA
AS THOUGH THE CURSES OF ONE YOUNG PUP MEANS ANYTHING TO ME AT THIS POINT!
BUT AFTER SEEING THE CAPABLE LADY SHUREI IN ACTION, DON'T YOU THINK MY PLAN MIGHT WORK?

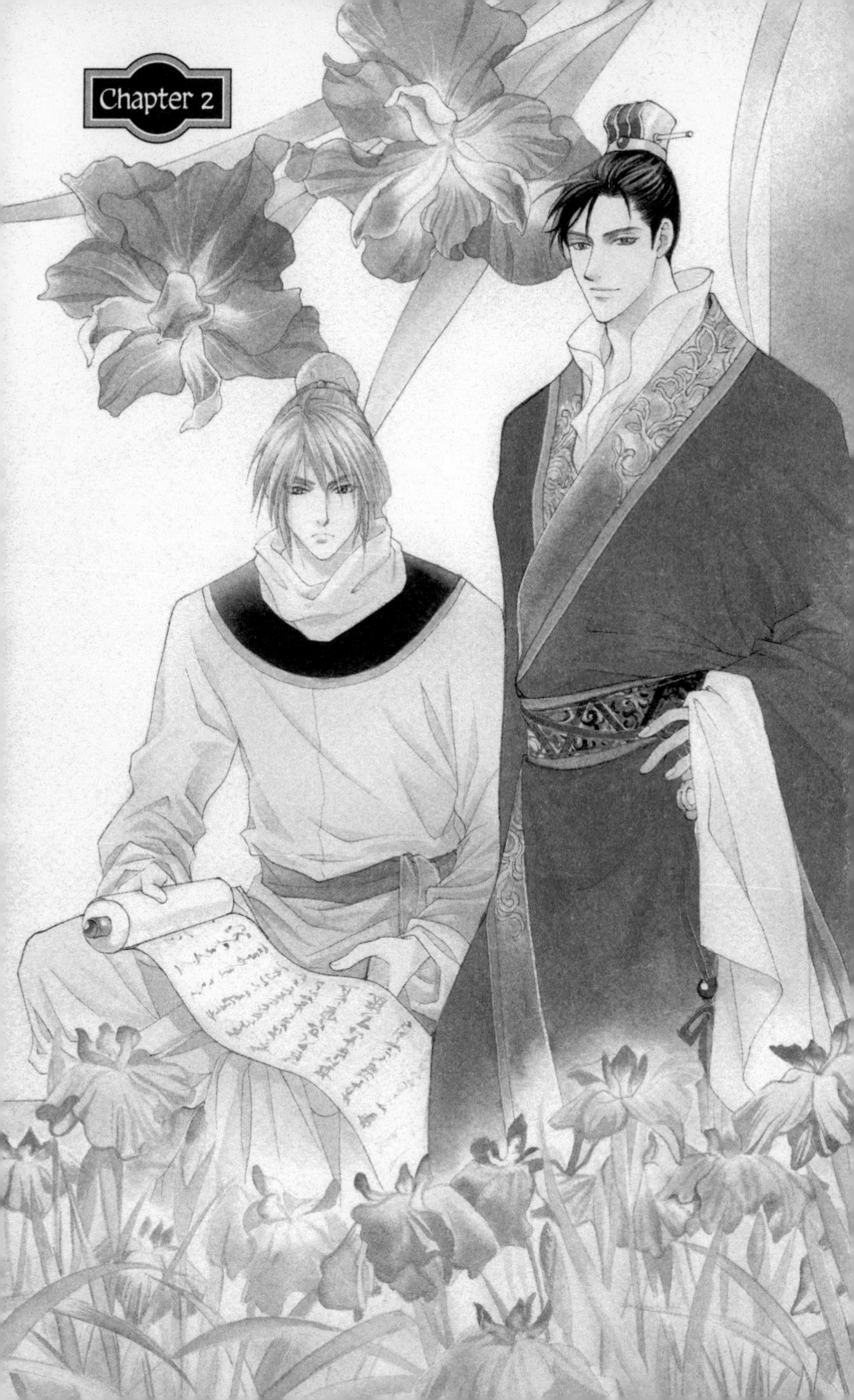
Chapter 2

The Story of
SAIUNKOKU

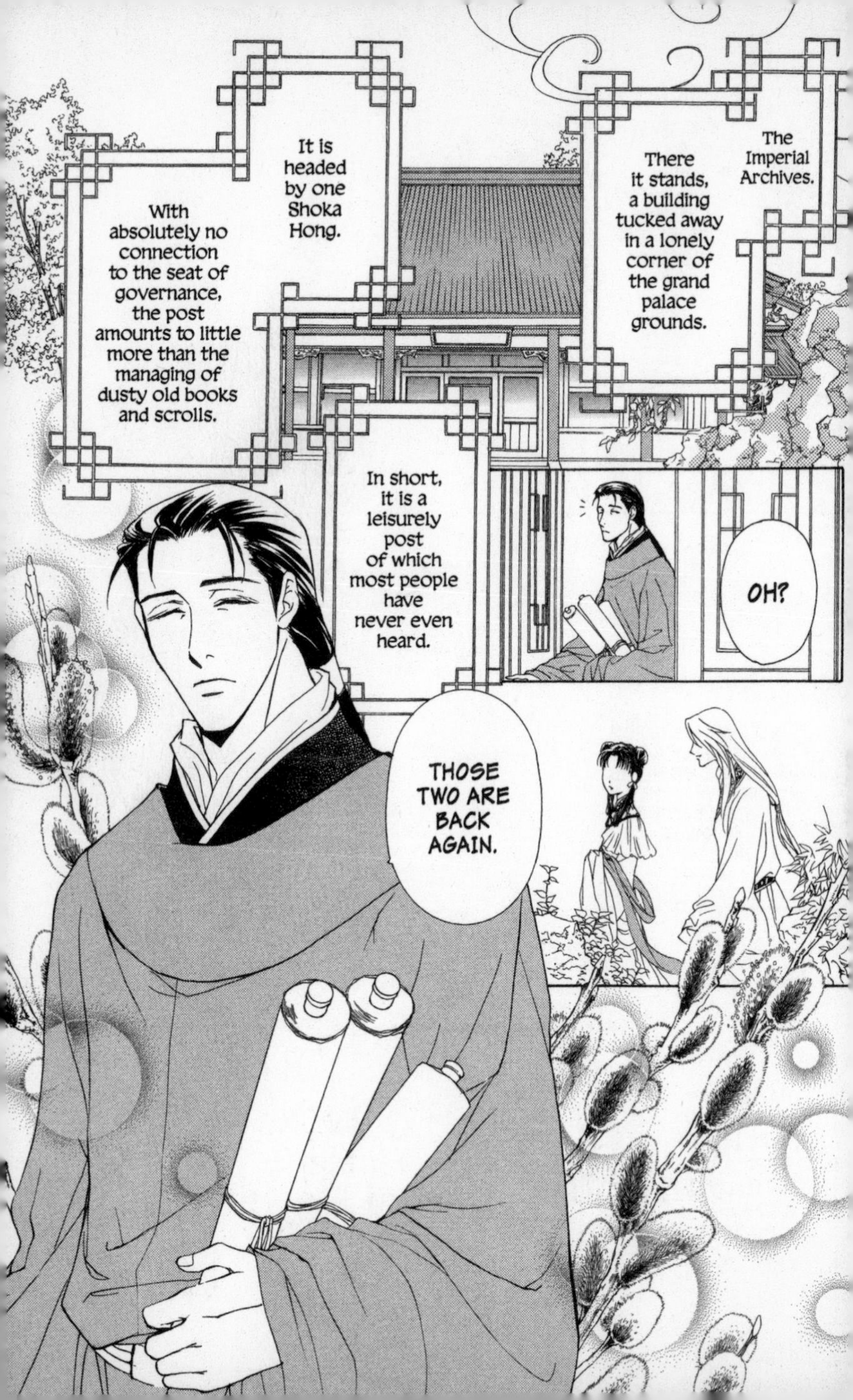
The Imperial Archives.
There it stands, a building tucked away in a lonely corner of the grand palace grounds.
It is headed by one Shoka Hong.
With absolutely no connection to the seat of governance, the post amounts to little more than the managing of dusty old books and scrolls.
In short, it is a leisurely post of which most people have never even heard.
OH?
THOSE TWO ARE BACK AGAIN.

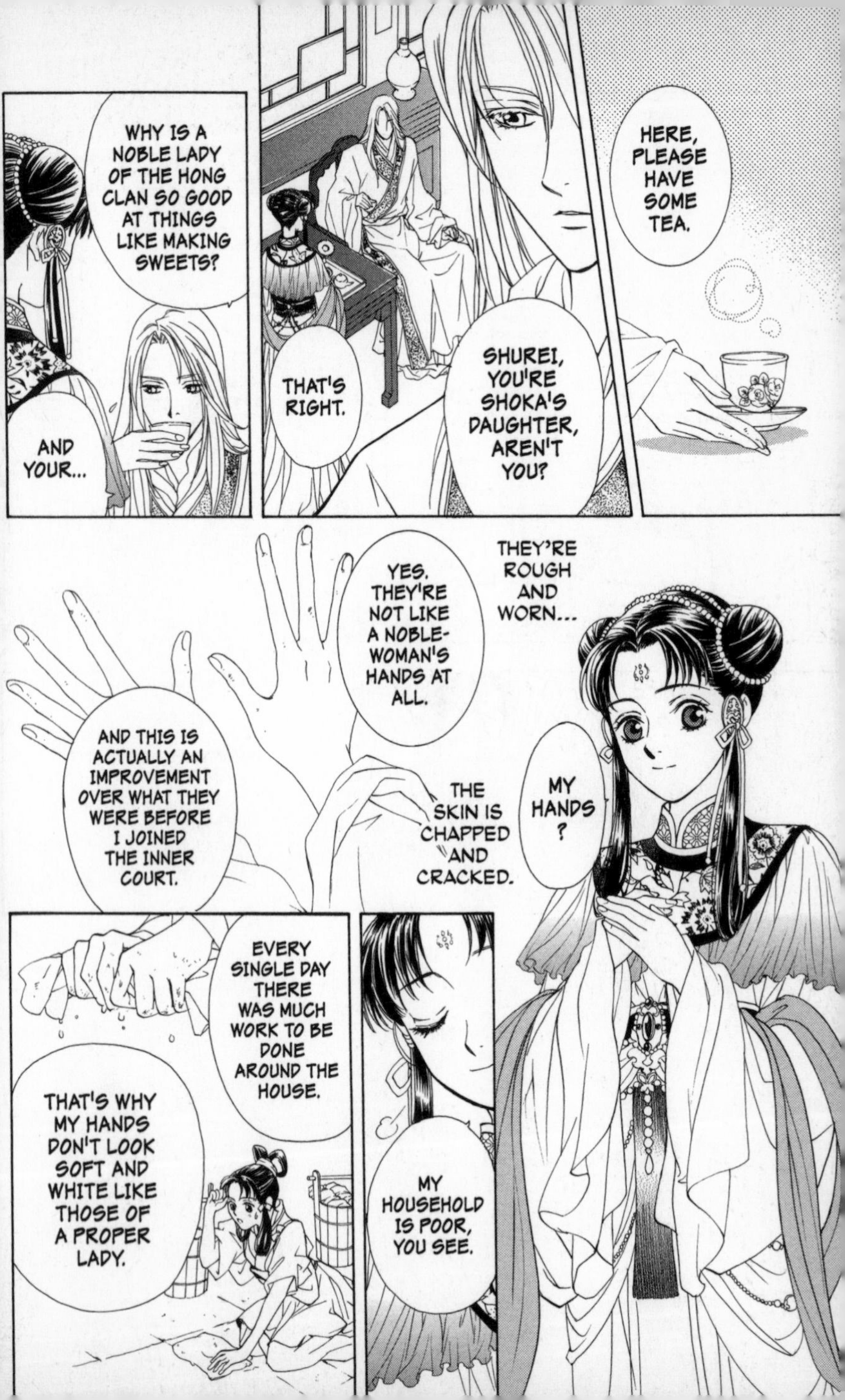
HERE, PLEASE HAVE SOME TEA.
SHUREI, YOU'RE SHOKA'S DAUGHTER, AREN'T YOU?
THAT'S RIGHT.
WHY IS A NOBLE LADY OF THE HONG CLAN SO GOOD AT THINGS LIKE MAKING SWEETS?
AND YOUR...
MY HANDS?
THEY'RE ROUGH AND WORN...
YES. THEY'RE NOT LIKE A NOBLE-WOMAN'S HANDS AT ALL.
THE SKIN IS CHAPPED AND CRACKED.
AND THIS IS ACTUALLY AN IMPROVEMENT OVER WHAT THEY WERE BEFORE I JOINED THE INNER COURT.
MY HOUSEHOLD IS POOR, YOU SEE.
EVERY SINGLE DAY THERE WAS MUCH WORK TO BE DONE AROUND THE HOUSE.
THAT'S WHY MY HANDS DON'T LOOK SOFT AND WHITE LIKE THOSE OF A PROPER LADY.

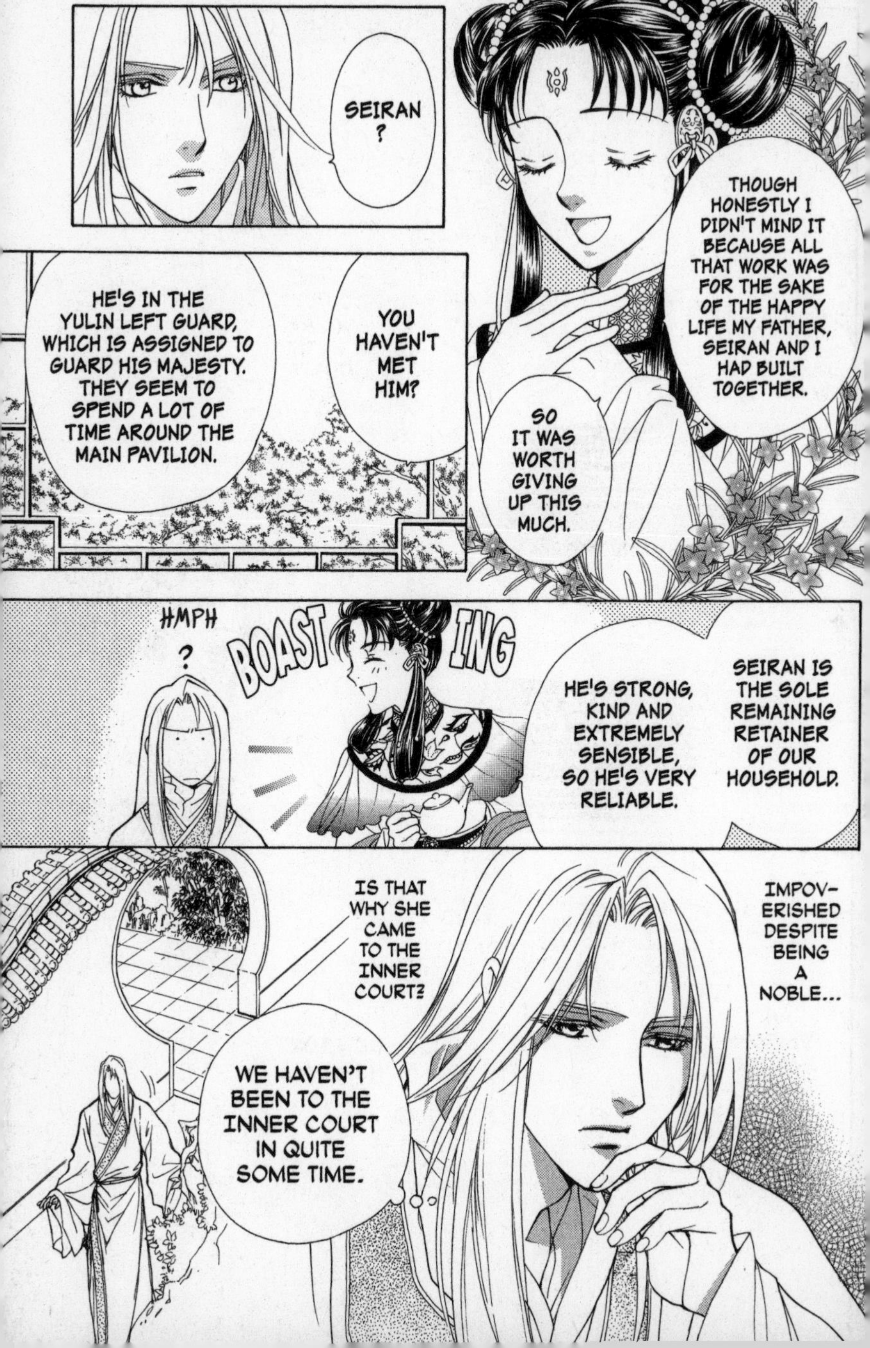
THOUGH HONESTLY I DIDN'T MIND IT BECAUSE ALL THAT WORK WAS FOR THE SAKE OF THE HAPPY LIFE MY FATHER, SEIRAN AND I HAD BUILT TOGETHER.
SO IT WAS WORTH GIVING UP THIS MUCH.
SEIRAN ?
YOU HAVEN'T MET HIM?
HE'S IN THE YULIN LEFT GUARD, WHICH IS ASSIGNED TO GUARD HIS MAJESTY. THEY SEEM TO SPEND A LOT OF TIME AROUND THE MAIN PAVILION.
SEIRAN IS THE SOLE REMAINING RETAINER OF OUR HOUSEHOLD.
HE'S STRONG, KIND AND EXTREMELY SENSIBLE, SO HE'S VERY RELIABLE.
BOASTING
HMPH
?
IMPOVERISHED DESPITE BEING A NOBLE...
IS THAT WHY SHE CAME TO THE INNER COURT?
WE HAVEN'T BEEN TO THE INNER COURT IN QUITE SOME TIME.

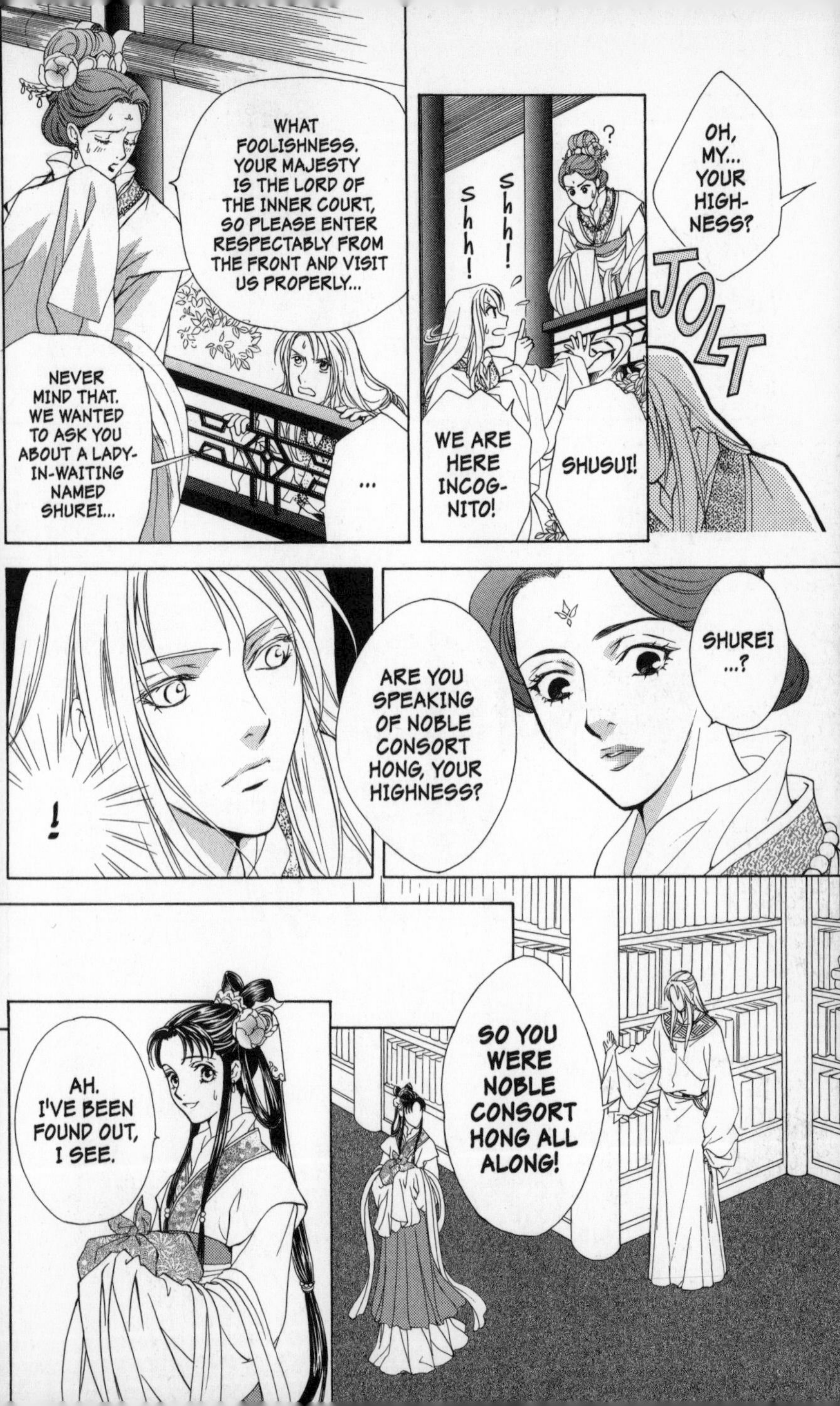
OH, MY... YOUR HIGHNESS?
JOLT
SHUSUI!
Shhh!
Shhh!
WE ARE HERE INCOGNITO!
WHAT FOOLISHNESS. YOUR MAJESTY IS THE LORD OF THE INNER COURT, SO PLEASE ENTER RESPECTABLY FROM THE FRONT AND VISIT US PROPERLY...
...
NEVER MIND THAT. WE WANTED TO ASK YOU ABOUT A LADY-IN-WAITING NAMED SHUREI...
SHUREI ...?
ARE YOU SPEAKING OF NOBLE CONSORT HONG, YOUR HIGHNESS?
!
SO YOU WERE NOBLE CONSORT HONG ALL ALONG!
AH. I'VE BEEN FOUND OUT, I SEE.

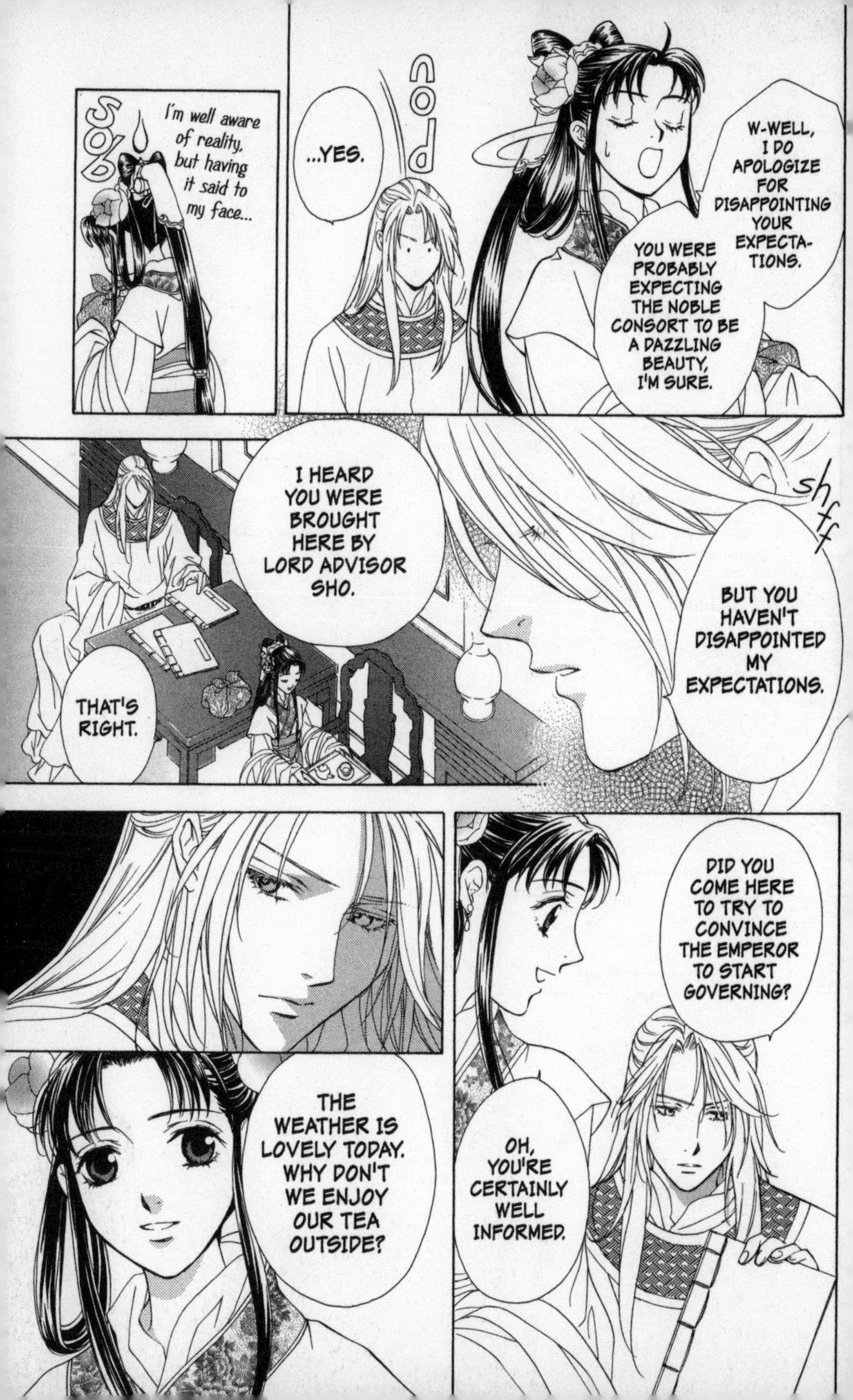
W-WELL, I DO APOLOGIZE FOR DISAPPOINTING YOUR EXPECTATIONS.
YOU WERE PROBABLY EXPECTING THE NOBLE CONSORT TO BE A DAZZLING BEAUTY, I'M SURE.
nod
...YES.
sob
I'm well aware of reality, but having it said to my face...
shff
BUT YOU HAVEN'T DISAPPOINTED MY EXPECTATIONS.
I HEARD YOU WERE BROUGHT HERE BY LORD ADVISOR SHO.
THAT'S RIGHT.
DID YOU COME HERE TO TRY TO CONVINCE THE EMPEROR TO START GOVERNING?
OH, YOU'RE CERTAINLY WELL INFORMED.
THE WEATHER IS LOVELY TODAY. WHY DON'T WE ENJOY OUR TEA OUTSIDE?

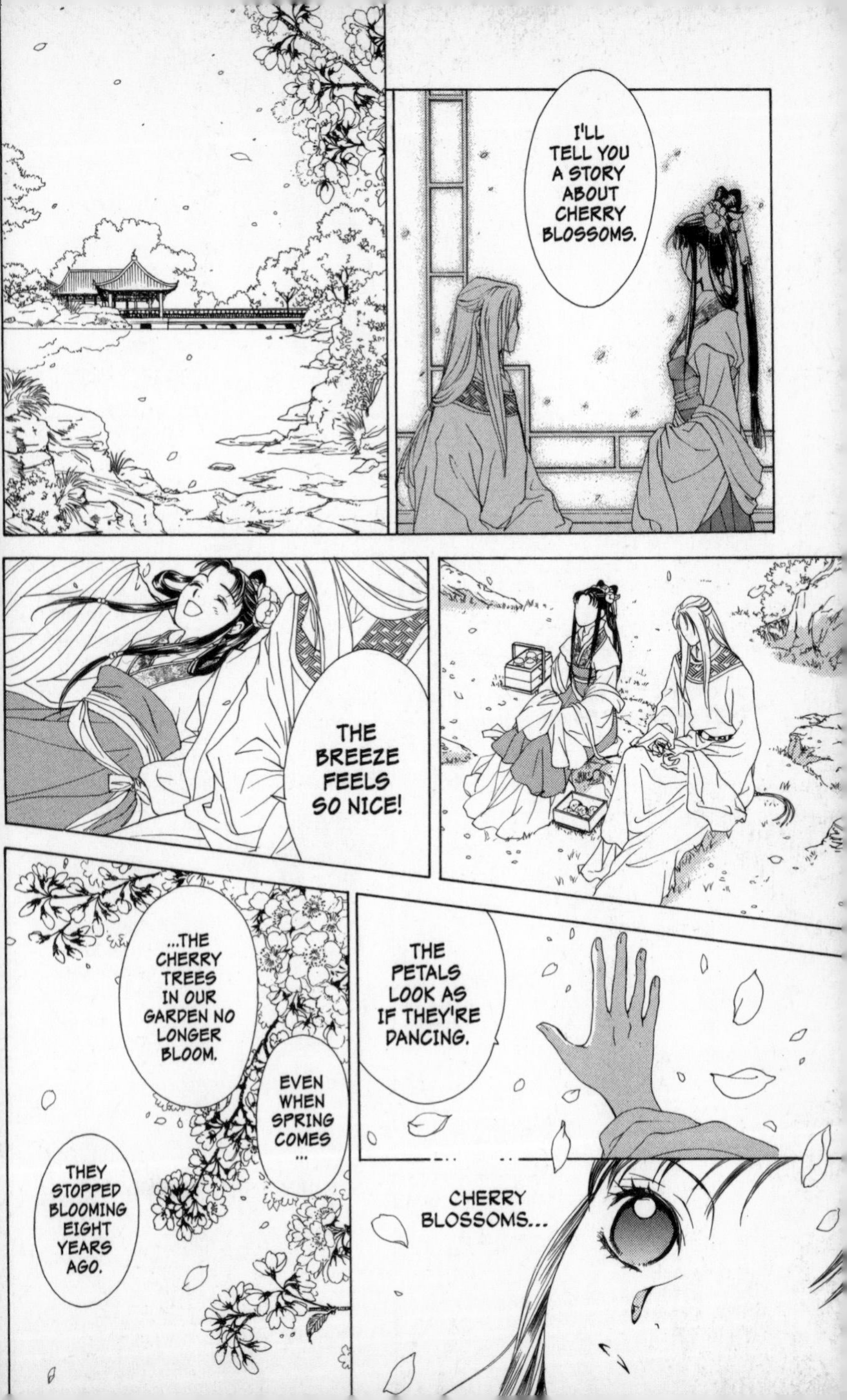
I'LL TELL YOU A STORY ABOUT CHERRY BLOSSOMS.
THE BREEZE FEELS SO NICE!
THE PETALS LOOK AS IF THEY'RE DANCING.
CHERRY BLOSSOMS...
...THE CHERRY TREES IN OUR GARDEN NO LONGER BLOOM.
EVEN WHEN SPRING COMES...
THEY STOPPED BLOOMING EIGHT YEARS AGO.

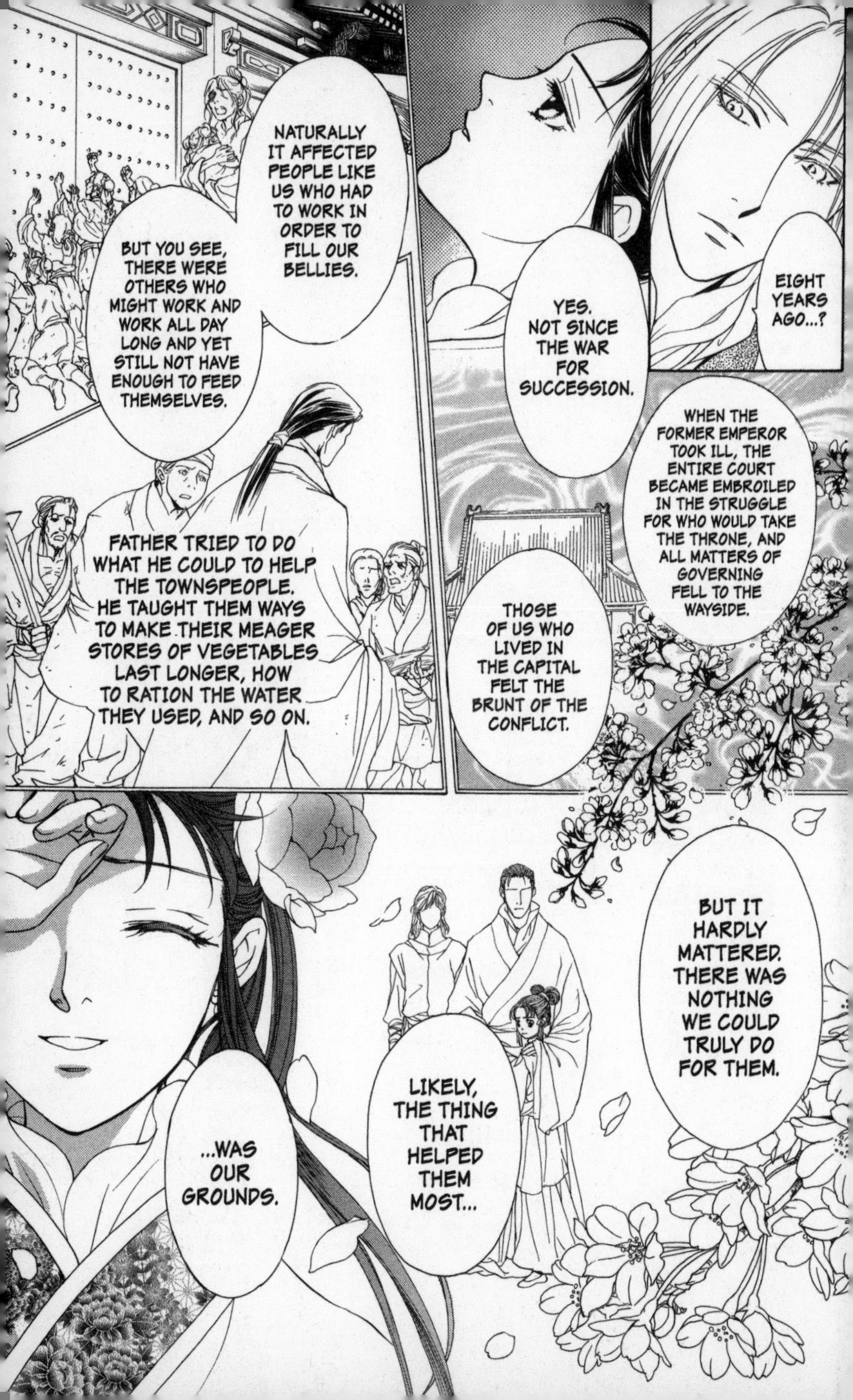

EIGHT YEARS AGO...?
YES. NOT SINCE THE WAR FOR SUCCESSION.
WHEN THE FORMER EMPEROR TOOK ILL, THE ENTIRE COURT BECAME EMBROILED IN THE STRUGGLE FOR WHO WOULD TAKE THE THRONE, AND ALL MATTERS OF GOVERNING FELL TO THE WAYSIDE.
THOSE OF US WHO LIVED IN THE CAPITAL FELT THE BRUNT OF THE CONFLICT.
NATURALLY IT AFFECTED PEOPLE LIKE US WHO HAD TO WORK IN ORDER TO FILL OUR BELLIES.
BUT YOU SEE, THERE WERE OTHERS WHO MIGHT WORK AND WORK ALL DAY LONG AND YET STILL NOT HAVE ENOUGH TO FEED THEMSELVES.
FATHER TRIED TO DO WHAT HE COULD TO HELP THE TOWNSPEOPLE. HE TAUGHT THEM WAYS TO MAKE THEIR MEAGER STORES OF VEGETABLES LAST LONGER, HOW TO RATION THE WATER THEY USED, AND SO ON.
BUT IT HARDLY MATTERED. THERE WAS NOTHING WE COULD TRULY DO FOR THEM.
LIKELY, THE THING THAT HELPED THEM MOST...
...WAS OUR GROUNDS.

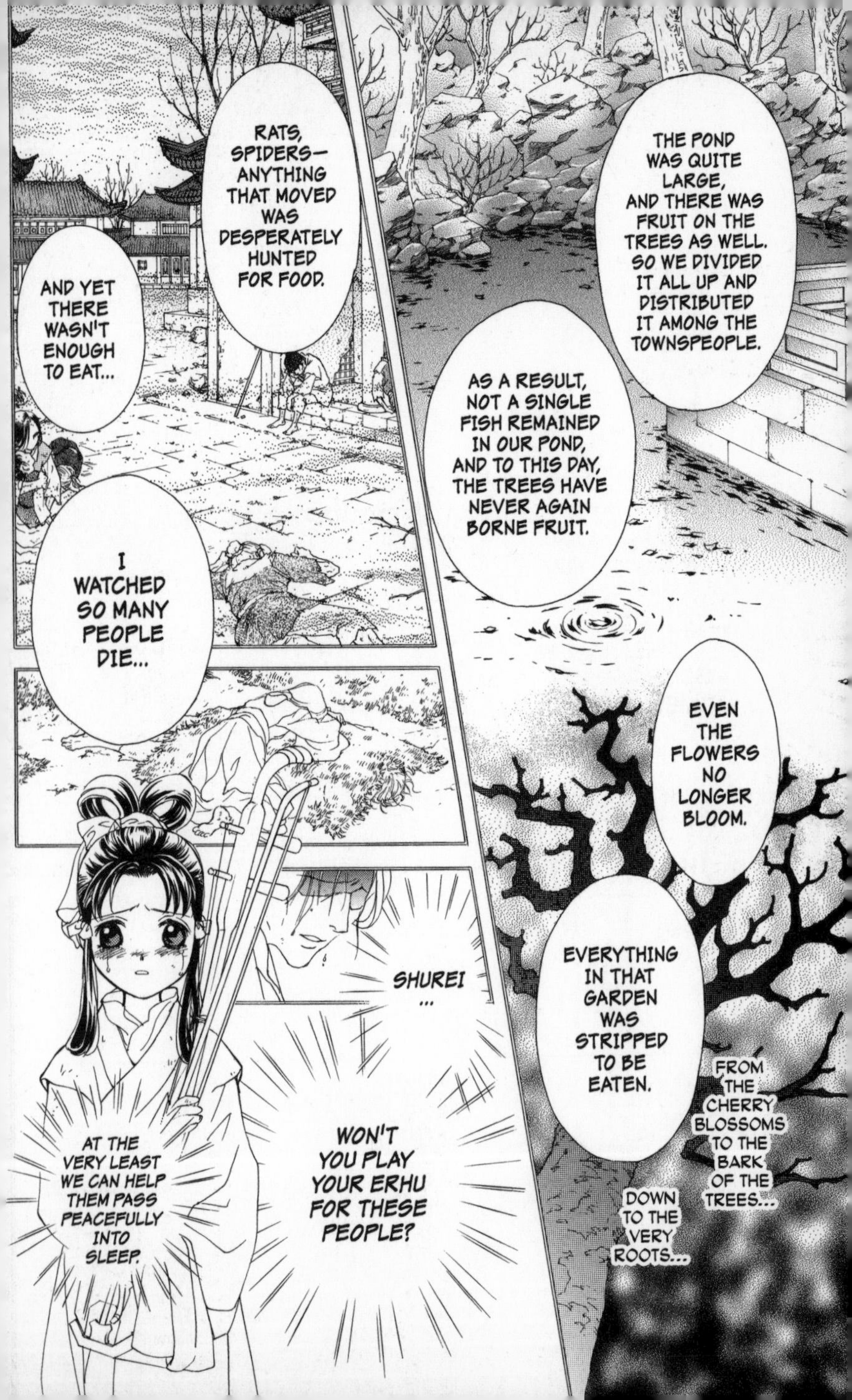
THE POND WAS QUITE LARGE, AND THERE WAS FRUIT ON THE TREES AS WELL. SO WE DIVIDED IT ALL UP AND DISTRIBUTED IT AMONG THE TOWNSPEOPLE.
AS A RESULT, NOT A SINGLE FISH REMAINED IN OUR POND, AND TO THIS DAY, THE TREES HAVE NEVER AGAIN BORNE FRUIT.
EVEN THE FLOWERS NO LONGER BLOOM.
EVERYTHING IN THAT GARDEN WAS STRIPPED TO BE EATEN.
FROM THE CHERRY BLOSSOMS TO THE BARK OF THE TREES...
DOWN TO THE VERY ROOTS...
RATS, SPIDERS—ANYTHING THAT MOVED WAS DESPERATELY HUNTED FOR FOOD.
AND YET THERE WASN'T ENOUGH TO EAT...
I WATCHED SO MANY PEOPLE DIE...
SHUREI ...
WON'T YOU PLAY YOUR ERHU FOR THESE PEOPLE?
AT THE VERY LEAST WE CAN HELP THEM PASS PEACEFULLY INTO SLEEP.

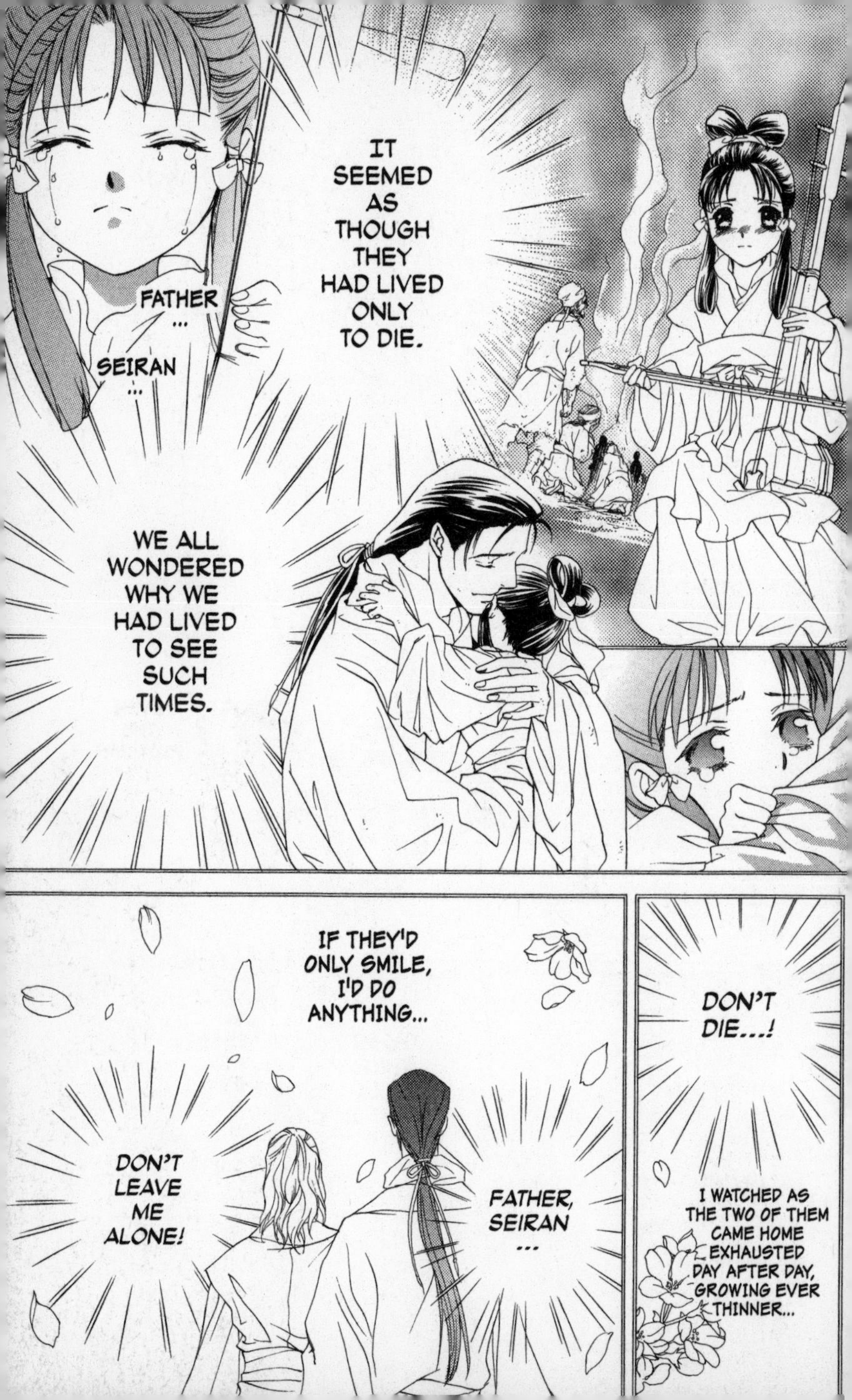
IT SEEMED AS THOUGH THEY HAD LIVED ONLY TO DIE.
FATHER...
SEIRAN...
WE ALL WONDERED WHY WE HAD LIVED TO SEE SUCH TIMES.
DON'T DIE...!
I WATCHED AS THE TWO OF THEM CAME HOME EXHAUSTED DAY AFTER DAY, GROWING EVER THINNER...
IF THEY'D ONLY SMILE, I'D DO ANYTHING...
FATHER, SEIRAN...
DON'T LEAVE ME ALONE!

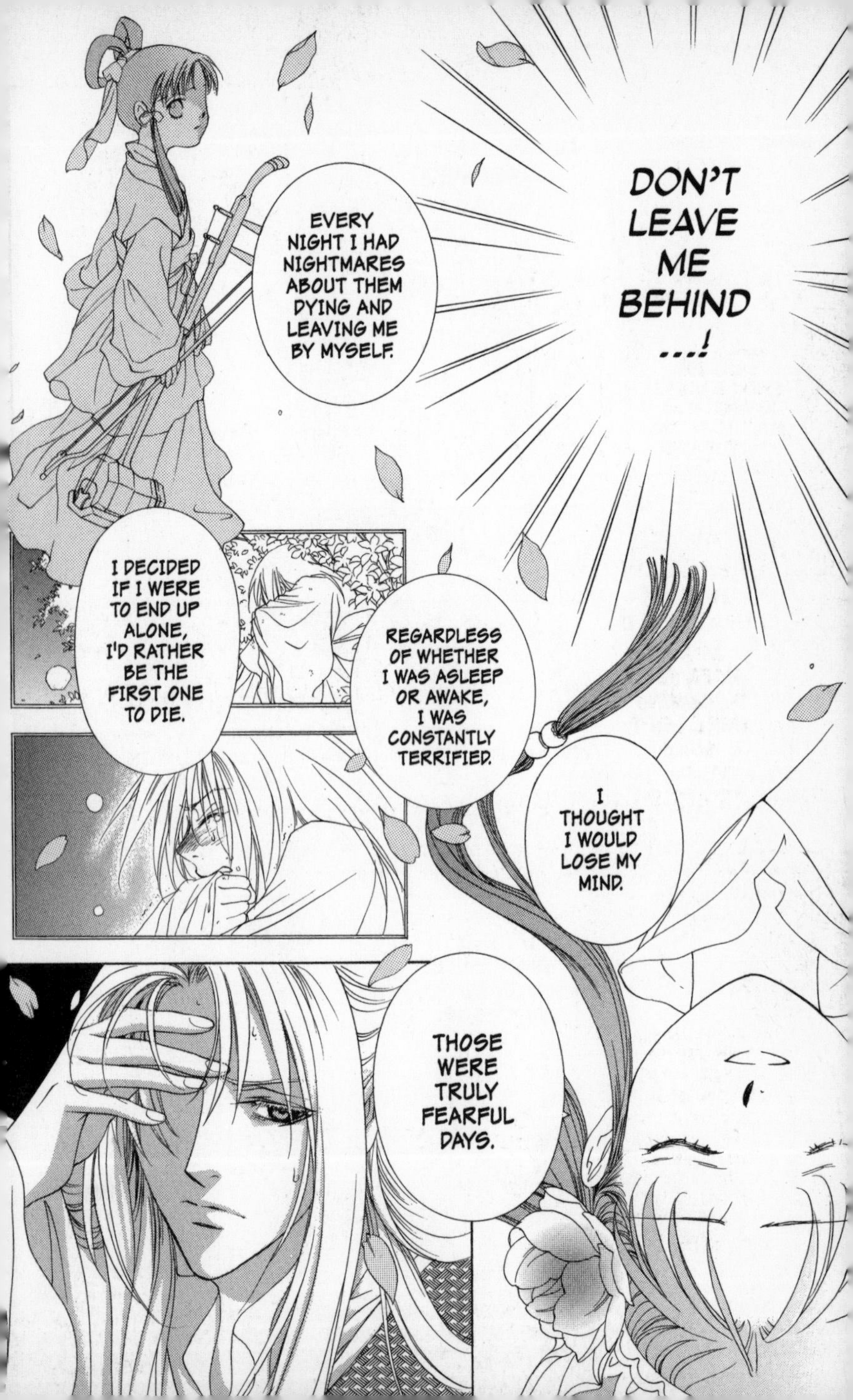

DON'T LEAVE ME BEHIND ...!
EVERY NIGHT I HAD NIGHTMARES ABOUT THEM DYING AND LEAVING ME BY MYSELF.
REGARDLESS OF WHETHER I WAS ASLEEP OR AWAKE, I WAS CONSTANTLY TERRIFIED.
I THOUGHT I WOULD LOSE MY MIND.
I DECIDED IF I WERE TO END UP ALONE, I'D RATHER BE THE FIRST ONE TO DIE.
THOSE WERE TRULY FEARFUL DAYS.

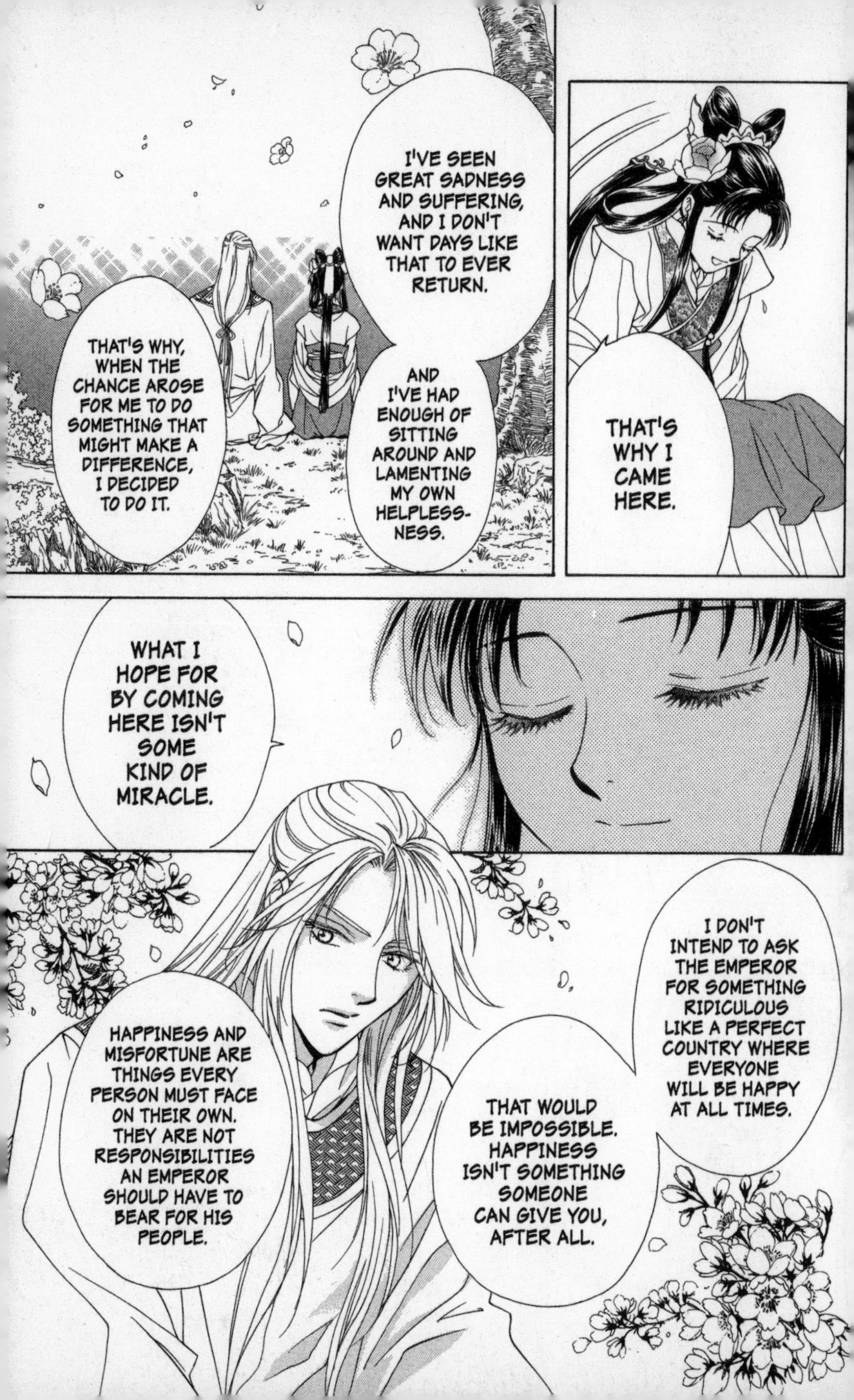
THAT'S WHY I CAME HERE.
I'VE SEEN GREAT SADNESS AND SUFFERING, AND I DON'T WANT DAYS LIKE THAT TO EVER RETURN.
AND I'VE HAD ENOUGH OF SITTING AROUND AND LAMENTING MY OWN HELPLESS-NESS.
THAT'S WHY, WHEN THE CHANCE AROSE FOR ME TO DO SOMETHING THAT MIGHT MAKE A DIFFERENCE, I DECIDED TO DO IT.
WHAT I HOPE FOR BY COMING HERE ISN'T SOME KIND OF MIRACLE.
I DON'T INTEND TO ASK THE EMPEROR FOR SOMETHING RIDICULOUS LIKE A PERFECT COUNTRY WHERE EVERYONE WILL BE HAPPY AT ALL TIMES.
THAT WOULD BE IMPOSSIBLE. HAPPINESS ISN'T SOMETHING SOMEONE CAN GIVE YOU, AFTER ALL.
HAPPINESS AND MISFORTUNE ARE THINGS EVERY PERSON MUST FACE ON THEIR OWN. THEY ARE NOT RESPONSIBILITIES AN EMPEROR SHOULD HAVE TO BEAR FOR HIS PEOPLE.

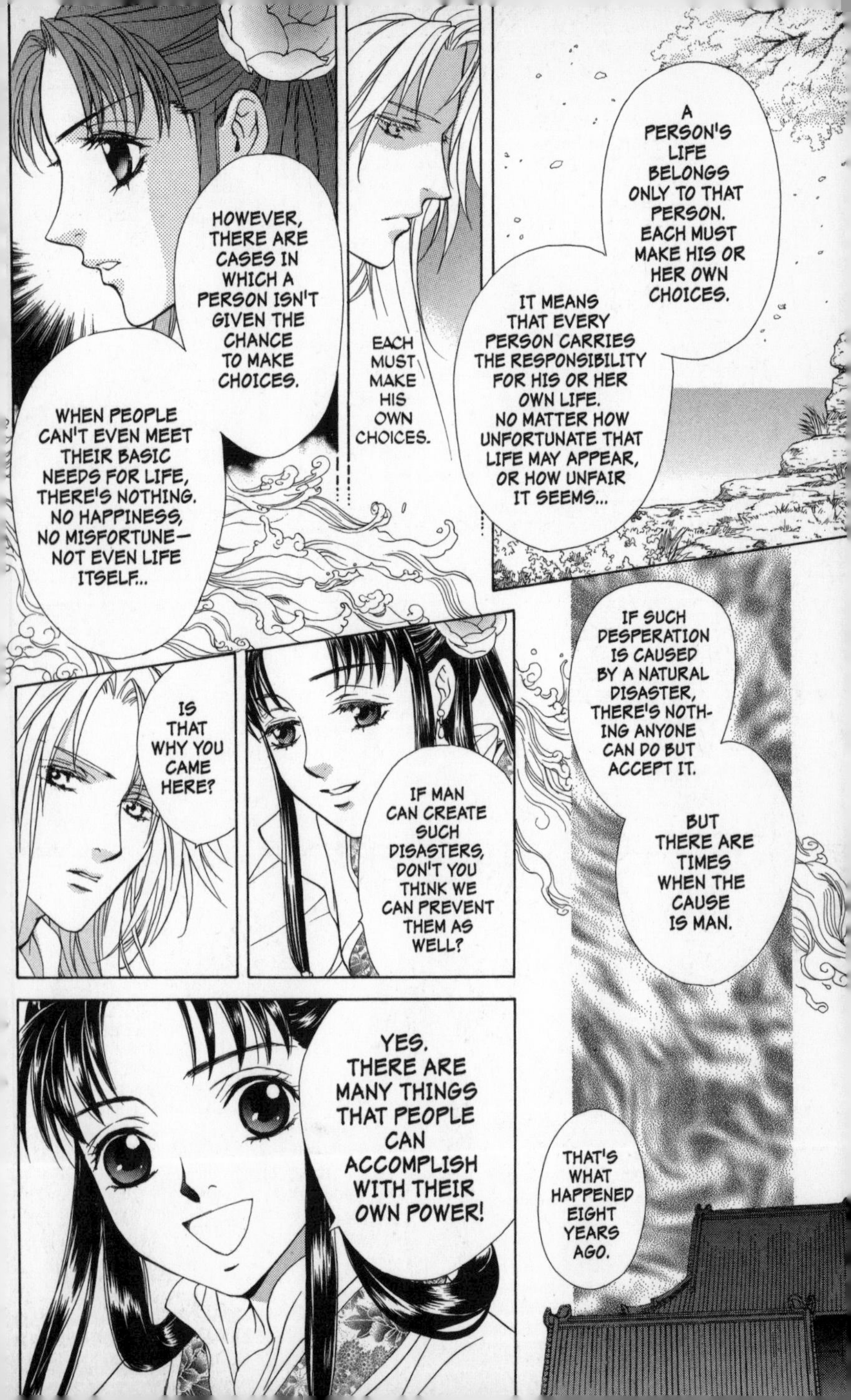
A PERSON'S LIFE BELONGS ONLY TO THAT PERSON. EACH MUST MAKE HIS OR HER OWN CHOICES.
IT MEANS THAT EVERY PERSON CARRIES THE RESPONSIBILITY FOR HIS OR HER OWN LIFE. NO MATTER HOW UNFORTUNATE THAT LIFE MAY APPEAR, OR HOW UNFAIR IT SEEMS...
EACH MUST MAKE HIS OWN CHOICES.
HOWEVER, THERE ARE CASES IN WHICH A PERSON ISN'T GIVEN THE CHANCE TO MAKE CHOICES.
WHEN PEOPLE CAN'T EVEN MEET THEIR BASIC NEEDS FOR LIFE, THERE'S NOTHING. NO HAPPINESS, NO MISFORTUNE— NOT EVEN LIFE ITSELF...
IF SUCH DESPERATION IS CAUSED BY A NATURAL DISASTER, THERE'S NOTHING ANYONE CAN DO BUT ACCEPT IT.
BUT THERE ARE TIMES WHEN THE CAUSE IS MAN.
THAT'S WHAT HAPPENED EIGHT YEARS AGO.
IF MAN CAN CREATE SUCH DISASTERS, DON'T YOU THINK WE CAN PREVENT THEM AS WELL?
IS THAT WHY YOU CAME HERE?
YES. THERE ARE MANY THINGS THAT PEOPLE CAN ACCOMPLISH WITH THEIR OWN POWER!

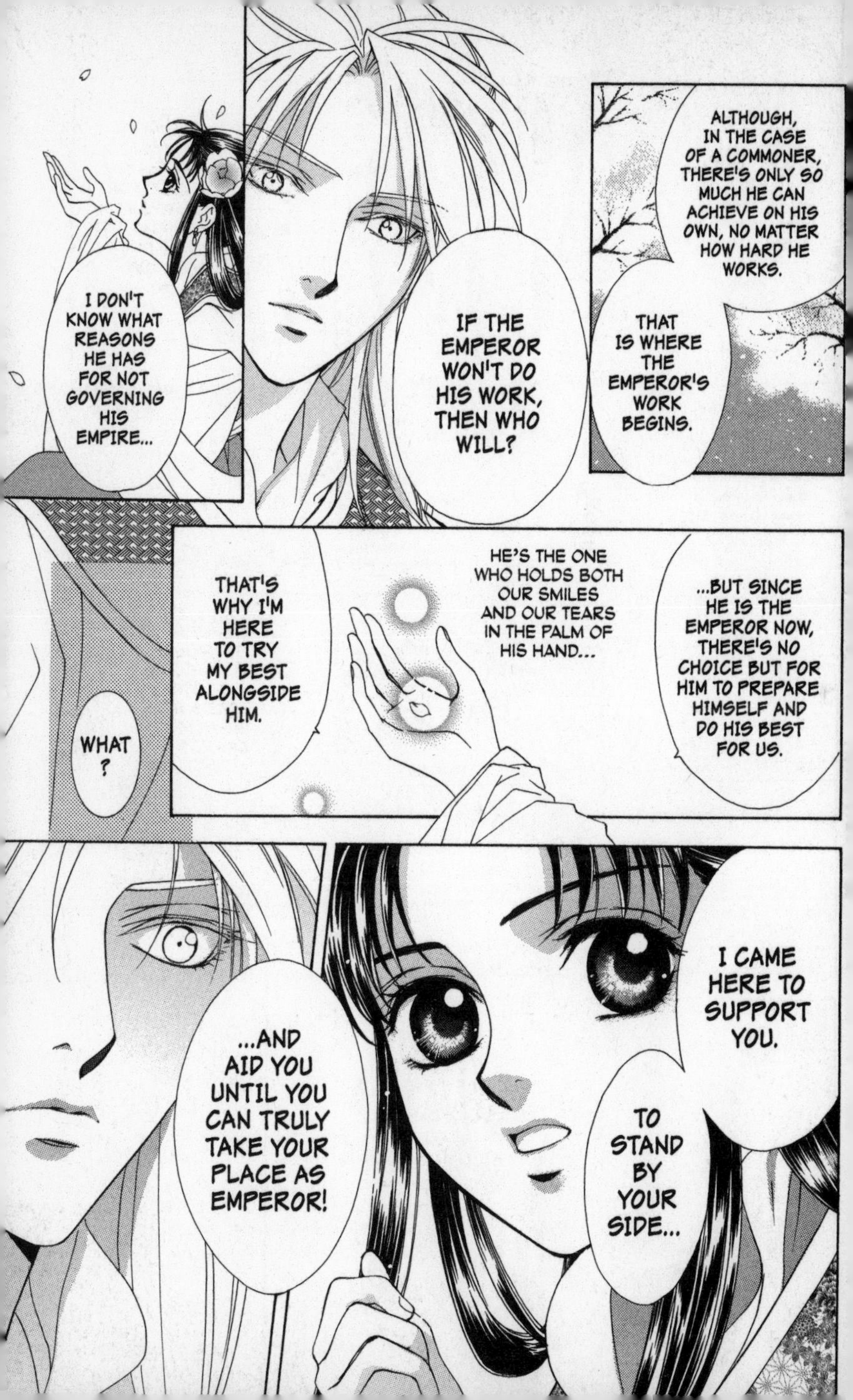
ALTHOUGH, IN THE CASE OF A COMMONER, THERE'S ONLY SO MUCH HE CAN ACHIEVE ON HIS OWN, NO MATTER HOW HARD HE WORKS.
THAT IS WHERE THE EMPEROR'S WORK BEGINS.
IF THE EMPEROR WON'T DO HIS WORK, THEN WHO WILL?
I DON'T KNOW WHAT REASONS HE HAS FOR NOT GOVERNING HIS EMPIRE...
...BUT SINCE HE IS THE EMPEROR NOW, THERE'S NO CHOICE BUT FOR HIM TO PREPARE HIMSELF AND DO HIS BEST FOR US.
HE'S THE ONE WHO HOLDS BOTH OUR SMILES AND OUR TEARS IN THE PALM OF HIS HAND...
THAT'S WHY I'M HERE TO TRY MY BEST ALONGSIDE HIM.
WHAT?
I CAME HERE TO SUPPORT YOU.
TO STAND BY YOUR SIDE...
...AND AID YOU UNTIL YOU CAN TRULY TAKE YOUR PLACE AS EMPEROR!

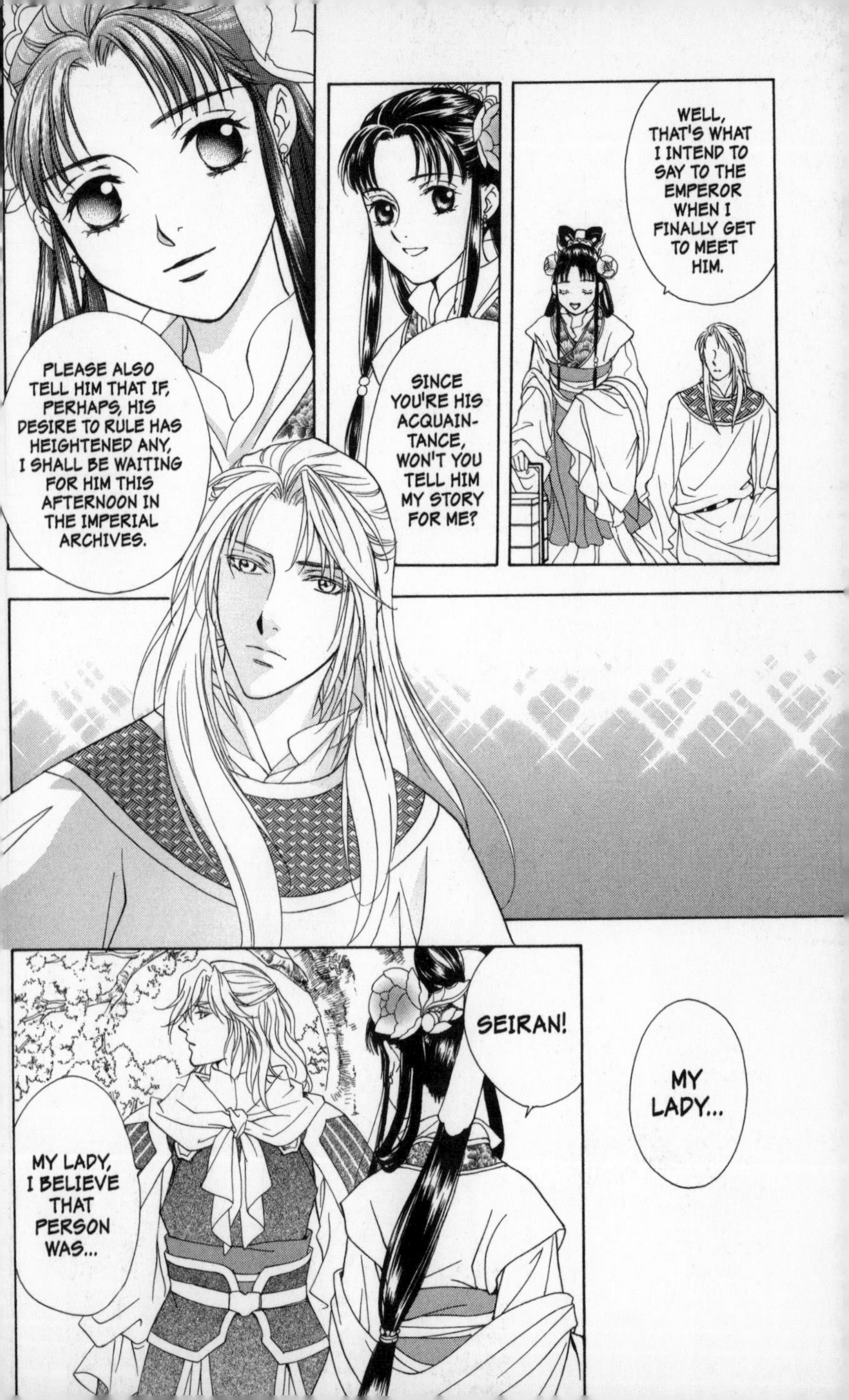
WELL, THAT'S WHAT I INTEND TO SAY TO THE EMPEROR WHEN I FINALLY GET TO MEET HIM.
SINCE YOU'RE HIS ACQUAIN-TANCE, WON'T YOU TELL HIM MY STORY FOR ME?
PLEASE ALSO TELL HIM THAT IF, PERHAPS, HIS DESIRE TO RULE HAS HEIGHTENED ANY, I SHALL BE WAITING FOR HIM THIS AFTERNOON IN THE IMPERIAL ARCHIVES.
MY LADY...
SEIRAN!
MY LADY, I BELIEVE THAT PERSON WAS...

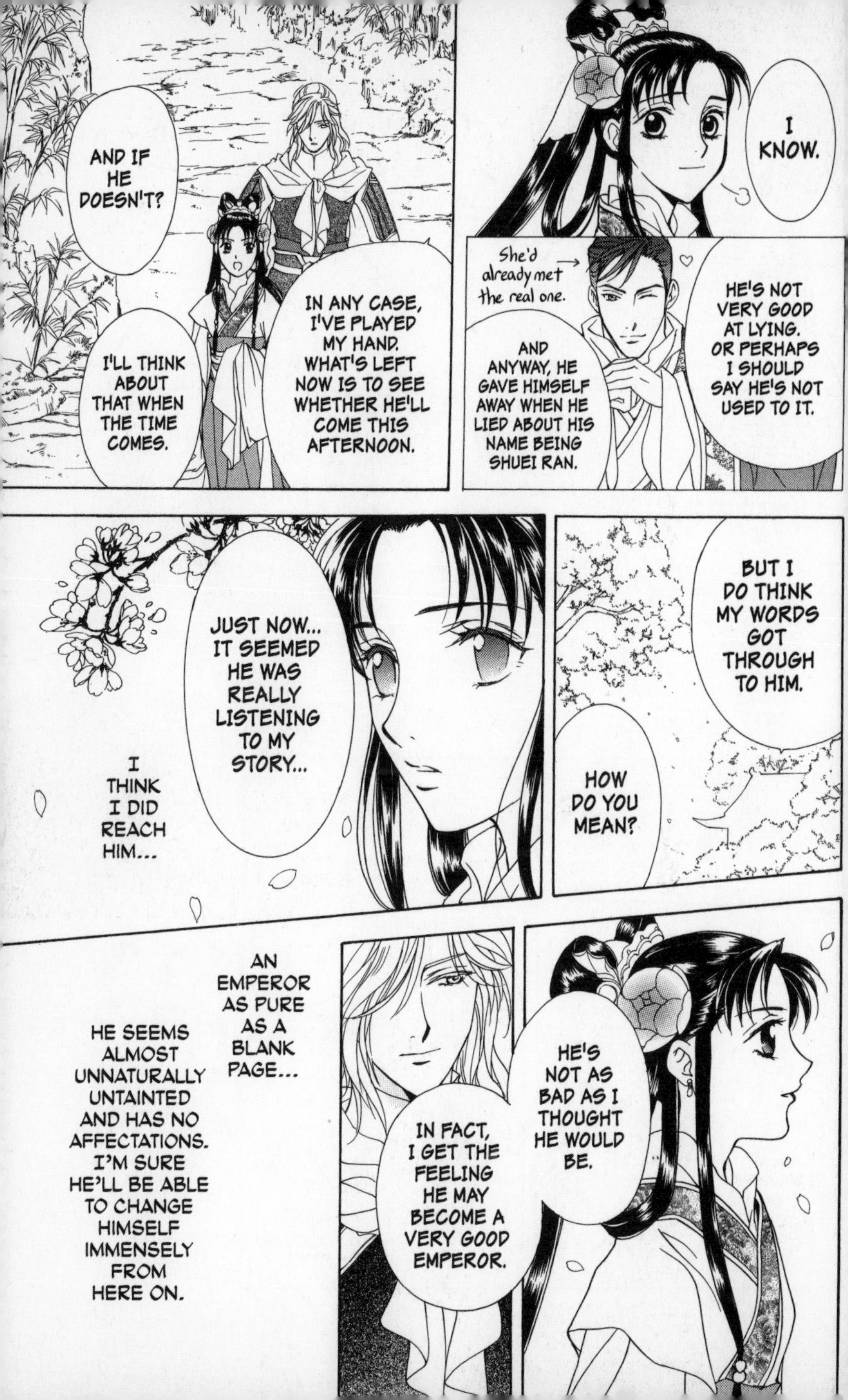
I KNOW.
HE'S NOT VERY GOOD AT LYING. OR PERHAPS I SHOULD SAY HE'S NOT USED TO IT.
AND ANYWAY, HE GAVE HIMSELF AWAY WHEN HE LIED ABOUT HIS NAME BEING SHUEI RAN.
She'd already met the real one.
IN ANY CASE, I'VE PLAYED MY HAND. WHAT'S LEFT NOW IS TO SEE WHETHER HE'LL COME THIS AFTERNOON.
AND IF HE DOESN'T?
I'LL THINK ABOUT THAT WHEN THE TIME COMES.
BUT I DO THINK MY WORDS GOT THROUGH TO HIM.
HOW DO YOU MEAN?
JUST NOW... IT SEEMED HE WAS REALLY LISTENING TO MY STORY...
I THINK I DID REACH HIM...
HE'S NOT AS BAD AS I THOUGHT HE WOULD BE.
IN FACT, I GET THE FEELING HE MAY BECOME A VERY GOOD EMPEROR.
AN EMPEROR AS PURE AS A BLANK PAGE...
HE SEEMS ALMOST UNNATURALLY UNTAINTED AND HAS NO AFFECTATIONS. I'M SURE HE'LL BE ABLE TO CHANGE HIMSELF IMMENSELY FROM HERE ON.

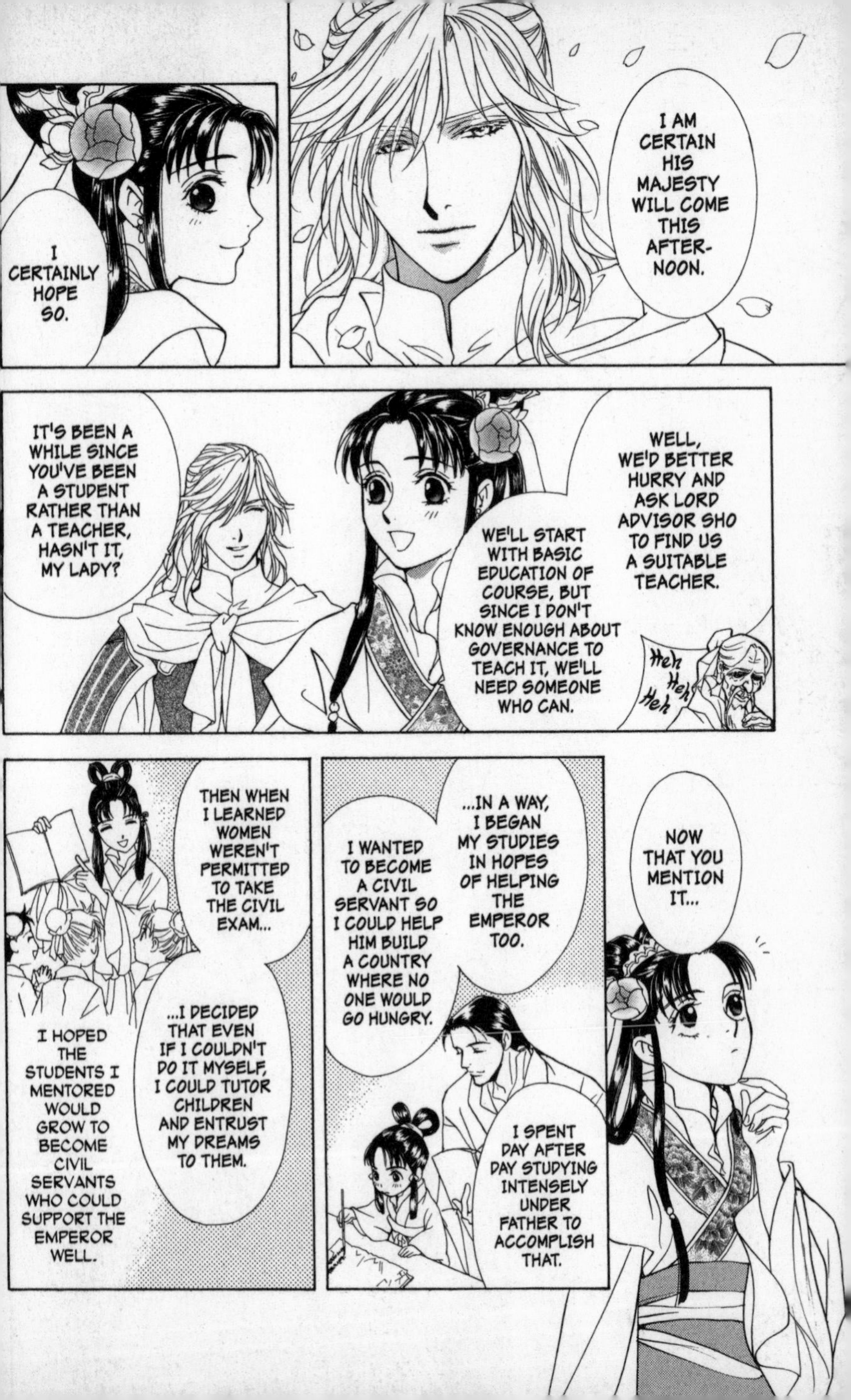
I AM CERTAIN HIS MAJESTY WILL COME THIS AFTER-NOON.
I CERTAINLY HOPE SO.
WELL, WE'D BETTER HURRY AND ASK LORD ADVISOR SHO TO FIND US A SUITABLE TEACHER.
Heh Heh Heh
WE'LL START WITH BASIC EDUCATION OF COURSE, BUT SINCE I DON'T KNOW ENOUGH ABOUT GOVERNANCE TO TEACH IT, WE'LL NEED SOMEONE WHO CAN.
IT'S BEEN A WHILE SINCE YOU'VE BEEN A STUDENT RATHER THAN A TEACHER, HASN'T IT, MY LADY?
NOW THAT YOU MENTION IT...
...IN A WAY, I BEGAN MY STUDIES IN HOPES OF HELPING THE EMPEROR TOO.
I WANTED TO BECOME A CIVIL SERVANT SO I COULD HELP HIM BUILD A COUNTRY WHERE NO ONE WOULD GO HUNGRY.
I SPENT DAY AFTER DAY STUDYING INTENSELY UNDER FATHER TO ACCOMPLISH THAT.
THEN WHEN I LEARNED WOMEN WEREN'T PERMITTED TO TAKE THE CIVIL EXAM...
...I DECIDED THAT EVEN IF I COULDN'T DO IT MYSELF, I COULD TUTOR CHILDREN AND ENTRUST MY DREAMS TO THEM.
I HOPED THE STUDENTS I MENTORED WOULD GROW TO BECOME CIVIL SERVANTS WHO COULD SUPPORT THE EMPEROR WELL.

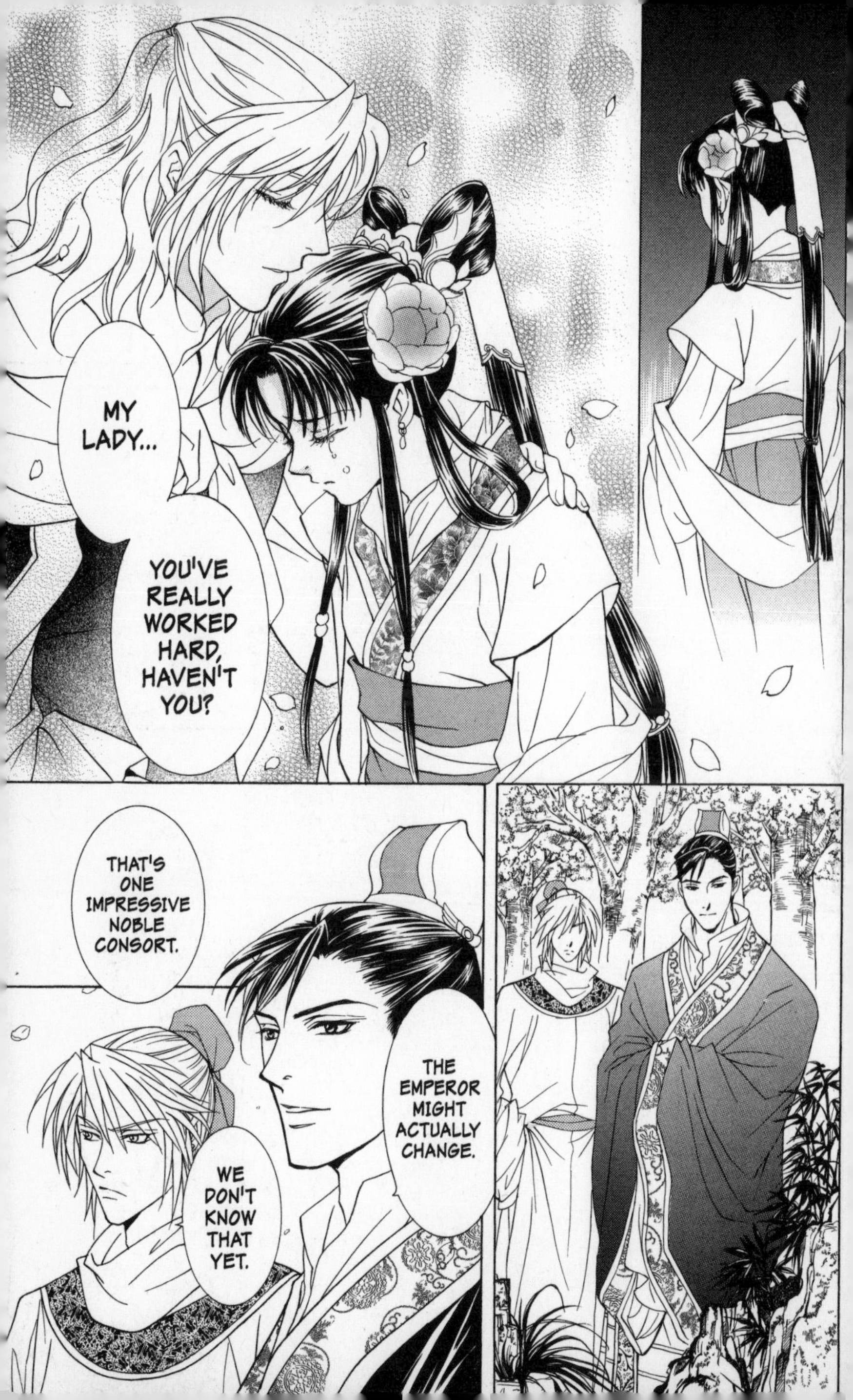
MY LADY...
YOU'VE REALLY WORKED HARD, HAVEN'T YOU?
THAT'S ONE IMPRESSIVE NOBLE CONSORT.
THE EMPEROR MIGHT ACTUALLY CHANGE.
WE DON'T KNOW THAT YET.

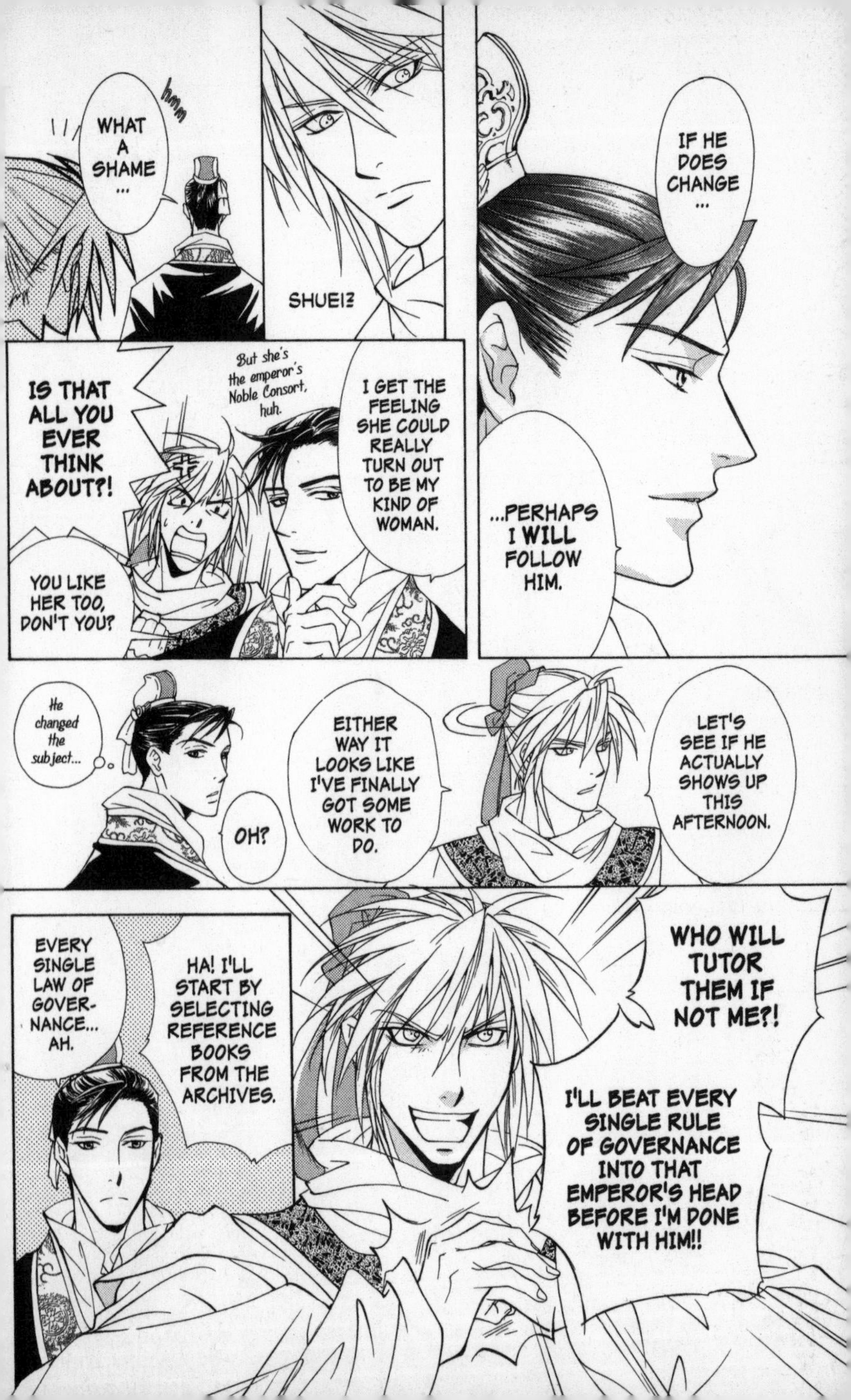
IF HE DOES CHANGE...
...PERHAPS I WILL FOLLOW HIM.
SHUEI!?
hmm
WHAT A SHAME...
I GET THE FEELING SHE COULD REALLY TURN OUT TO BE MY KIND OF WOMAN.
But she's the emperor's Noble Consort, huh.
IS THAT ALL YOU EVER THINK ABOUT?!
YOU LIKE HER TOO, DON'T YOU?
LET'S SEE IF HE ACTUALLY SHOWS UP THIS AFTERNOON.
EITHER WAY IT LOOKS LIKE I'VE FINALLY GOT SOME WORK TO DO.
OH?
He changed the subject...
WHO WILL TUTOR THEM IF NOT ME?!
I'LL BEAT EVERY SINGLE RULE OF GOVERNANCE INTO THAT EMPEROR'S HEAD BEFORE I'M DONE WITH HIM!!
HA! I'LL START BY SELECTING REFERENCE BOOKS FROM THE ARCHIVES.
EVERY SINGLE LAW OF GOVER-NANCE... AH.

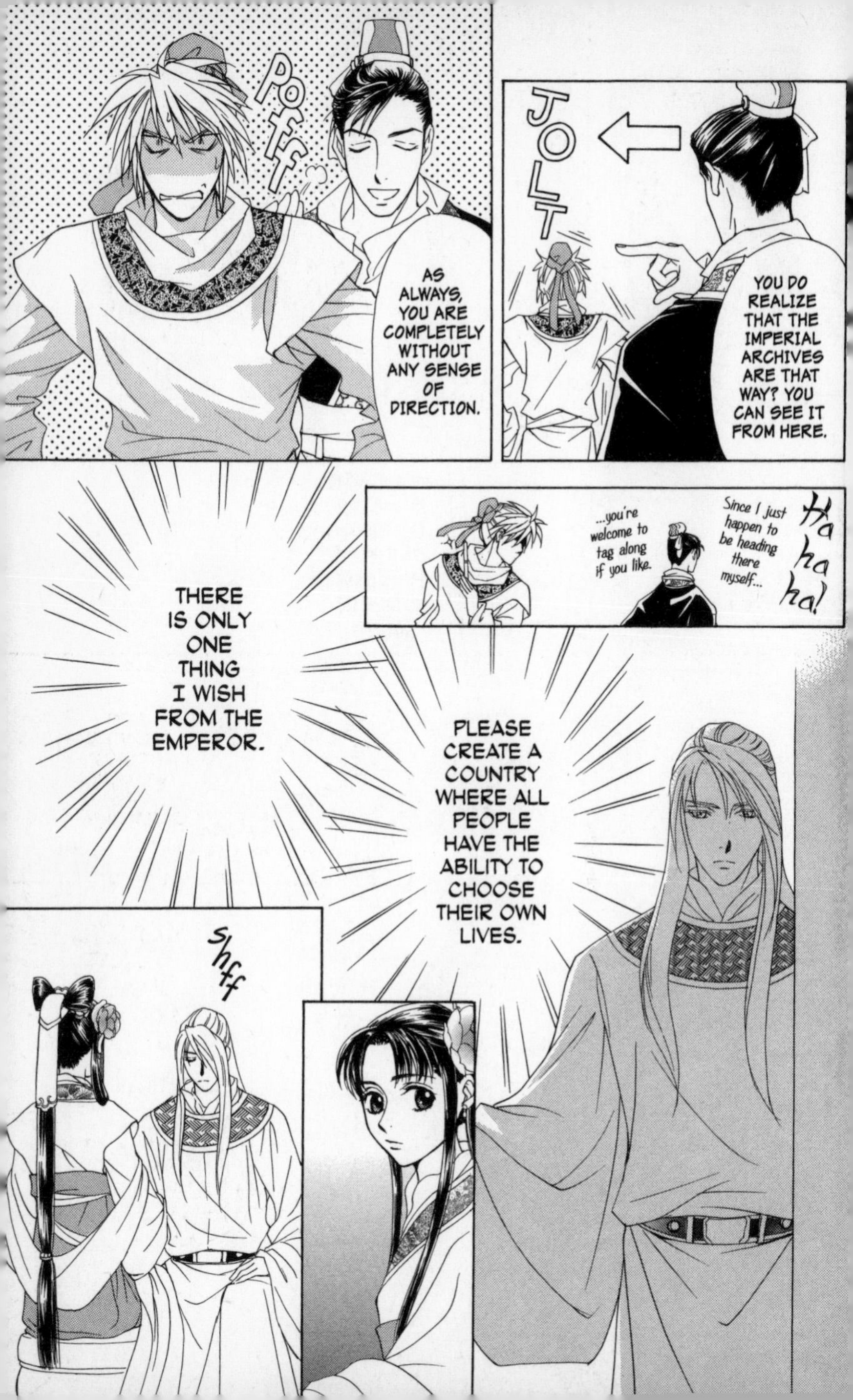
JOLT
YOU DO REALIZE THAT THE IMPERIAL ARCHIVES ARE THAT WAY? YOU CAN SEE IT FROM HERE.
Poff
AS ALWAYS, YOU ARE COMPLETELY WITHOUT ANY SENSE OF DIRECTION.
Ha ha ha!
Since I just happen to be heading there myself...
...you're welcome to tag along if you like.
THERE IS ONLY ONE THING I WISH FROM THE EMPEROR.
PLEASE CREATE A COUNTRY WHERE ALL PEOPLE HAVE THE ABILITY TO CHOOSE THEIR OWN LIVES.
Shff

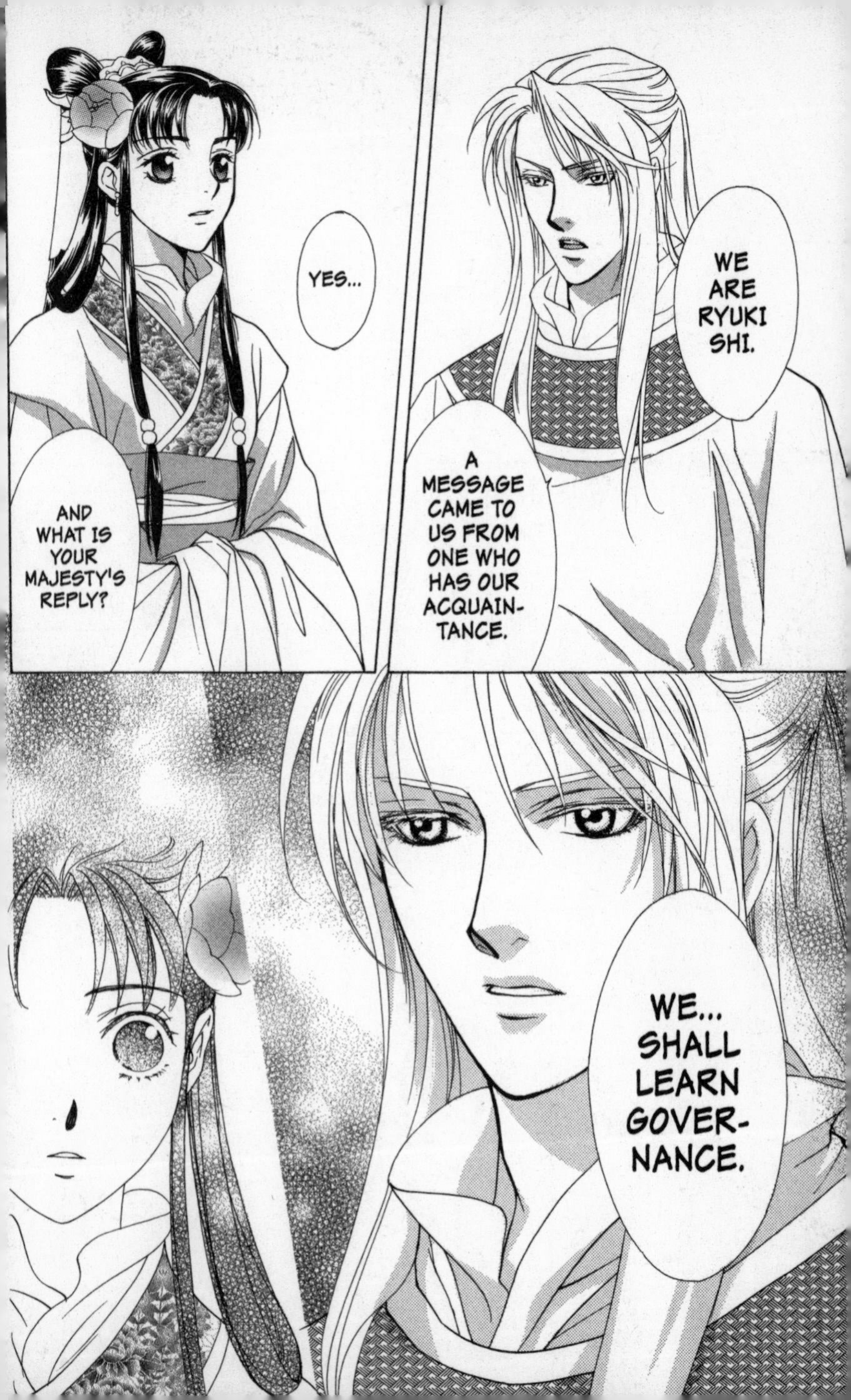

WE ARE RYUKI SHI.
A MESSAGE CAME TO US FROM ONE WHO HAS OUR ACQUAINTANCE.
YES...
AND WHAT IS YOUR MAJESTY'S REPLY?
WE... SHALL LEARN GOVERNANCE.

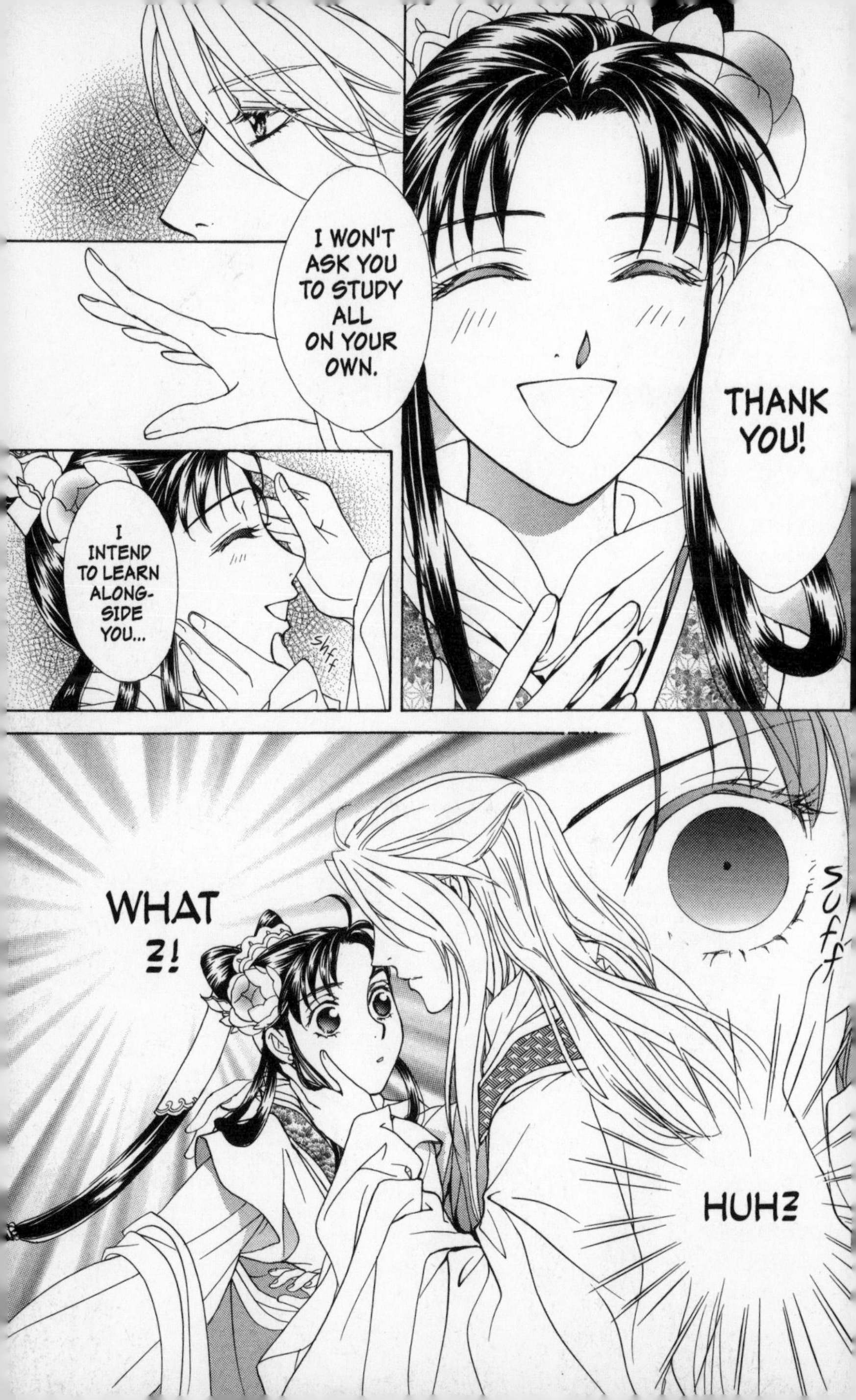

THANK YOU!
I WON'T ASK YOU TO STUDY ALL ON YOUR OWN.
I INTEND TO LEARN ALONG-SIDE YOU...
shff
suff
WHAT?!
HUH?

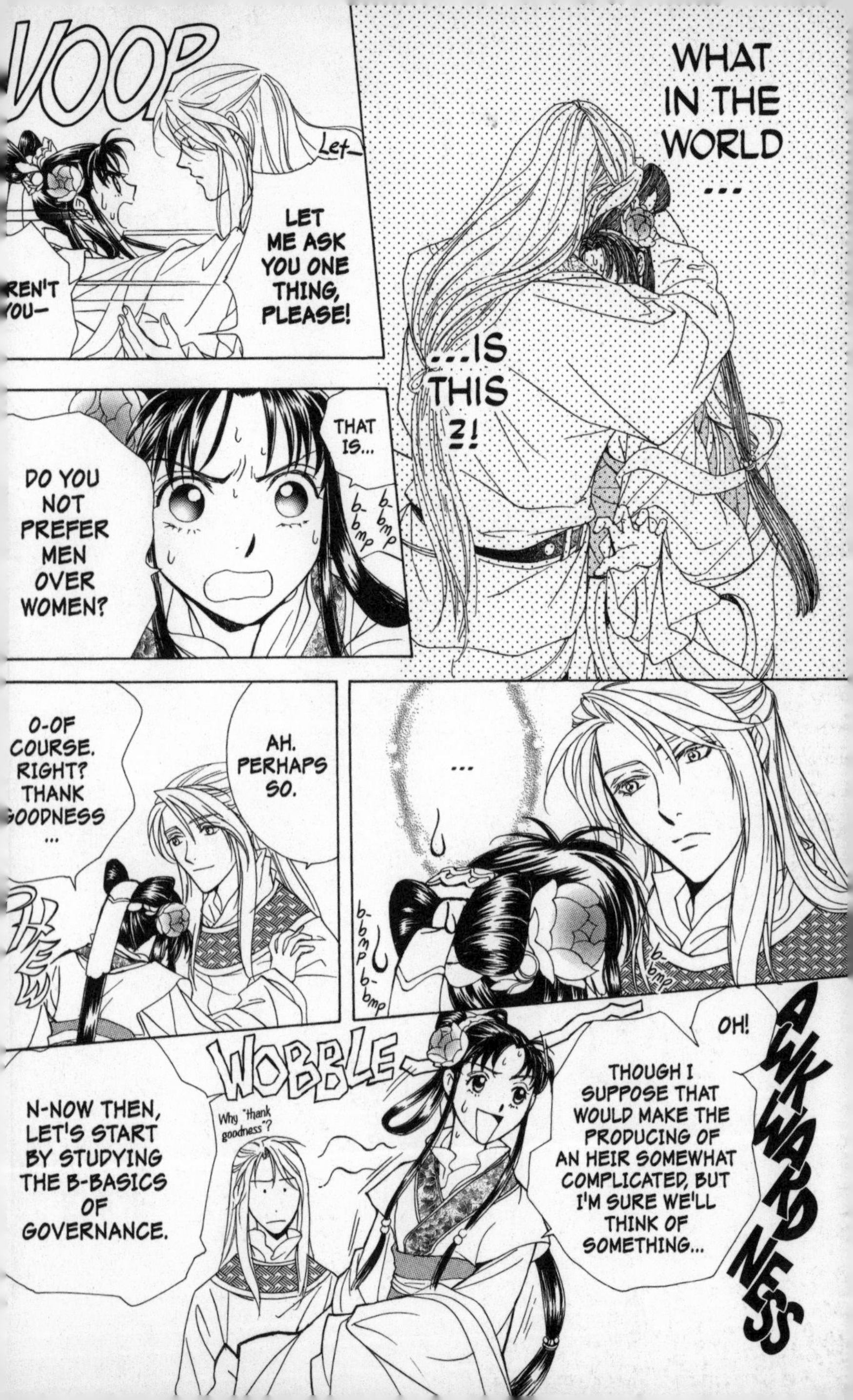
WHAT IN THE WORLD...
...IS THIS?!
VOOP
Let—
LET ME ASK YOU ONE THING, PLEASE!
REN'T YOU—
THAT IS...
b-bmp b-bmp
DO YOU NOT PREFER MEN OVER WOMEN?
...
b-bmp
b-bmp b-bmp
AH. PERHAPS SO.
O-OF COURSE. RIGHT? THANK GOODNESS...
PHEW
AWKWARDNESS
OH!
THOUGH I SUPPOSE THAT WOULD MAKE THE PRODUCING OF AN HEIR SOMEWHAT COMPLICATED, BUT I'M SURE WE'LL THINK OF SOMETHING...
WOBBLE
Why "thank goodness"?
N-NOW THEN, LET'S START BY STUDYING THE B-BASICS OF GOVERNANCE.

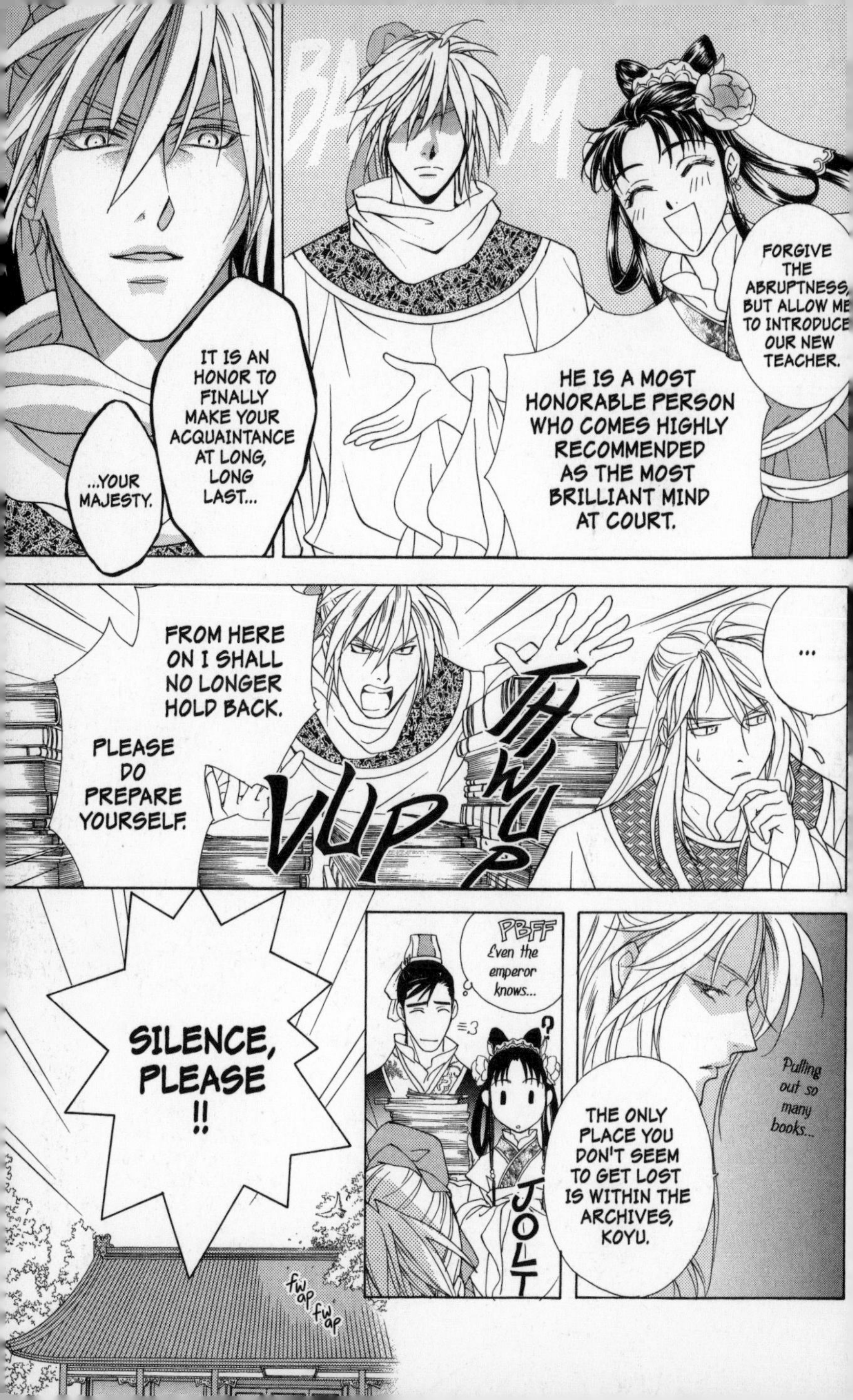
FORGIVE THE ABRUPTNESS, BUT ALLOW ME TO INTRODUCE OUR NEW TEACHER.
HE IS A MOST HONORABLE PERSON WHO COMES HIGHLY RECOMMENDED AS THE MOST BRILLIANT MIND AT COURT.
IT IS AN HONOR TO FINALLY MAKE YOUR ACQUAINTANCE AT LONG, LONG LAST...
...YOUR MAJESTY.
...
FROM HERE ON I SHALL NO LONGER HOLD BACK.
PLEASE DO PREPARE YOURSELF.
THWUP
VUP
Pulling out so many books...
THE ONLY PLACE YOU DON'T SEEM TO GET LOST IS WITHIN THE ARCHIVES, KOYU.
PBFF
Even the emperor knows...
?
JOLT
SILENCE, PLEASE!!
fwap fwap

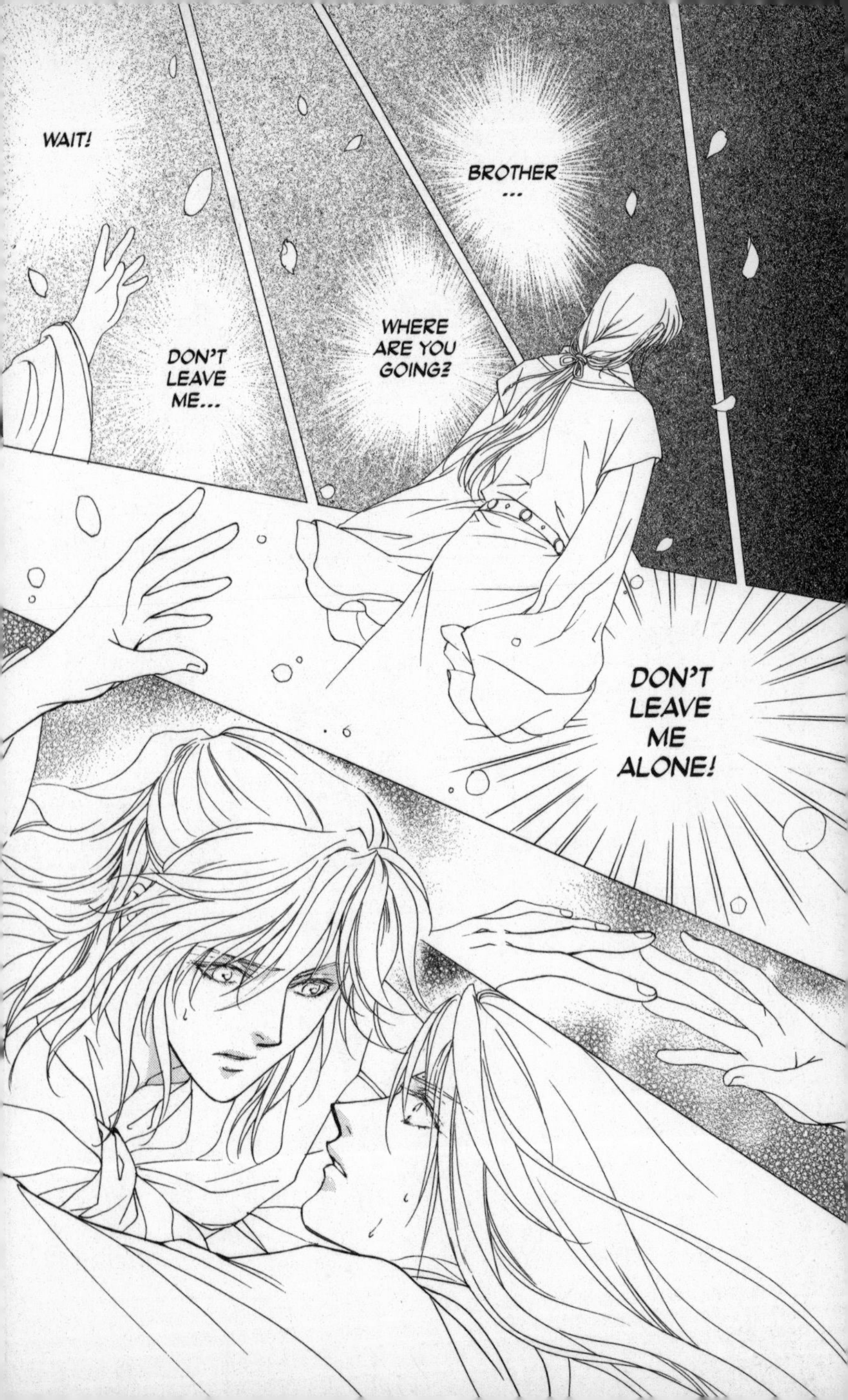
BROTHER ...
WHERE ARE YOU GOING?
DON'T LEAVE ME...
WAIT!
DON'T LEAVE ME ALONE!

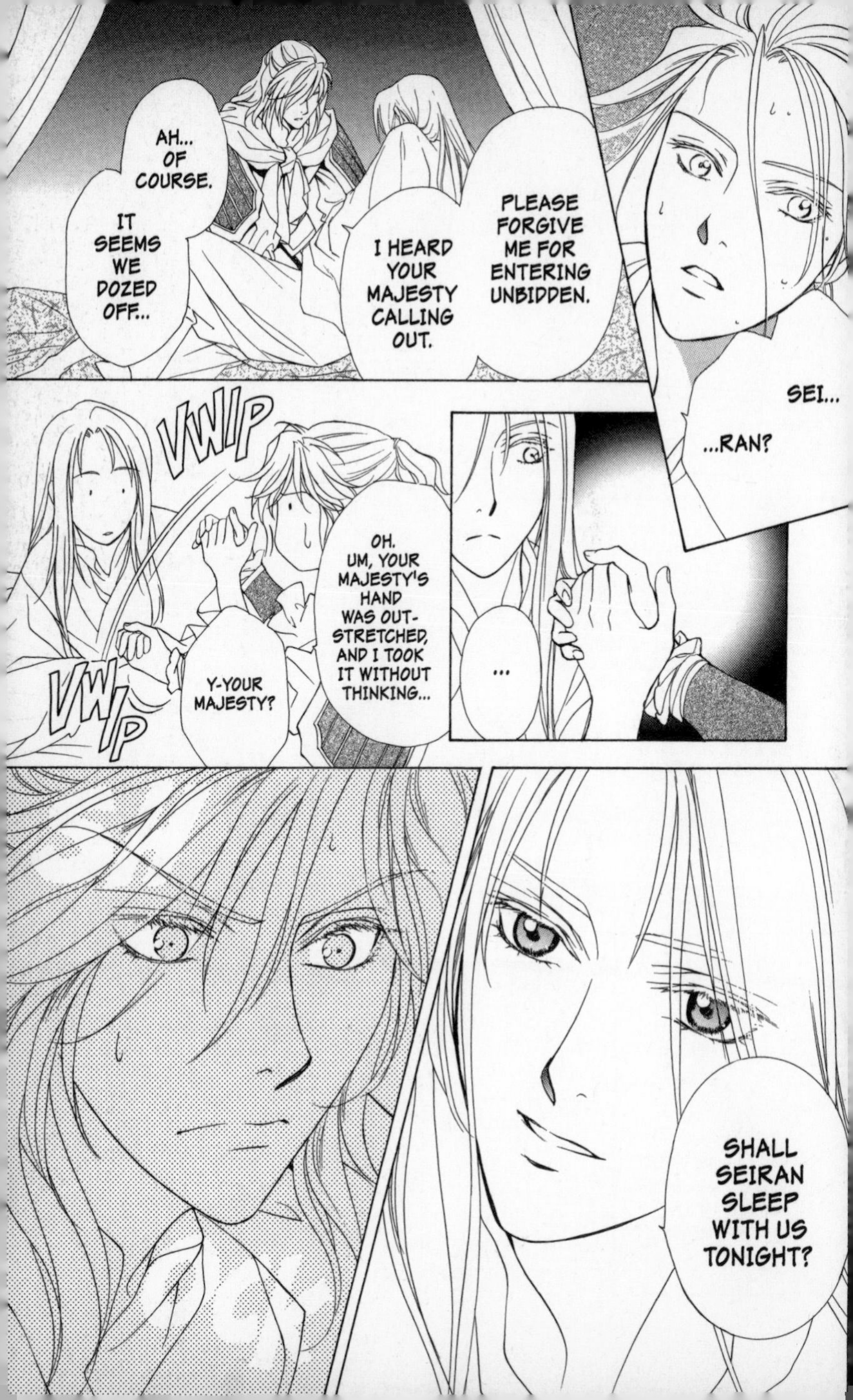
SEI...
...RAN?
PLEASE FORGIVE ME FOR ENTERING UNBIDDEN.
I HEARD YOUR MAJESTY CALLING OUT.
AH... OF COURSE.
IT SEEMS WE DOZED OFF...
...
OH. UM, YOUR MAJESTY'S HAND WAS OUT-STRETCHED, AND I TOOK IT WITHOUT THINKING...
VWIP
Y-YOUR MAJESTY?
VWIP
SHALL SEIRAN SLEEP WITH US TONIGHT?

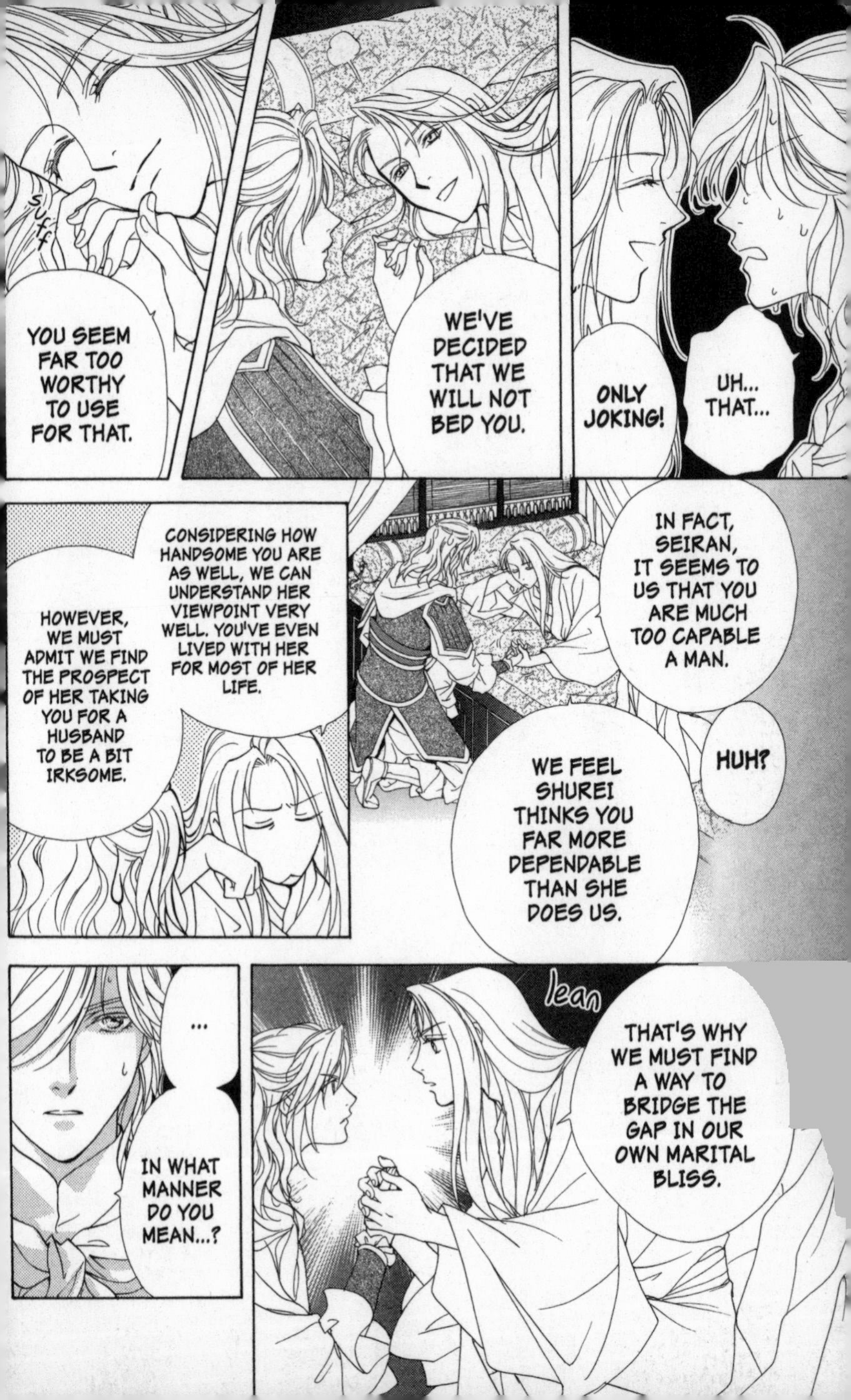
UH... THAT...
ONLY JOKING!
WE'VE DECIDED THAT WE WILL NOT BED YOU.
suff
YOU SEEM FAR TOO WORTHY TO USE FOR THAT.
IN FACT, SEIRAN, IT SEEMS TO US THAT YOU ARE MUCH TOO CAPABLE A MAN.
HUH?
WE FEEL SHUREI THINKS YOU FAR MORE DEPENDABLE THAN SHE DOES US.
CONSIDERING HOW HANDSOME YOU ARE AS WELL, WE CAN UNDERSTAND HER VIEWPOINT VERY WELL. YOU'VE EVEN LIVED WITH HER FOR MOST OF HER LIFE.
HOWEVER, WE MUST ADMIT WE FIND THE PROSPECT OF HER TAKING YOU FOR A HUSBAND TO BE A BIT IRKSOME.
lean
THAT'S WHY WE MUST FIND A WAY TO BRIDGE THE GAP IN OUR OWN MARITAL BLISS.
...
IN WHAT MANNER DO YOU MEAN...?

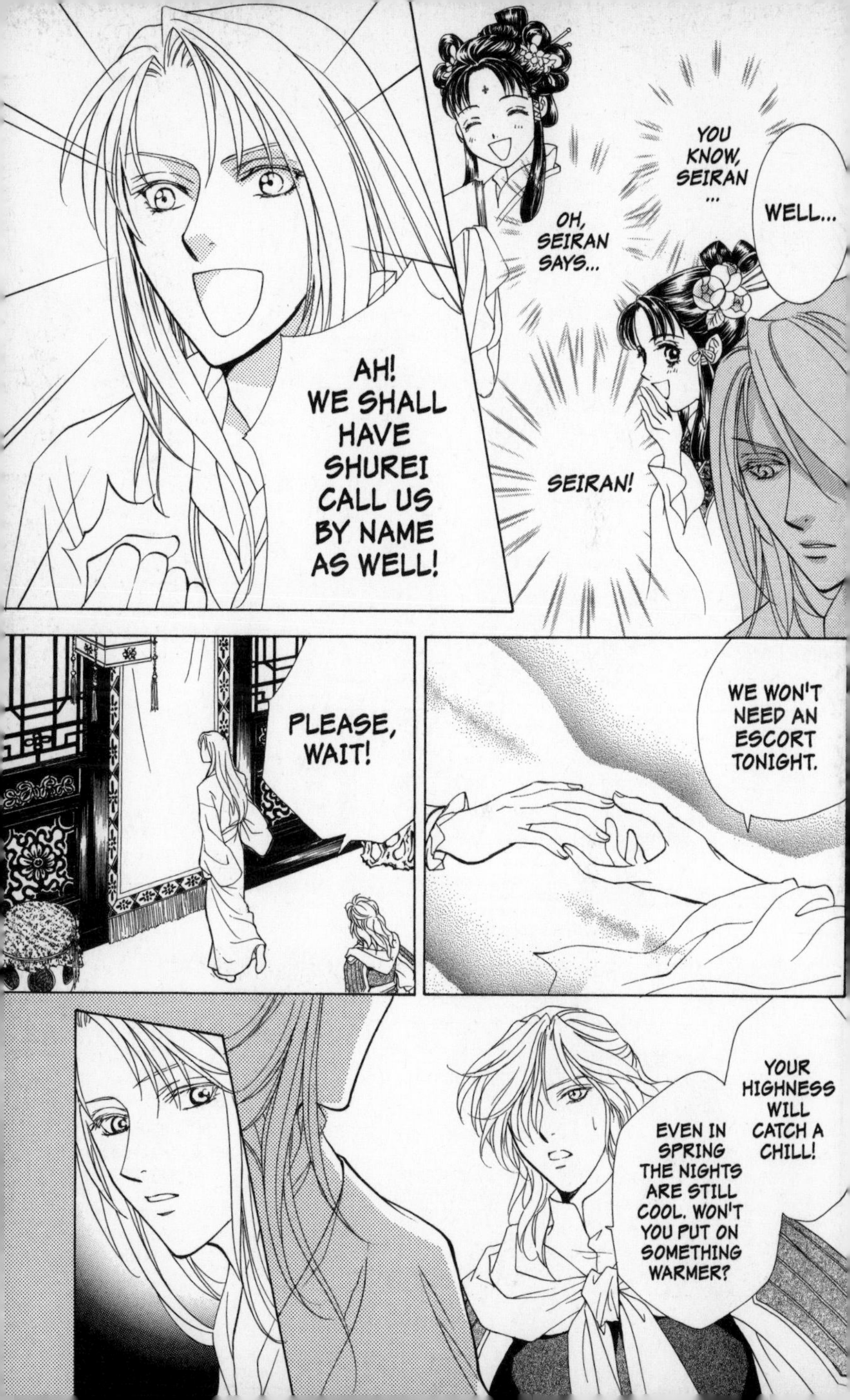
WELL...
YOU KNOW, SEIRAN ...
OH, SEIRAN SAYS...
SEIRAN!
AH! WE SHALL HAVE SHUREI CALL US BY NAME AS WELL!
WE WON'T NEED AN ESCORT TONIGHT.
PLEASE, WAIT!
YOUR HIGHNESS WILL CATCH A CHILL!
EVEN IN SPRING THE NIGHTS ARE STILL COOL. WON'T YOU PUT ON SOMETHING WARMER?

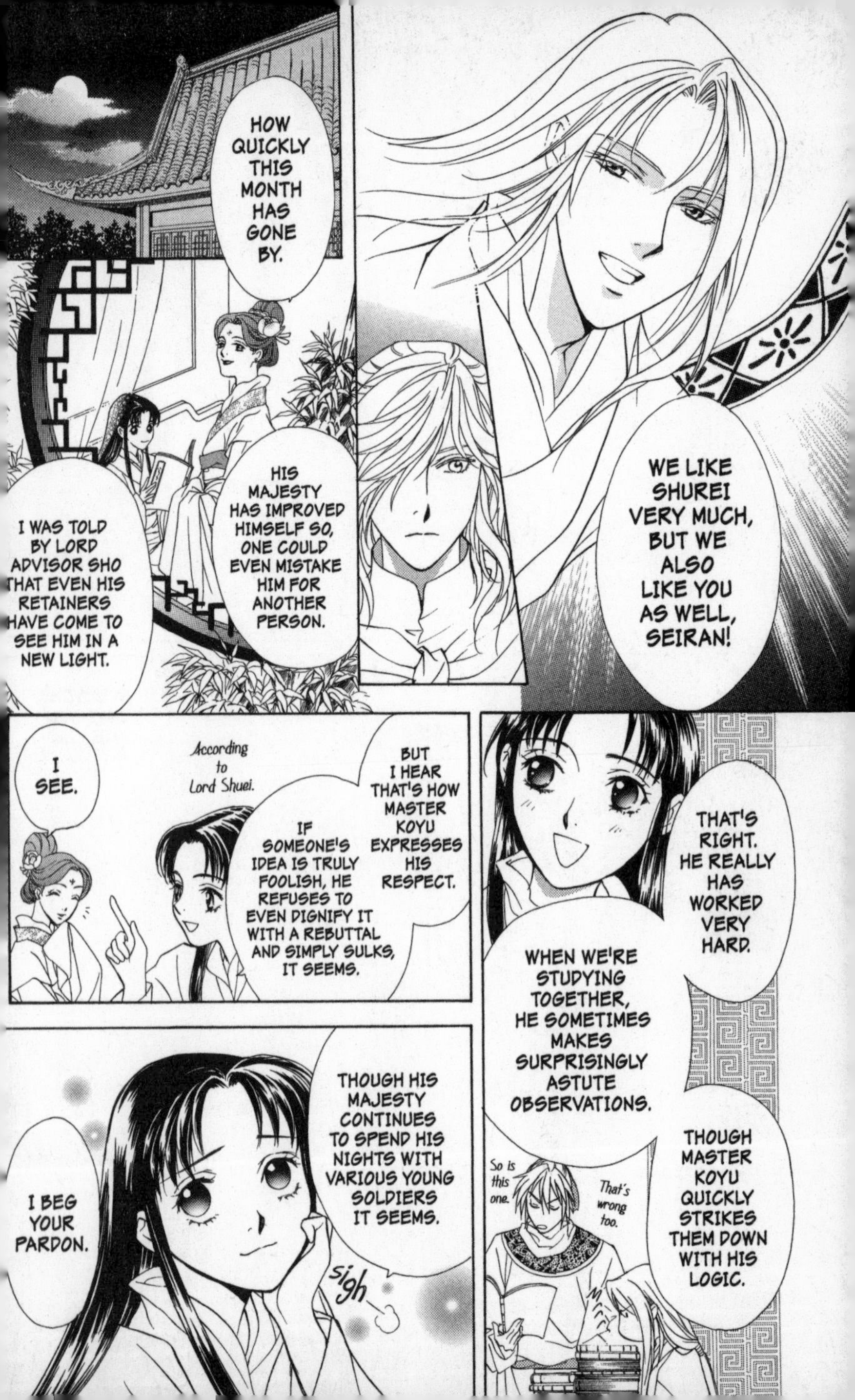
WE LIKE SHUREI VERY MUCH, BUT WE ALSO LIKE YOU AS WELL, SEIRAN!
HOW QUICKLY THIS MONTH HAS GONE BY.
HIS MAJESTY HAS IMPROVED HIMSELF SO, ONE COULD EVEN MISTAKE HIM FOR ANOTHER PERSON.
I WAS TOLD BY LORD ADVISOR SHO THAT EVEN HIS RETAINERS HAVE COME TO SEE HIM IN A NEW LIGHT.
THAT'S RIGHT. HE REALLY HAS WORKED VERY HARD.
WHEN WE'RE STUDYING TOGETHER, HE SOMETIMES MAKES SURPRISINGLY ASTUTE OBSERVATIONS.
THOUGH MASTER KOYU QUICKLY STRIKES THEM DOWN WITH HIS LOGIC.
That's wrong too.
So is this one.
BUT I HEAR THAT'S HOW MASTER KOYU EXPRESSES HIS RESPECT.
IF SOMEONE'S IDEA IS TRULY FOOLISH, HE REFUSES TO EVEN DIGNIFY IT WITH A REBUTTAL AND SIMPLY SULKS, IT SEEMS.
According to Lord Shuei.
I SEE.
THOUGH HIS MAJESTY CONTINUES TO SPEND HIS NIGHTS WITH VARIOUS YOUNG SOLDIERS IT SEEMS.
sigh
I BEG YOUR PARDON.

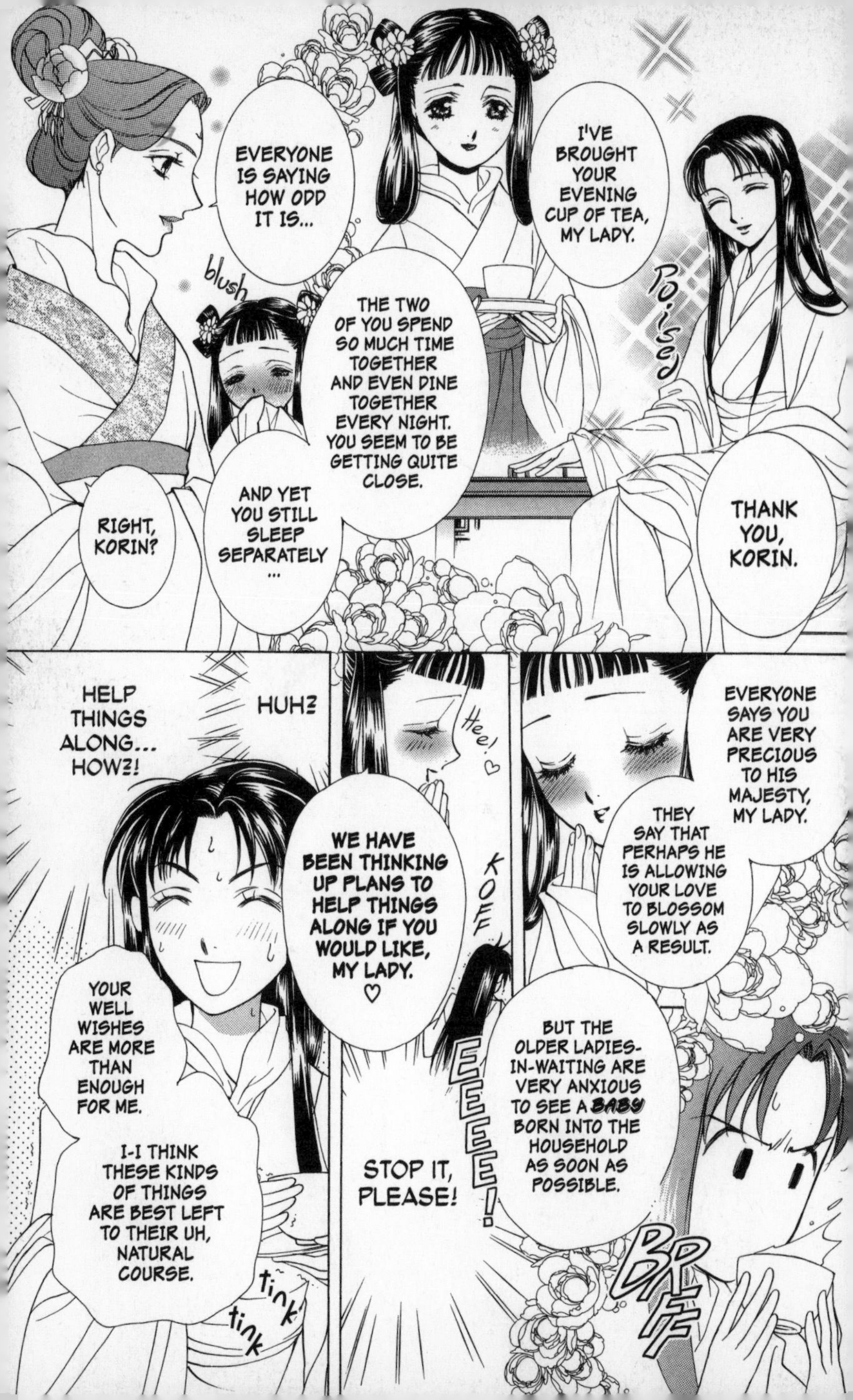
I'VE BROUGHT YOUR EVENING CUP OF TEA, MY LADY.
Poised
EVERYONE IS SAYING HOW ODD IT IS...
THE TWO OF YOU SPEND SO MUCH TIME TOGETHER AND EVEN DINE TOGETHER EVERY NIGHT. YOU SEEM TO BE GETTING QUITE CLOSE.
blush
THANK YOU, KORIN.
AND YET YOU STILL SLEEP SEPARATELY...
RIGHT, KORIN?
EVERYONE SAYS YOU ARE VERY PRECIOUS TO HIS MAJESTY, MY LADY.
THEY SAY THAT PERHAPS HE IS ALLOWING YOUR LOVE TO BLOSSOM SLOWLY AS A RESULT.
BUT THE OLDER LADIES-IN-WAITING ARE VERY ANXIOUS TO SEE A BABY BORN INTO THE HOUSEHOLD AS SOON AS POSSIBLE.
BRFF
KOFF
Hee! ♡
WE HAVE BEEN THINKING UP PLANS TO HELP THINGS ALONG IF YOU WOULD LIKE, MY LADY. ♡
EEEEE!
STOP IT, PLEASE!
HUH?
HELP THINGS ALONG... HOW?!
YOUR WELL WISHES ARE MORE THAN ENOUGH FOR ME.
I-I THINK THESE KINDS OF THINGS ARE BEST LEFT TO THEIR UH, NATURAL COURSE.
tink tink

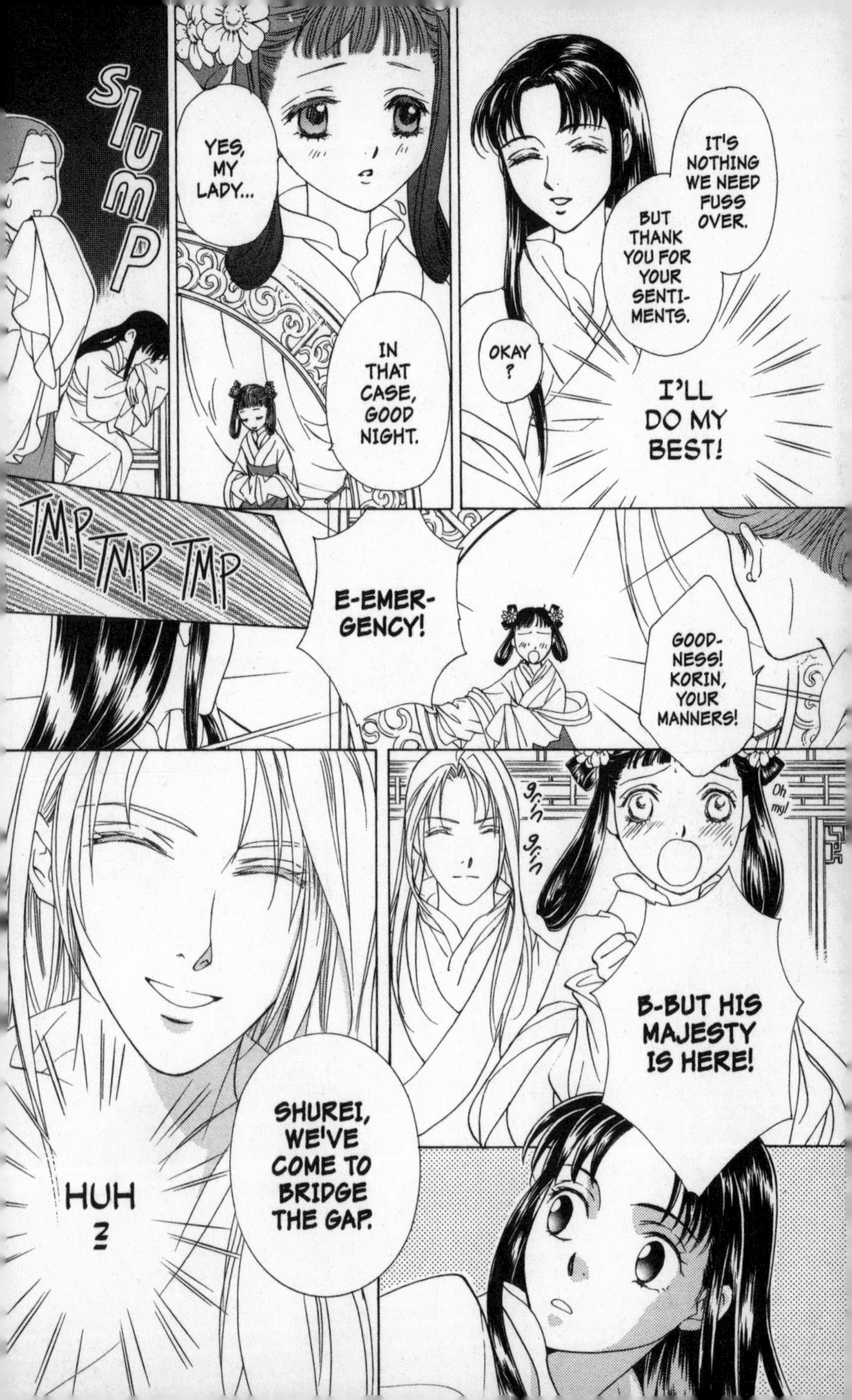
IT'S NOTHING WE NEED FUSS OVER.
BUT THANK YOU FOR YOUR SENTIMENTS.
OKAY?
I'LL DO MY BEST!
IN THAT CASE, GOOD NIGHT.
YES, MY LADY...
SLUMP
E-EMERGENCY!
GOODNESS! KORIN, YOUR MANNERS!
TMP TMP TMP
Oh my!
grin grin
B-BUT HIS MAJESTY IS HERE!
SHUREI, WE'VE COME TO BRIDGE THE GAP.
HUH?

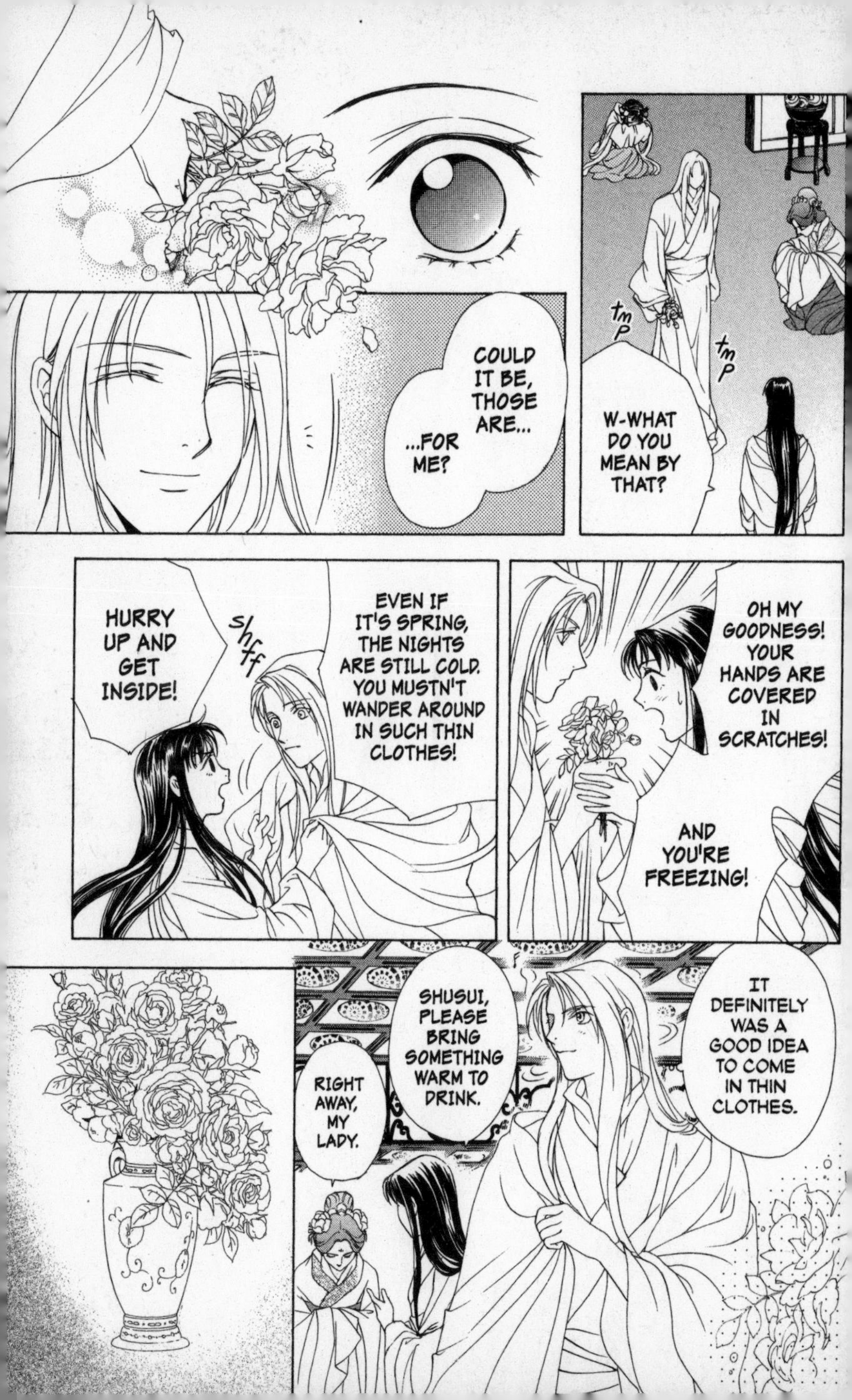
tmp
tmp
W-WHAT DO YOU MEAN BY THAT?
COULD IT BE, THOSE ARE...
...FOR ME?
OH MY GOODNESS! YOUR HANDS ARE COVERED IN SCRATCHES!
AND YOU'RE FREEZING!
EVEN IF IT'S SPRING, THE NIGHTS ARE STILL COLD. YOU MUSTN'T WANDER AROUND IN SUCH THIN CLOTHES!
shff
HURRY UP AND GET INSIDE!
IT DEFINITELY WAS A GOOD IDEA TO COME IN THIN CLOTHES.
SHUSUI, PLEASE BRING SOMETHING WARM TO DRINK.
RIGHT AWAY, MY LADY.

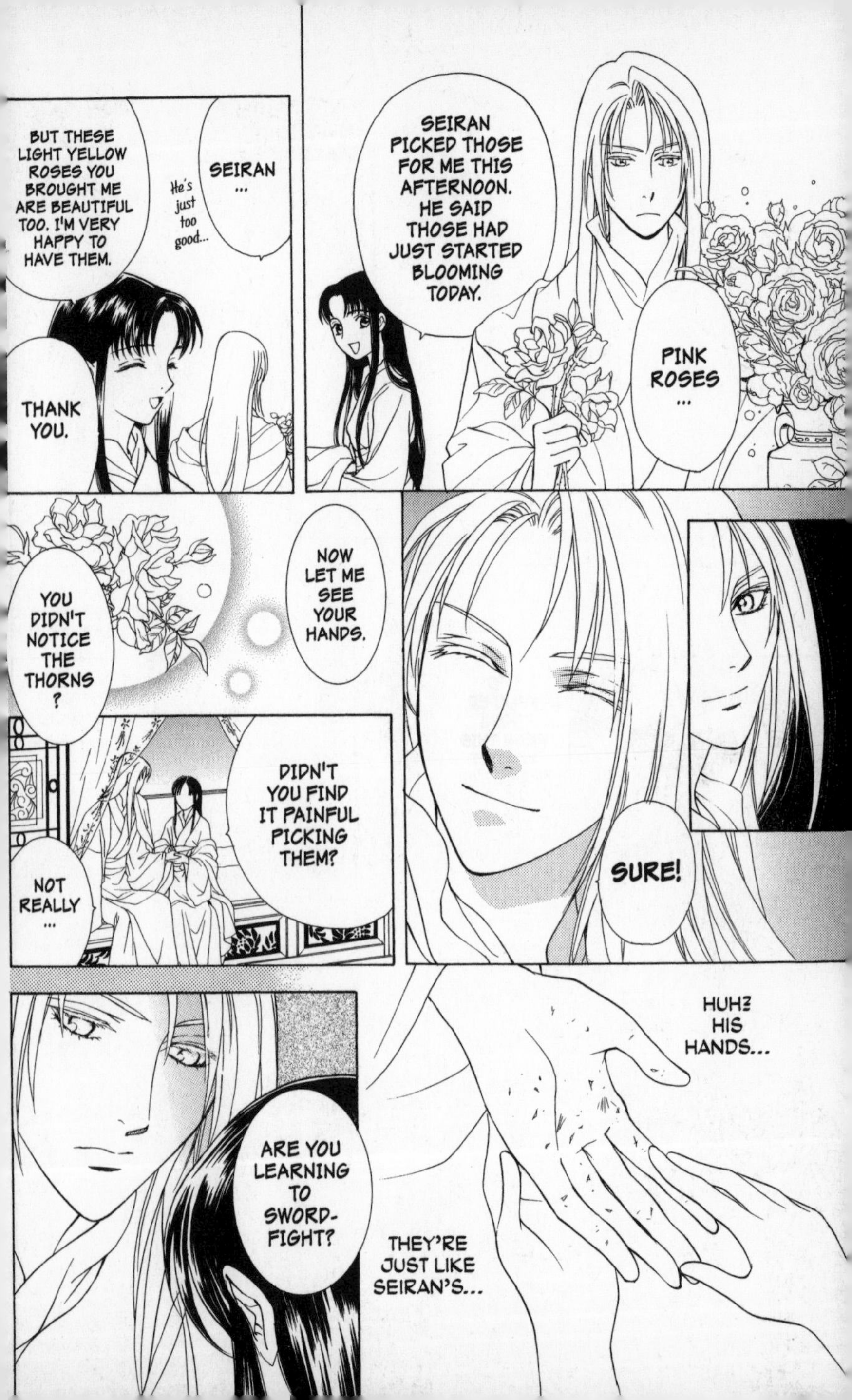

SEIRAN PICKED THOSE FOR ME THIS AFTERNOON. HE SAID THOSE HAD JUST STARTED BLOOMING TODAY.
PINK ROSES ...
SEIRAN ...
He's just too good...
BUT THESE LIGHT YELLOW ROSES YOU BROUGHT ME ARE BEAUTIFUL TOO. I'M VERY HAPPY TO HAVE THEM.
THANK YOU.
SURE!
NOW LET ME SEE YOUR HANDS.
YOU DIDN'T NOTICE THE THORNS ?
DIDN'T YOU FIND IT PAINFUL PICKING THEM?
NOT REALLY ...
HUH? HIS HANDS...
THEY'RE JUST LIKE SEIRAN'S...
ARE YOU LEARNING TO SWORD-FIGHT?

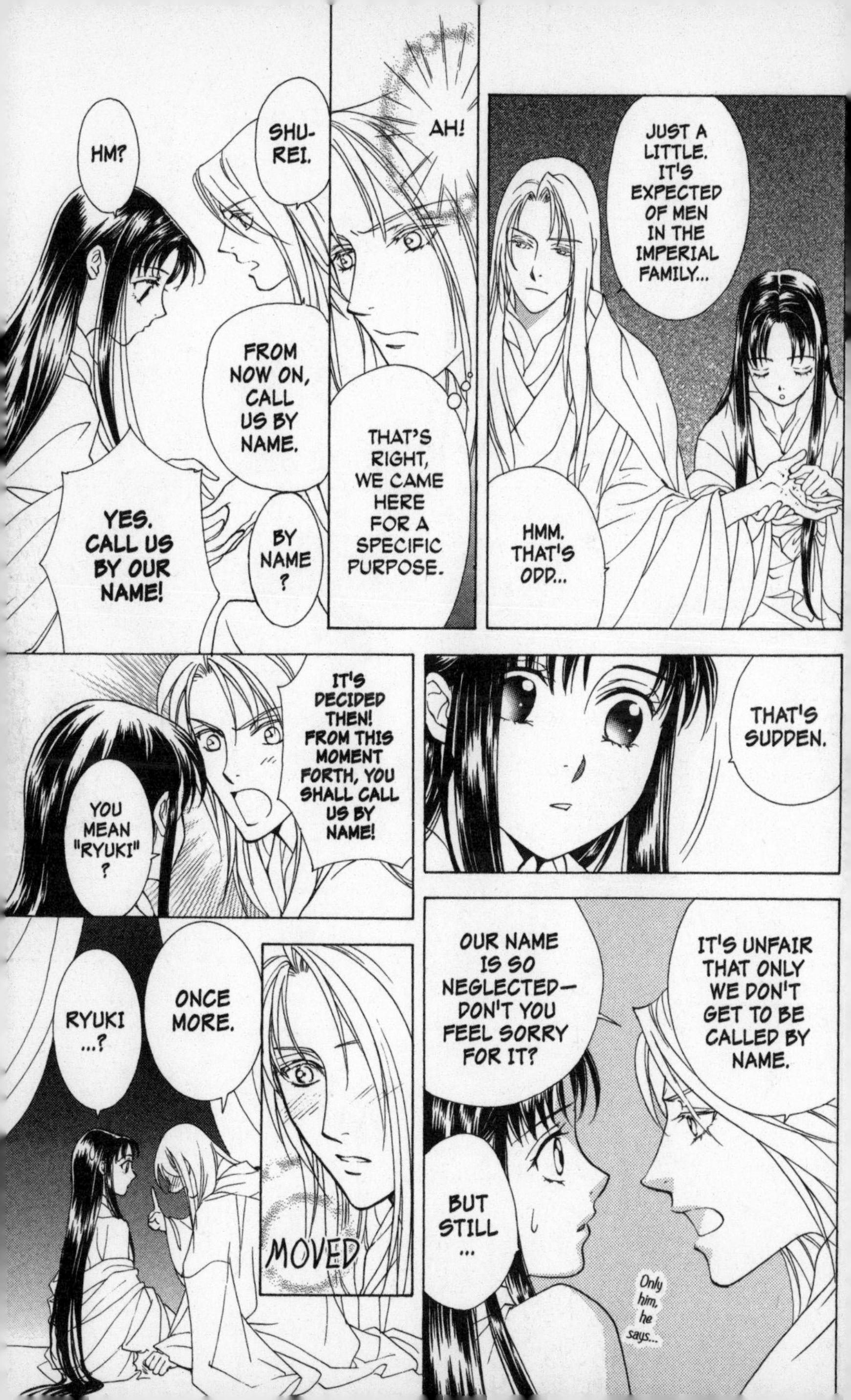
JUST A LITTLE. IT'S EXPECTED OF MEN IN THE IMPERIAL FAMILY...
HMM. THAT'S ODD...
AH!
THAT'S RIGHT, WE CAME HERE FOR A SPECIFIC PURPOSE.
SHU-REI.
HM?
FROM NOW ON, CALL US BY NAME.
BY NAME?
YES. CALL US BY OUR NAME!
THAT'S SUDDEN.
IT'S DECIDED THEN! FROM THIS MOMENT FORTH, YOU SHALL CALL US BY NAME!
YOU MEAN "RYUKI"?
IT'S UNFAIR THAT ONLY WE DON'T GET TO BE CALLED BY NAME.
OUR NAME IS SO NEGLECTED— DON'T YOU FEEL SORRY FOR IT?
BUT STILL...
Only him, he says...
MOVED
ONCE MORE.
RYUKI ...?

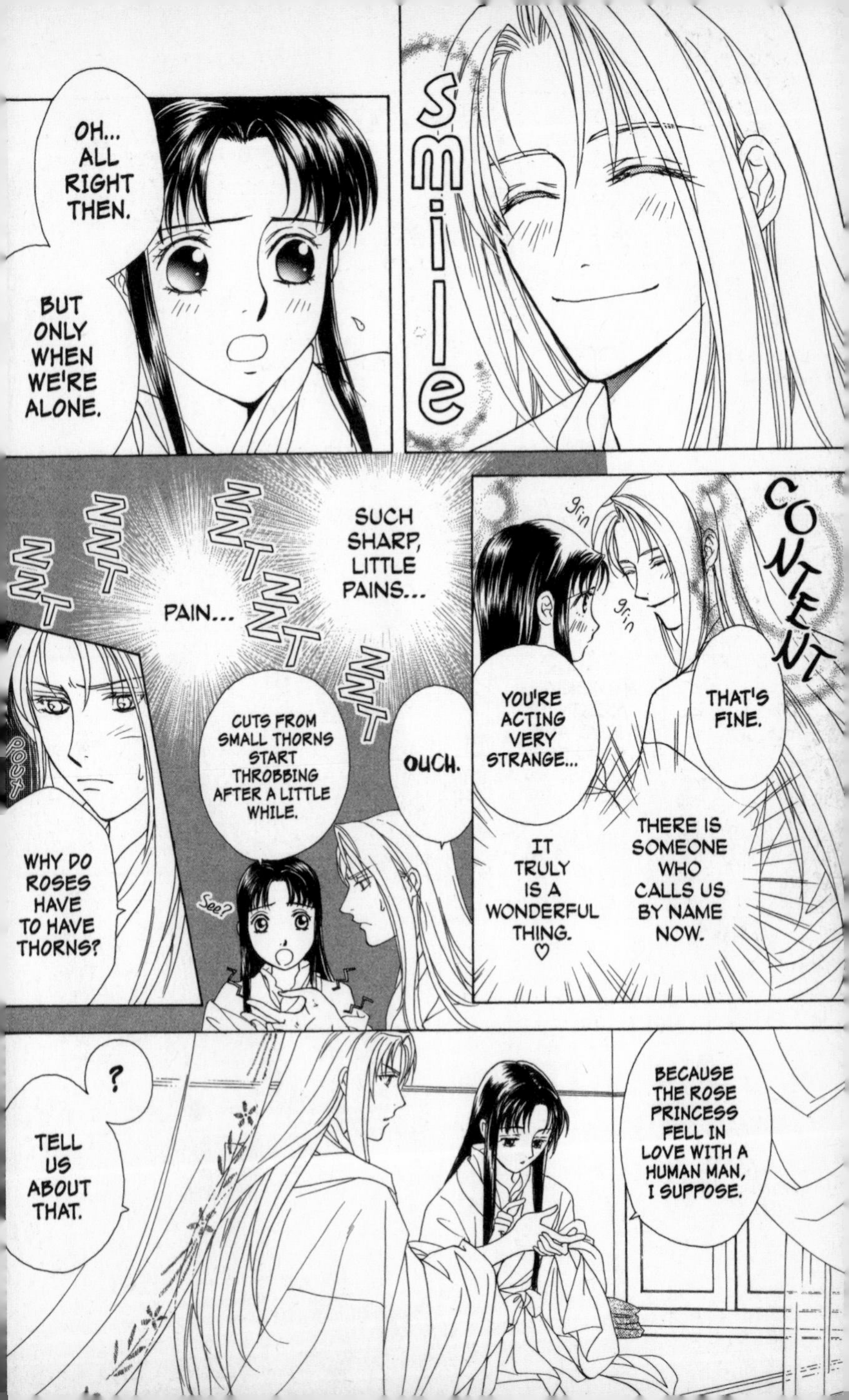
smile
OH... ALL RIGHT THEN.
BUT ONLY WHEN WE'RE ALONE.
CONTENT
grin
grin
THAT'S FINE.
YOU'RE ACTING VERY STRANGE...
THERE IS SOMEONE WHO CALLS US BY NAME NOW.
IT TRULY IS A WONDERFUL THING. ♡
SUCH SHARP, LITTLE PAINS...
ZZT
ZZT
PAIN...
ZZT
ZZT
ZZT
ZZT
OUCH.
CUTS FROM SMALL THORNS START THROBBING AFTER A LITTLE WHILE.
See?
POUT
WHY DO ROSES HAVE TO HAVE THORNS?
BECAUSE THE ROSE PRINCESS FELL IN LOVE WITH A HUMAN MAN, I SUPPOSE.
?
TELL US ABOUT THAT.

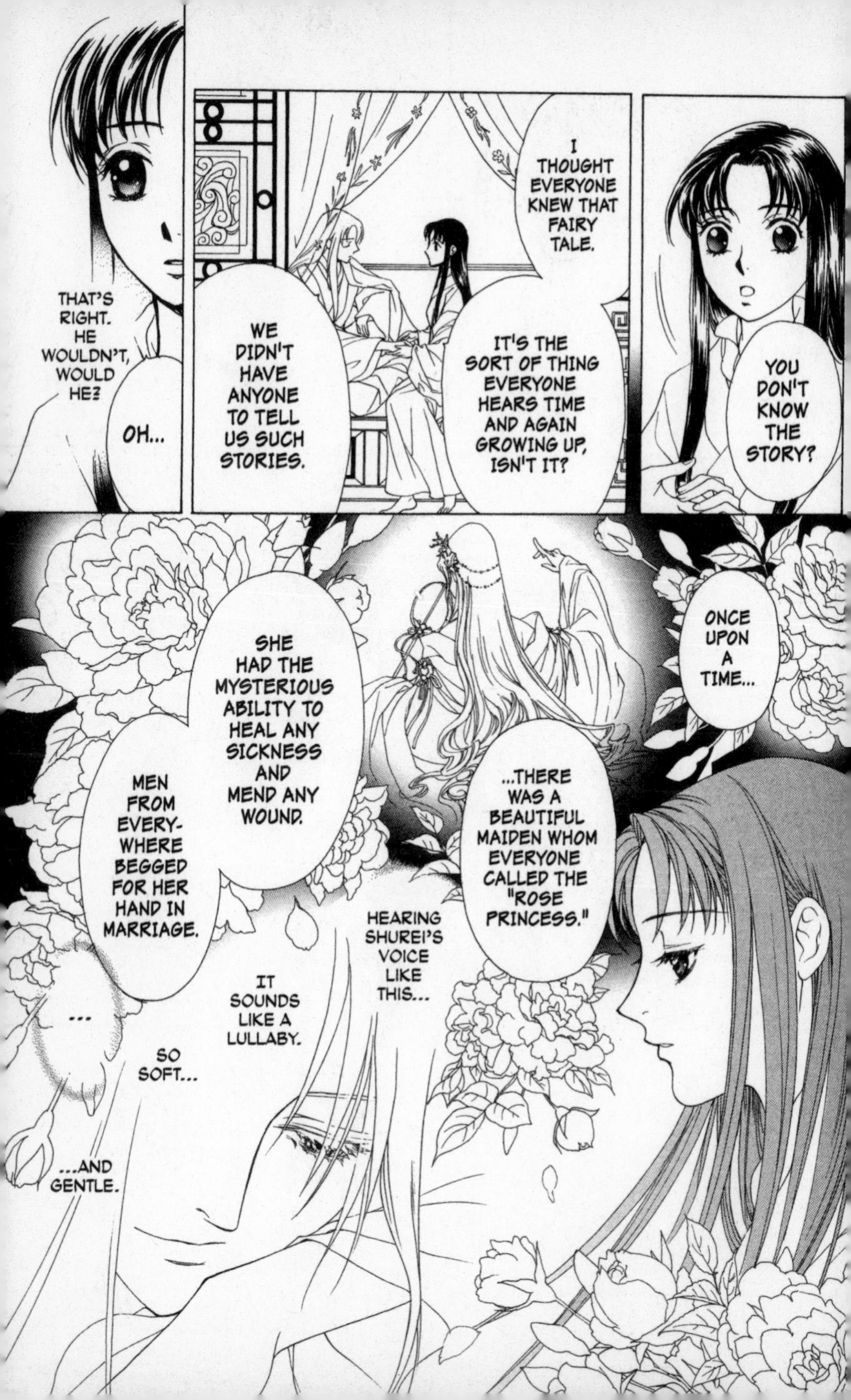
YOU DON'T KNOW THE STORY?
I THOUGHT EVERYONE KNEW THAT FAIRY TALE.
IT'S THE SORT OF THING EVERYONE HEARS TIME AND AGAIN GROWING UP, ISN'T IT?
WE DIDN'T HAVE ANYONE TO TELL US SUCH STORIES.
OH...
THAT'S RIGHT. HE WOULDN'T, WOULD HE?
ONCE UPON A TIME...
...THERE WAS A BEAUTIFUL MAIDEN WHOM EVERYONE CALLED THE "ROSE PRINCESS."
SHE HAD THE MYSTERIOUS ABILITY TO HEAL ANY SICKNESS AND MEND ANY WOUND.
MEN FROM EVERY-WHERE BEGGED FOR HER HAND IN MARRIAGE.
HEARING SHUREI'S VOICE LIKE THIS...
IT SOUNDS LIKE A LULLABY.
SO SOFT...
...
...AND GENTLE.

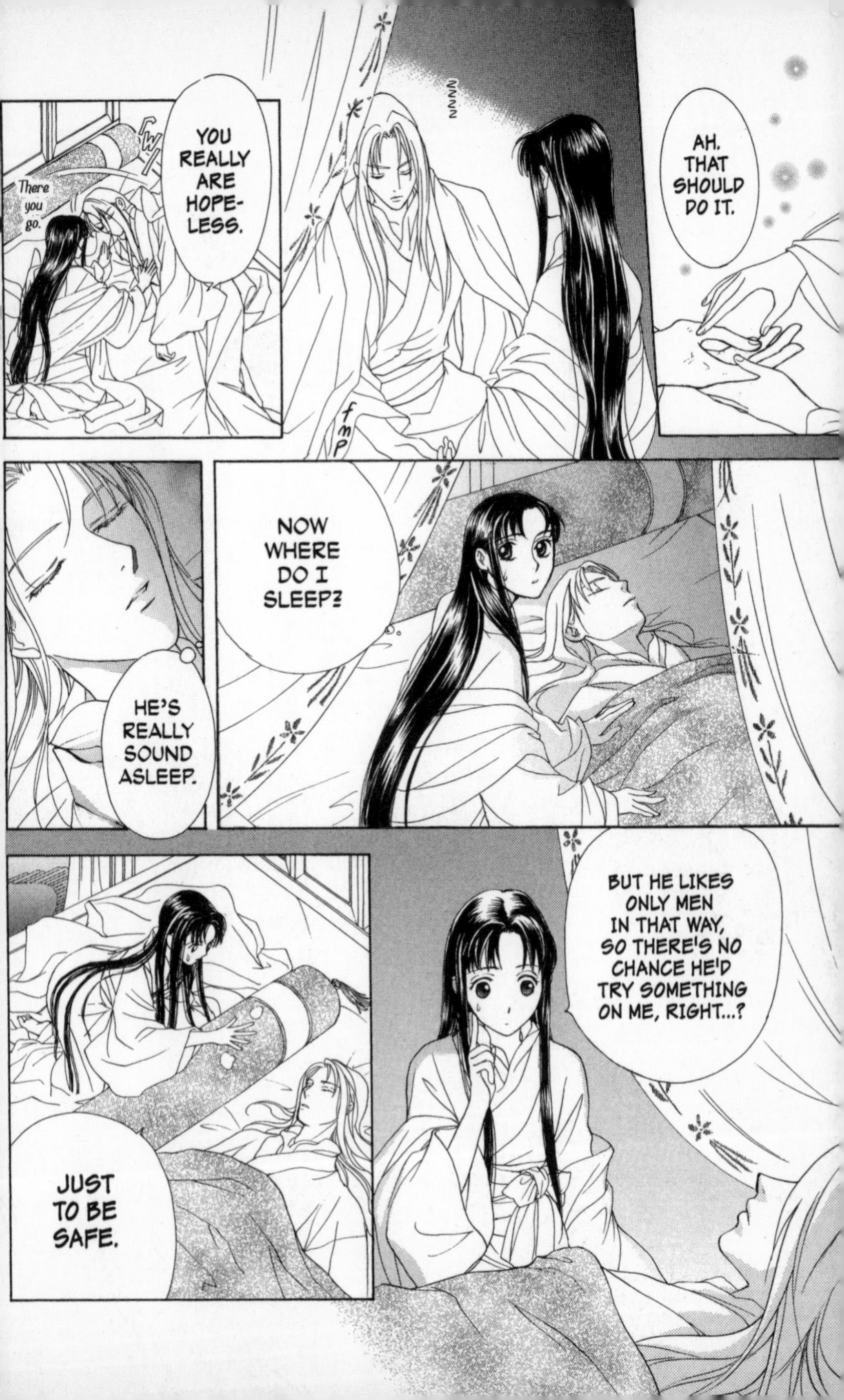
AH. THAT SHOULD DO IT.
ZZZ
fmp
YOU REALLY ARE HOPE-LESS.
FW
There you go.
NOW WHERE DO I SLEEP?
HE'S REALLY SOUND ASLEEP.
BUT HE LIKES ONLY MEN IN THAT WAY, SO THERE'S NO CHANCE HE'D TRY SOMETHING ON ME, RIGHT...?
JUST TO BE SAFE.

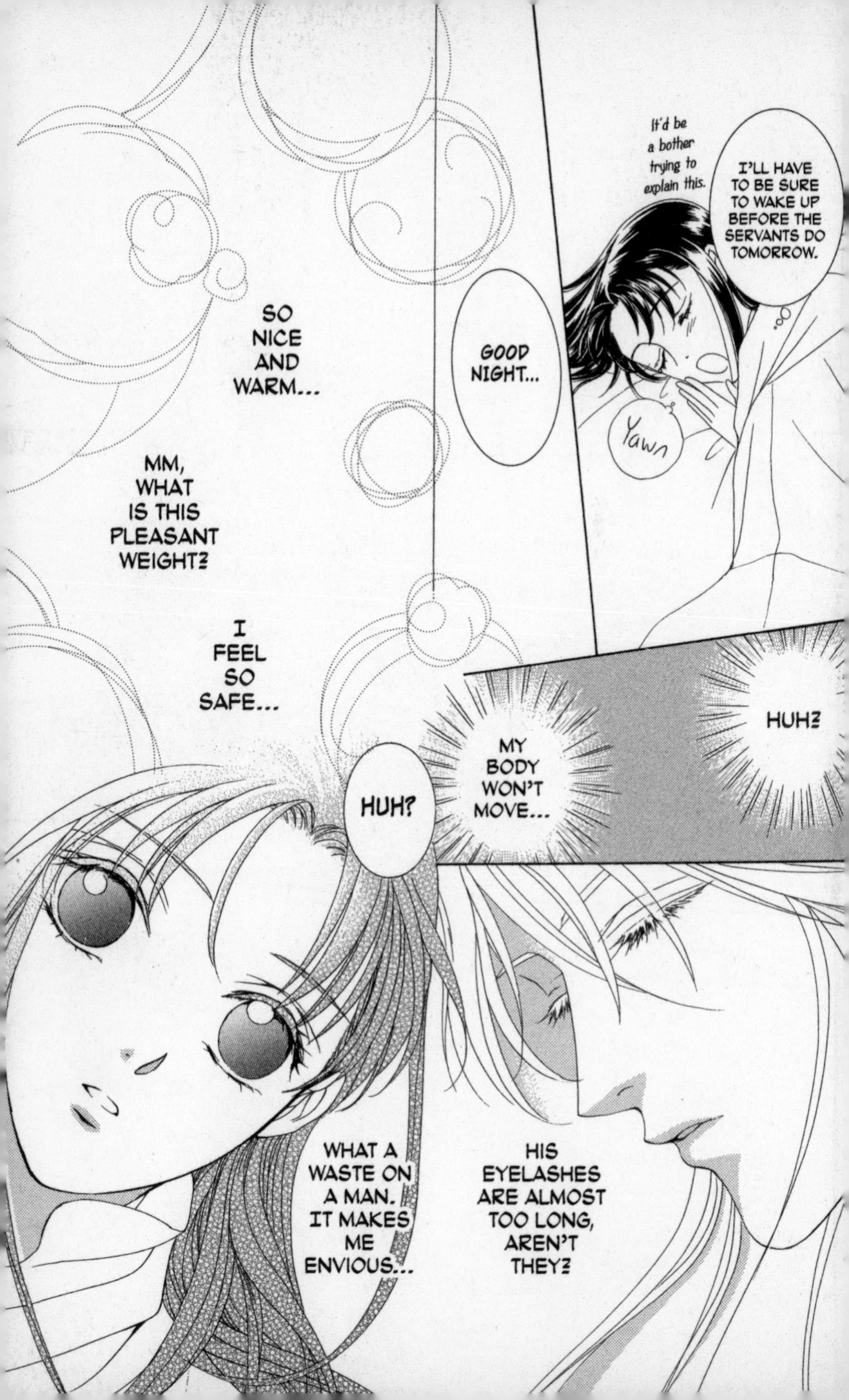
It'd be a bother trying to explain this.
I'LL HAVE TO BE SURE TO WAKE UP BEFORE THE SERVANTS DO TOMORROW.
Yawn
GOOD NIGHT...
SO NICE AND WARM...
MM, WHAT IS THIS PLEASANT WEIGHT?
I FEEL SO SAFE...
HUH?
MY BODY WON'T MOVE...
HUH?
HIS EYELASHES ARE ALMOST TOO LONG, AREN'T THEY?
WHAT A WASTE ON A MAN. IT MAKES ME ENVIOUS...

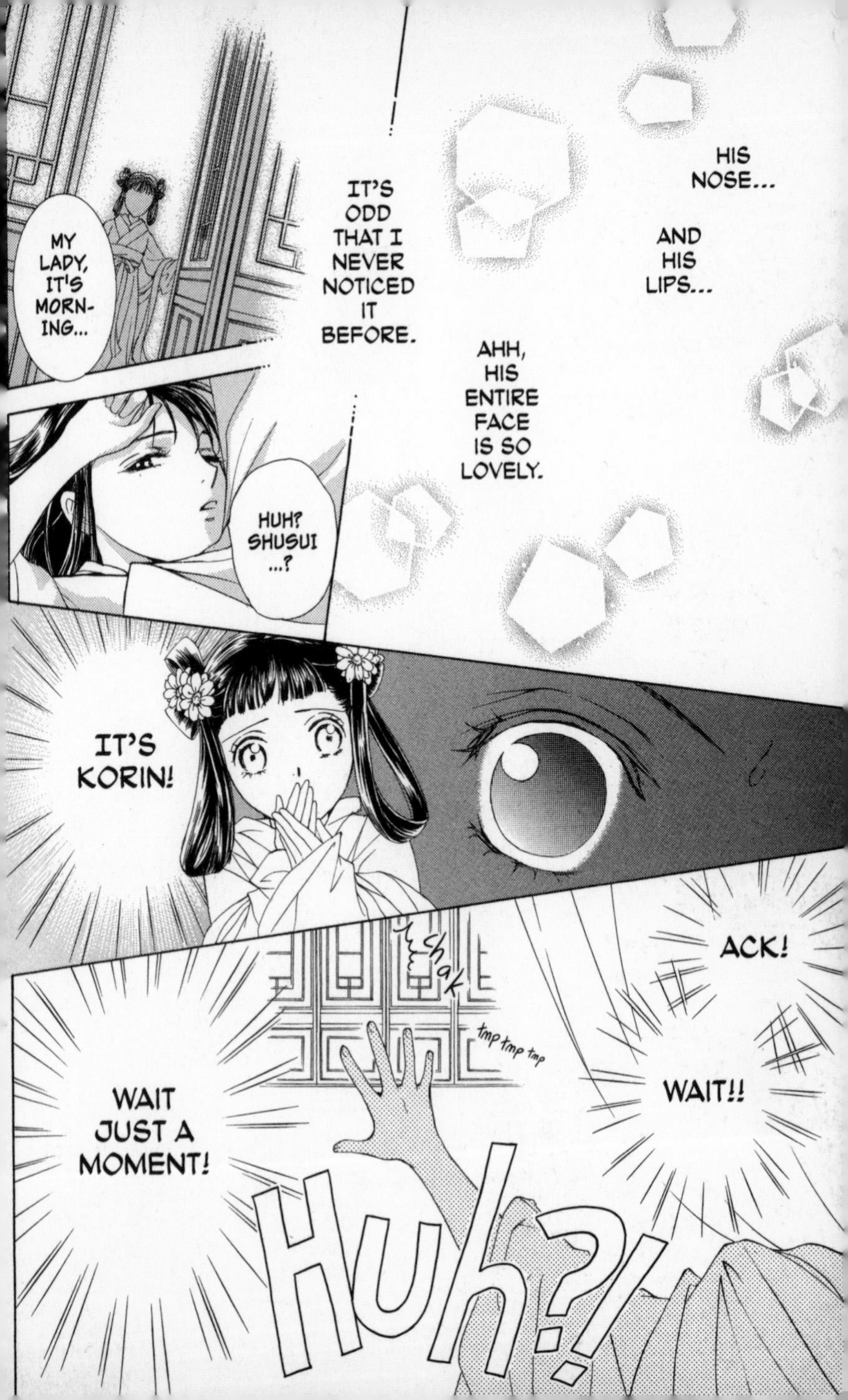
HIS NOSE...
AND HIS LIPS...
AHH, HIS ENTIRE FACE IS SO LOVELY.
IT'S ODD THAT I NEVER NOTICED IT BEFORE.
MY LADY, IT'S MORN-ING...
HUH? SHUSUI ...?
IT'S KORIN!
ACK!
chak
tmp tmp tmp
WAIT!!
WAIT JUST A MOMENT!
HUH?!

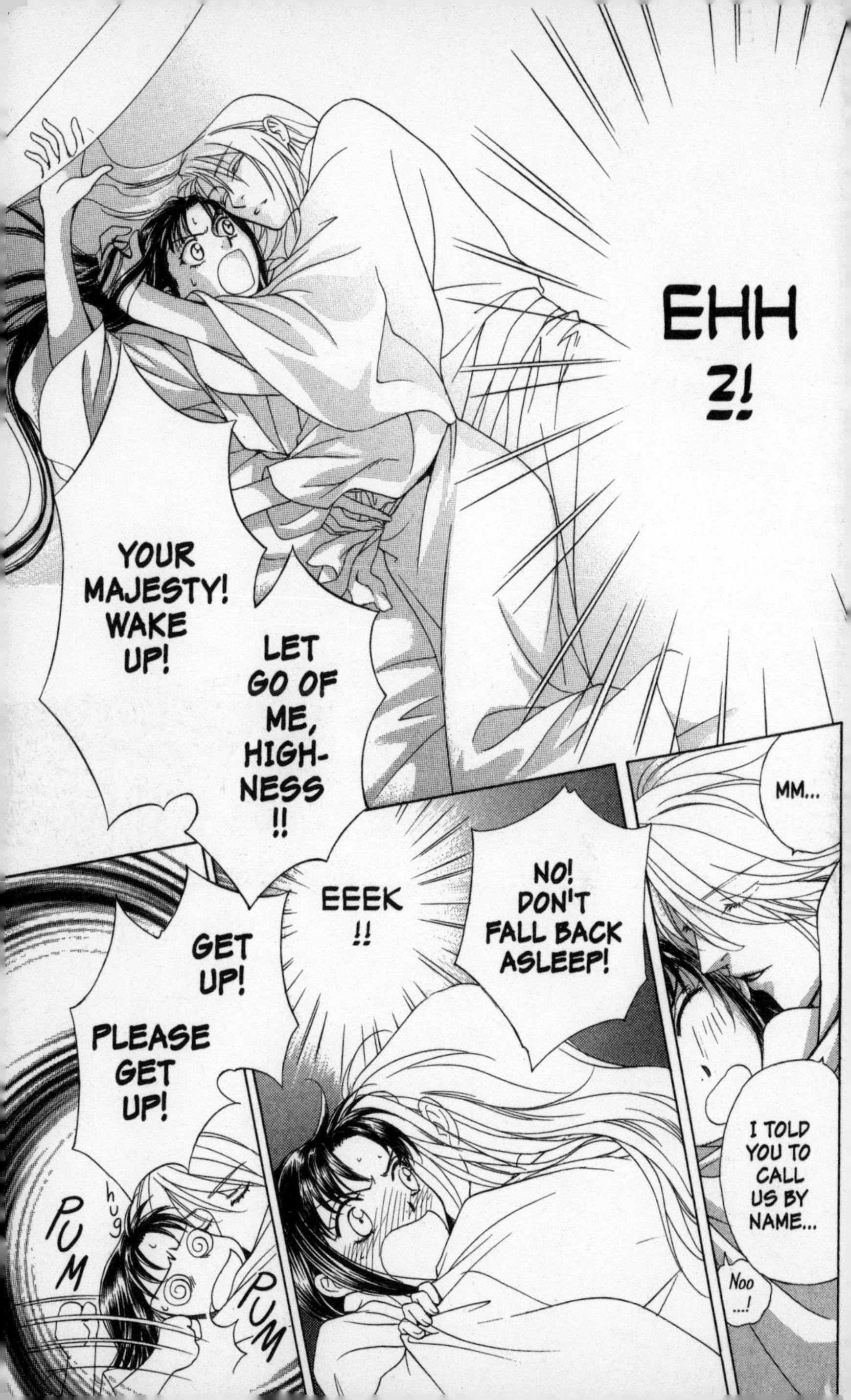
EHH ?!
YOUR MAJESTY! WAKE UP!
LET GO OF ME, HIGHNESS!!
MM...
I TOLD YOU TO CALL US BY NAME...
Noo ...!
NO! DON'T FALL BACK ASLEEP!
EEEK!!
GET UP!
PLEASE GET UP!
hug
PUM
PUM

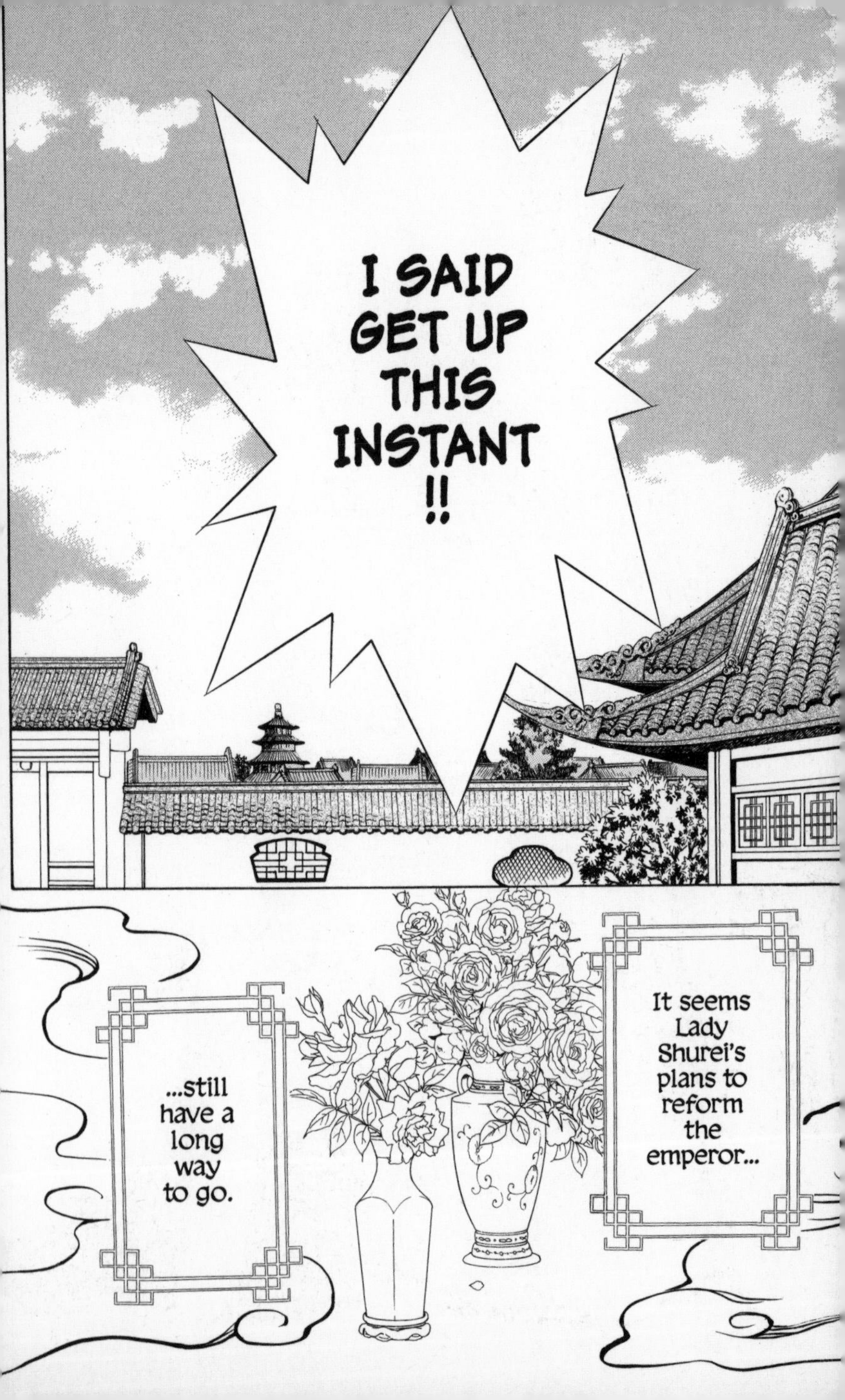
I SAID GET UP THIS INSTANT !!
It seems Lady Shurei's plans to reform the emperor...
...still have a long way to go.

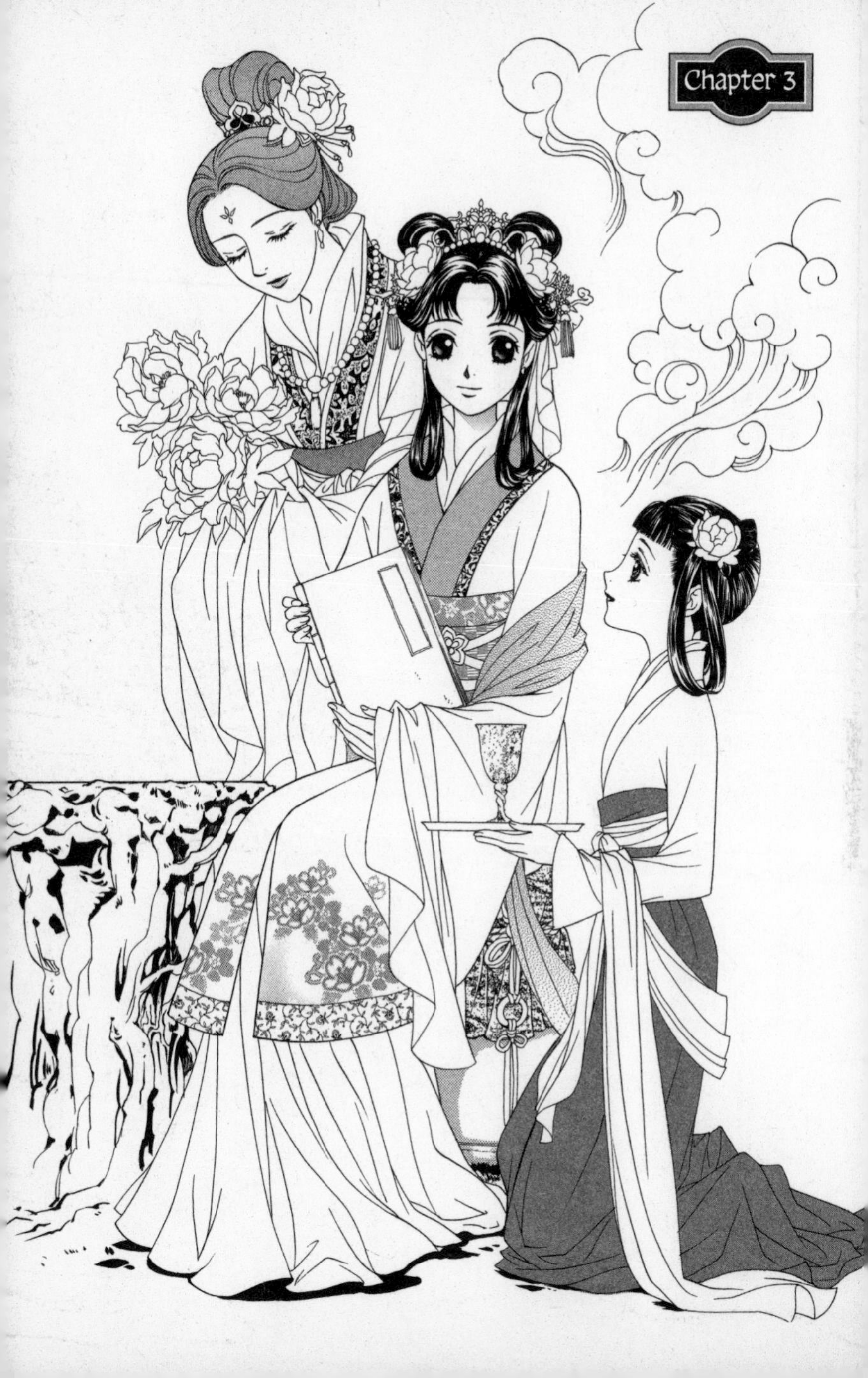
Chapter 3

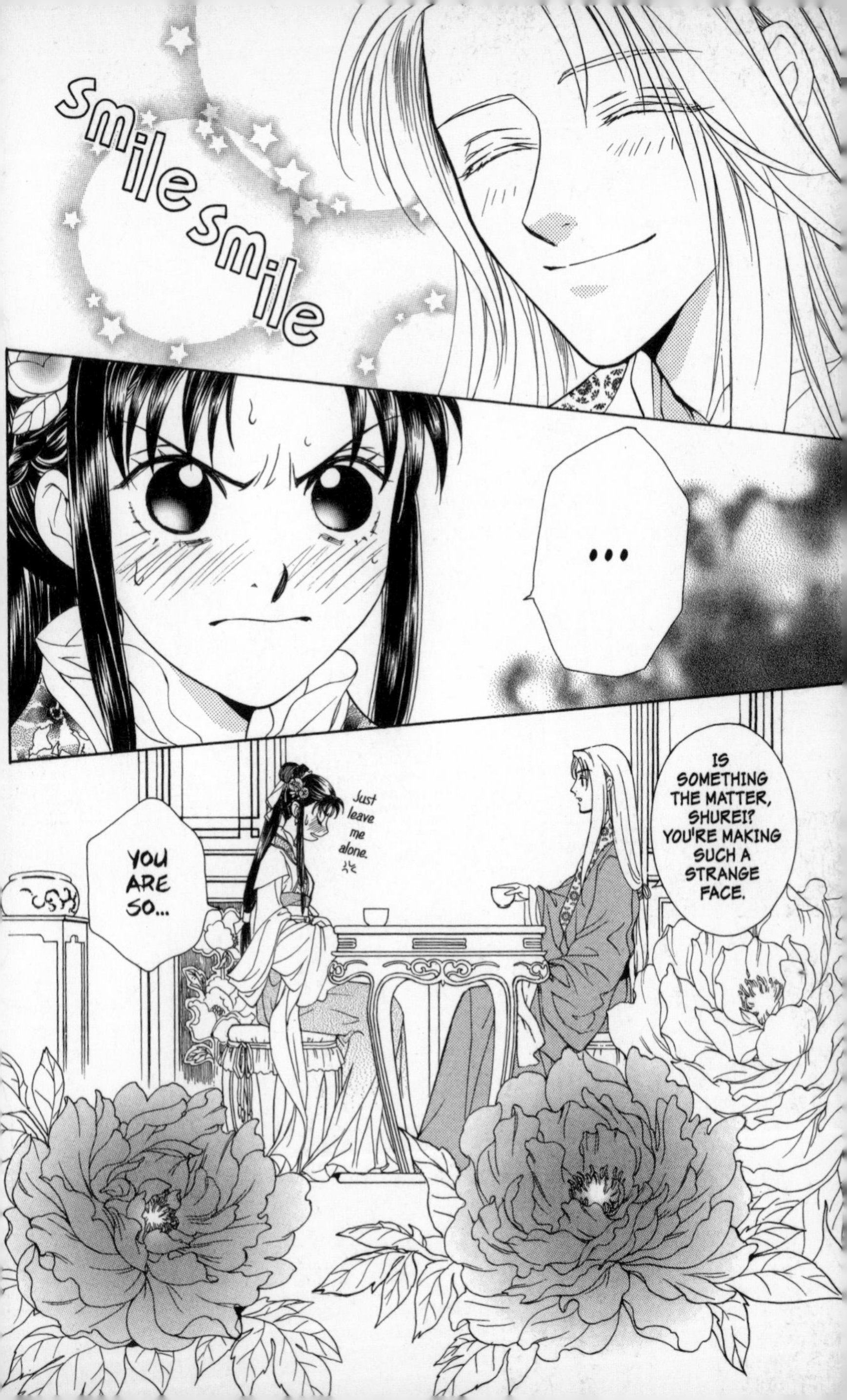
smile smile
...
IS SOMETHING THE MATTER, SHUREI!? YOU'RE MAKING SUCH A STRANGE FACE.
Just leave me alone.
YOU ARE SO...

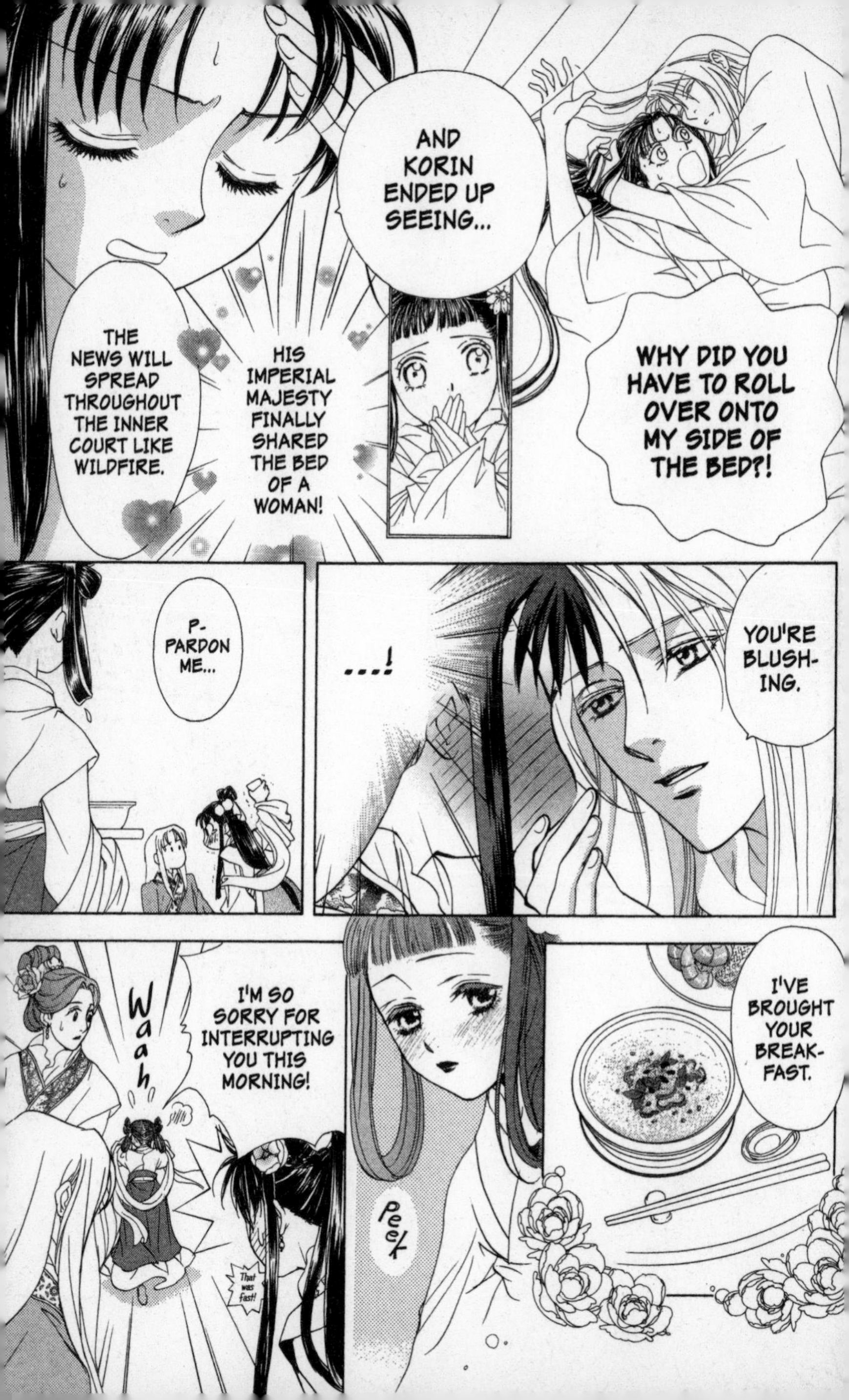

WHY DID YOU HAVE TO ROLL OVER ONTO MY SIDE OF THE BED?!
AND KORIN ENDED UP SEEING...
HIS IMPERIAL MAJESTY FINALLY SHARED THE BED OF A WOMAN!
THE NEWS WILL SPREAD THROUGHOUT THE INNER COURT LIKE WILDFIRE.
YOU'RE BLUSH-ING.
...!
P-PARDON ME...
I'VE BROUGHT YOUR BREAK-FAST.
Peek
I'M SO SORRY FOR INTERRUPTING YOU THIS MORNING!
Waah
That was fast!

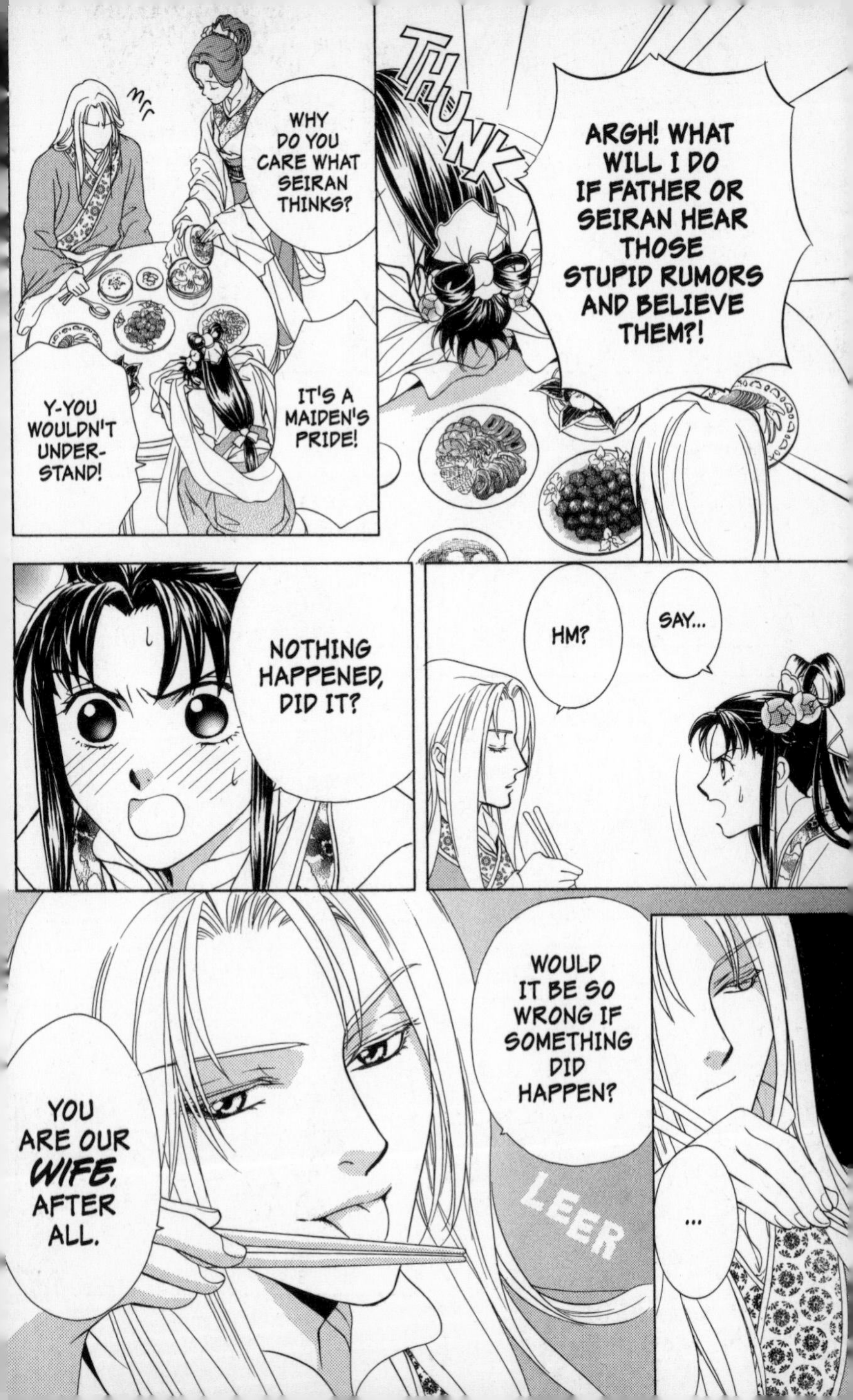
THUNK
ARGH! WHAT WILL I DO IF FATHER OR SEIRAN HEAR THOSE STUPID RUMORS AND BELIEVE THEM?!
WHY DO YOU CARE WHAT SEIRAN THINKS?
mrr
IT'S A MAIDEN'S PRIDE!
Y-YOU WOULDN'T UNDER-STAND!
SAY...
HM?
NOTHING HAPPENED, DID IT?
...
WOULD IT BE SO WRONG IF SOMETHING DID HAPPEN?
LEER
YOU ARE OUR *WIFE*, AFTER ALL.

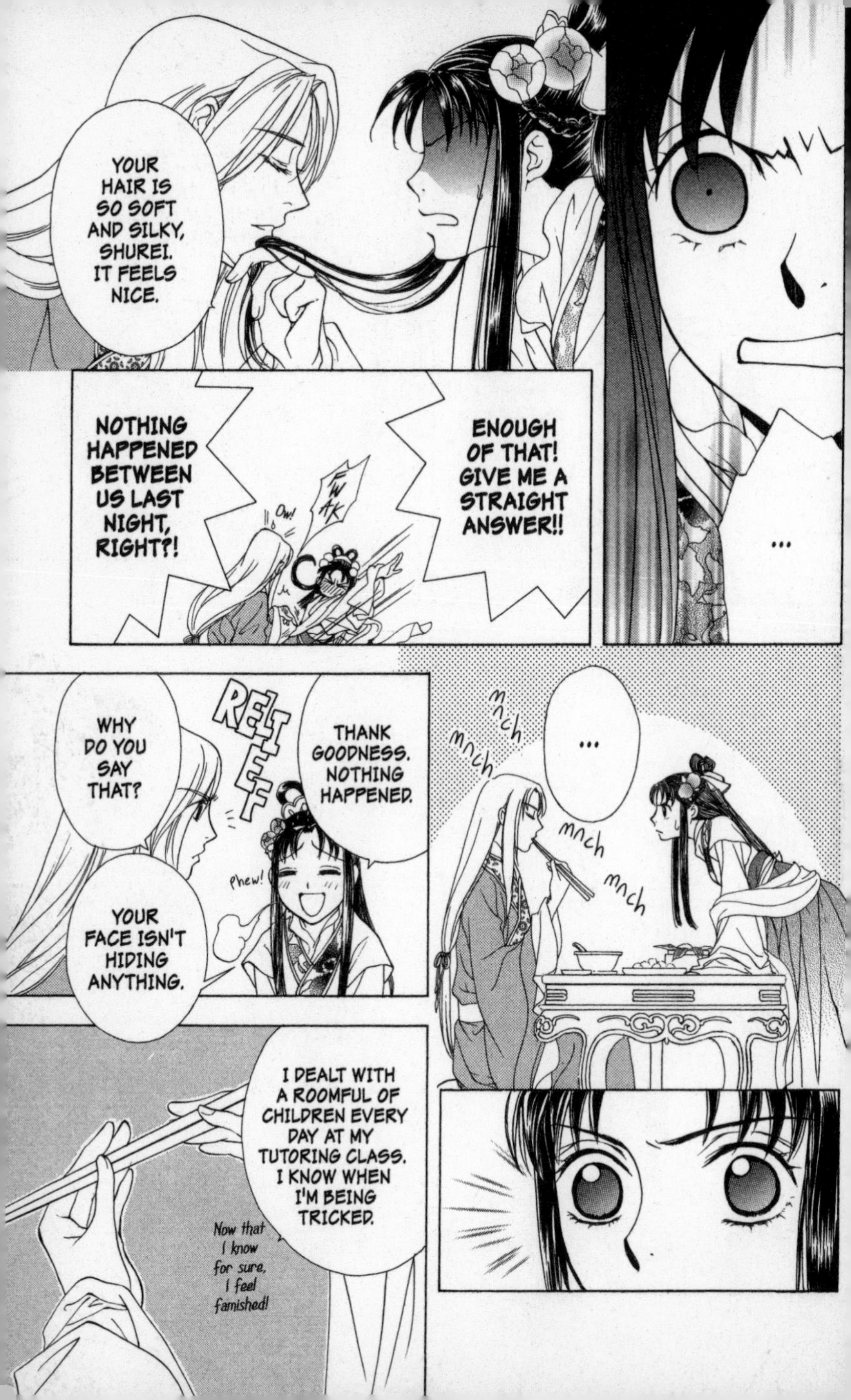
YOUR HAIR IS SO SOFT AND SILKY, SHUREI. IT FEELS NICE.
...
ENOUGH OF THAT! GIVE ME A STRAIGHT ANSWER!!
NOTHING HAPPENED BETWEEN US LAST NIGHT, RIGHT?!
FWAK
Ow!
mnch
mnch
...
mnch
mnch
THANK GOODNESS. NOTHING HAPPENED.
RELIEF
Phew!
WHY DO YOU SAY THAT?
YOUR FACE ISN'T HIDING ANYTHING.
I DEALT WITH A ROOMFUL OF CHILDREN EVERY DAY AT MY TUTORING CLASS. I KNOW WHEN I'M BEING TRICKED.
Now that I know for sure, I feel famished!

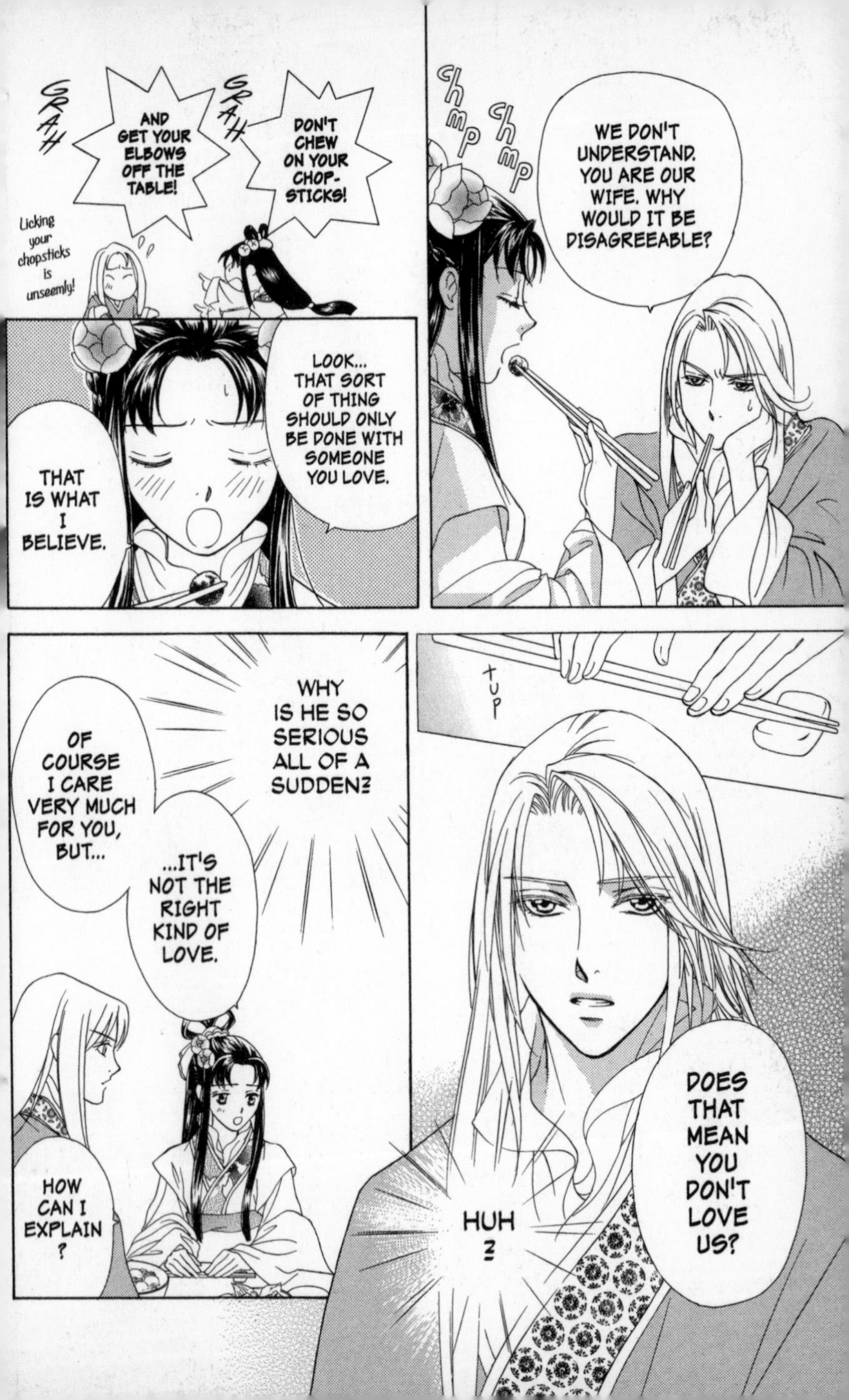
CHMP CHMP CHMP CHMP
WE DON'T UNDERSTAND. YOU ARE OUR WIFE. WHY WOULD IT BE DISAGREEABLE?
GRAH
DON'T CHEW ON YOUR CHOP-STICKS!
GRAH
AND GET YOUR ELBOWS OFF THE TABLE!
Licking your chopsticks is unseemly!
LOOK... THAT SORT OF THING SHOULD ONLY BE DONE WITH SOMEONE YOU LOVE.
THAT IS WHAT I BELIEVE.
TUP
DOES THAT MEAN YOU DON'T LOVE US?
HUH?
WHY IS HE SO SERIOUS ALL OF A SUDDEN?
OF COURSE I CARE VERY MUCH FOR YOU, BUT...
...IT'S NOT THE RIGHT KIND OF LOVE.
HOW CAN I EXPLAIN?

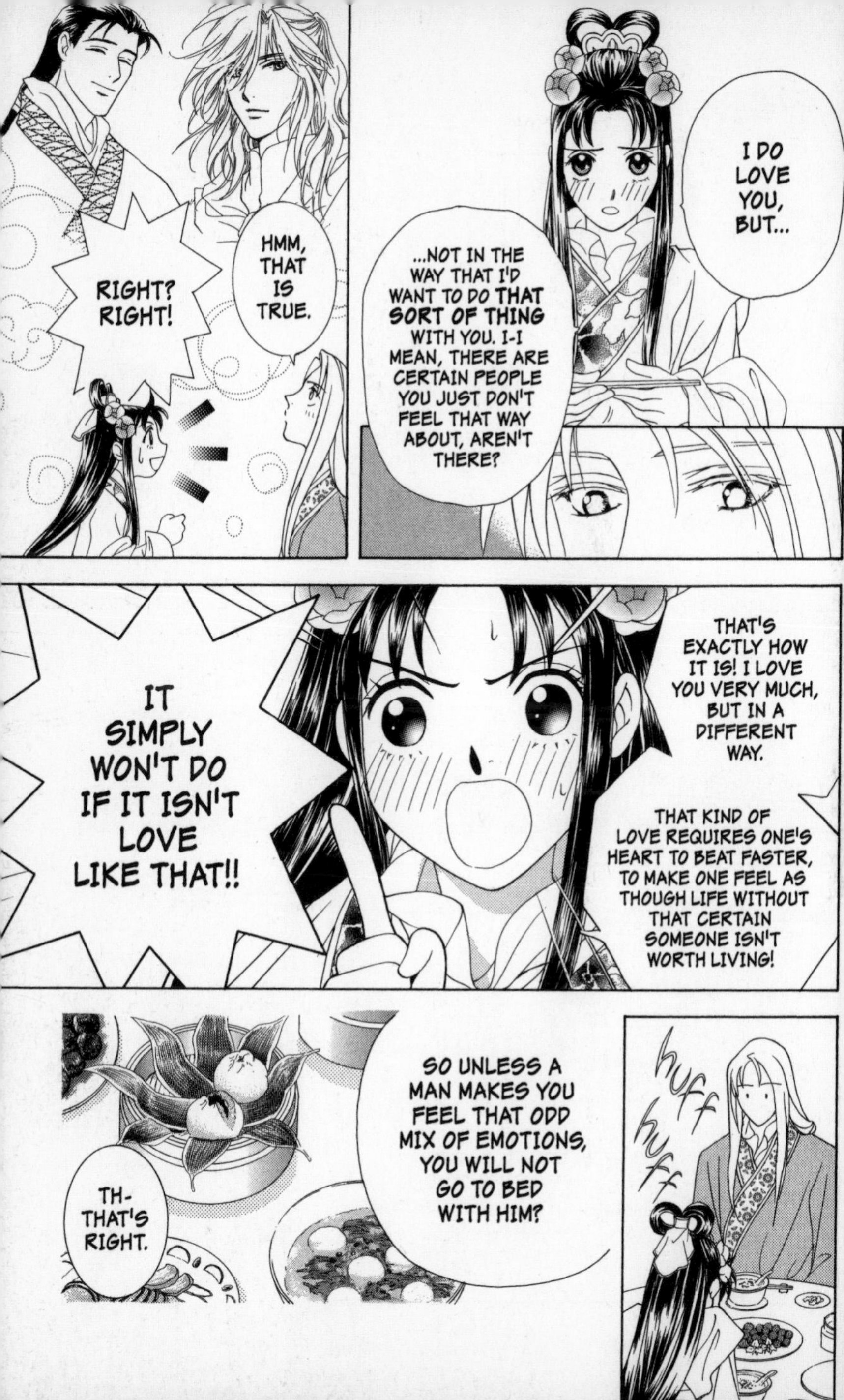
I DO LOVE YOU, BUT...
...NOT IN THE WAY THAT I'D WANT TO DO THAT SORT OF THING WITH YOU. I-I MEAN, THERE ARE CERTAIN PEOPLE YOU JUST DON'T FEEL THAT WAY ABOUT, AREN'T THERE?
HMM, THAT IS TRUE.
RIGHT? RIGHT!
THAT'S EXACTLY HOW IT IS! I LOVE YOU VERY MUCH, BUT IN A DIFFERENT WAY.
THAT KIND OF LOVE REQUIRES ONE'S HEART TO BEAT FASTER, TO MAKE ONE FEEL AS THOUGH LIFE WITHOUT THAT CERTAIN SOMEONE ISN'T WORTH LIVING!
IT SIMPLY WON'T DO IF IT ISN'T LOVE LIKE THAT!!
huff huff
SO UNLESS A MAN MAKES YOU FEEL THAT ODD MIX OF EMOTIONS, YOU WILL NOT GO TO BED WITH HIM?
TH-THAT'S RIGHT.

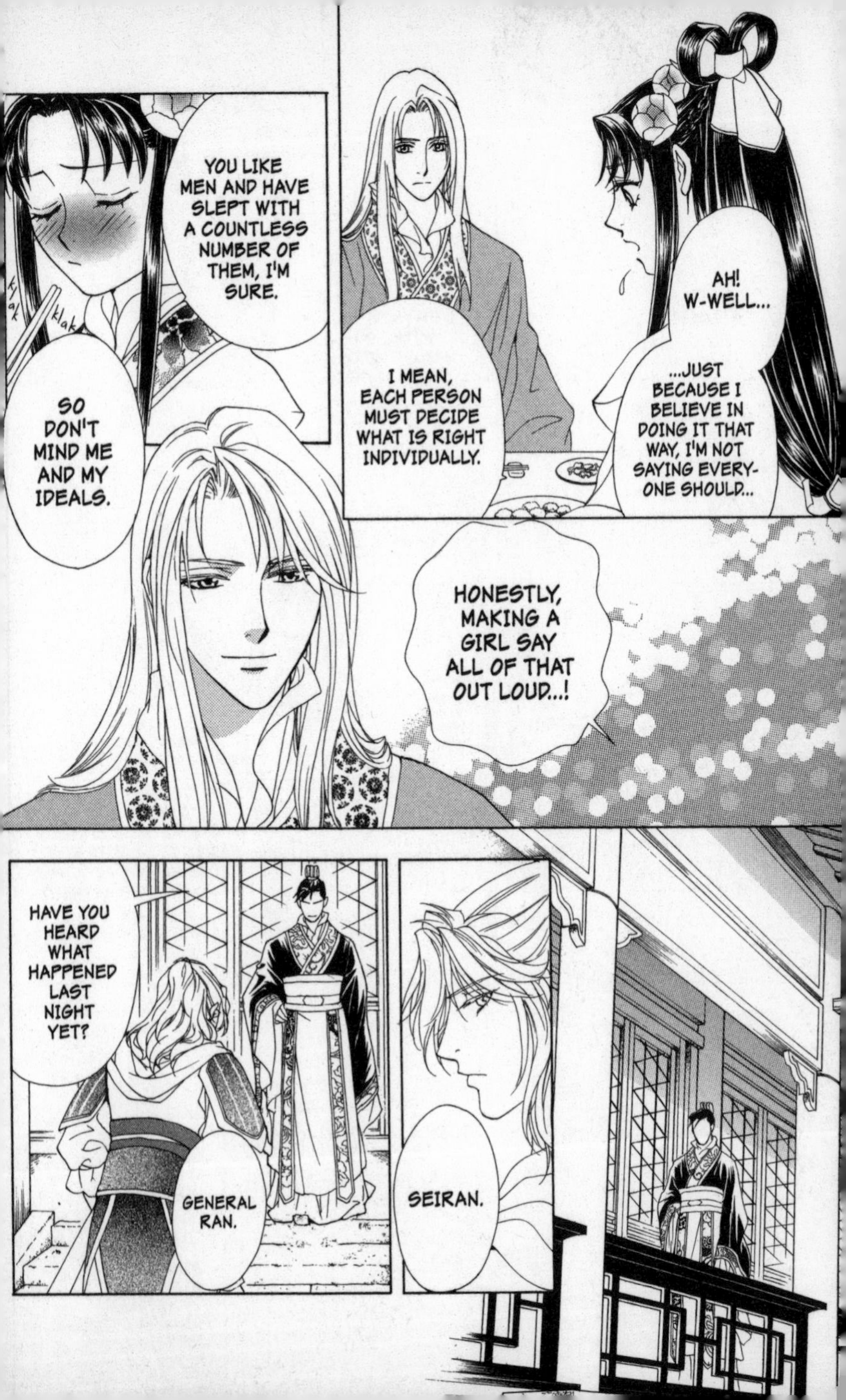
AH! W-WELL...
...JUST BECAUSE I BELIEVE IN DOING IT THAT WAY, I'M NOT SAYING EVERY-ONE SHOULD...
I MEAN, EACH PERSON MUST DECIDE WHAT IS RIGHT INDIVIDUALLY.
YOU LIKE MEN AND HAVE SLEPT WITH A COUNTLESS NUMBER OF THEM, I'M SURE.
klak
klak
SO DON'T MIND ME AND MY IDEALS.
HONESTLY, MAKING A GIRL SAY ALL OF THAT OUT LOUD...!
SEIRAN.
GENERAL RAN.
HAVE YOU HEARD WHAT HAPPENED LAST NIGHT YET?

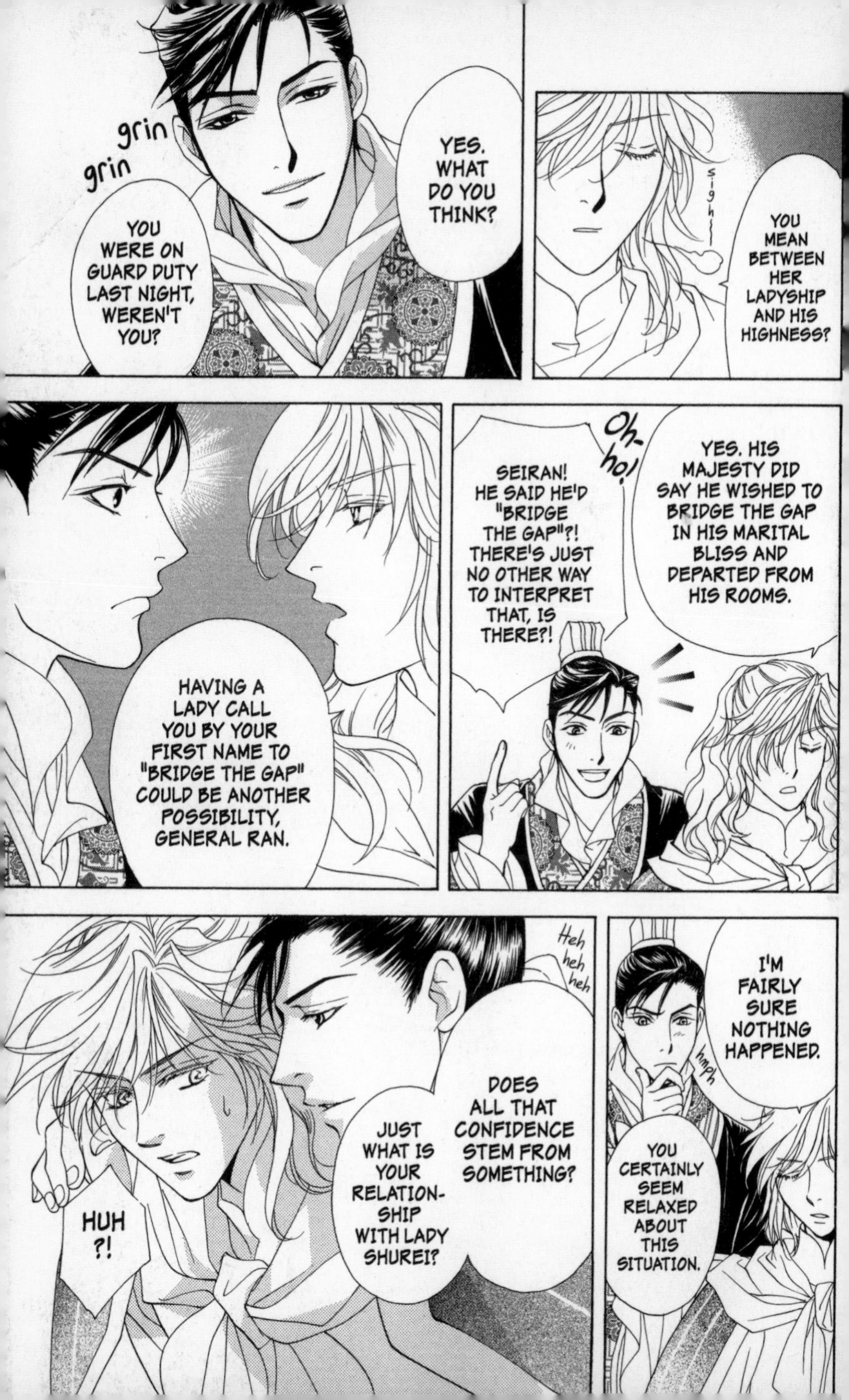
sigh
YOU MEAN BETWEEN HER LADYSHIP AND HIS HIGHNESS?
YES. WHAT DO YOU THINK?
grin grin
YOU WERE ON GUARD DUTY LAST NIGHT, WEREN'T YOU?
YES. HIS MAJESTY DID SAY HE WISHED TO BRIDGE THE GAP IN HIS MARITAL BLISS AND DEPARTED FROM HIS ROOMS.
Oh-ho!
SEIRAN! HE SAID HE'D "BRIDGE THE GAP"?! THERE'S JUST NO OTHER WAY TO INTERPRET THAT, IS THERE?!
HAVING A LADY CALL YOU BY YOUR FIRST NAME TO "BRIDGE THE GAP" COULD BE ANOTHER POSSIBILITY, GENERAL RAN.
I'M FAIRLY SURE NOTHING HAPPENED.
hmph
YOU CERTAINLY SEEM RELAXED ABOUT THIS SITUATION.
Heh heh heh
DOES ALL THAT CONFIDENCE STEM FROM SOMETHING?
JUST WHAT IS YOUR RELATION-SHIP WITH LADY SHUREI?
HUH?!

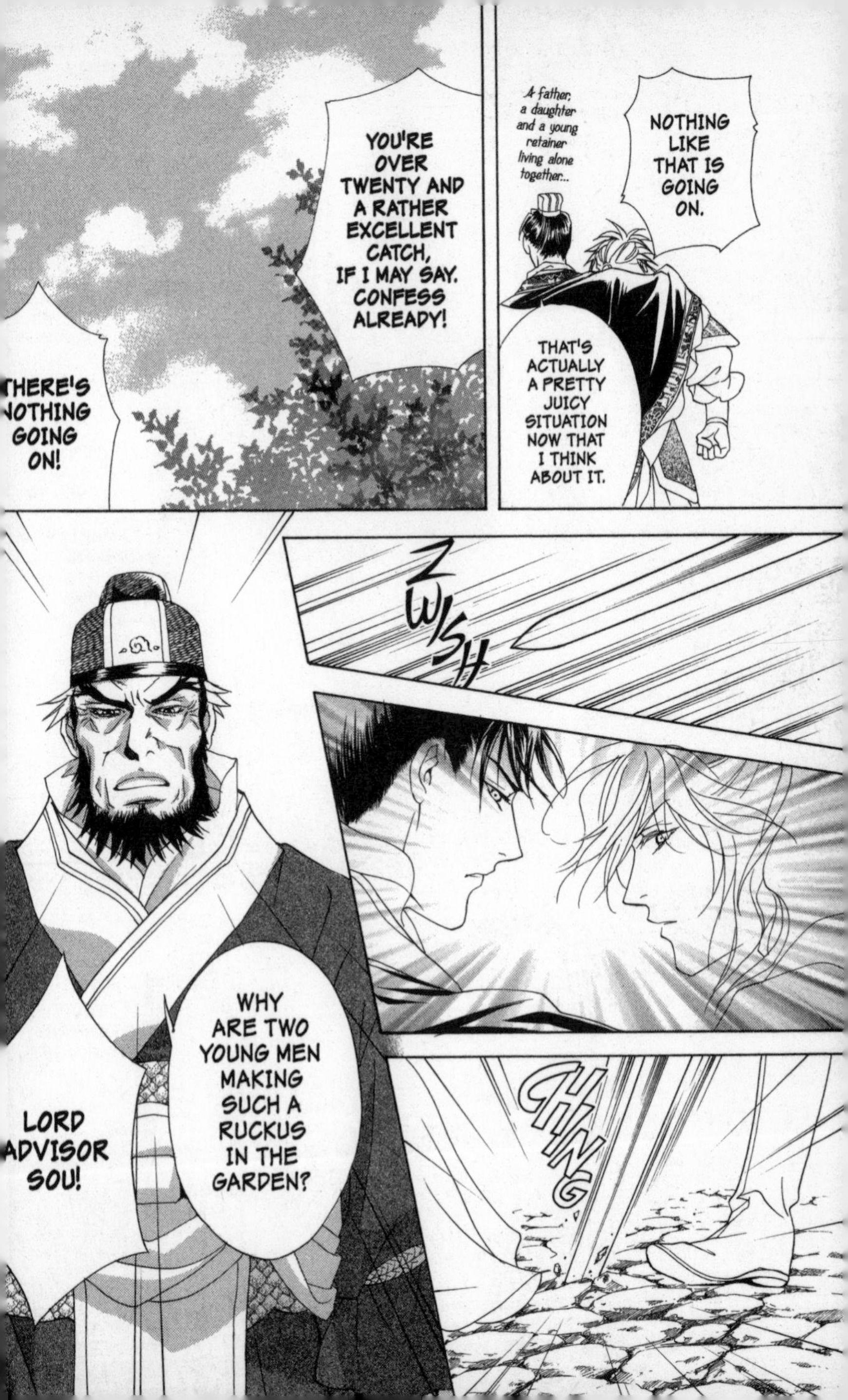
NOTHING LIKE THAT IS GOING ON.
A father, a daughter and a young retainer living alone together...
THAT'S ACTUALLY A PRETTY JUICY SITUATION NOW THAT I THINK ABOUT IT.
YOU'RE OVER TWENTY AND A RATHER EXCELLENT CATCH, IF I MAY SAY. CONFESS ALREADY!
THERE'S NOTHING GOING ON!
ZWISH
CHING
WHY ARE TWO YOUNG MEN MAKING SUCH A RUCKUS IN THE GARDEN?
LORD ADVISOR SOU!

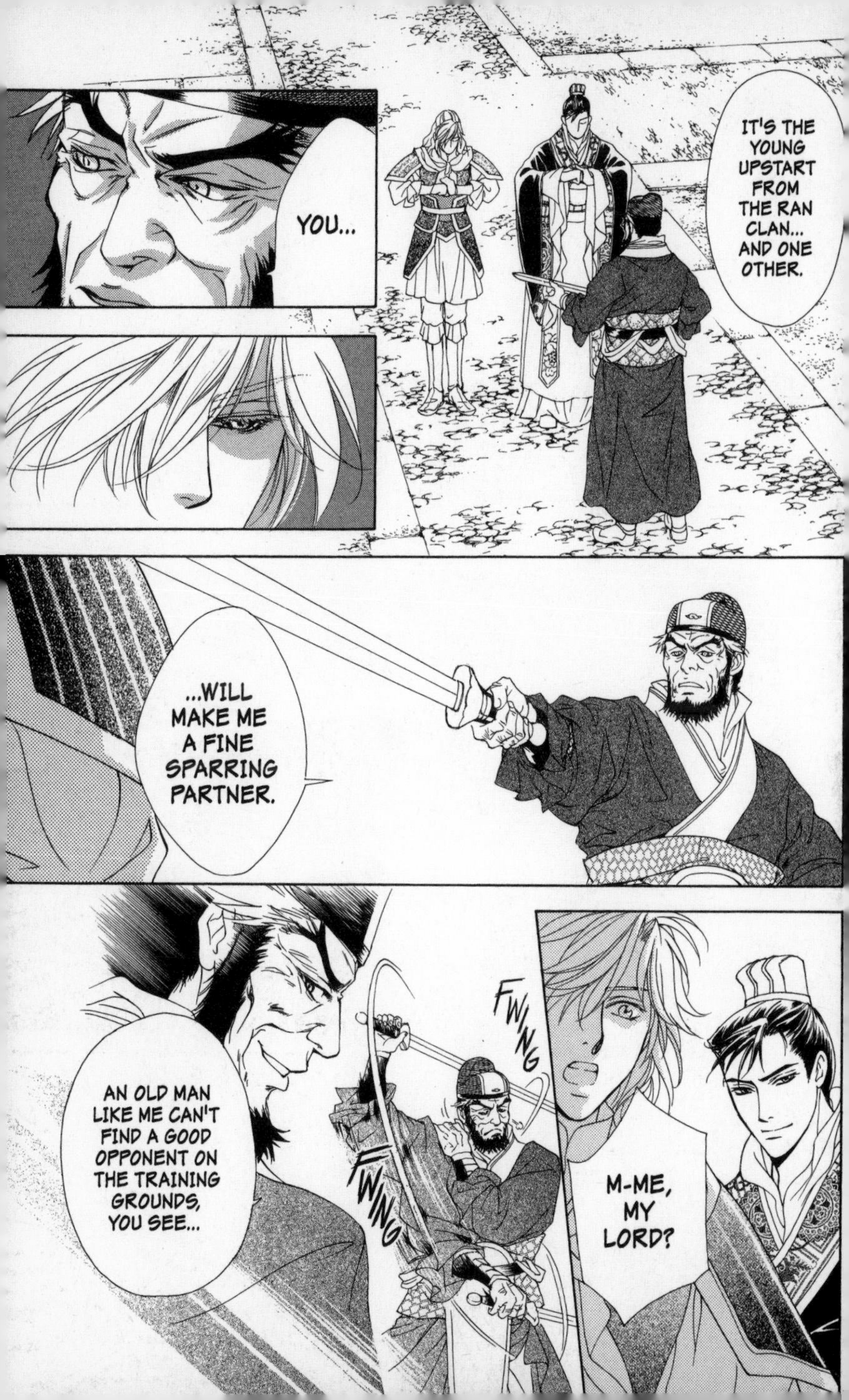
IT'S THE YOUNG UPSTART FROM THE RAN CLAN... AND ONE OTHER.
YOU...
...WILL MAKE ME A FINE SPARRING PARTNER.
M-ME, MY LORD?
FWING
FWING
AN OLD MAN LIKE ME CAN'T FIND A GOOD OPPONENT ON THE TRAINING GROUNDS, YOU SEE...

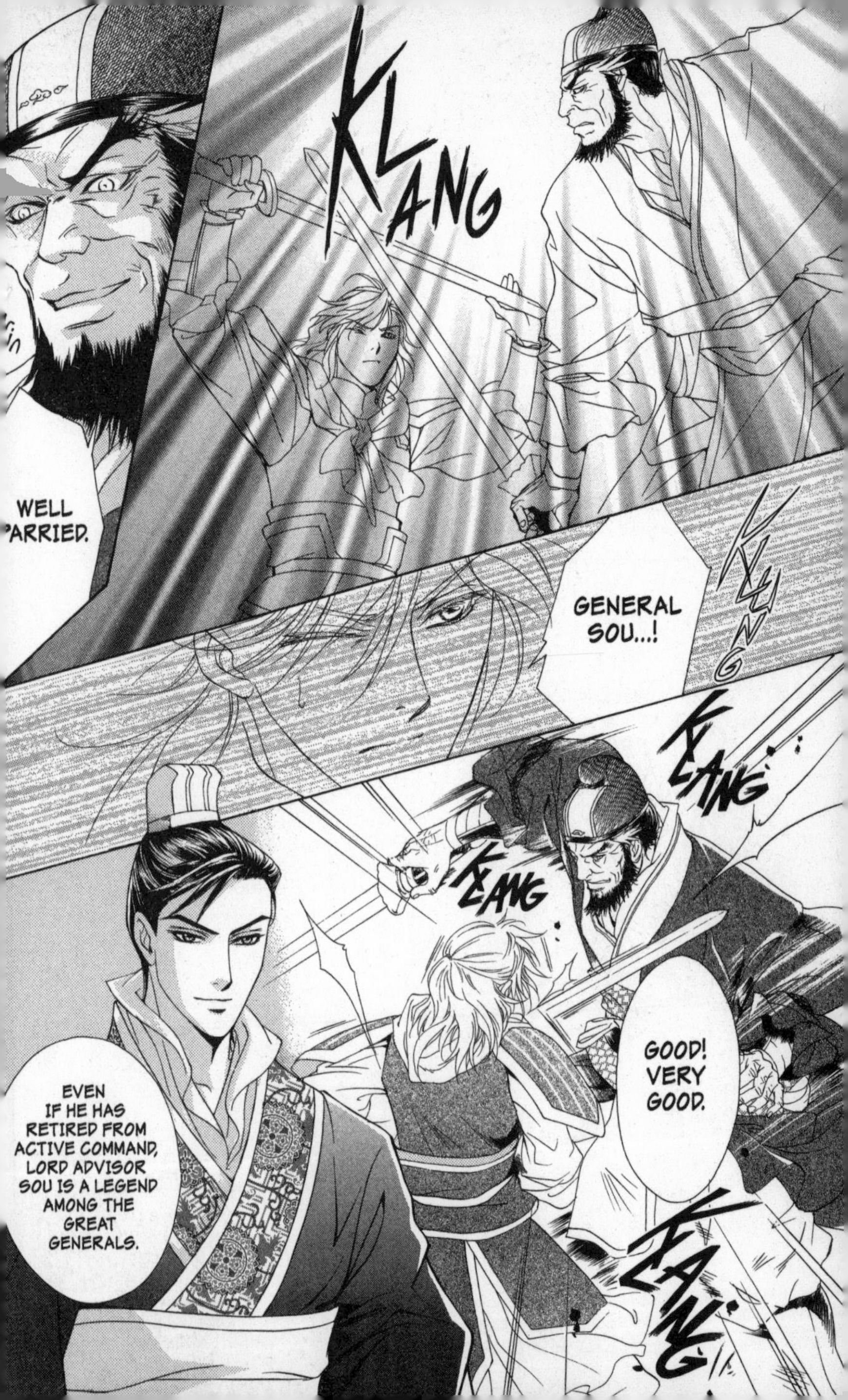
KLANG
WELL PARRIED.
KLUNG
GENERAL SOU...!
KLANG
KLANG
GOOD! VERY GOOD.
EVEN IF HE HAS RETIRED FROM ACTIVE COMMAND, LORD ADVISOR SOU IS A LEGEND AMONG THE GREAT GENERALS.
KLANG!!

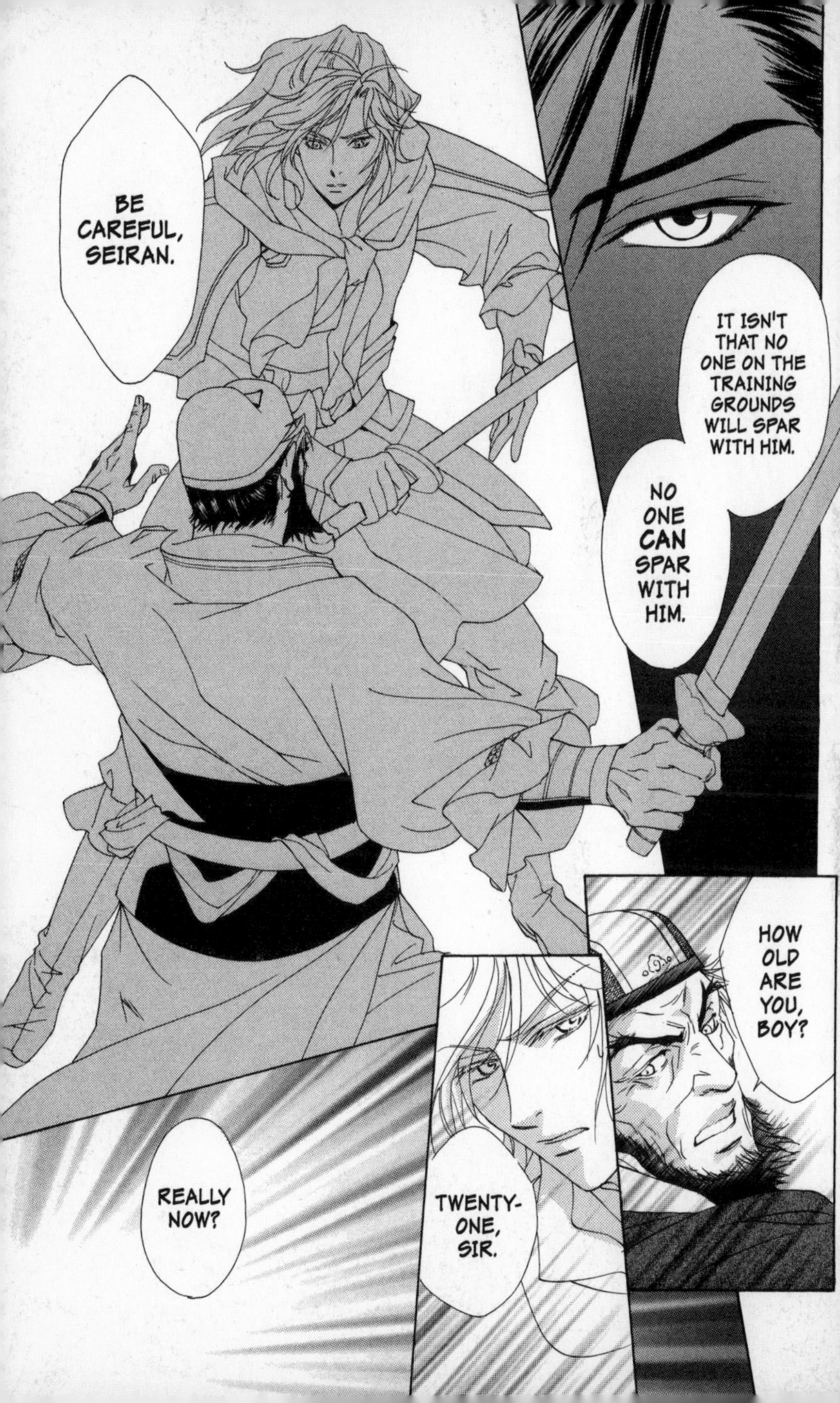
IT ISN'T THAT NO ONE ON THE TRAINING GROUNDS WILL SPAR WITH HIM.
NO ONE CAN SPAR WITH HIM.
BE CAREFUL, SEIRAN.
HOW OLD ARE YOU, BOY?
TWENTY-ONE, SIR.
REALLY NOW?

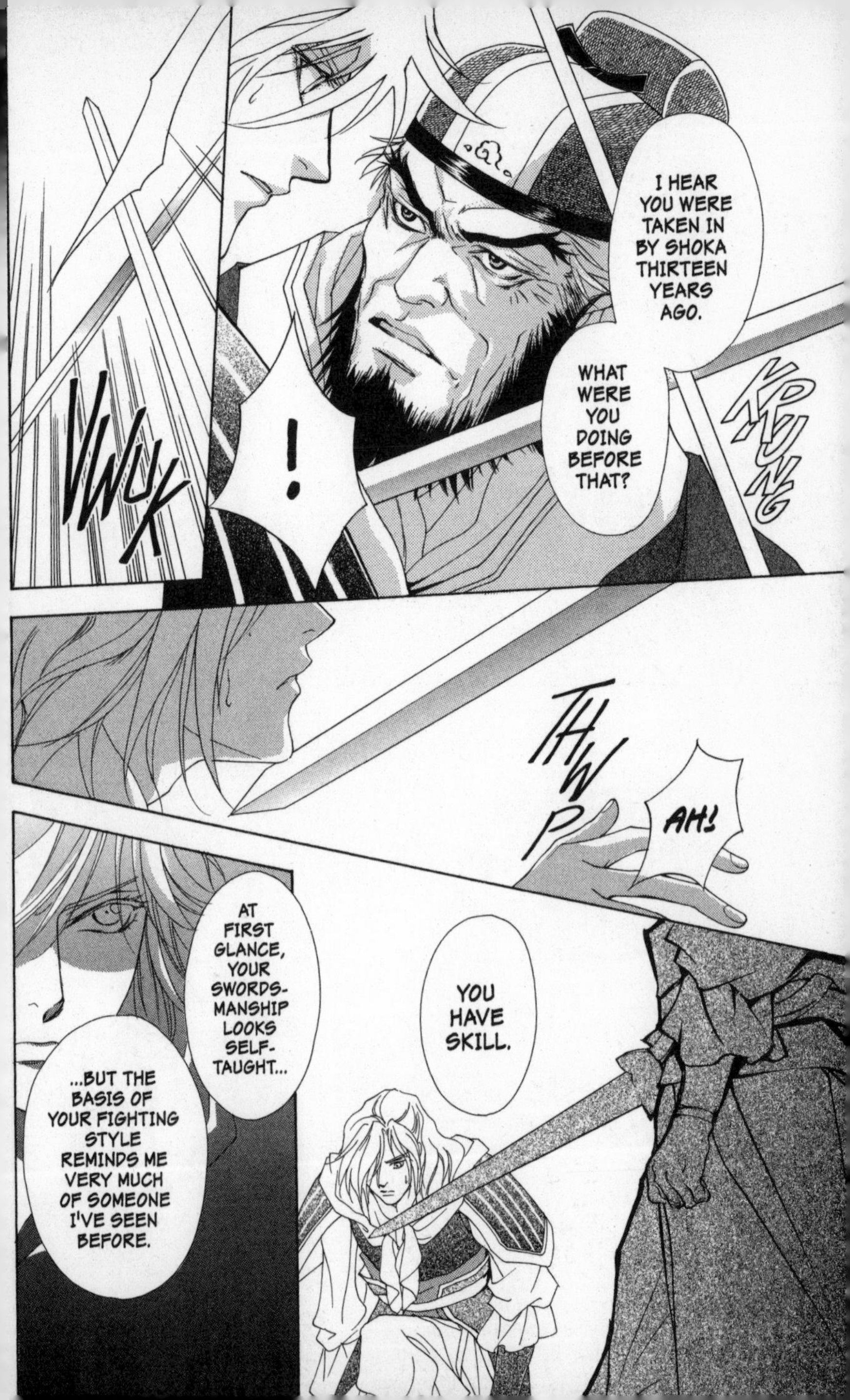
I HEAR YOU WERE TAKEN IN BY SHOKA THIRTEEN YEARS AGO.
KRUNG
WHAT WERE YOU DOING BEFORE THAT?
!
VWUK
THWP
AH!
YOU HAVE SKILL.
AT FIRST GLANCE, YOUR SWORDS-MANSHIP LOOKS SELF-TAUGHT...
...BUT THE BASIS OF YOUR FIGHTING STYLE REMINDS ME VERY MUCH OF SOMEONE I'VE SEEN BEFORE.

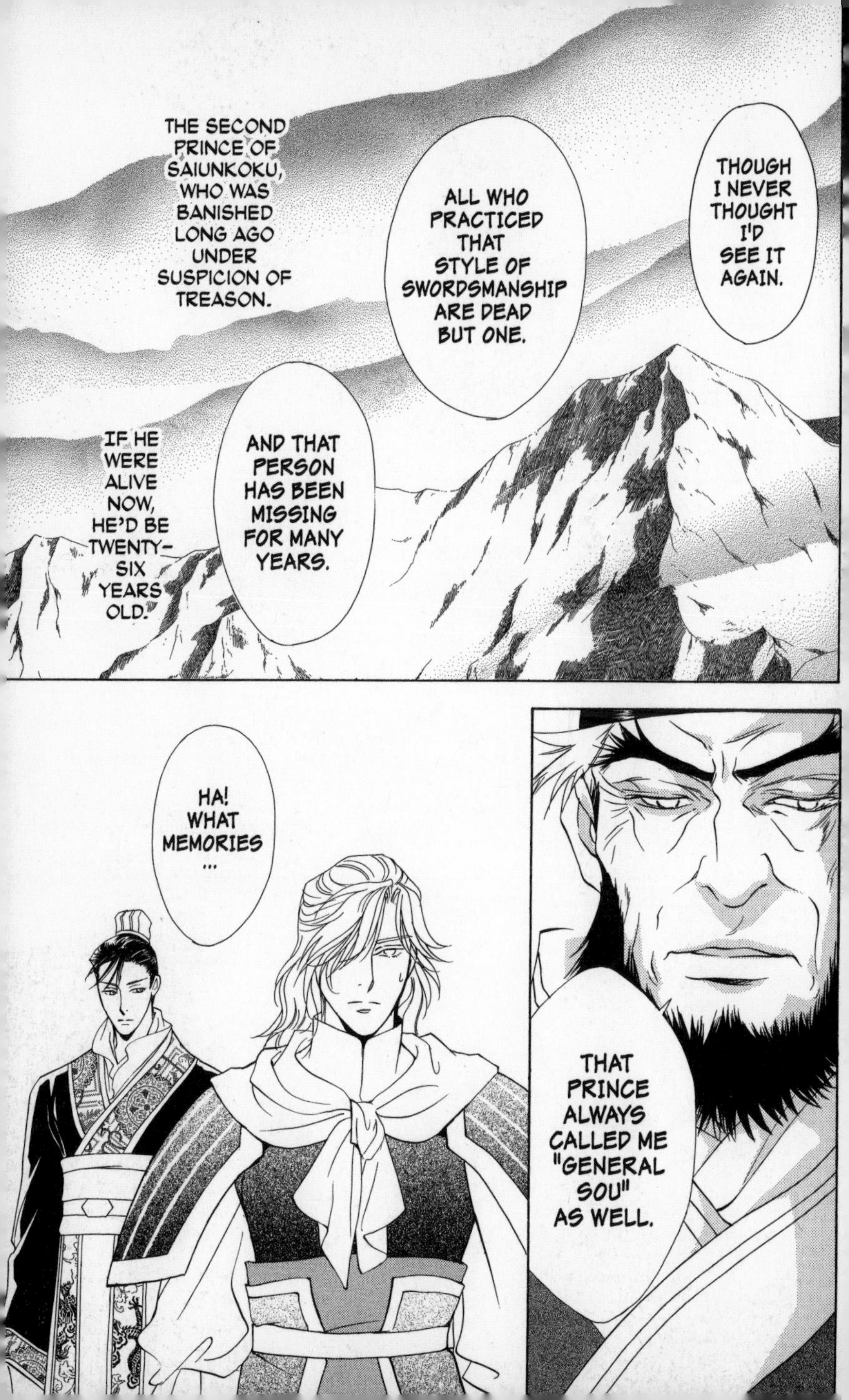
THOUGH I NEVER THOUGHT I'D SEE IT AGAIN.
ALL WHO PRACTICED THAT STYLE OF SWORDSMANSHIP ARE DEAD BUT ONE.
AND THAT PERSON HAS BEEN MISSING FOR MANY YEARS.
THE SECOND PRINCE OF SAIUNKOKU, WHO WAS BANISHED LONG AGO UNDER SUSPICION OF TREASON.
IF HE WERE ALIVE NOW, HE'D BE TWENTY-SIX YEARS OLD.
THAT PRINCE ALWAYS CALLED ME "GENERAL SOU" AS WELL.
HA! WHAT MEMORIES...

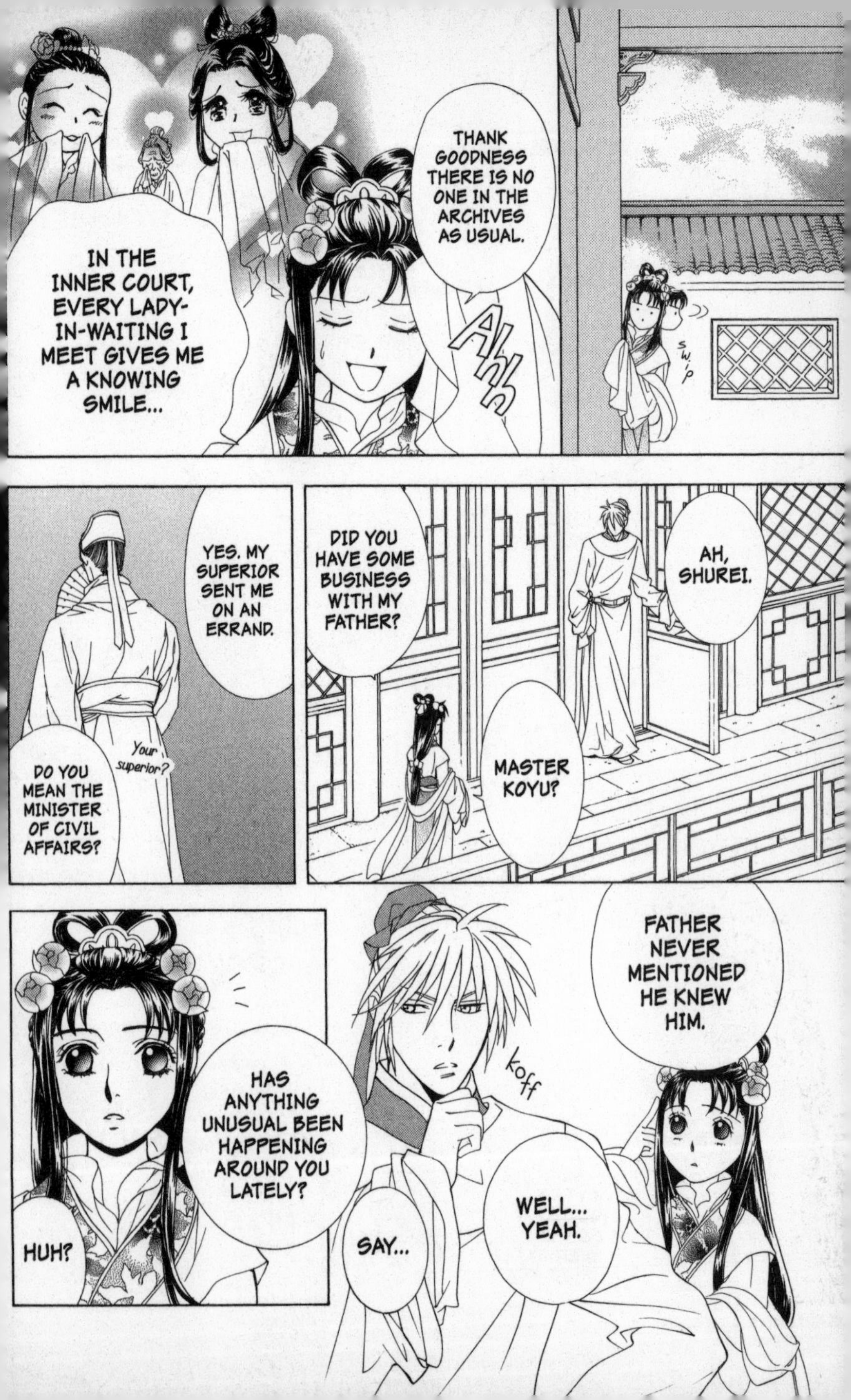
S W I P
THANK GOODNESS THERE IS NO ONE IN THE ARCHIVES AS USUAL.
Ahh
IN THE INNER COURT, EVERY LADY-IN-WAITING I MEET GIVES ME A KNOWING SMILE...
AH, SHUREI.
MASTER KOYU?
DID YOU HAVE SOME BUSINESS WITH MY FATHER?
YES. MY SUPERIOR SENT ME ON AN ERRAND.
Your superior?
DO YOU MEAN THE MINISTER OF CIVIL AFFAIRS?
FATHER NEVER MENTIONED HE KNEW HIM.
koff
WELL... YEAH.
SAY...
HAS ANYTHING UNUSUAL BEEN HAPPENING AROUND YOU LATELY?
HUH?

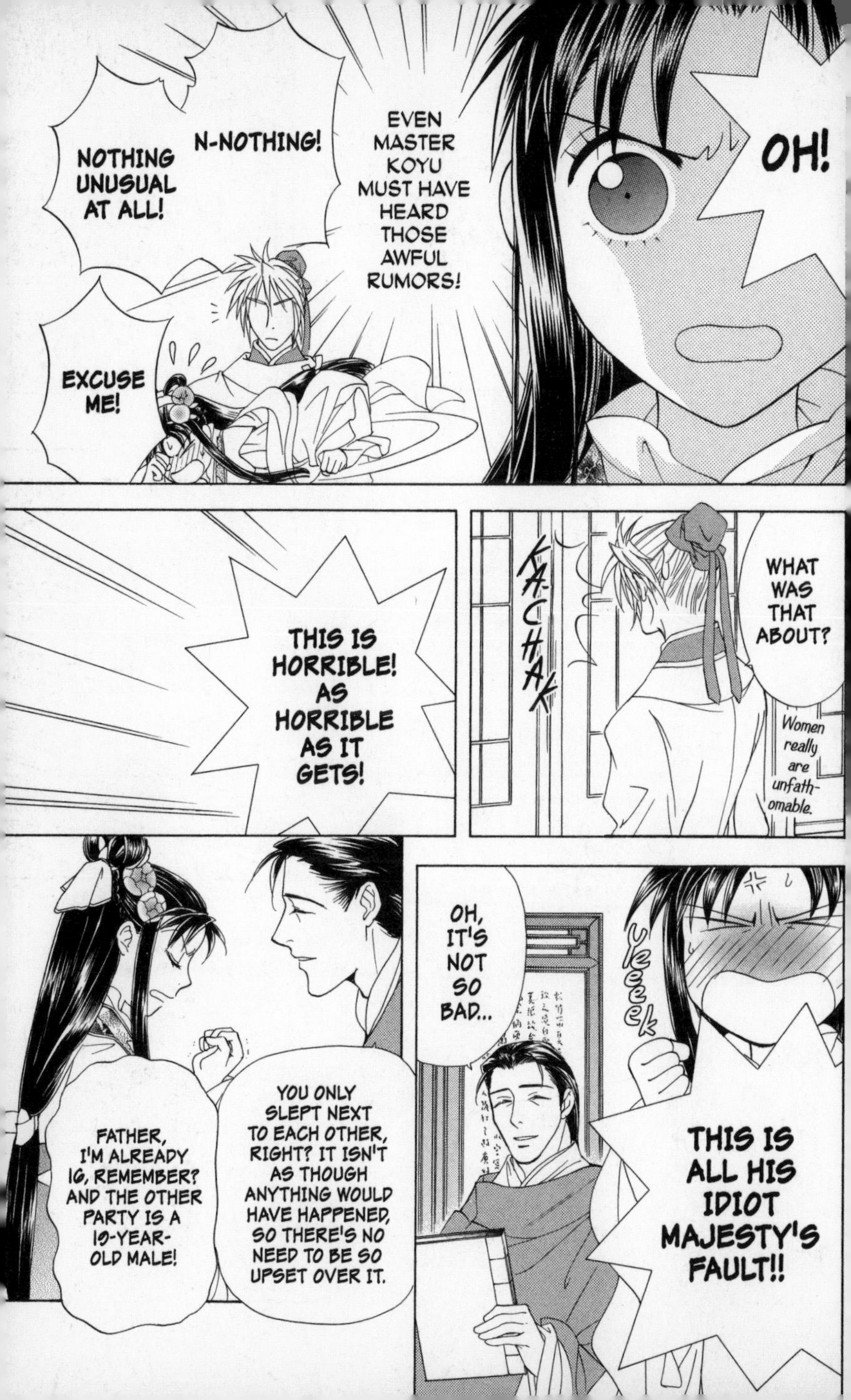
OH!
EVEN MASTER KOYU MUST HAVE HEARD THOSE AWFUL RUMORS!
N-NOTHING!
NOTHING UNUSUAL AT ALL!
EXCUSE ME!
KA-CHAK
WHAT WAS THAT ABOUT?
Women really are unfathomable.
THIS IS HORRIBLE! AS HORRIBLE AS IT GETS!
Yeeek
OH, IT'S NOT SO BAD...
THIS IS ALL HIS IDIOT MAJESTY'S FAULT!!
YOU ONLY SLEPT NEXT TO EACH OTHER, RIGHT? IT ISN'T AS THOUGH ANYTHING WOULD HAVE HAPPENED, SO THERE'S NO NEED TO BE SO UPSET OVER IT.
FATHER, I'M ALREADY 16, REMEMBER? AND THE OTHER PARTY IS A 19-YEAR-OLD MALE!

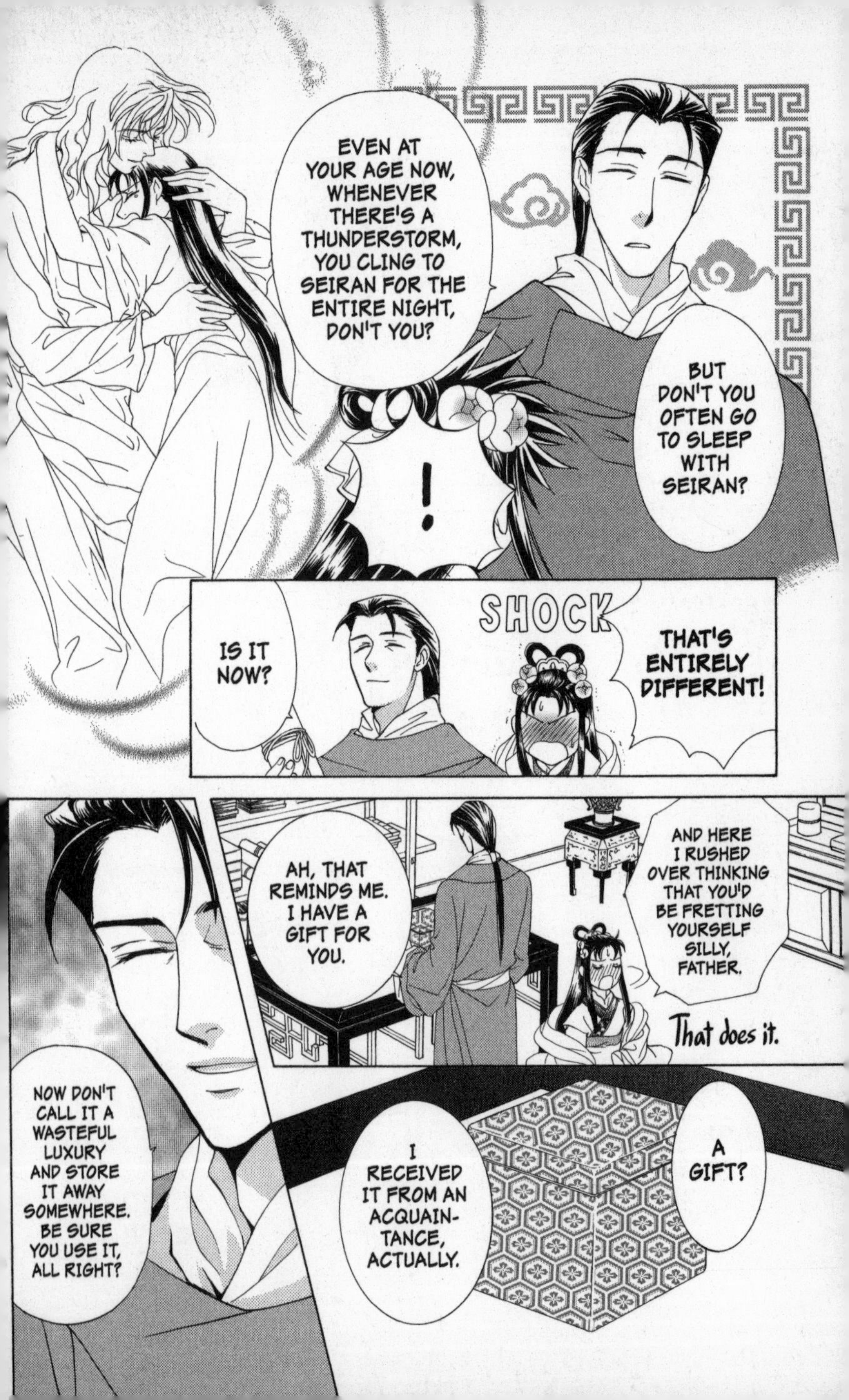
BUT DON'T YOU OFTEN GO TO SLEEP WITH SEIRAN?
!
EVEN AT YOUR AGE NOW, WHENEVER THERE'S A THUNDERSTORM, YOU CLING TO SEIRAN FOR THE ENTIRE NIGHT, DON'T YOU?
THAT'S ENTIRELY DIFFERENT!
SHOCK
IS IT NOW?
AND HERE I RUSHED OVER THINKING THAT YOU'D BE FRETTING YOURSELF SILLY, FATHER.
That does it.
AH, THAT REMINDS ME. I HAVE A GIFT FOR YOU.
A GIFT?
I RECEIVED IT FROM AN ACQUAIN-TANCE, ACTUALLY.
NOW DON'T CALL IT A WASTEFUL LUXURY AND STORE IT AWAY SOMEWHERE. BE SURE YOU USE IT, ALL RIGHT?

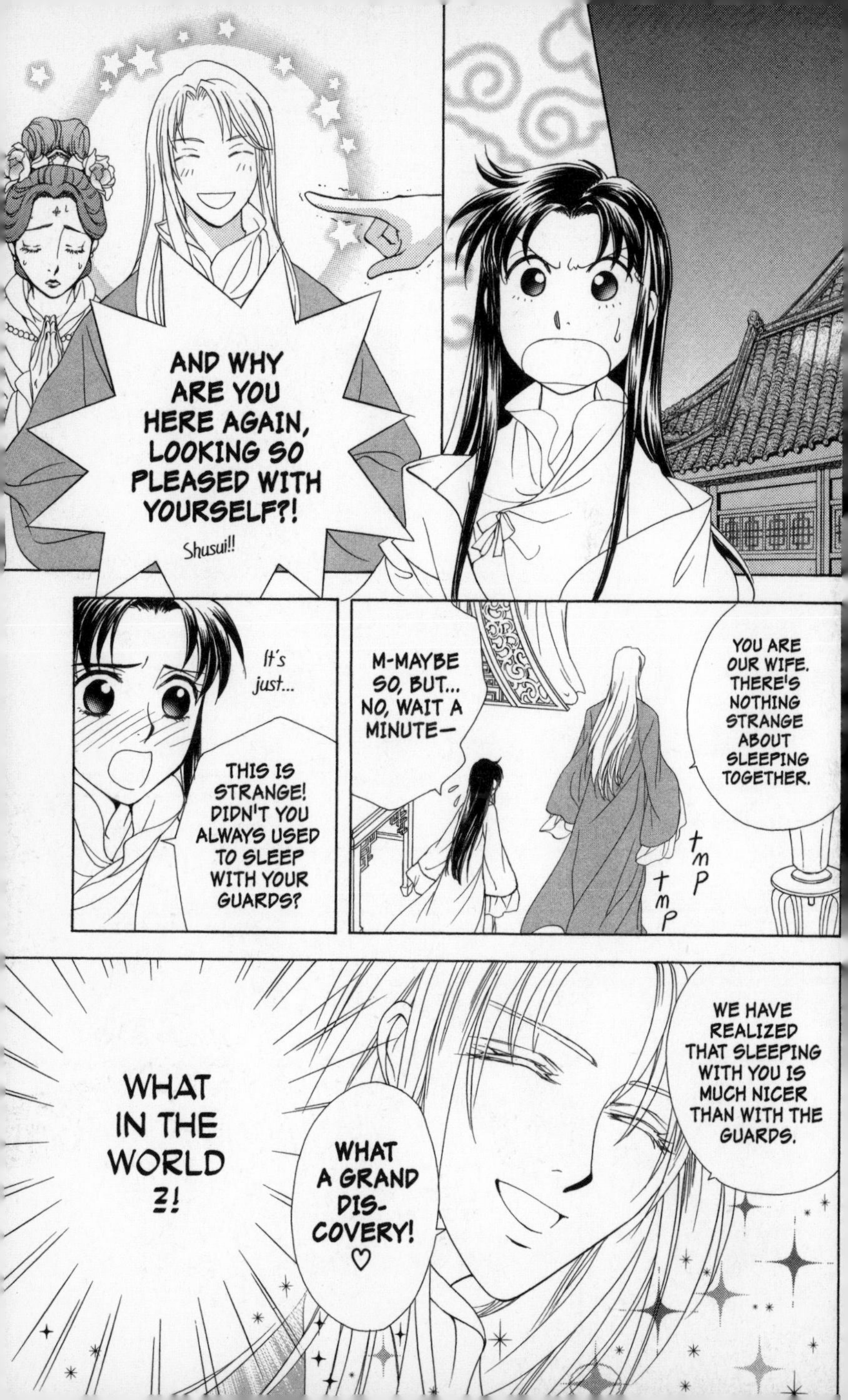
AND WHY ARE YOU HERE AGAIN, LOOKING SO PLEASED WITH YOURSELF?!
Shusui!!
YOU ARE OUR WIFE. THERE'S NOTHING STRANGE ABOUT SLEEPING TOGETHER.
tmp tmp
M-MAYBE SO, BUT... NO, WAIT A MINUTE—
It's just...
THIS IS STRANGE! DIDN'T YOU ALWAYS USED TO SLEEP WITH YOUR GUARDS?
WE HAVE REALIZED THAT SLEEPING WITH YOU IS MUCH NICER THAN WITH THE GUARDS.
WHAT A GRAND DIS-COVERY! ♡
WHAT IN THE WORLD ?!

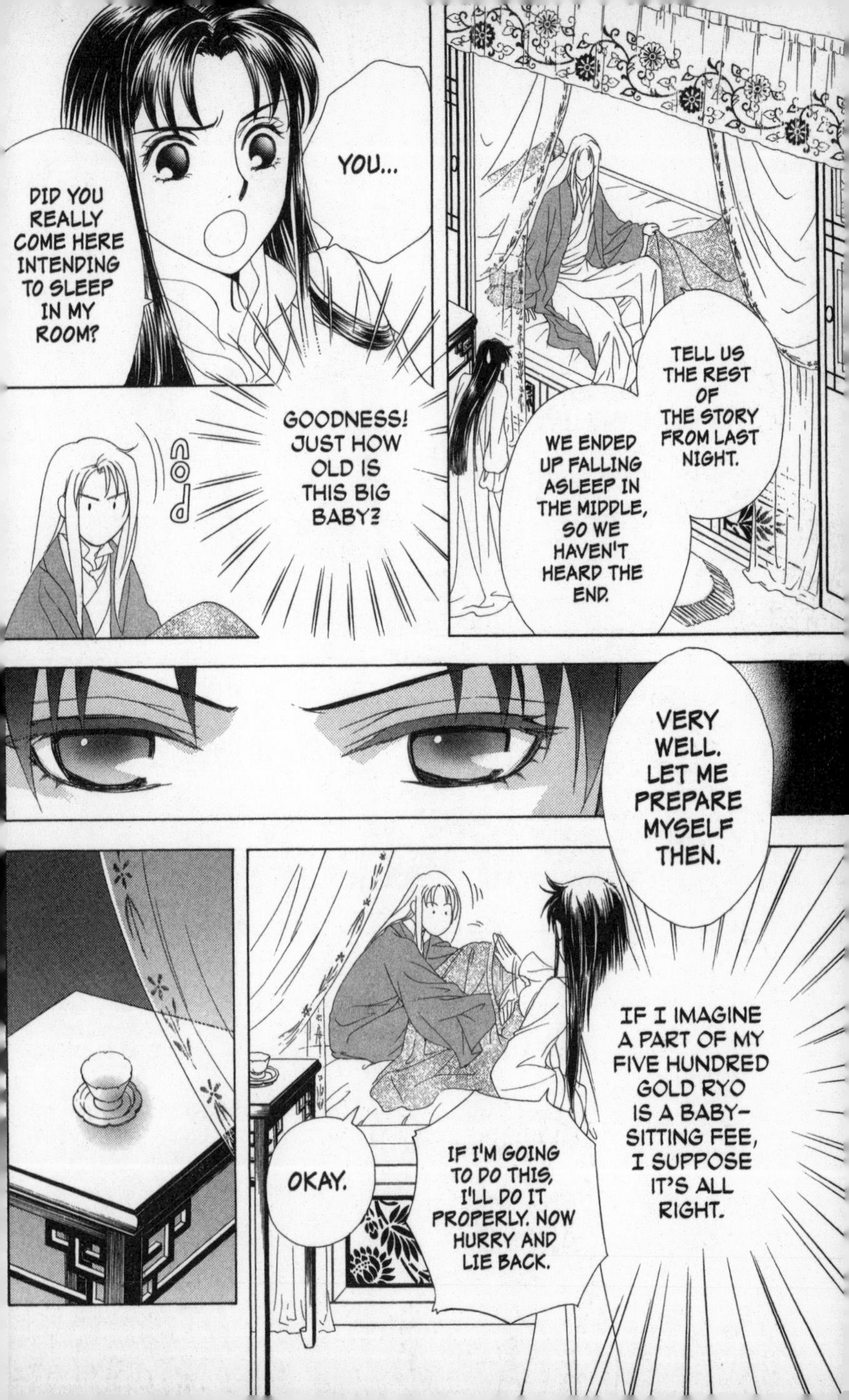
TELL US THE REST OF THE STORY FROM LAST NIGHT.
WE ENDED UP FALLING ASLEEP IN THE MIDDLE, SO WE HAVEN'T HEARD THE END.
YOU...
DID YOU REALLY COME HERE INTENDING TO SLEEP IN MY ROOM?
GOODNESS! JUST HOW OLD IS THIS BIG BABY?
VERY WELL. LET ME PREPARE MYSELF THEN.
IF I IMAGINE A PART OF MY FIVE HUNDRED GOLD RYO IS A BABY-SITTING FEE, I SUPPOSE IT'S ALL RIGHT.
IF I'M GOING TO DO THIS, I'LL DO IT PROPERLY. NOW HURRY AND LIE BACK.
OKAY.

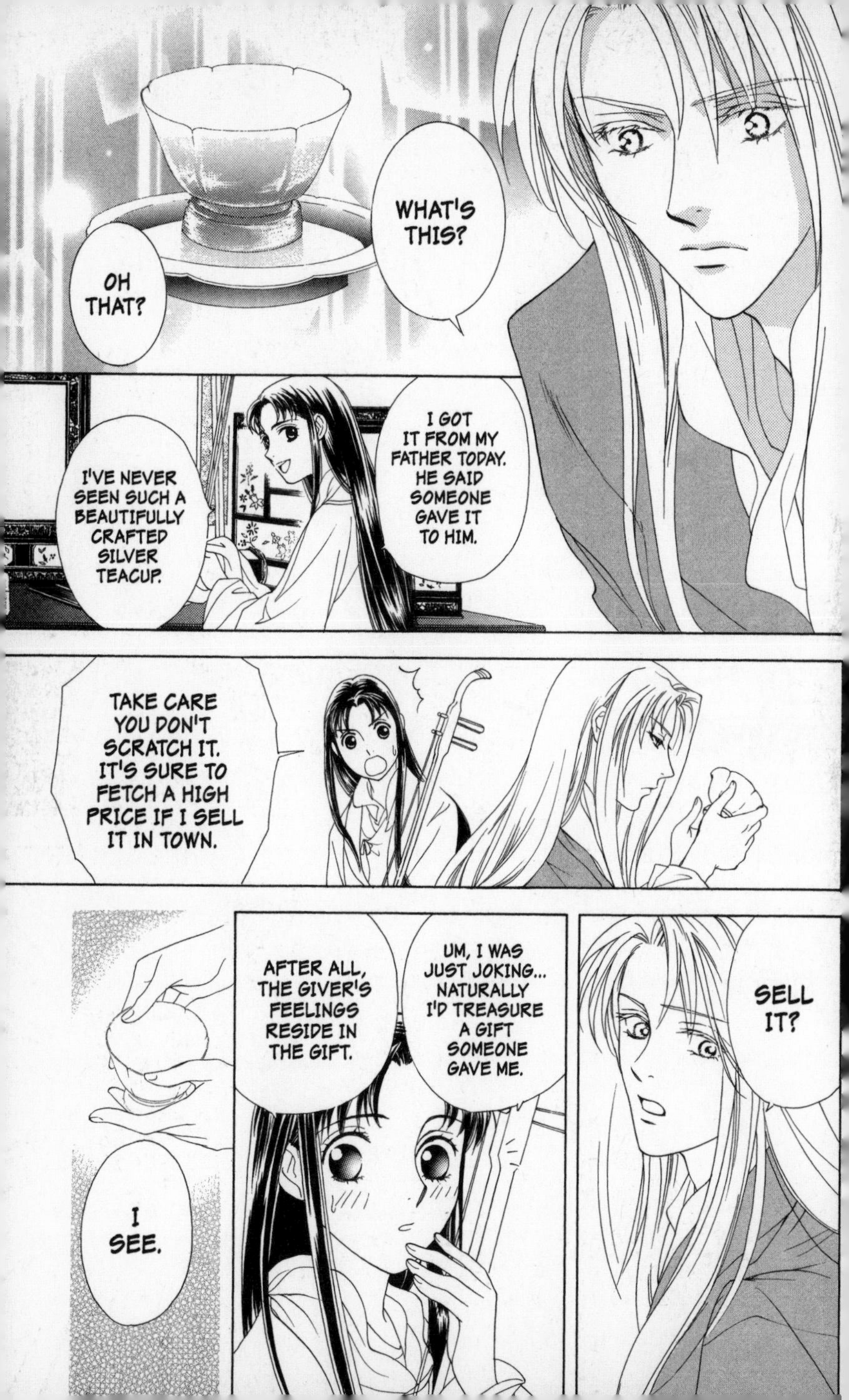
WHAT'S THIS?
OH THAT?
I GOT IT FROM MY FATHER TODAY. HE SAID SOMEONE GAVE IT TO HIM.
I'VE NEVER SEEN SUCH A BEAUTIFULLY CRAFTED SILVER TEACUP.
TAKE CARE YOU DON'T SCRATCH IT. IT'S SURE TO FETCH A HIGH PRICE IF I SELL IT IN TOWN.
SELL IT?
UM, I WAS JUST JOKING... NATURALLY I'D TREASURE A GIFT SOMEONE GAVE ME.
AFTER ALL, THE GIVER'S FEELINGS RESIDE IN THE GIFT.
I SEE.

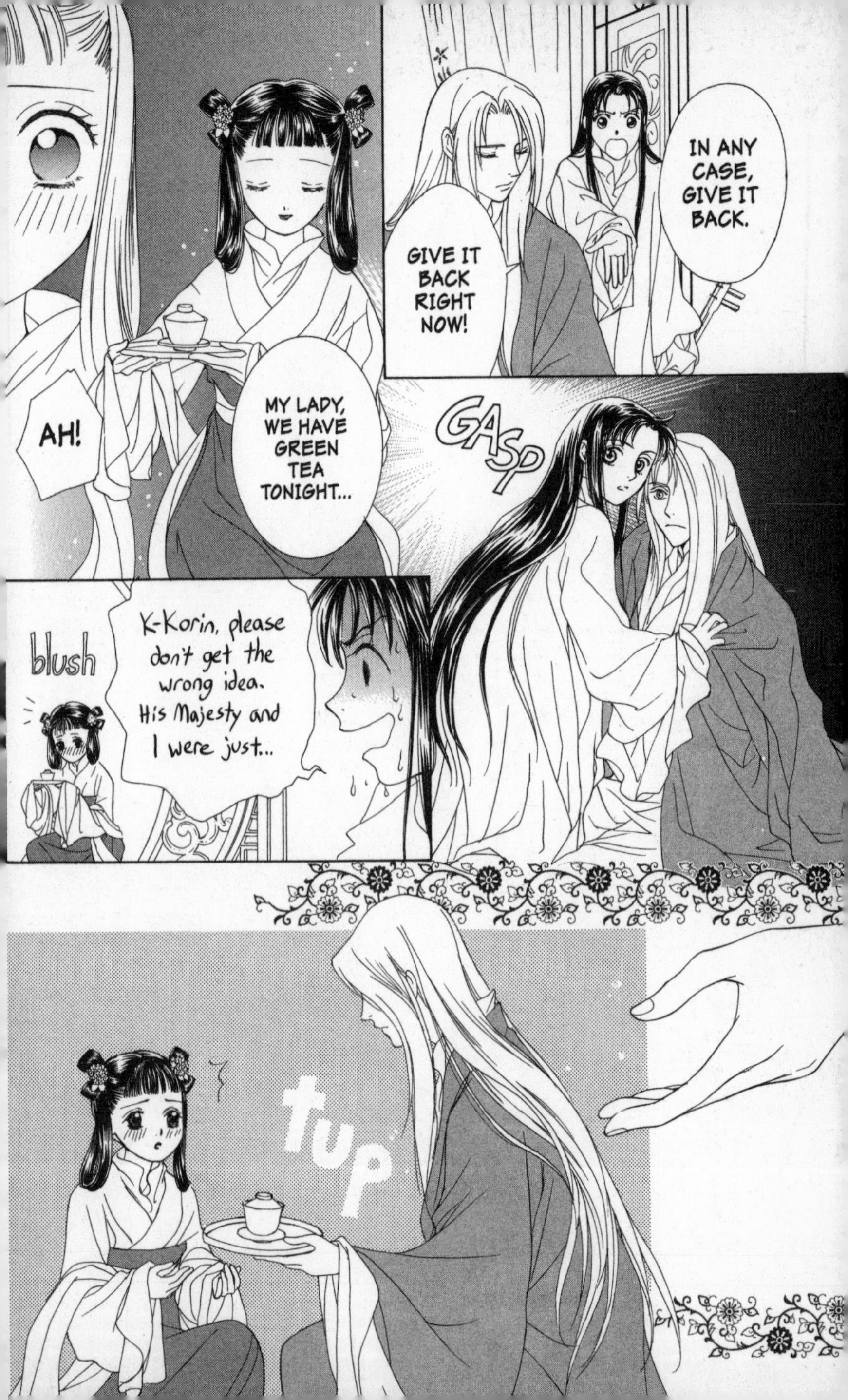
IN ANY CASE, GIVE IT BACK.
GIVE IT BACK RIGHT NOW!
MY LADY, WE HAVE GREEN TEA TONIGHT...
AH!
GASP
blush
K-Korin, please don't get the wrong idea. His Majesty and I were just...
tup

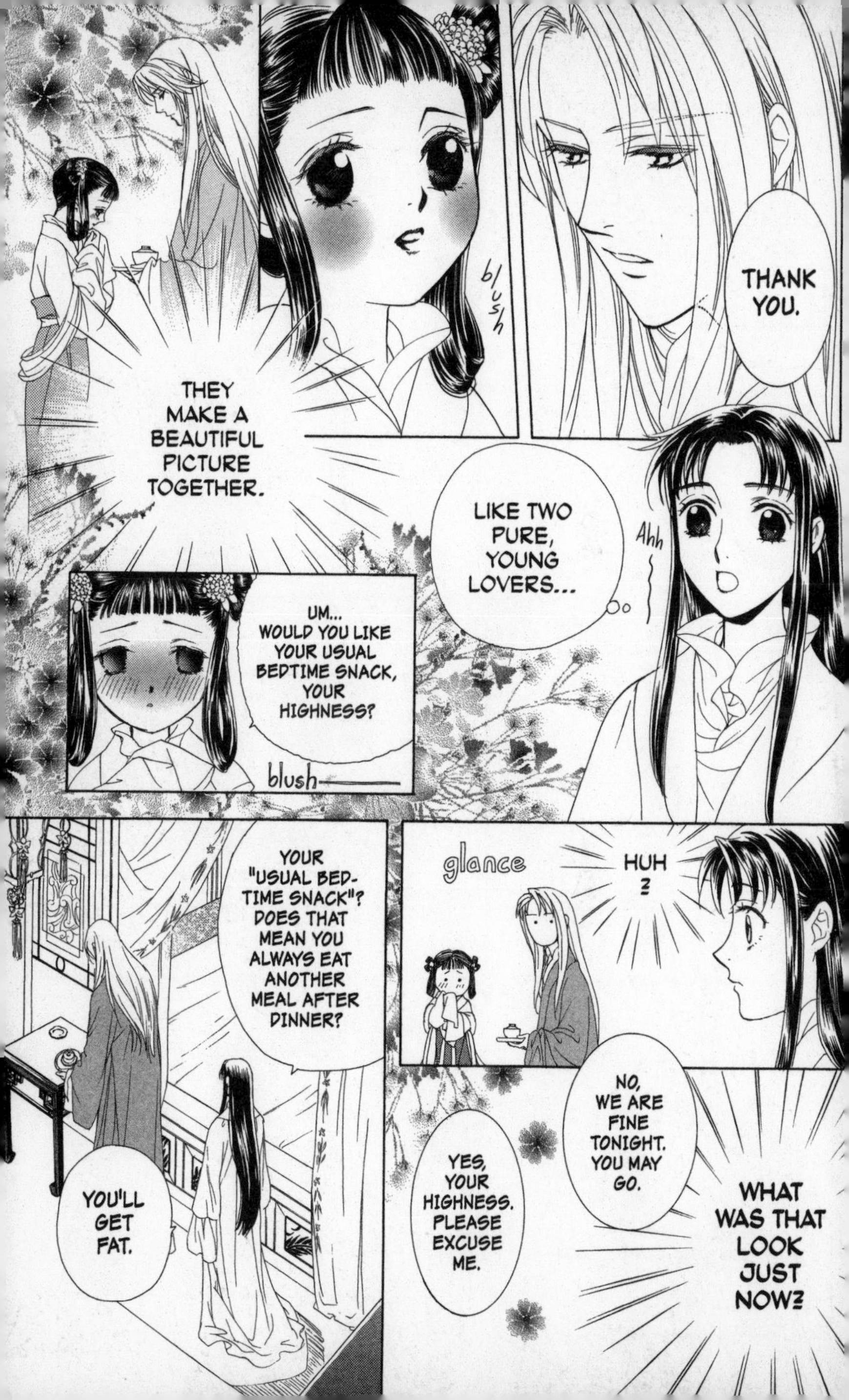
THANK YOU.
blush
THEY MAKE A BEAUTIFUL PICTURE TOGETHER.
Ahh
LIKE TWO PURE, YOUNG LOVERS...
UM... WOULD YOU LIKE YOUR USUAL BEDTIME SNACK, YOUR HIGHNESS?
blush
HUH?
glance
WHAT WAS THAT LOOK JUST NOW?
NO, WE ARE FINE TONIGHT. YOU MAY GO.
YES, YOUR HIGHNESS. PLEASE EXCUSE ME.
YOUR "USUAL BED-TIME SNACK"? DOES THAT MEAN YOU ALWAYS EAT ANOTHER MEAL AFTER DINNER?
YOU'LL GET FAT.

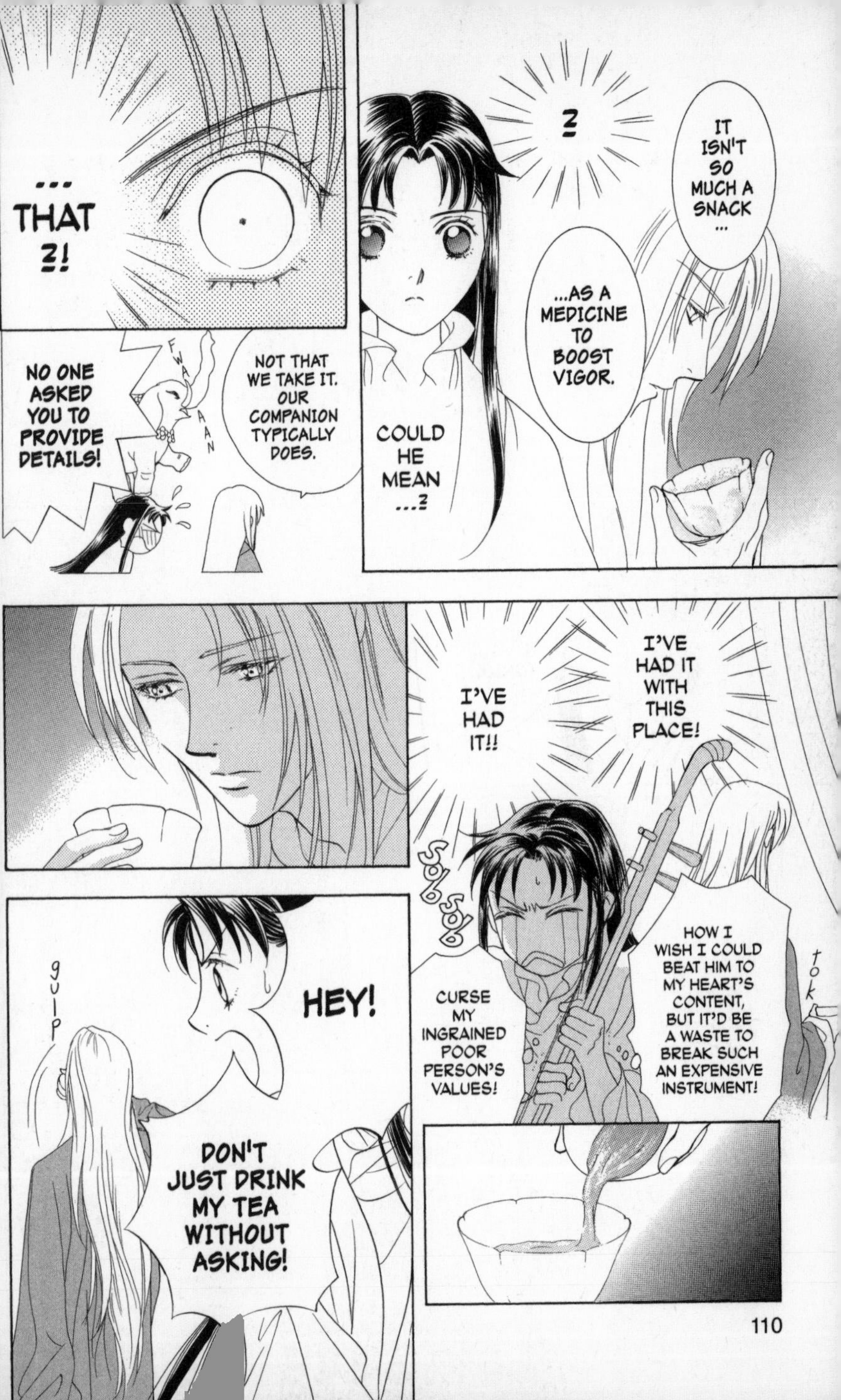
?
IT ISN'T SO MUCH A SNACK...
...AS A MEDICINE TO BOOST VIGOR.
COULD HE MEAN ...?
...THAT?!
NOT THAT WE TAKE IT. OUR COMPANION TYPICALLY DOES.
FWAAAN
NO ONE ASKED YOU TO PROVIDE DETAILS!
I'VE HAD IT WITH THIS PLACE!
I'VE HAD IT!!
SOB SOB
tok
HOW I WISH I COULD BEAT HIM TO MY HEART'S CONTENT, BUT IT'D BE A WASTE TO BREAK SUCH AN EXPENSIVE INSTRUMENT!
CURSE MY INGRAINED POOR PERSON'S VALUES!
HEY!
gulp
DON'T JUST DRINK MY TEA WITHOUT ASKING!

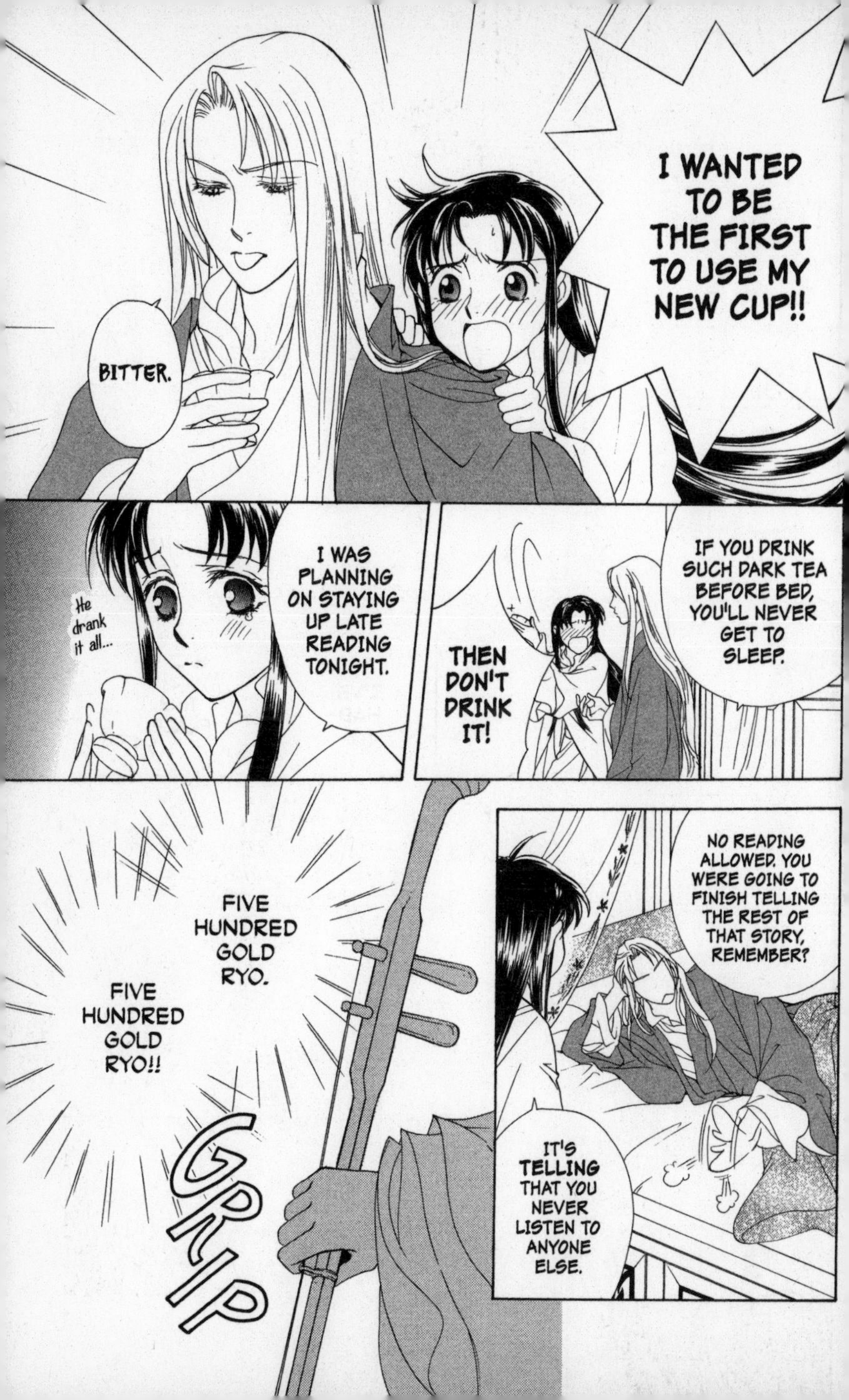
I WANTED TO BE THE FIRST TO USE MY NEW CUP!!
BITTER.
IF YOU DRINK SUCH DARK TEA BEFORE BED, YOU'LL NEVER GET TO SLEEP.
THEN DON'T DRINK IT!
I WAS PLANNING ON STAYING UP LATE READING TONIGHT.
He drank it all...
NO READING ALLOWED. YOU WERE GOING TO FINISH TELLING THE REST OF THAT STORY, REMEMBER?
IT'S TELLING THAT YOU NEVER LISTEN TO ANYONE ELSE.
FIVE HUNDRED GOLD RYO.
FIVE HUNDRED GOLD RYO!!
GRIP

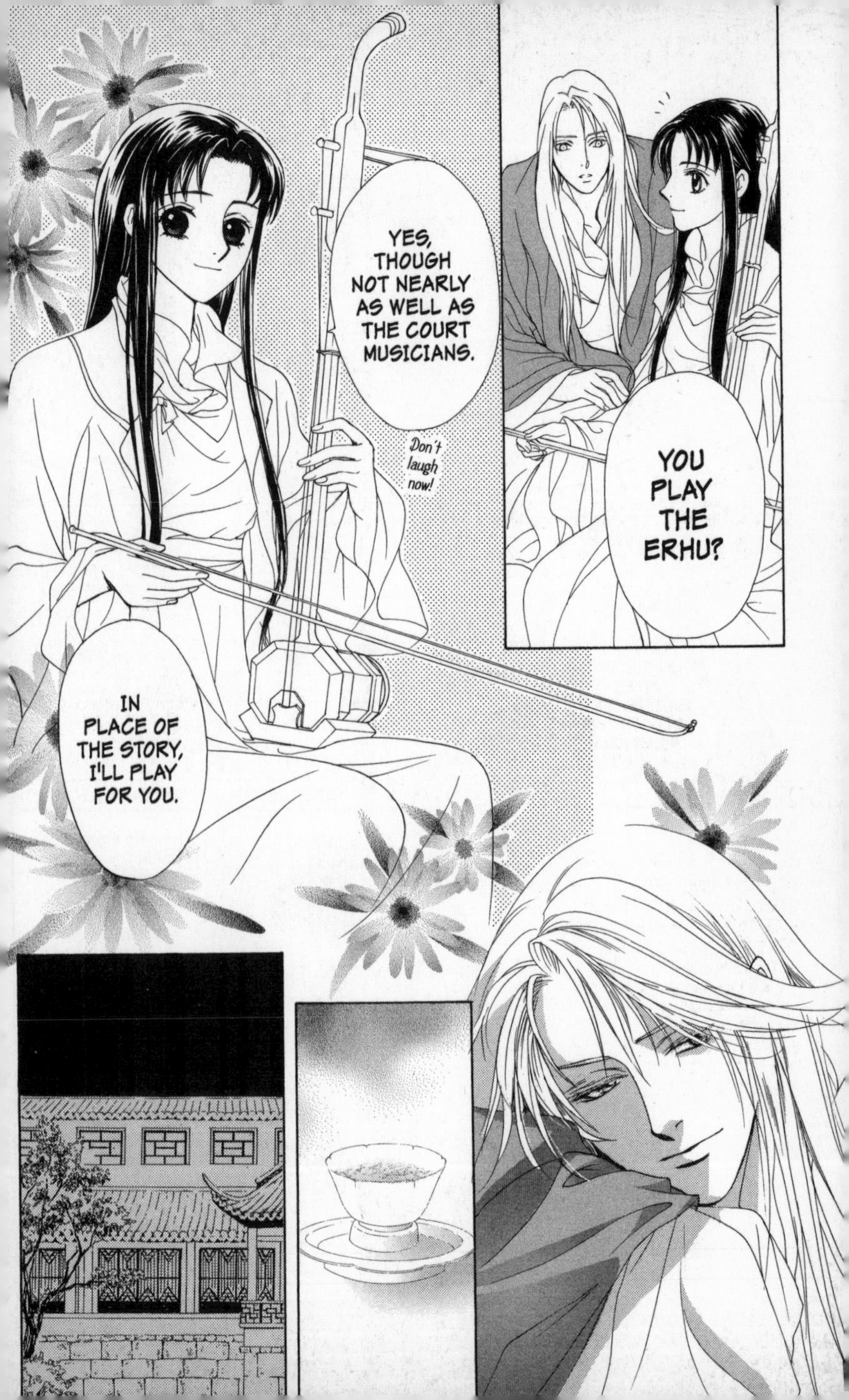
YOU PLAY THE ERHU?
YES, THOUGH NOT NEARLY AS WELL AS THE COURT MUSICIANS.
Don't laugh now!
IN PLACE OF THE STORY, I'LL PLAY FOR YOU.

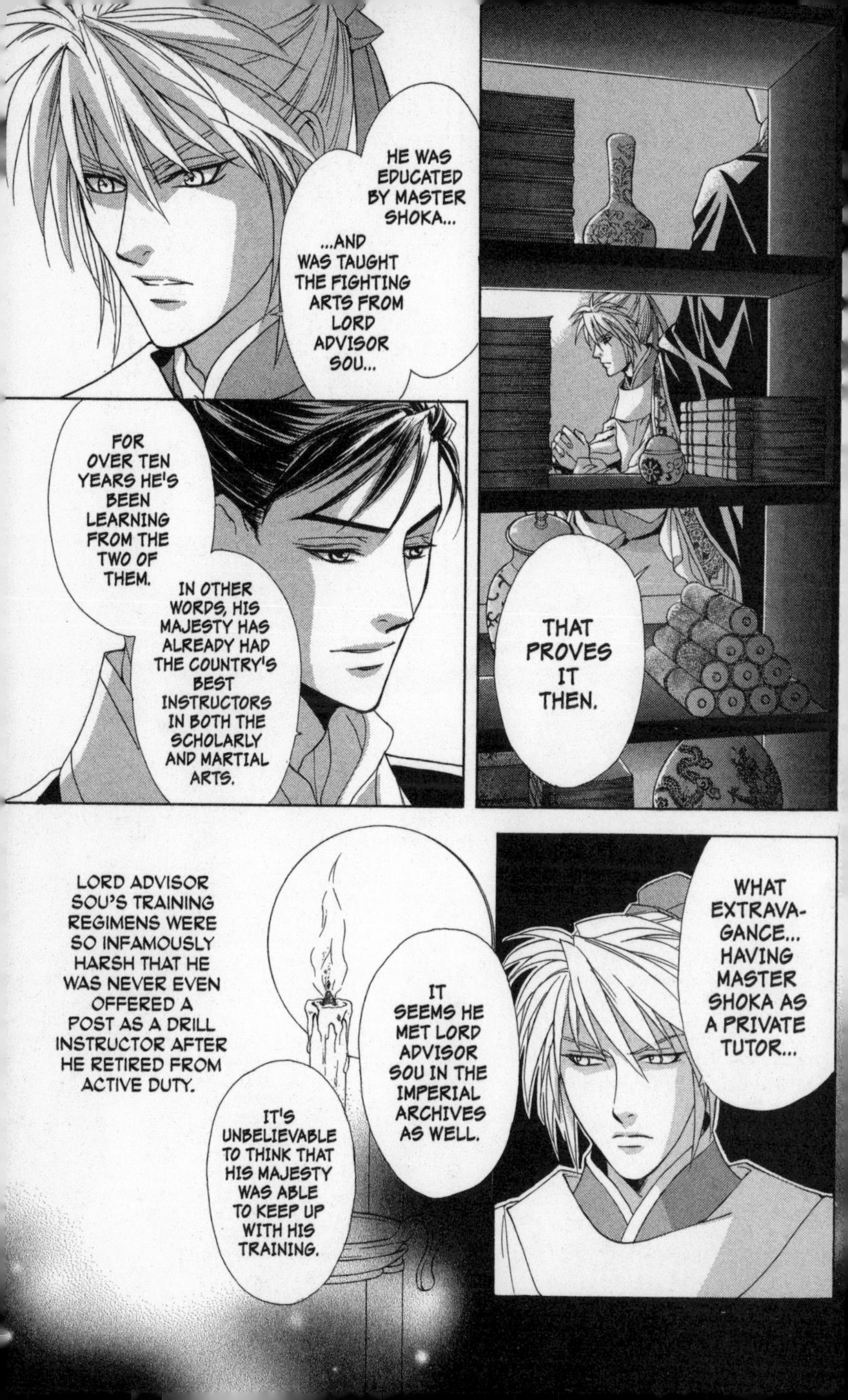
THAT PROVES IT THEN.
HE WAS EDUCATED BY MASTER SHOKA...
...AND WAS TAUGHT THE FIGHTING ARTS FROM LORD ADVISOR SOU...
FOR OVER TEN YEARS HE'S BEEN LEARNING FROM THE TWO OF THEM.
IN OTHER WORDS, HIS MAJESTY HAS ALREADY HAD THE COUNTRY'S BEST INSTRUCTORS IN BOTH THE SCHOLARLY AND MARTIAL ARTS.
WHAT EXTRAVA-GANCE... HAVING MASTER SHOKA AS A PRIVATE TUTOR...
IT SEEMS HE MET LORD ADVISOR SOU IN THE IMPERIAL ARCHIVES AS WELL.
LORD ADVISOR SOU'S TRAINING REGIMENS WERE SO INFAMOUSLY HARSH THAT HE WAS NEVER EVEN OFFERED A POST AS A DRILL INSTRUCTOR AFTER HE RETIRED FROM ACTIVE DUTY.
IT'S UNBELIEVABLE TO THINK THAT HIS MAJESTY WAS ABLE TO KEEP UP WITH HIS TRAINING.

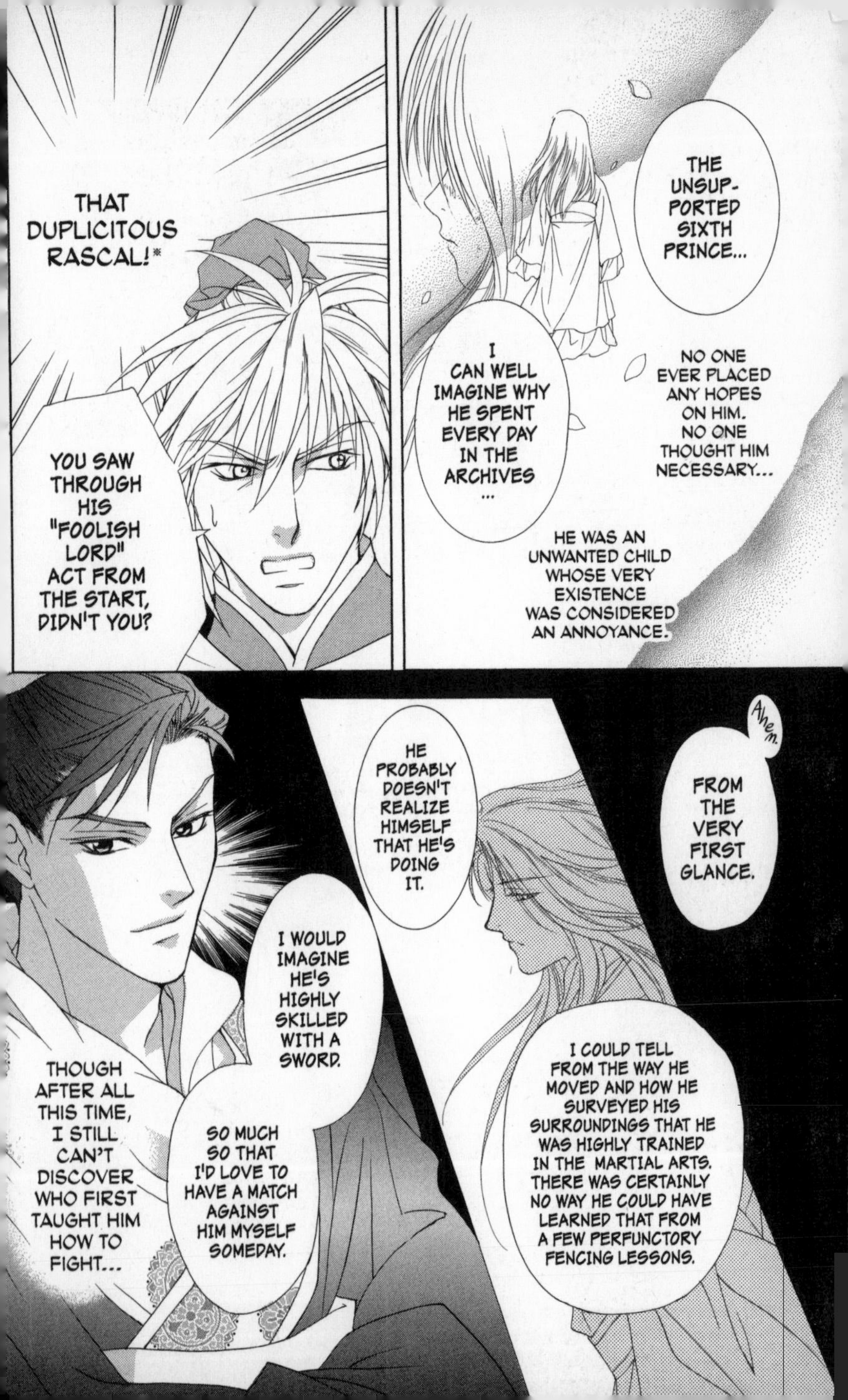
THE UNSUPPORTED SIXTH PRINCE...
NO ONE EVER PLACED ANY HOPES ON HIM. NO ONE THOUGHT HIM NECESSARY...
I CAN WELL IMAGINE WHY HE SPENT EVERY DAY IN THE ARCHIVES...
HE WAS AN UNWANTED CHILD WHOSE VERY EXISTENCE WAS CONSIDERED AN ANNOYANCE.
THAT DUPLICITOUS RASCAL!*
YOU SAW THROUGH HIS "FOOLISH LORD" ACT FROM THE START, DIDN'T YOU?
Ahem.
FROM THE VERY FIRST GLANCE.
HE PROBABLY DOESN'T REALIZE HIMSELF THAT HE'S DOING IT.
I COULD TELL FROM THE WAY HE MOVED AND HOW HE SURVEYED HIS SURROUNDINGS THAT HE WAS HIGHLY TRAINED IN THE MARTIAL ARTS. THERE WAS CERTAINLY NO WAY HE COULD HAVE LEARNED THAT FROM A FEW PERFUNCTORY FENCING LESSONS.
I WOULD IMAGINE HE'S HIGHLY SKILLED WITH A SWORD.
SO MUCH SO THAT I'D LOVE TO HAVE A MATCH AGAINST HIM MYSELF SOMEDAY.
THOUGH AFTER ALL THIS TIME, I STILL CAN'T DISCOVER WHO FIRST TAUGHT HIM HOW TO FIGHT...

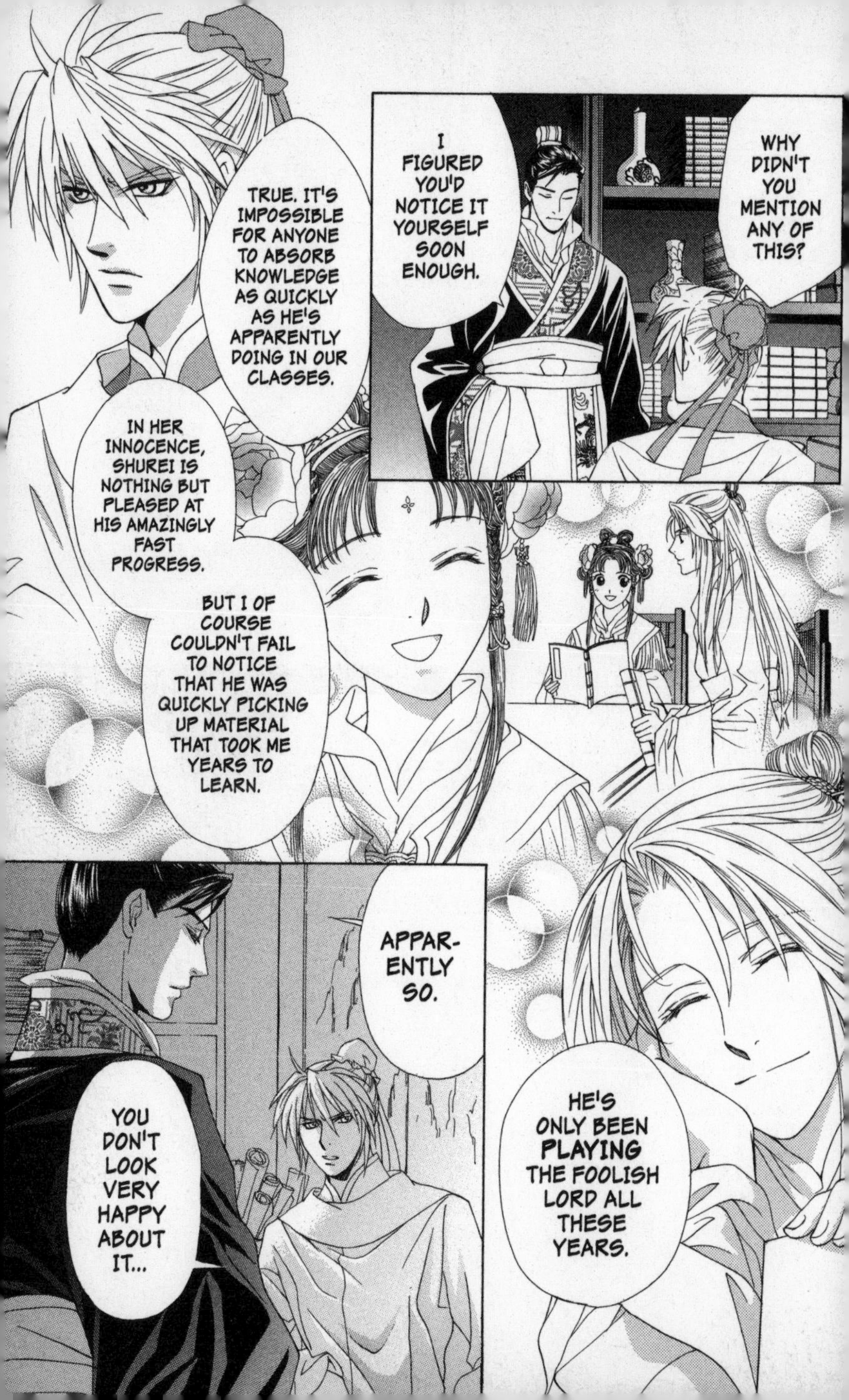
WHY DIDN'T YOU MENTION ANY OF THIS?
I FIGURED YOU'D NOTICE IT YOURSELF SOON ENOUGH.
TRUE. IT'S IMPOSSIBLE FOR ANYONE TO ABSORB KNOWLEDGE AS QUICKLY AS HE'S APPARENTLY DOING IN OUR CLASSES.
IN HER INNOCENCE, SHUREI IS NOTHING BUT PLEASED AT HIS AMAZINGLY FAST PROGRESS.
BUT I OF COURSE COULDN'T FAIL TO NOTICE THAT HE WAS QUICKLY PICKING UP MATERIAL THAT TOOK ME YEARS TO LEARN.
HE'S ONLY BEEN PLAYING THE FOOLISH LORD ALL THESE YEARS.
APPAR-ENTLY SO.
YOU DON'T LOOK VERY HAPPY ABOUT IT...

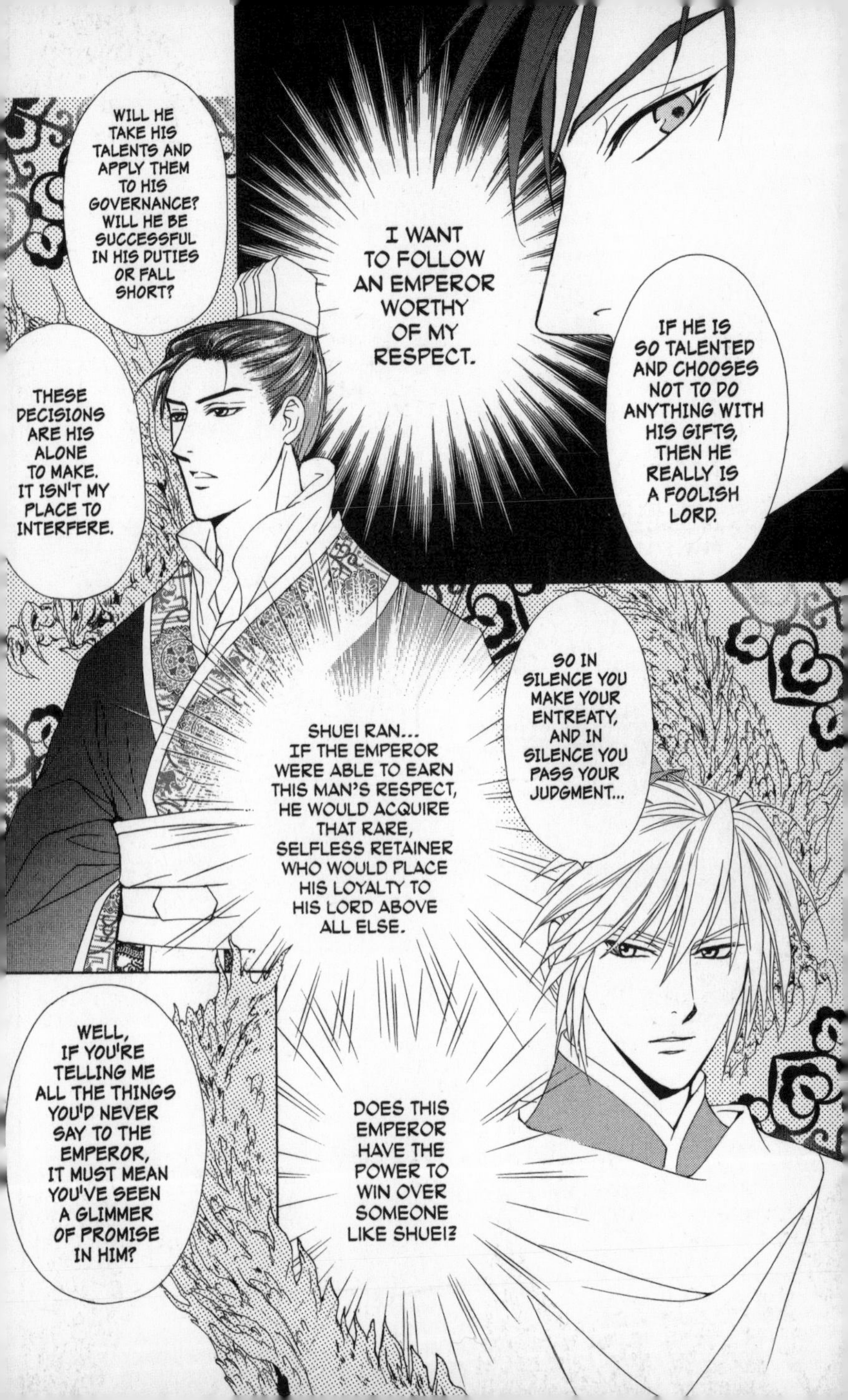
WILL HE TAKE HIS TALENTS AND APPLY THEM TO HIS GOVERNANCE? WILL HE BE SUCCESSFUL IN HIS DUTIES OR FALL SHORT?
THESE DECISIONS ARE HIS ALONE TO MAKE. IT ISN'T MY PLACE TO INTERFERE.
IF HE IS SO TALENTED AND CHOOSES NOT TO DO ANYTHING WITH HIS GIFTS, THEN HE REALLY IS A FOOLISH LORD.
I WANT TO FOLLOW AN EMPEROR WORTHY OF MY RESPECT.
SO IN SILENCE YOU MAKE YOUR ENTREATY, AND IN SILENCE YOU PASS YOUR JUDGMENT...
SHUEI RAN... IF THE EMPEROR WERE ABLE TO EARN THIS MAN'S RESPECT, HE WOULD ACQUIRE THAT RARE, SELFLESS RETAINER WHO WOULD PLACE HIS LOYALTY TO HIS LORD ABOVE ALL ELSE.
DOES THIS EMPEROR HAVE THE POWER TO WIN OVER SOMEONE LIKE SHUEI!?
WELL, IF YOU'RE TELLING ME ALL THE THINGS YOU'D NEVER SAY TO THE EMPEROR, IT MUST MEAN YOU'VE SEEN A GLIMMER OF PROMISE IN HIM?

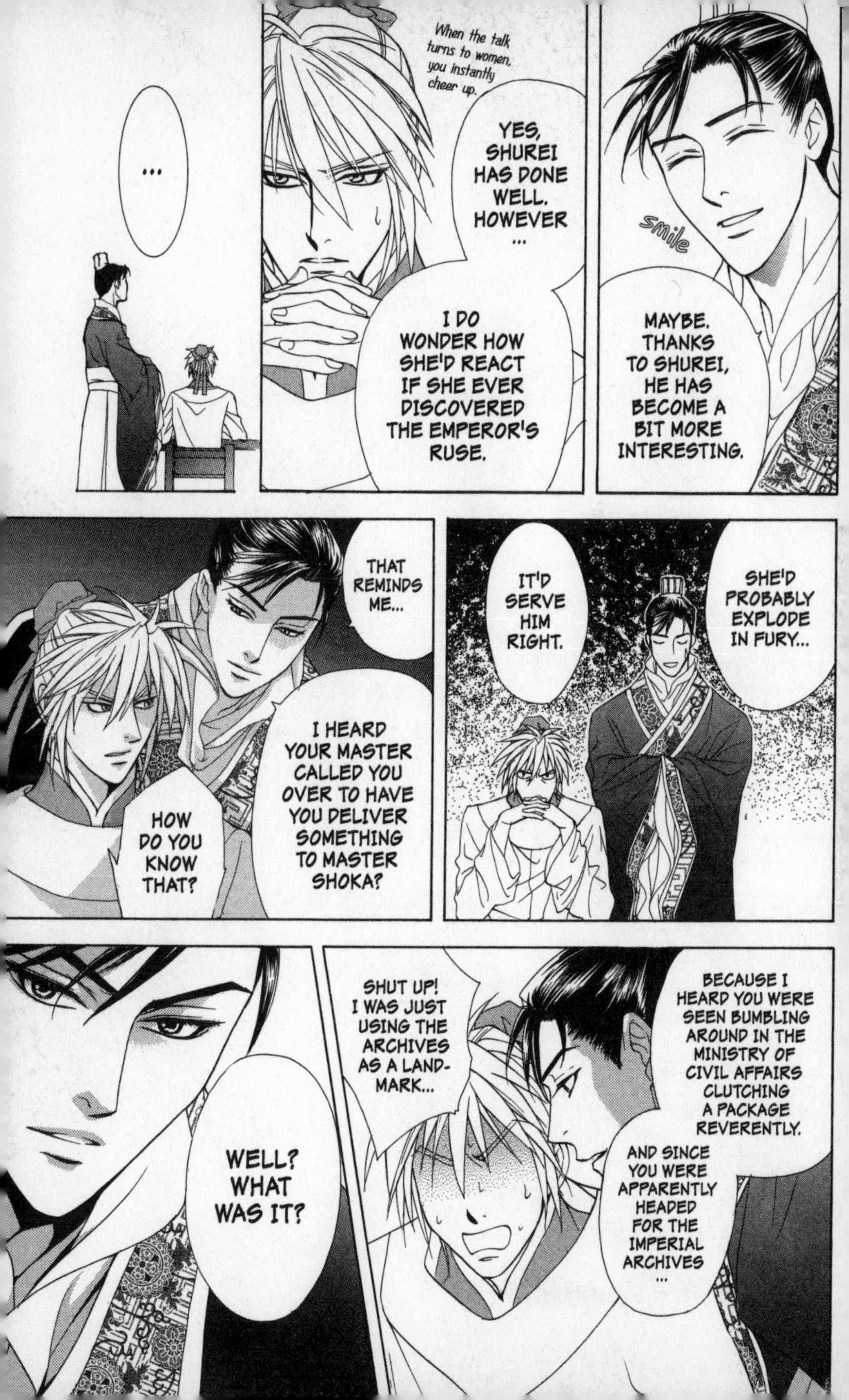
Smile
MAYBE. THANKS TO SHUREI, HE HAS BECOME A BIT MORE INTERESTING.
When the talk turns to women, you instantly cheer up.
YES, SHUREI HAS DONE WELL. HOWEVER ...
I DO WONDER HOW SHE'D REACT IF SHE EVER DISCOVERED THE EMPEROR'S RUSE.
...
SHE'D PROBABLY EXPLODE IN FURY...
IT'D SERVE HIM RIGHT.
THAT REMINDS ME...
I HEARD YOUR MASTER CALLED YOU OVER TO HAVE YOU DELIVER SOMETHING TO MASTER SHOKA?
HOW DO YOU KNOW THAT?
BECAUSE I HEARD YOU WERE SEEN BUMBLING AROUND IN THE MINISTRY OF CIVIL AFFAIRS CLUTCHING A PACKAGE REVERENTLY.
SHUT UP! I WAS JUST USING THE ARCHIVES AS A LAND-MARK...
AND SINCE YOU WERE APPARENTLY HEADED FOR THE IMPERIAL ARCHIVES ...
WELL? WHAT WAS IT?

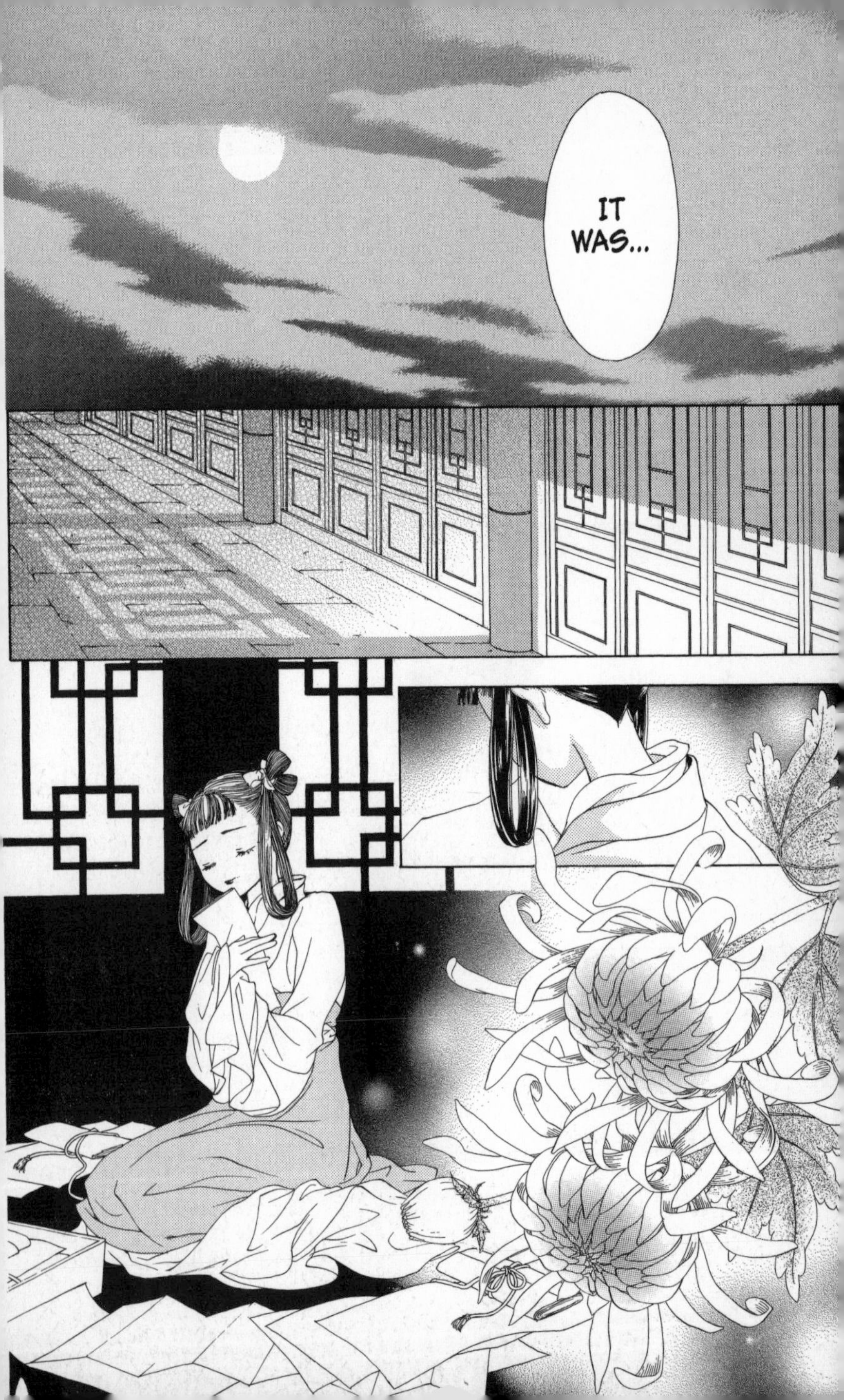
IT WAS...

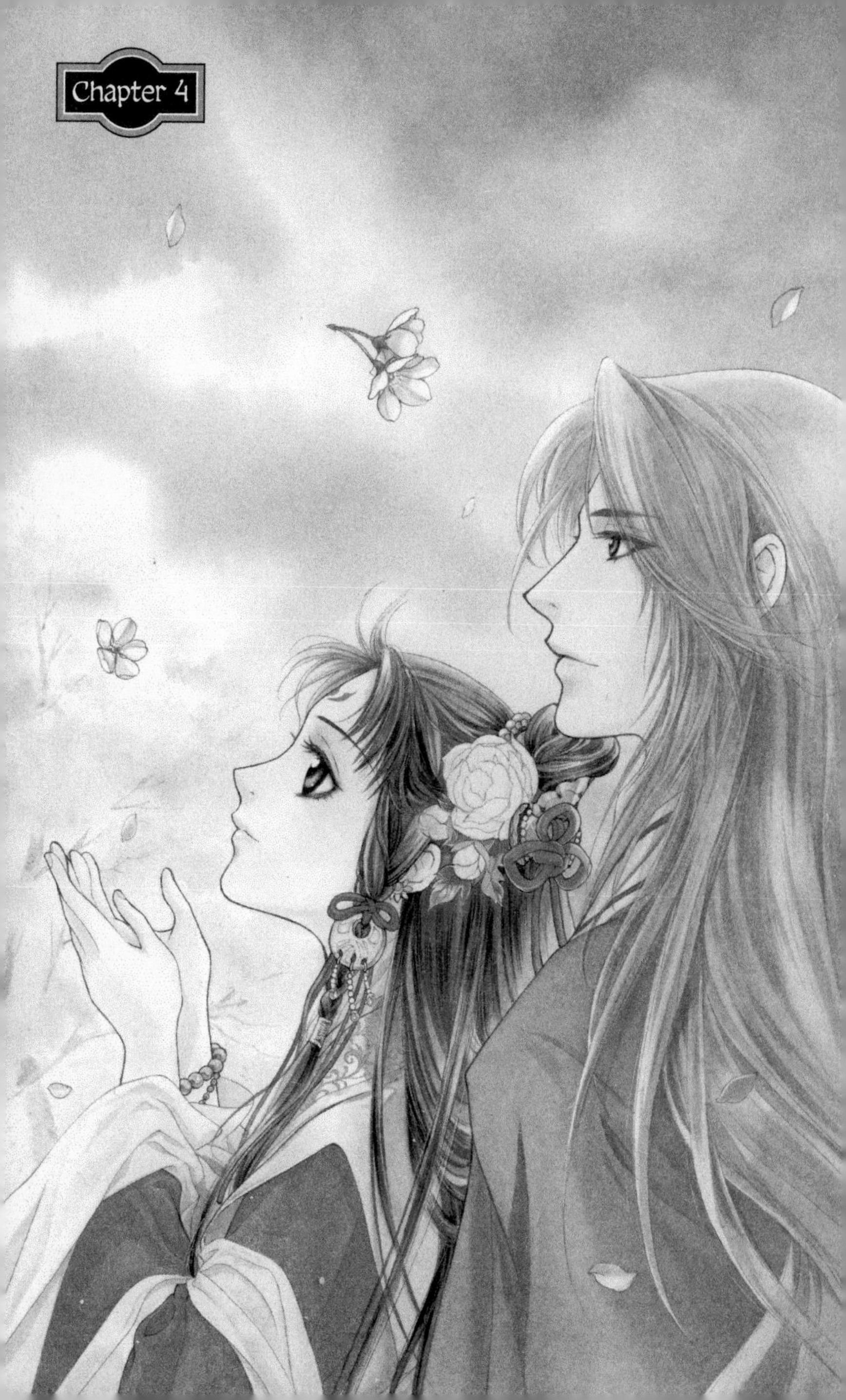
Chapter 4

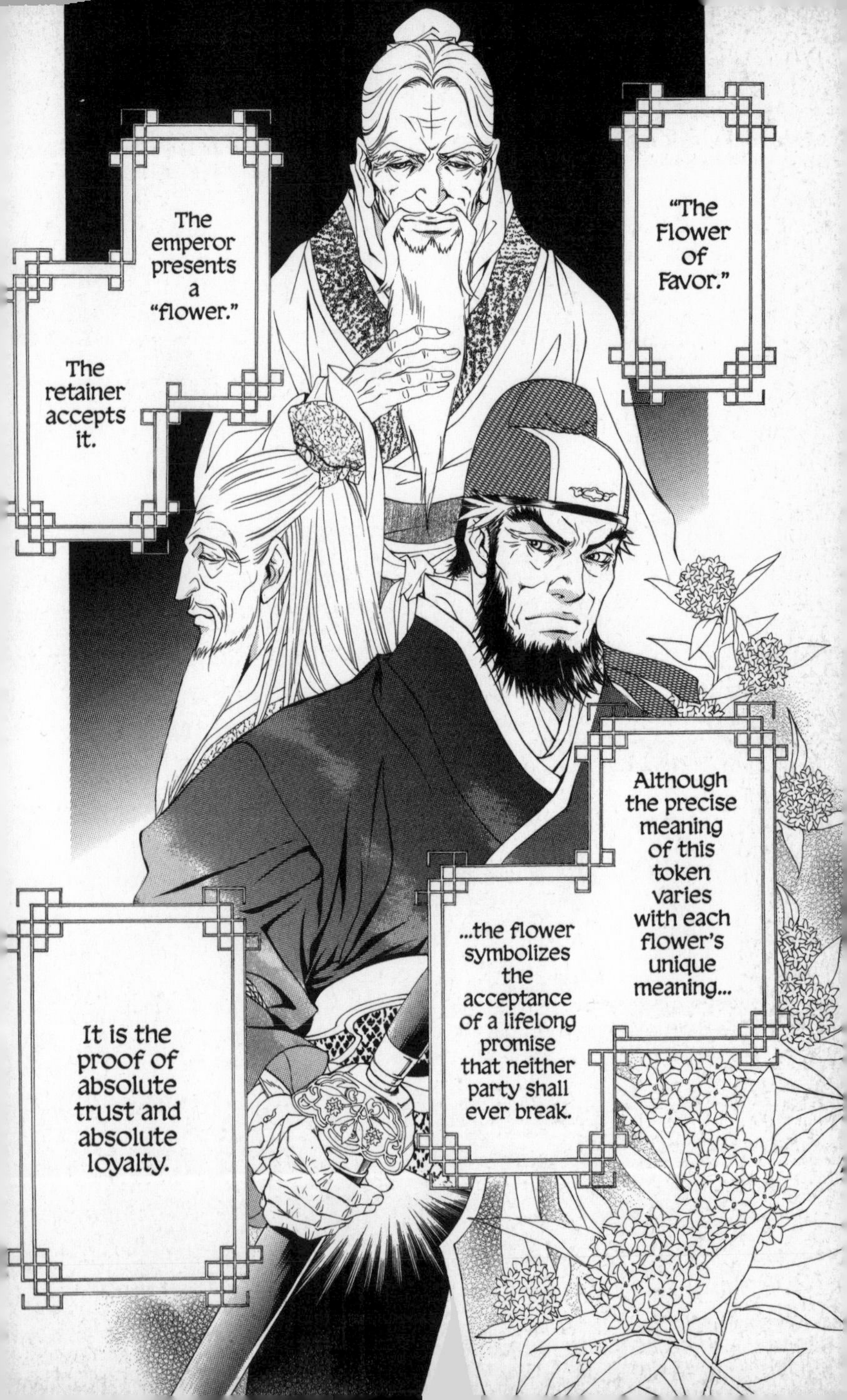
"The Flower of Favor."
The emperor presents a "flower."
The retainer accepts it.
Although the precise meaning of this token varies with each flower's unique meaning...
...the flower symbolizes the acceptance of a lifelong promise that neither party shall ever break.
It is the proof of absolute trust and absolute loyalty.

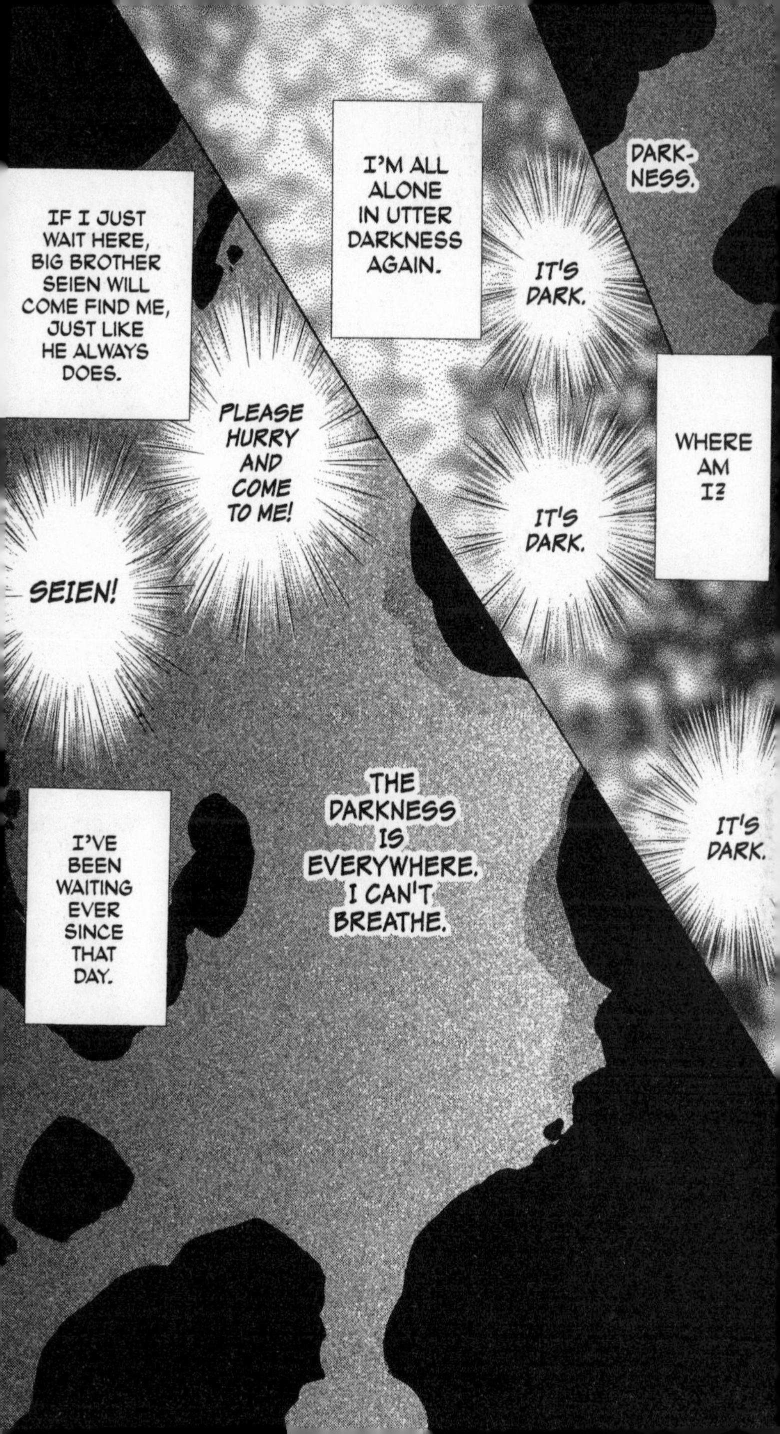
DARK-NESS.
WHERE AM I?
IT'S DARK.
I'M ALL ALONE IN UTTER DARKNESS AGAIN.
IT'S DARK.
IT'S DARK.
IF I JUST WAIT HERE, BIG BROTHER SEIEN WILL COME FIND ME, JUST LIKE HE ALWAYS DOES.
PLEASE HURRY AND COME TO ME!
SEIEN!
THE DARKNESS IS EVERYWHERE. I CAN'T BREATHE.
I'VE BEEN WAITING EVER SINCE THAT DAY.

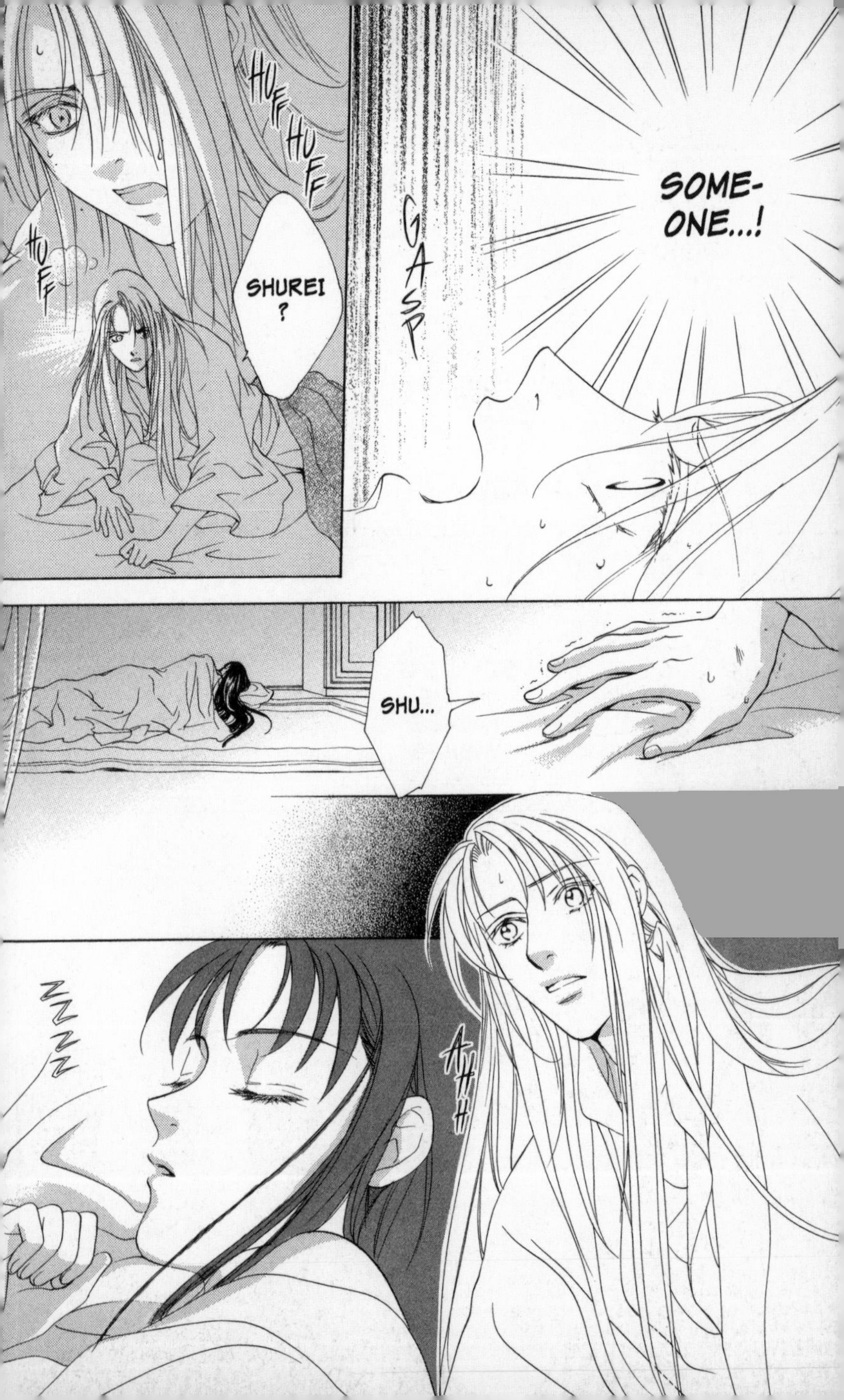
SOME-ONE...!
GASP
HUFF HUFF
SHUREI?
HUFF
SHU...
AHH
ZZZZ

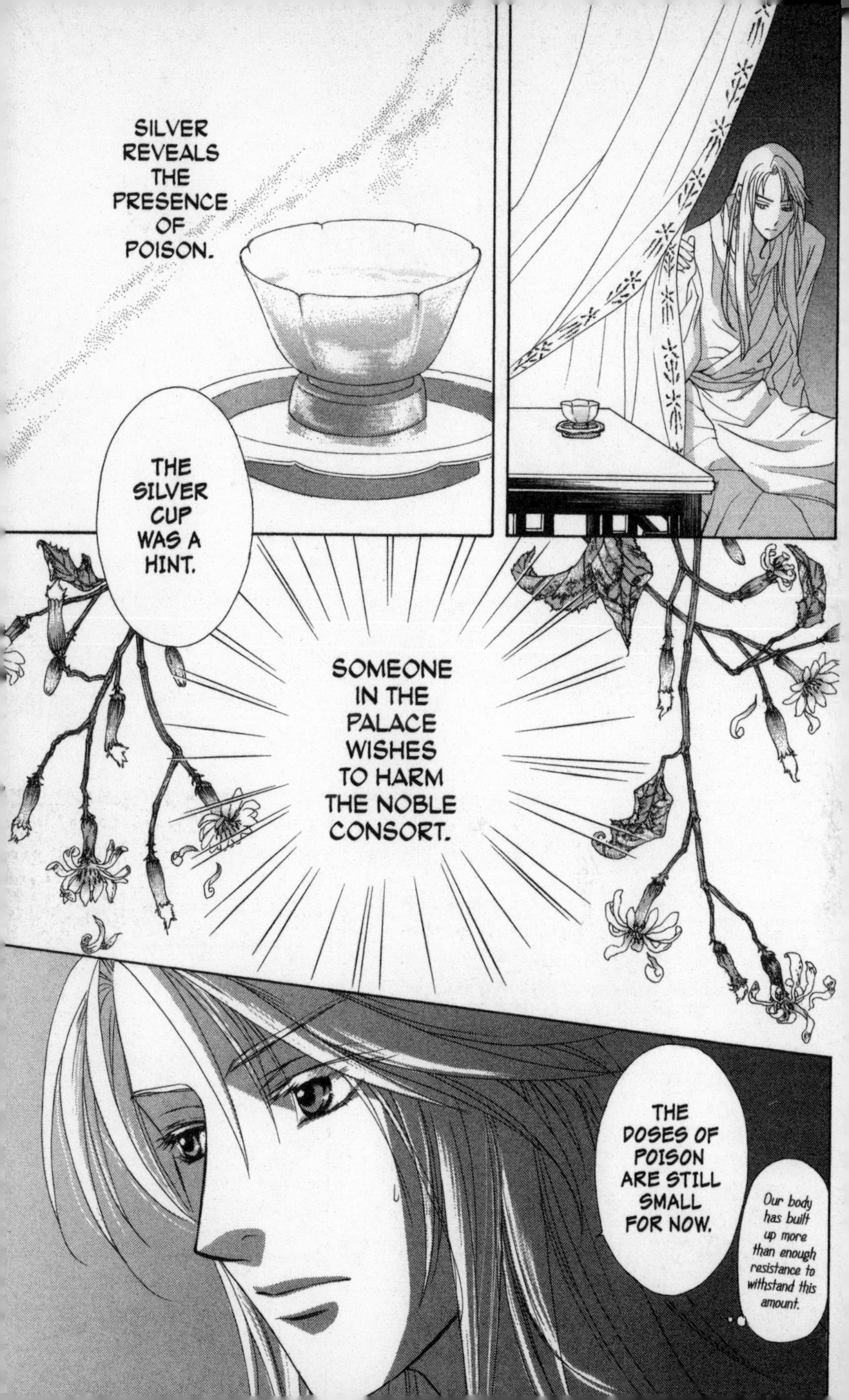
SILVER REVEALS THE PRESENCE OF POISON.
THE SILVER CUP WAS A HINT.
SOMEONE IN THE PALACE WISHES TO HARM THE NOBLE CONSORT.
THE DOSES OF POISON ARE STILL SMALL FOR NOW.
Our body has built up more than enough resistance to withstand this amount.

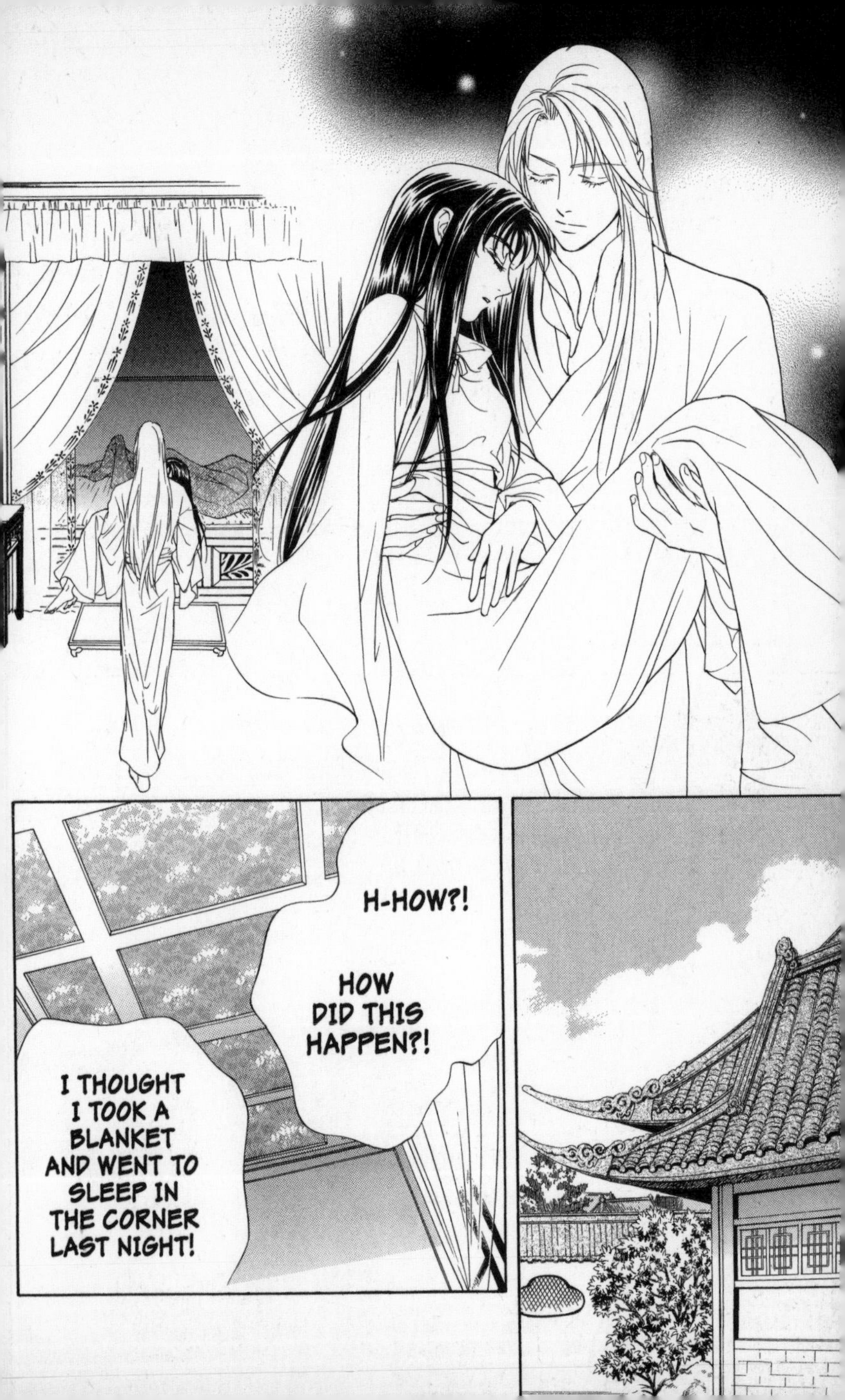
H-HOW?!
HOW DID THIS HAPPEN?!
I THOUGHT I TOOK A BLANKET AND WENT TO SLEEP IN THE CORNER LAST NIGHT!

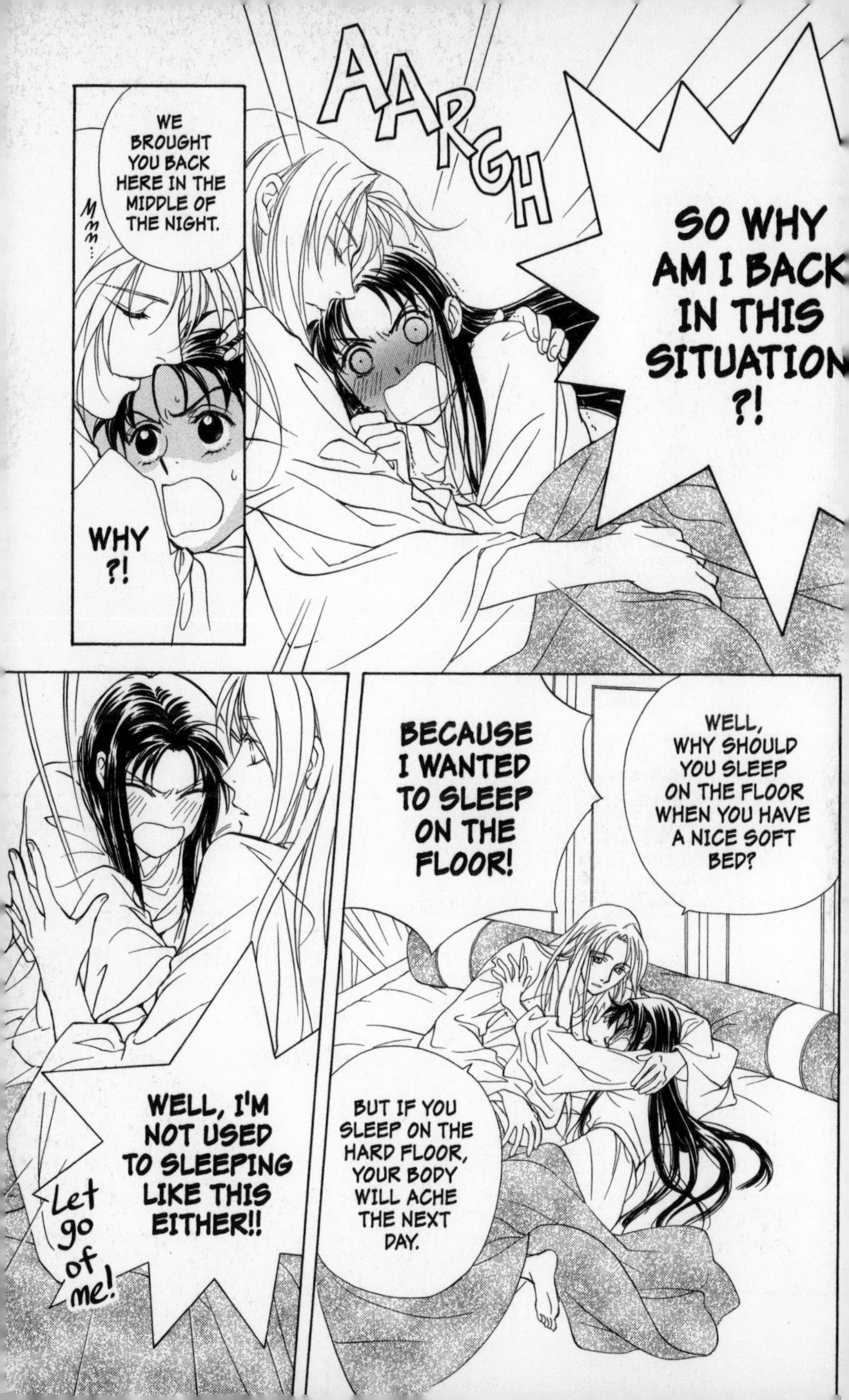
AARGH
SO WHY AM I BACK IN THIS SITUATION ?!
WE BROUGHT YOU BACK HERE IN THE MIDDLE OF THE NIGHT.
Mnn...
WHY ?!
WELL, WHY SHOULD YOU SLEEP ON THE FLOOR WHEN YOU HAVE A NICE SOFT BED?
BECAUSE I WANTED TO SLEEP ON THE FLOOR!
BUT IF YOU SLEEP ON THE HARD FLOOR, YOUR BODY WILL ACHE THE NEXT DAY.
WELL, I'M NOT USED TO SLEEPING LIKE THIS EITHER!!
Let go of me!

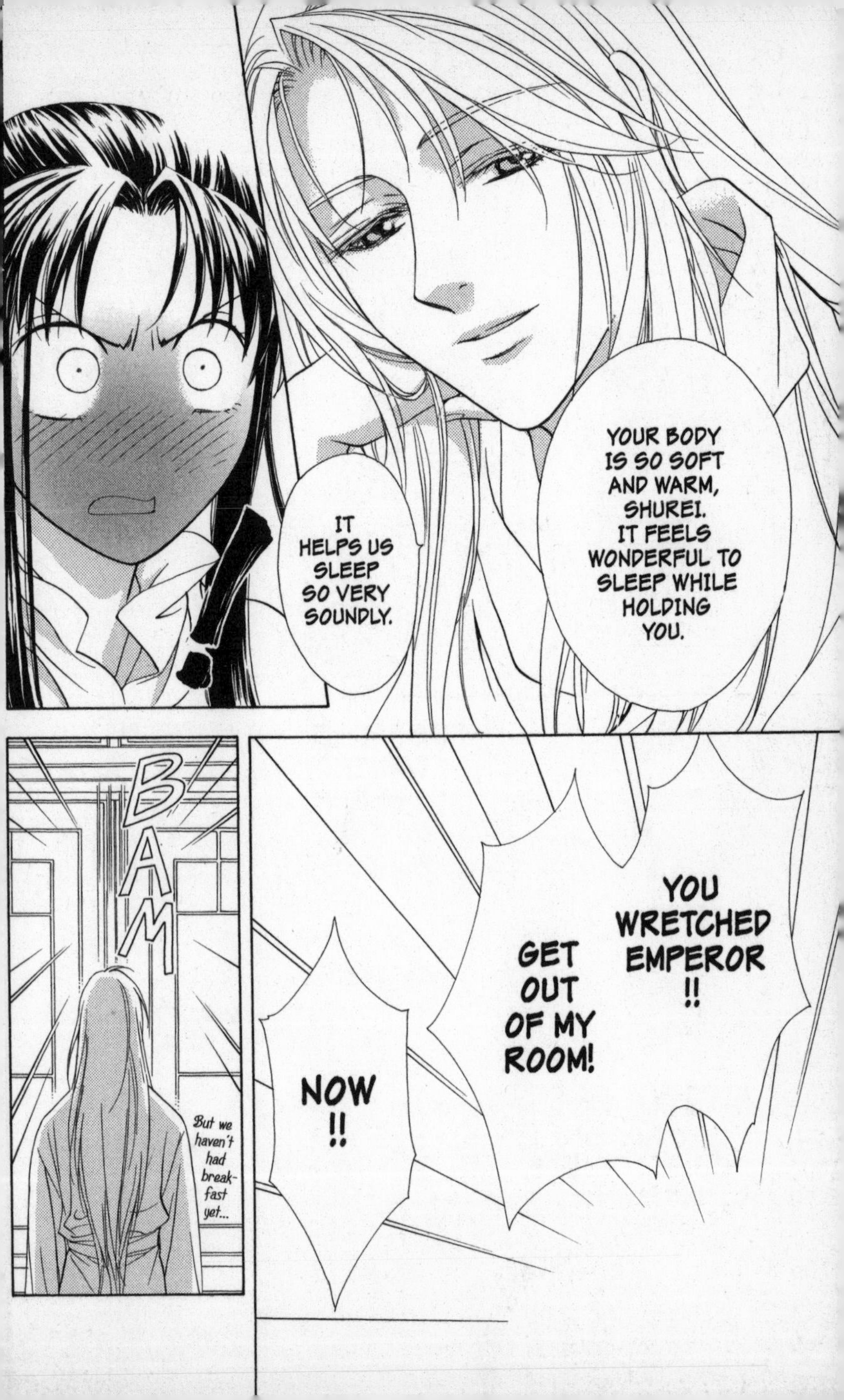
YOUR BODY IS SO SOFT AND WARM, SHUREI. IT FEELS WONDERFUL TO SLEEP WHILE HOLDING YOU.
IT HELPS US SLEEP SO VERY SOUNDLY.
YOU WRETCHED EMPEROR !!
GET OUT OF MY ROOM!
NOW !!
BAM
But we haven't had breakfast yet...

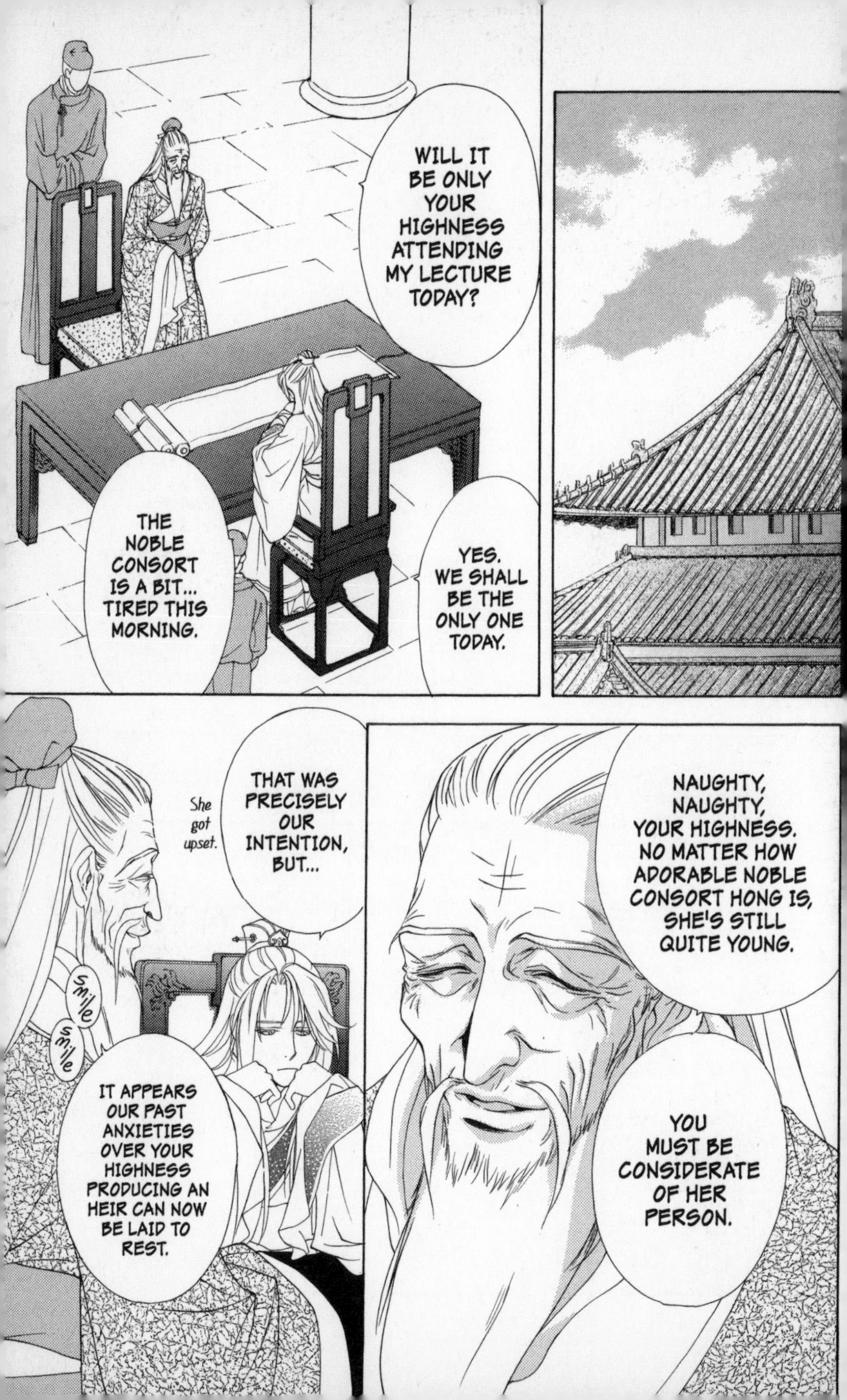
WILL IT BE ONLY YOUR HIGHNESS ATTENDING MY LECTURE TODAY?
YES. WE SHALL BE THE ONLY ONE TODAY.
THE NOBLE CONSORT IS A BIT... TIRED THIS MORNING.
NAUGHTY, NAUGHTY, YOUR HIGHNESS. NO MATTER HOW ADORABLE NOBLE CONSORT HONG IS, SHE'S STILL QUITE YOUNG.
YOU MUST BE CONSIDERATE OF HER PERSON.
THAT WAS PRECISELY OUR INTENTION, BUT...
She got upset.
smile
smile
IT APPEARS OUR PAST ANXIETIES OVER YOUR HIGHNESS PRODUCING AN HEIR CAN NOW BE LAID TO REST.

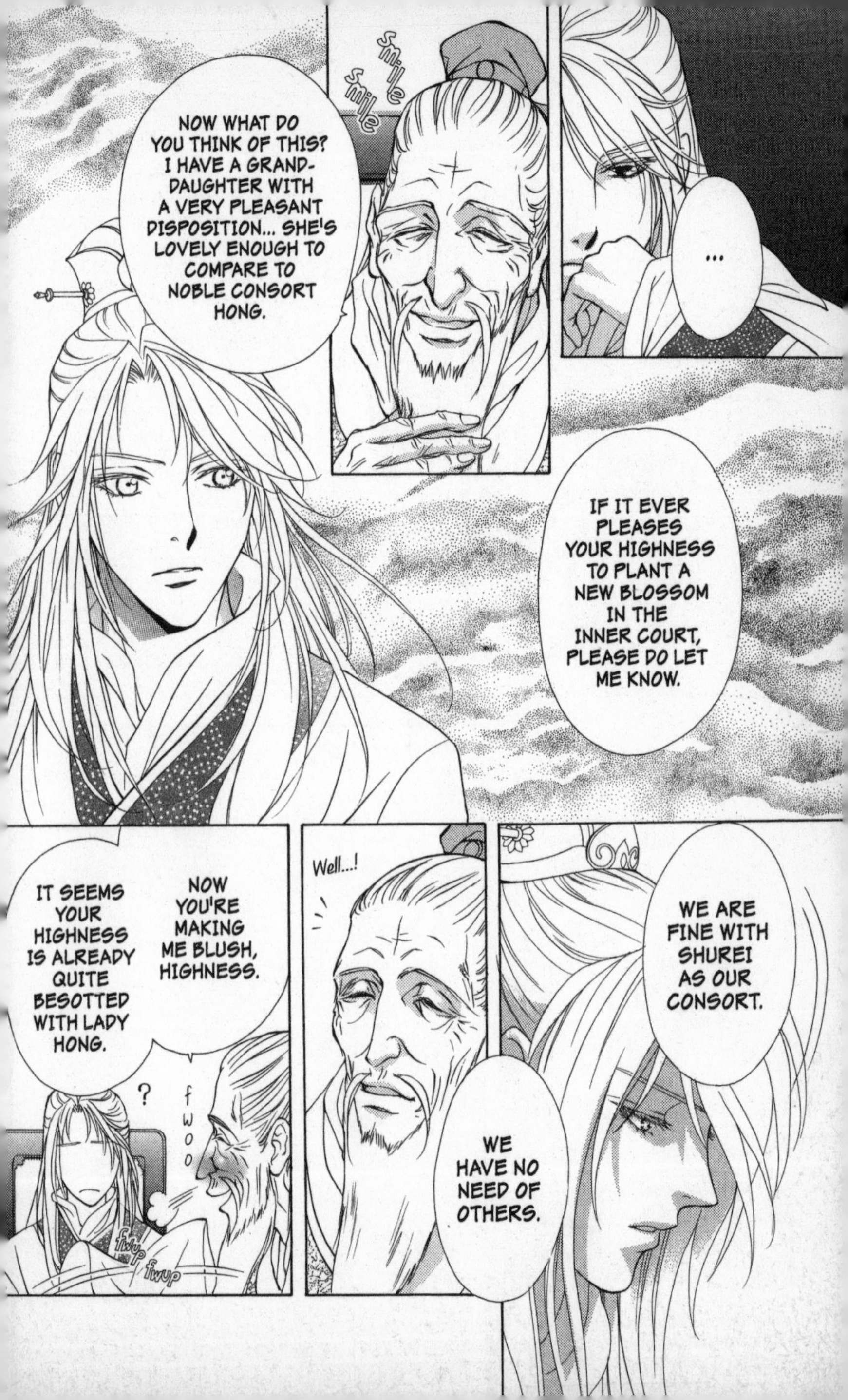
...
Smile
Smile
NOW WHAT DO YOU THINK OF THIS? I HAVE A GRAND-DAUGHTER WITH A VERY PLEASANT DISPOSITION... SHE'S LOVELY ENOUGH TO COMPARE TO NOBLE CONSORT HONG.
IF IT EVER PLEASES YOUR HIGHNESS TO PLANT A NEW BLOSSOM IN THE INNER COURT, PLEASE DO LET ME KNOW.
WE ARE FINE WITH SHUREI AS OUR CONSORT.
WE HAVE NO NEED OF OTHERS.
Well...!
NOW YOU'RE MAKING ME BLUSH, HIGHNESS.
IT SEEMS YOUR HIGHNESS IS ALREADY QUITE BESOTTED WITH LADY HONG.
?
fwoo
fwup
fwup

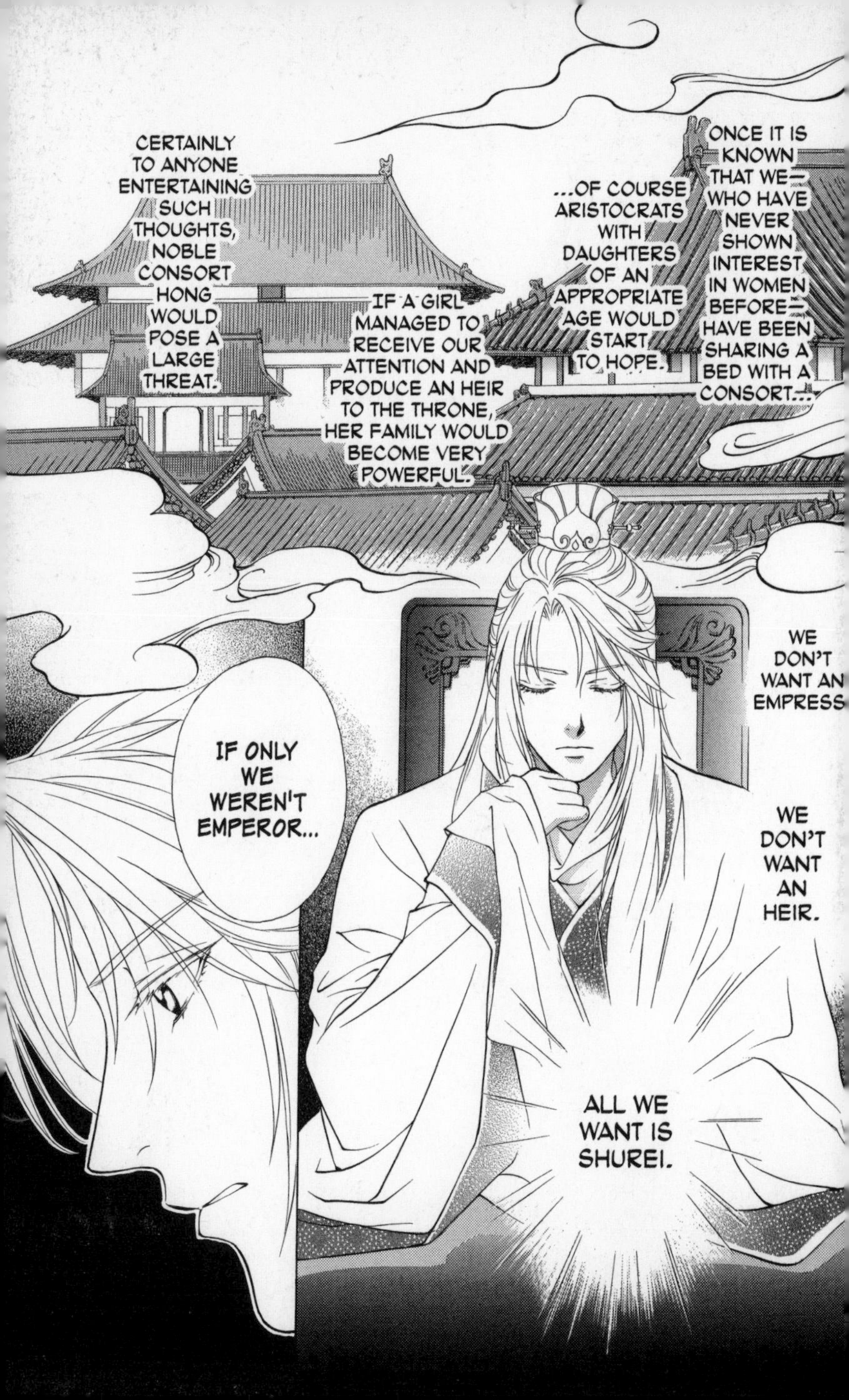
ONCE IT IS KNOWN THAT WE—WHO HAVE NEVER SHOWN INTEREST IN WOMEN BEFORE—HAVE BEEN SHARING A BED WITH A CONSORT...
...OF COURSE ARISTOCRATS WITH DAUGHTERS OF AN APPROPRIATE AGE WOULD START TO HOPE.
IF A GIRL MANAGED TO RECEIVE OUR ATTENTION AND PRODUCE AN HEIR TO THE THRONE, HER FAMILY WOULD BECOME VERY POWERFUL.
CERTAINLY TO ANYONE ENTERTAINING SUCH THOUGHTS, NOBLE CONSORT HONG WOULD POSE A LARGE THREAT.
WE DON'T WANT AN EMPRESS
WE DON'T WANT AN HEIR.
ALL WE WANT IS SHUREI.
IF ONLY WE WEREN'T EMPEROR...

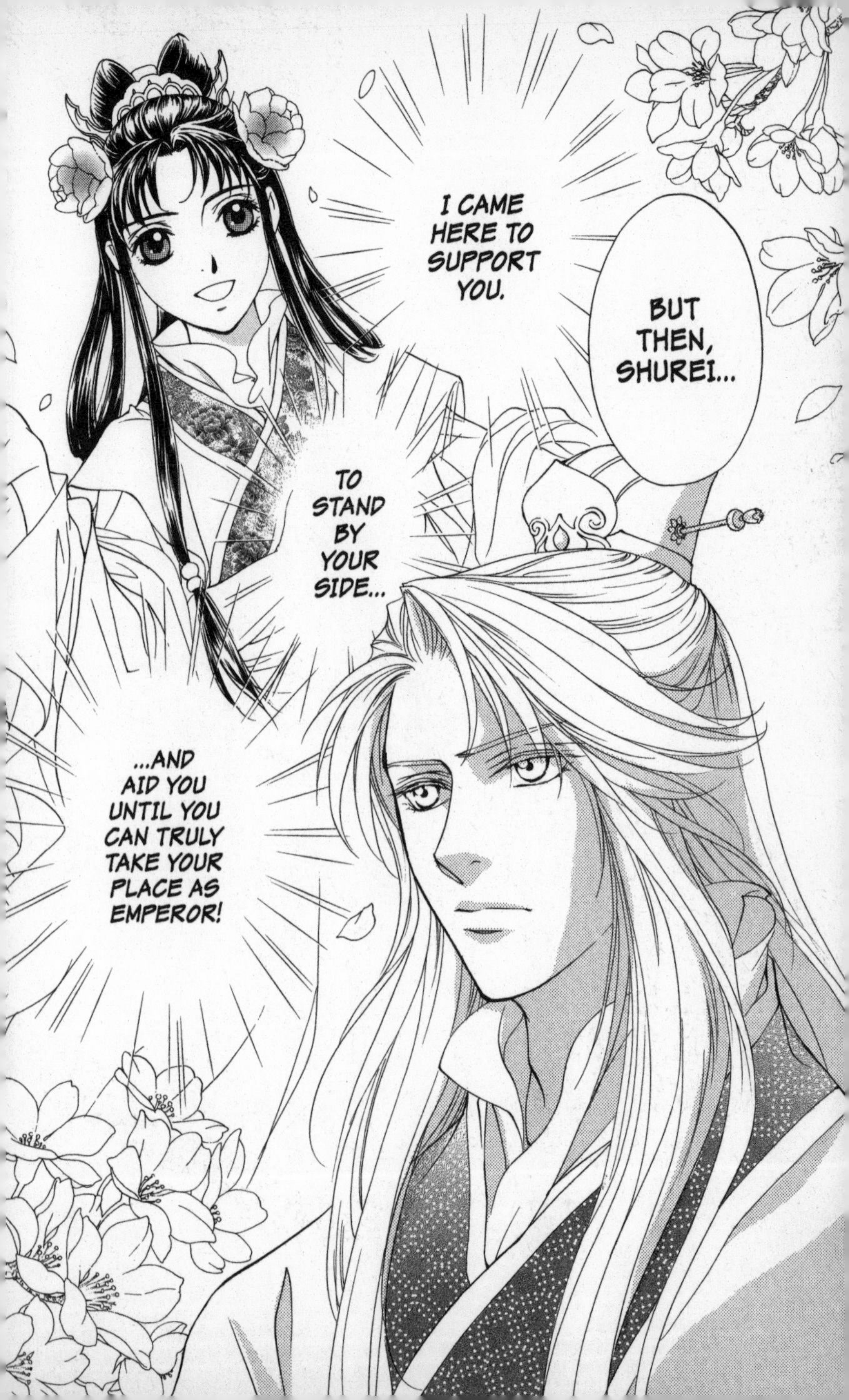
I CAME HERE TO SUPPORT YOU.
TO STAND BY YOUR SIDE...
...AND AID YOU UNTIL YOU CAN TRULY TAKE YOUR PLACE AS EMPEROR!
BUT THEN, SHUREI...

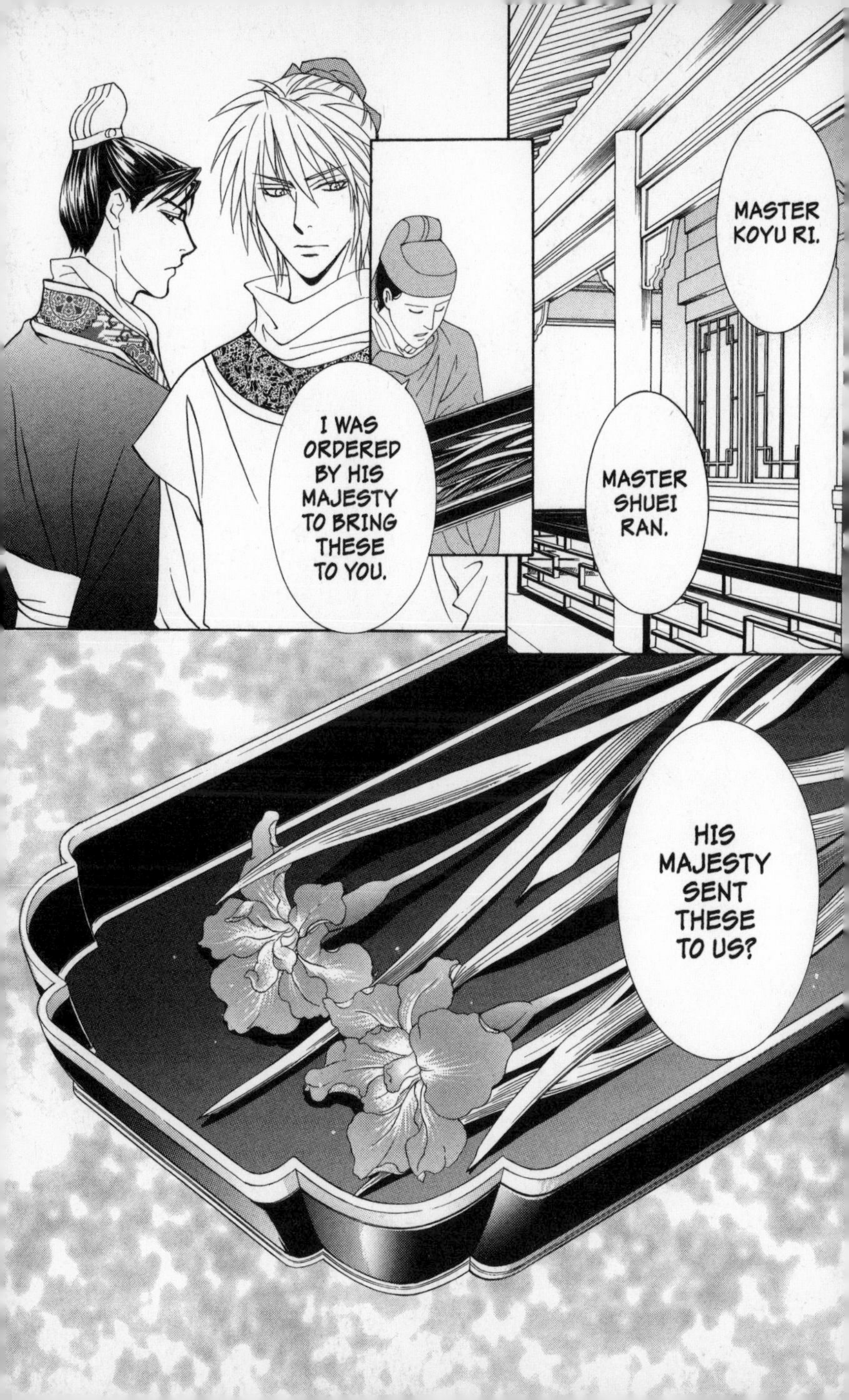
MASTER KOYU RI.
MASTER SHUEI RAN.
I WAS ORDERED BY HIS MAJESTY TO BRING THESE TO YOU.
HIS MAJESTY SENT THESE TO US?

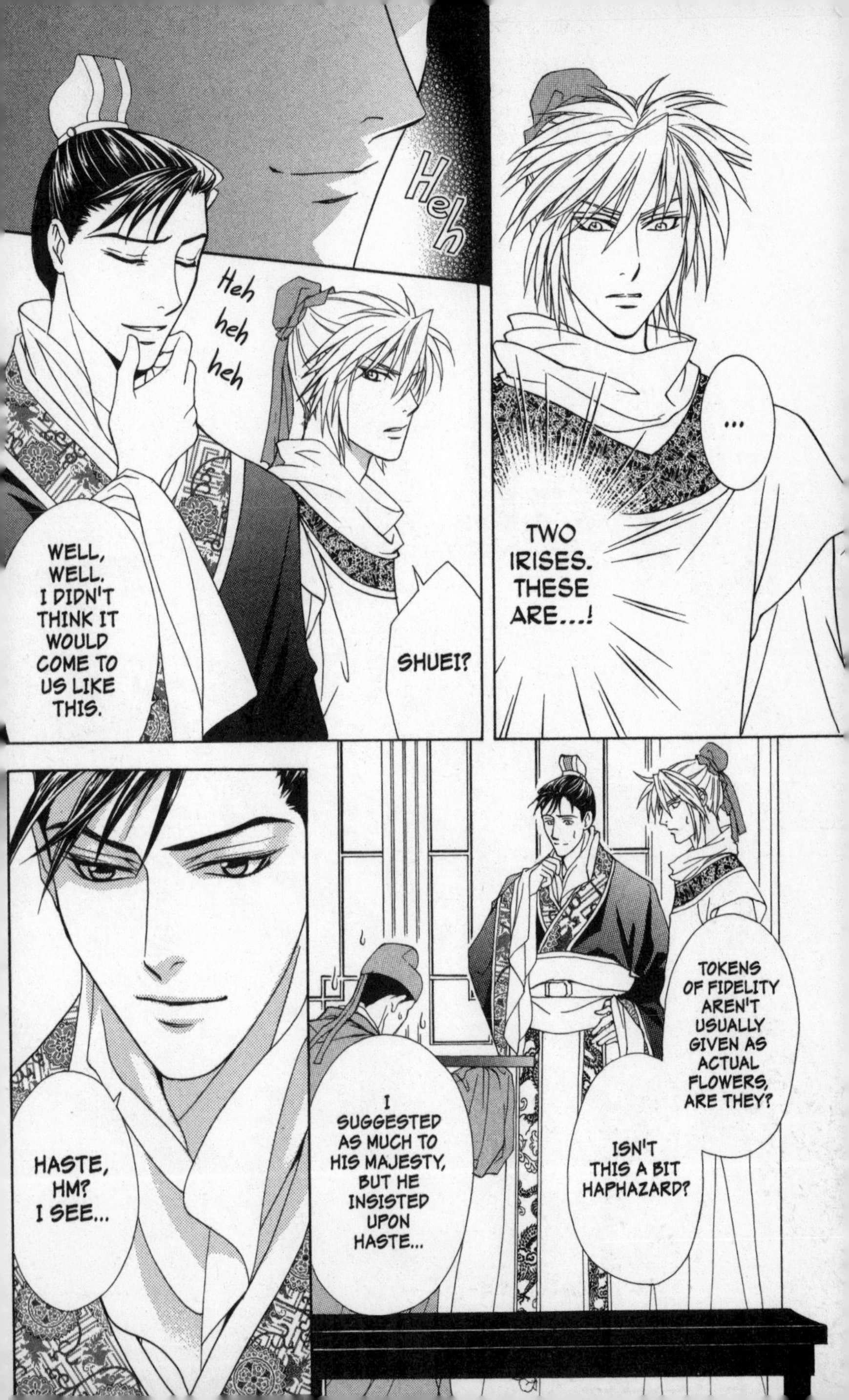
...
TWO IRISES. THESE ARE...!
Heh
SHUEI?
Heh heh heh
WELL, WELL. I DIDN'T THINK IT WOULD COME TO US LIKE THIS.
TOKENS OF FIDELITY AREN'T USUALLY GIVEN AS ACTUAL FLOWERS, ARE THEY?
ISN'T THIS A BIT HAPHAZARD?
I SUGGESTED AS MUCH TO HIS MAJESTY, BUT HE INSISTED UPON HASTE...
HASTE, HM? I SEE...

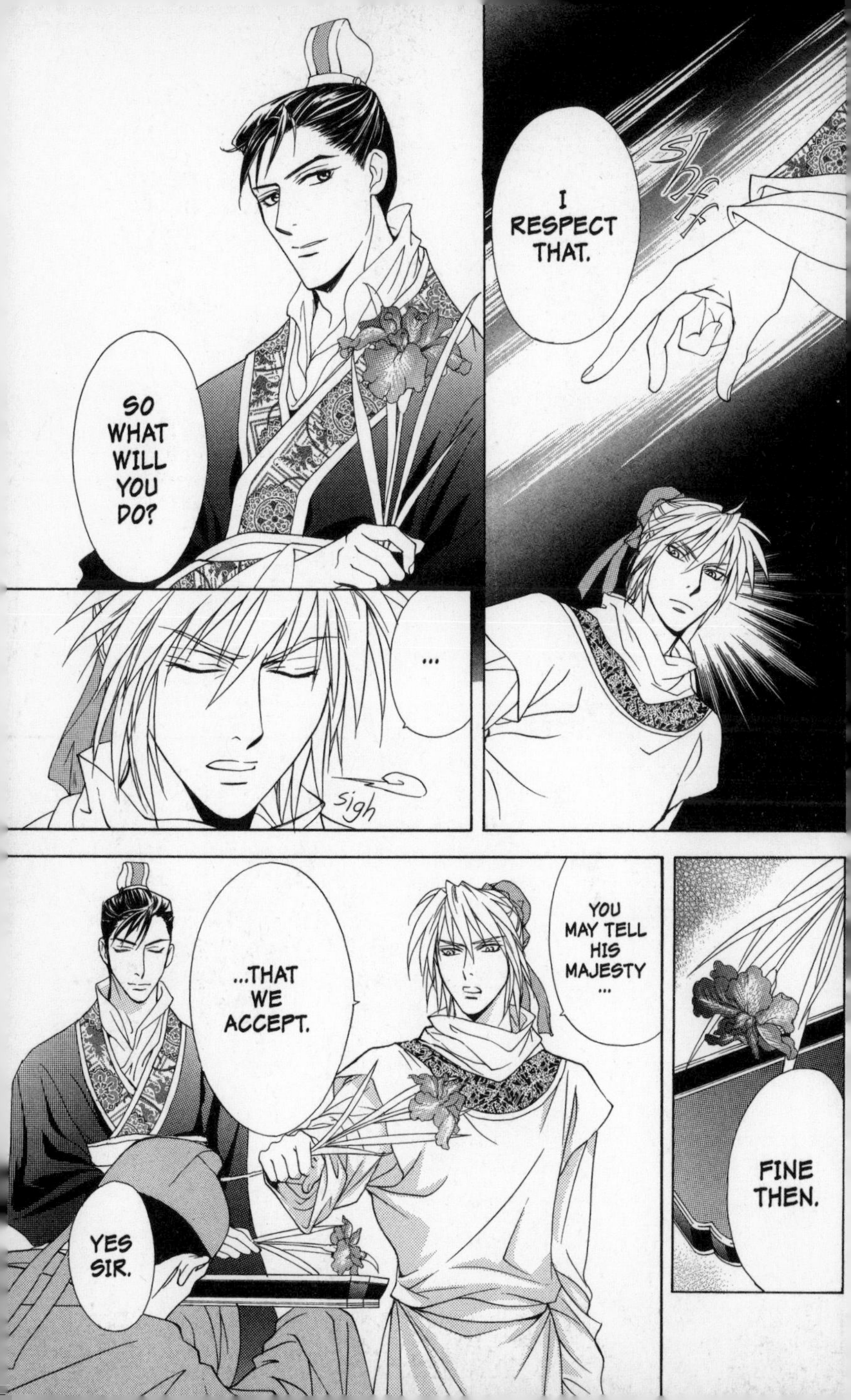
I RESPECT THAT.
shff
SO WHAT WILL YOU DO?
...
sigh
FINE THEN.
YOU MAY TELL HIS MAJESTY ...
...THAT WE ACCEPT.
YES SIR.

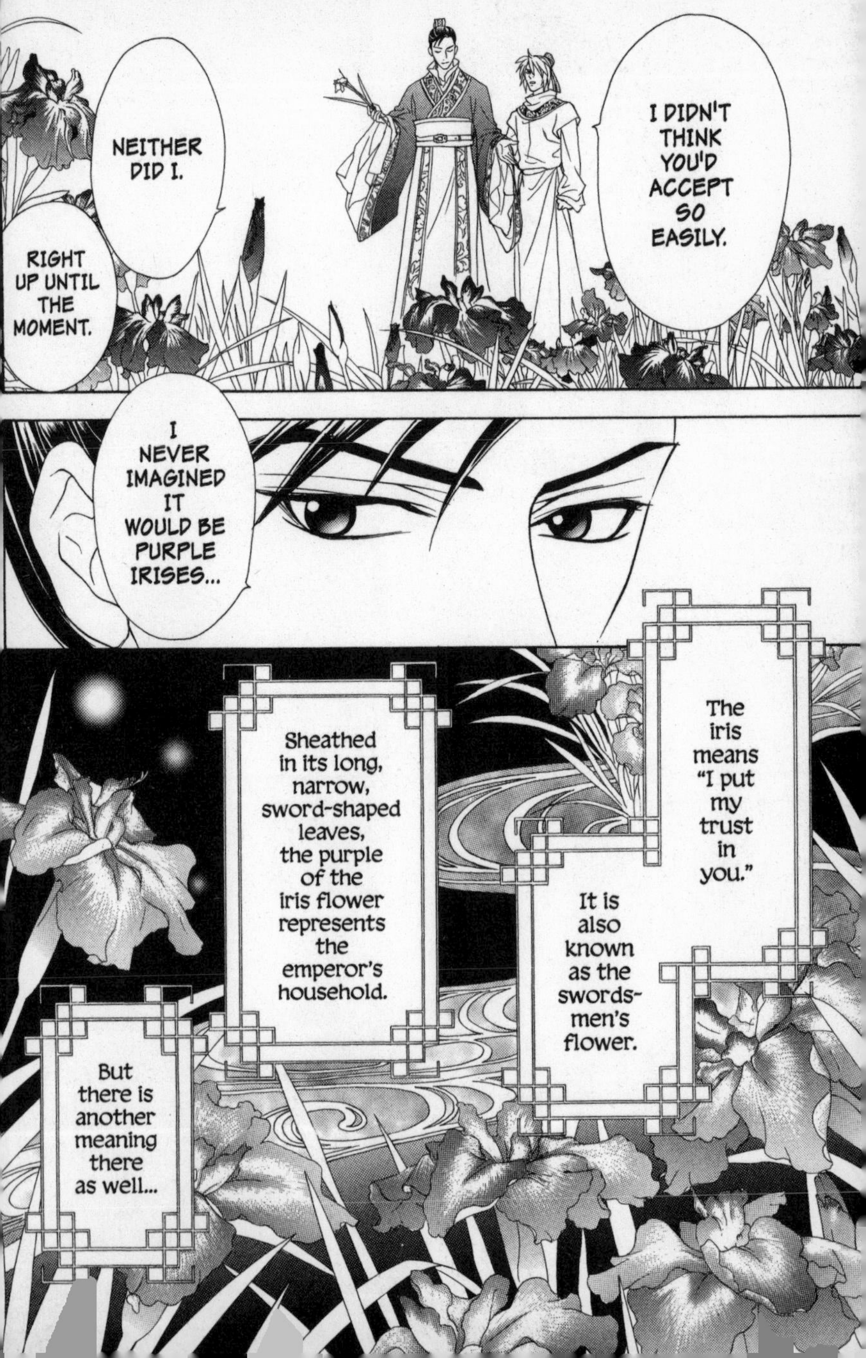

I DIDN'T THINK YOU'D ACCEPT SO EASILY.
NEITHER DID I.
RIGHT UP UNTIL THE MOMENT.
I NEVER IMAGINED IT WOULD BE PURPLE IRISES...
The iris means "I put my trust in you."
It is also known as the swords-men's flower.
Sheathed in its long, narrow, sword-shaped leaves, the purple of the iris flower represents the emperor's household.
But there is another meaning there as well...

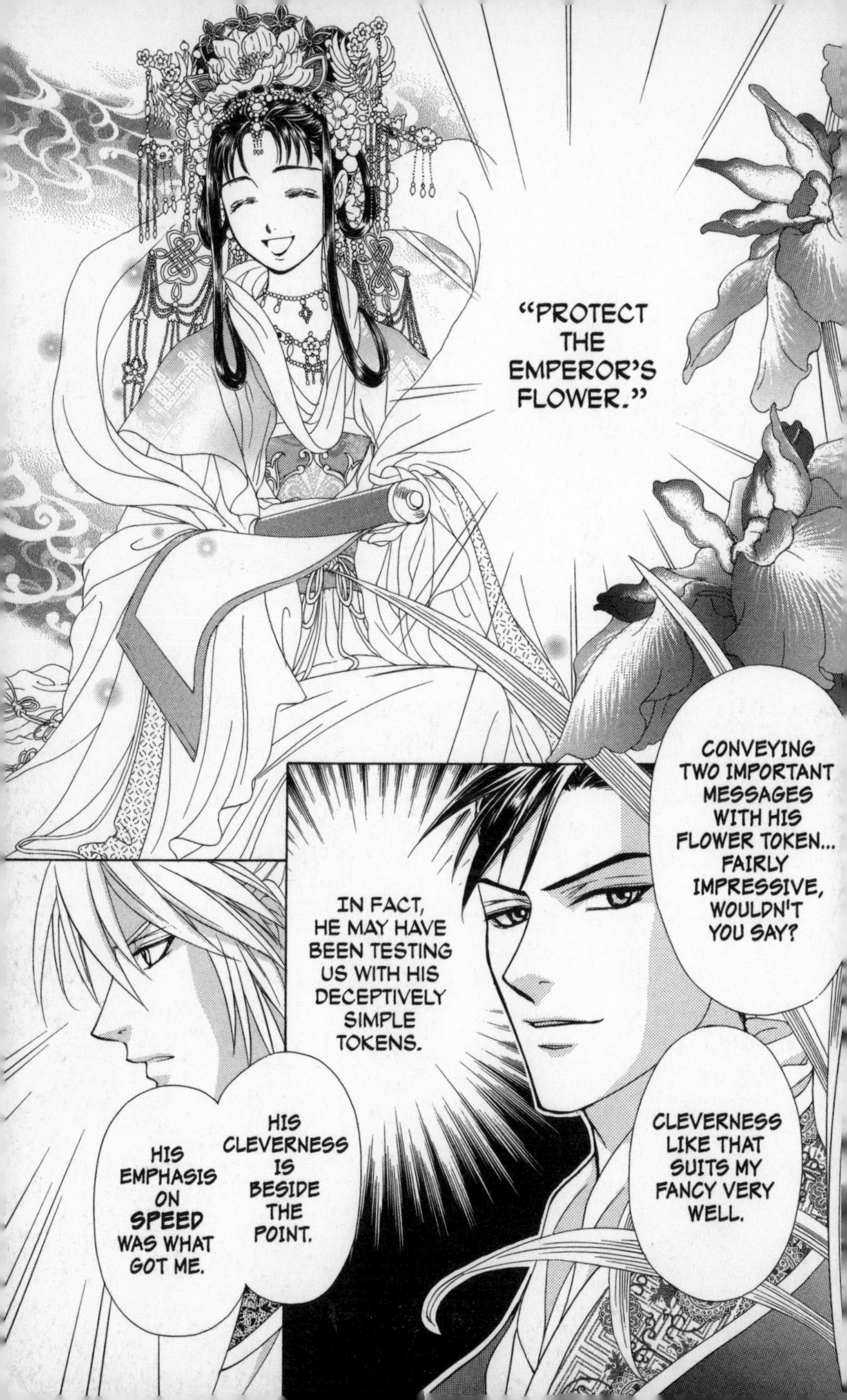
"PROTECT THE EMPEROR'S FLOWER."
CONVEYING TWO IMPORTANT MESSAGES WITH HIS FLOWER TOKEN... FAIRLY IMPRESSIVE, WOULDN'T YOU SAY?
IN FACT, HE MAY HAVE BEEN TESTING US WITH HIS DECEPTIVELY SIMPLE TOKENS.
CLEVERNESS LIKE THAT SUITS MY FANCY VERY WELL.
HIS CLEVERNESS IS BESIDE THE POINT.
HIS EMPHASIS ON **SPEED** WAS WHAT GOT ME.

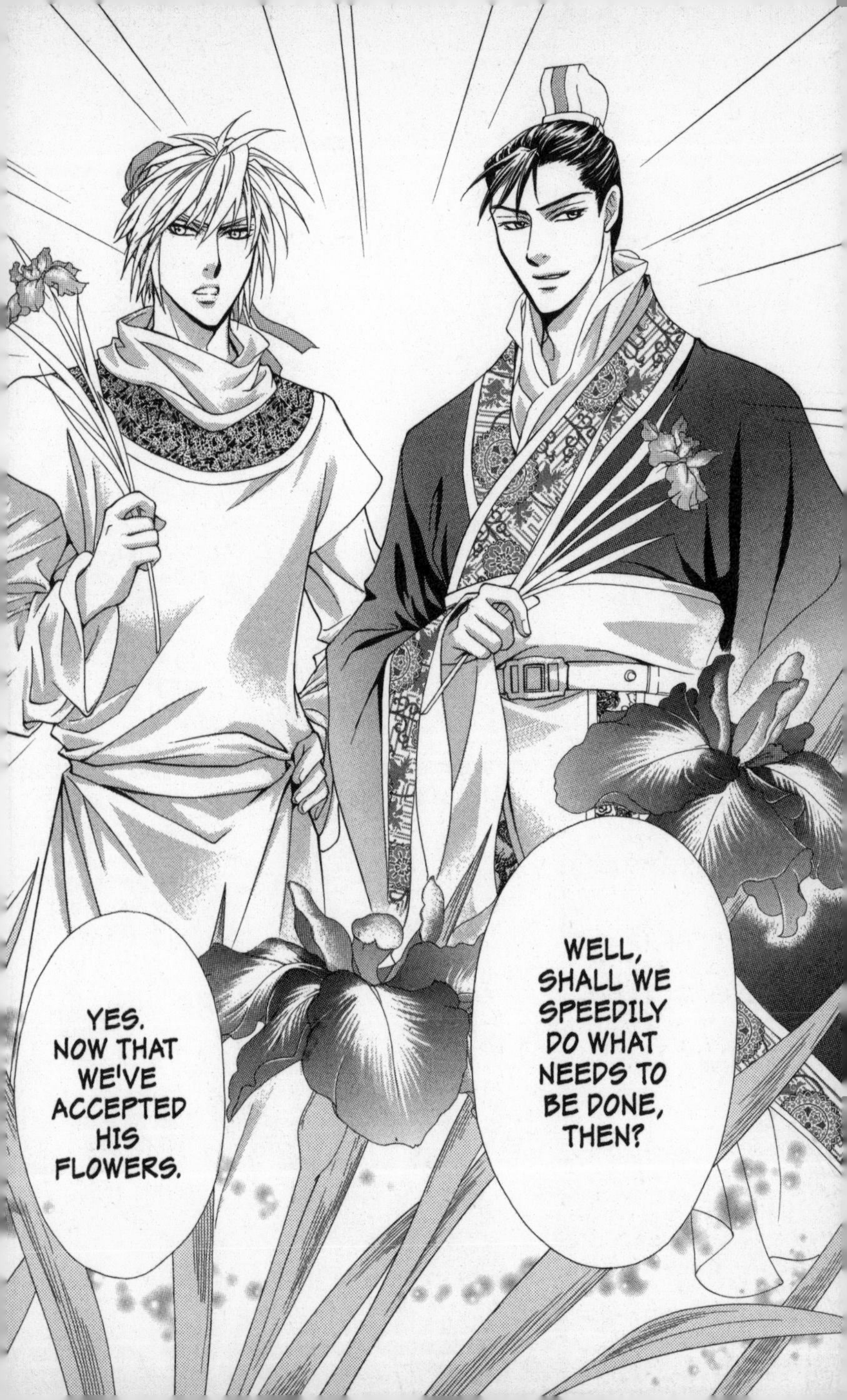
WELL, SHALL WE SPEEDILY DO WHAT NEEDS TO BE DONE, THEN?
YES. NOW THAT WE'VE ACCEPTED HIS FLOWERS.

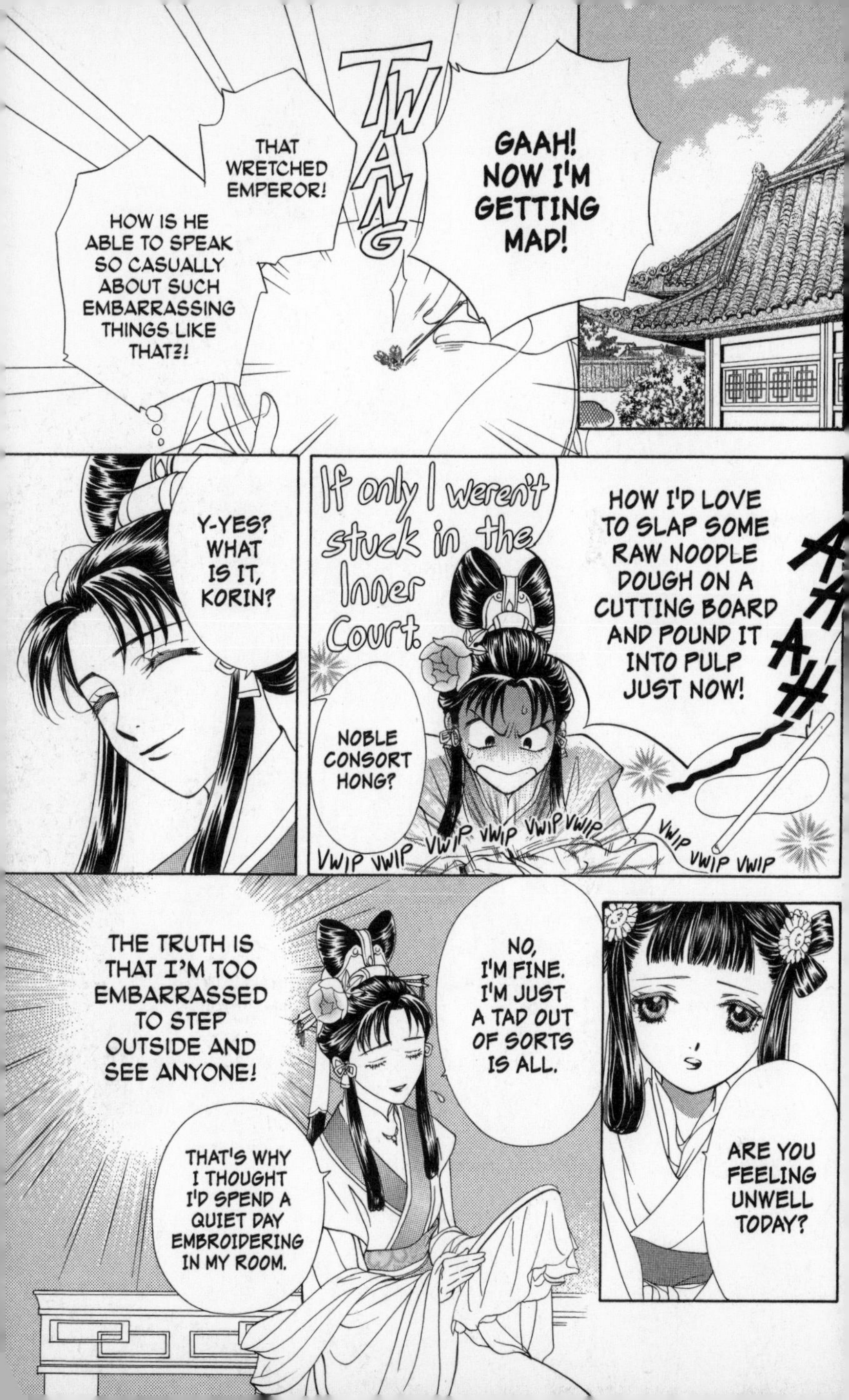
GAAH! NOW I'M GETTING MAD!
TWANG
THAT WRETCHED EMPEROR!
HOW IS HE ABLE TO SPEAK SO CASUALLY ABOUT SUCH EMBARRASSING THINGS LIKE THAT?!
HOW I'D LOVE TO SLAP SOME RAW NOODLE DOUGH ON A CUTTING BOARD AND POUND IT INTO PULP JUST NOW!
AAAH
If only I weren't stuck in the Inner Court.
NOBLE CONSORT HONG?
VWIP VWIP VWIP
VWIP VWIP VWIP VWIP VWIP VWIP VWIP
Y-YES? WHAT IS IT, KORIN?
ARE YOU FEELING UNWELL TODAY?
NO, I'M FINE. I'M JUST A TAD OUT OF SORTS IS ALL.
THE TRUTH IS THAT I'M TOO EMBARRASSED TO STEP OUTSIDE AND SEE ANYONE!
THAT'S WHY I THOUGHT I'D SPEND A QUIET DAY EMBROIDERING IN MY ROOM.

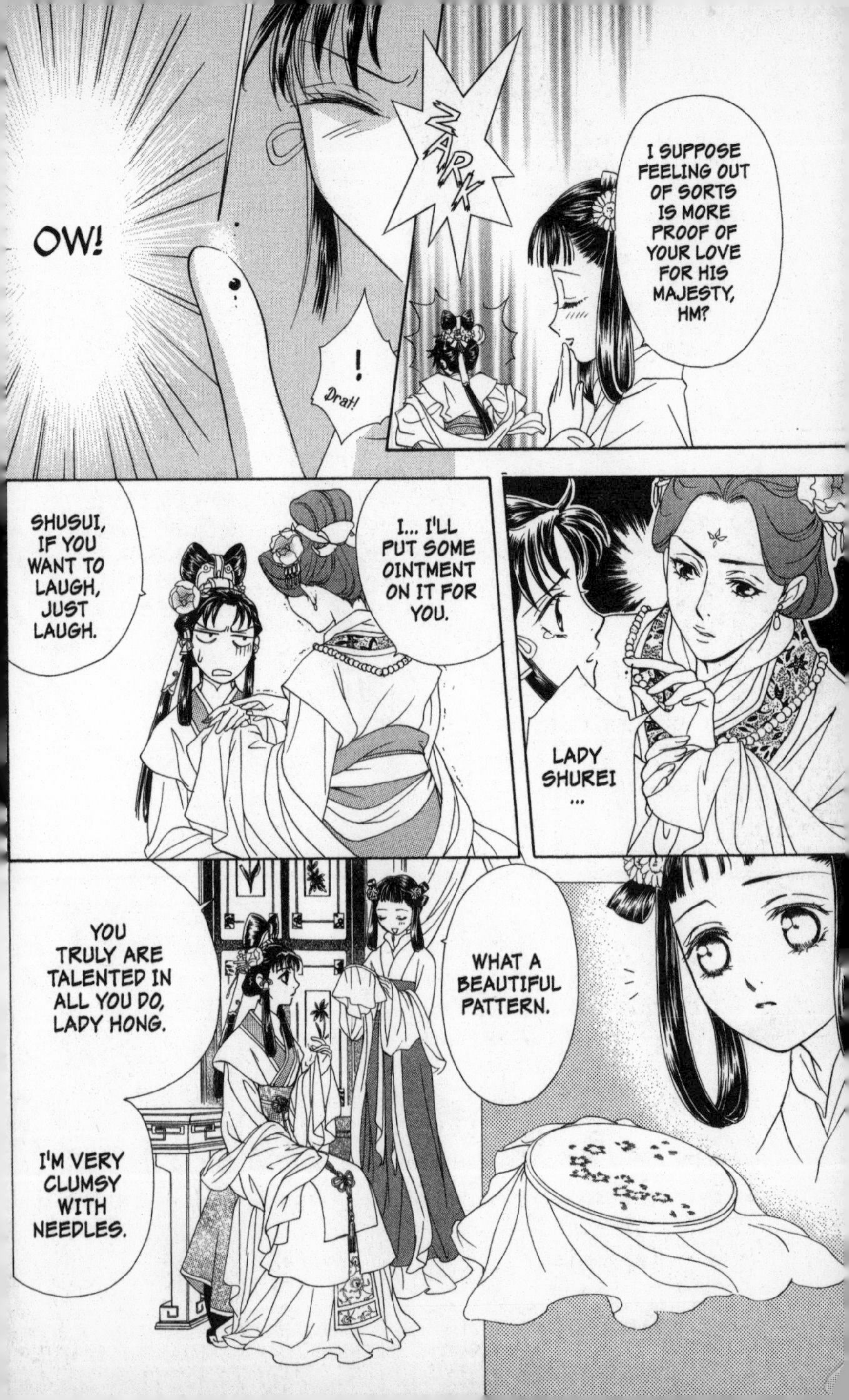
I SUPPOSE FEELING OUT OF SORTS IS MORE PROOF OF YOUR LOVE FOR HIS MAJESTY, HM?
ZARK
!
Drat!
OW!
LADY SHUREI ...
I... I'LL PUT SOME OINTMENT ON IT FOR YOU.
SHUSUI, IF YOU WANT TO LAUGH, JUST LAUGH.
WHAT A BEAUTIFUL PATTERN.
YOU TRULY ARE TALENTED IN ALL YOU DO, LADY HONG.
I'M VERY CLUMSY WITH NEEDLES.

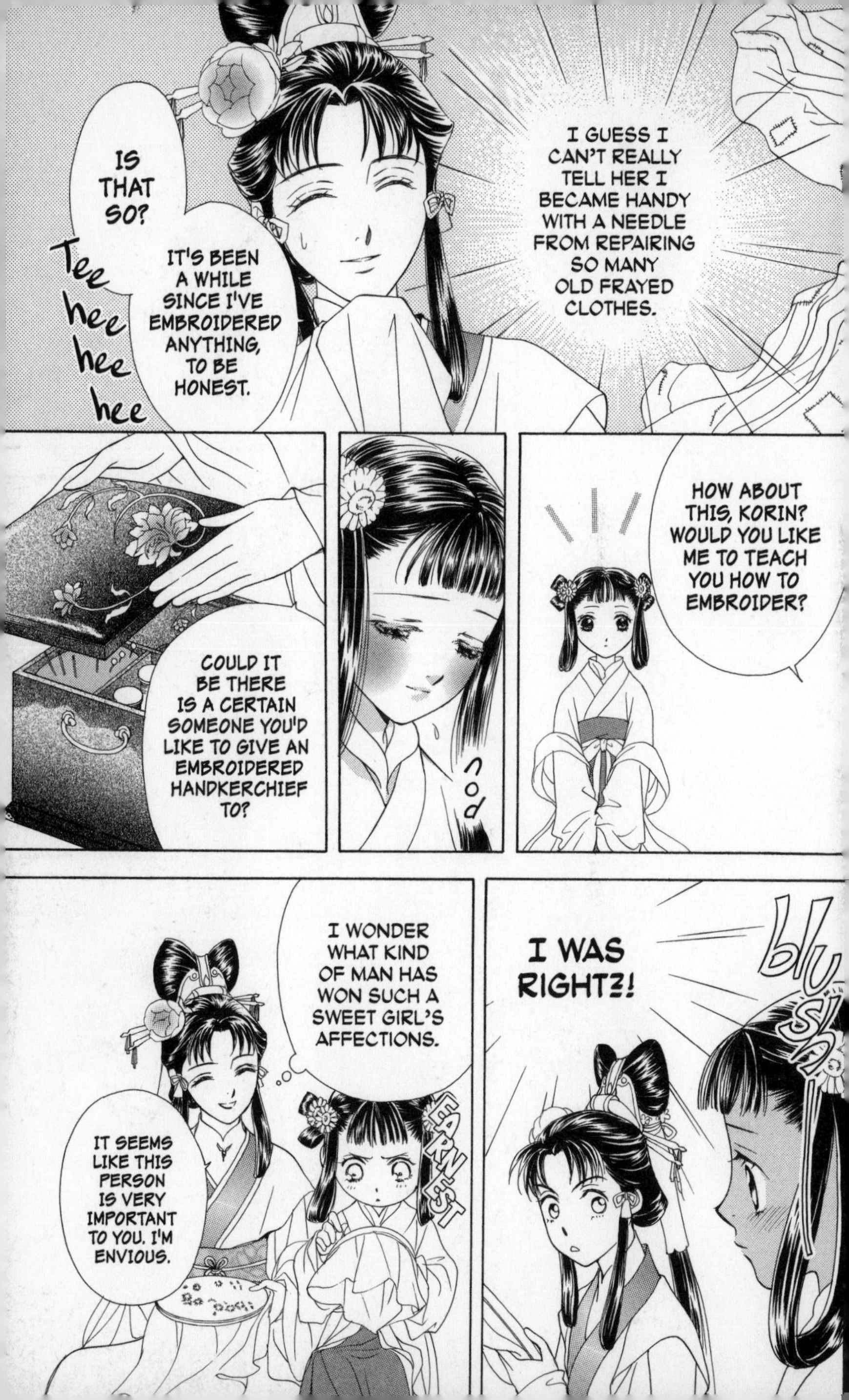
I GUESS I CAN'T REALLY TELL HER I BECAME HANDY WITH A NEEDLE FROM REPAIRING SO MANY OLD FRAYED CLOTHES.
IS THAT SO?
IT'S BEEN A WHILE SINCE I'VE EMBROIDERED ANYTHING, TO BE HONEST.
Tee hee hee hee
HOW ABOUT THIS, KORIN? WOULD YOU LIKE ME TO TEACH YOU HOW TO EMBROIDER?
nod
COULD IT BE THERE IS A CERTAIN SOMEONE YOU'D LIKE TO GIVE AN EMBROIDERED HANDKERCHIEF TO?
blush
I WAS RIGHT?!
I WONDER WHAT KIND OF MAN HAS WON SUCH A SWEET GIRL'S AFFECTIONS.
EARNEST
IT SEEMS LIKE THIS PERSON IS VERY IMPORTANT TO YOU. I'M ENVIOUS.

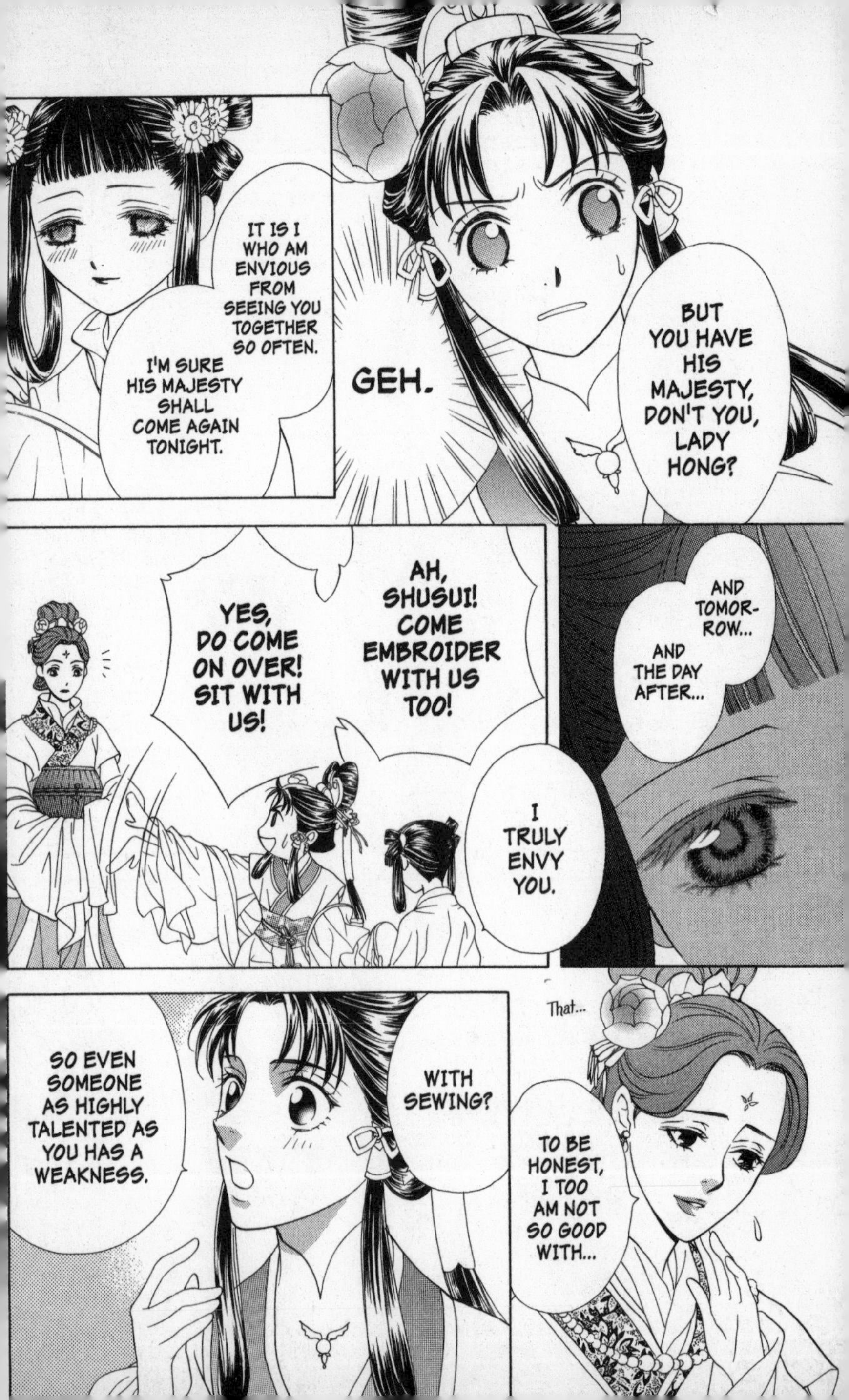
BUT YOU HAVE HIS MAJESTY, DON'T YOU, LADY HONG?
GEH.
IT IS I WHO AM ENVIOUS FROM SEEING YOU TOGETHER SO OFTEN.
I'M SURE HIS MAJESTY SHALL COME AGAIN TONIGHT.
AND TOMOR-ROW...
AND THE DAY AFTER...
I TRULY ENVY YOU.
AH, SHUSUI! COME EMBROIDER WITH US TOO!
YES, DO COME ON OVER! SIT WITH US!
That...
TO BE HONEST, I TOO AM NOT SO GOOD WITH...
WITH SEWING?
SO EVEN SOMEONE AS HIGHLY TALENTED AS YOU HAS A WEAKNESS.

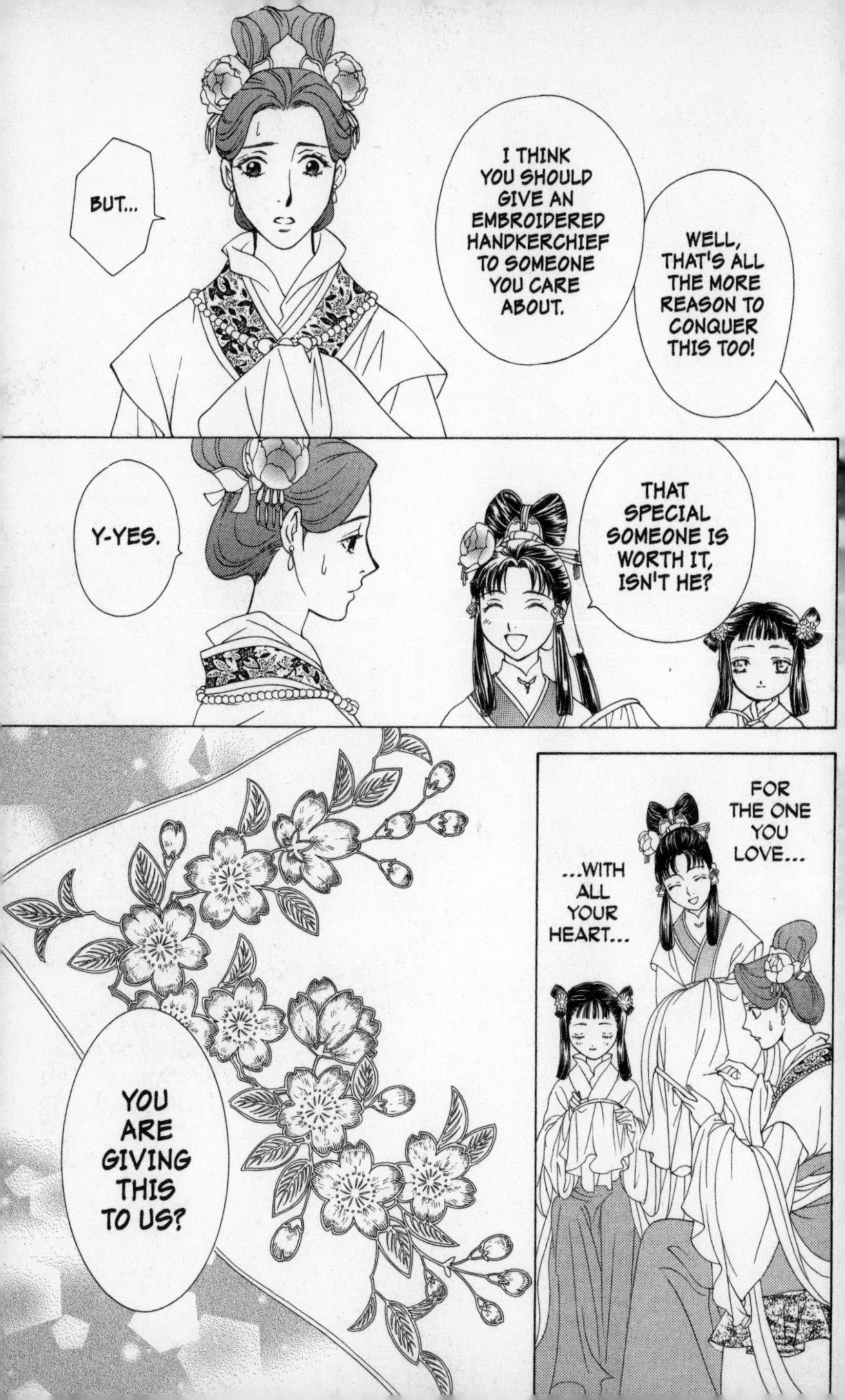
WELL, THAT'S ALL THE MORE REASON TO CONQUER THIS TOO!
I THINK YOU SHOULD GIVE AN EMBROIDERED HANDKERCHIEF TO SOMEONE YOU CARE ABOUT.
BUT...
THAT SPECIAL SOMEONE IS WORTH IT, ISN'T HE?
Y-YES.
FOR THE ONE YOU LOVE...
...WITH ALL YOUR HEART...
YOU ARE GIVING THIS TO US?

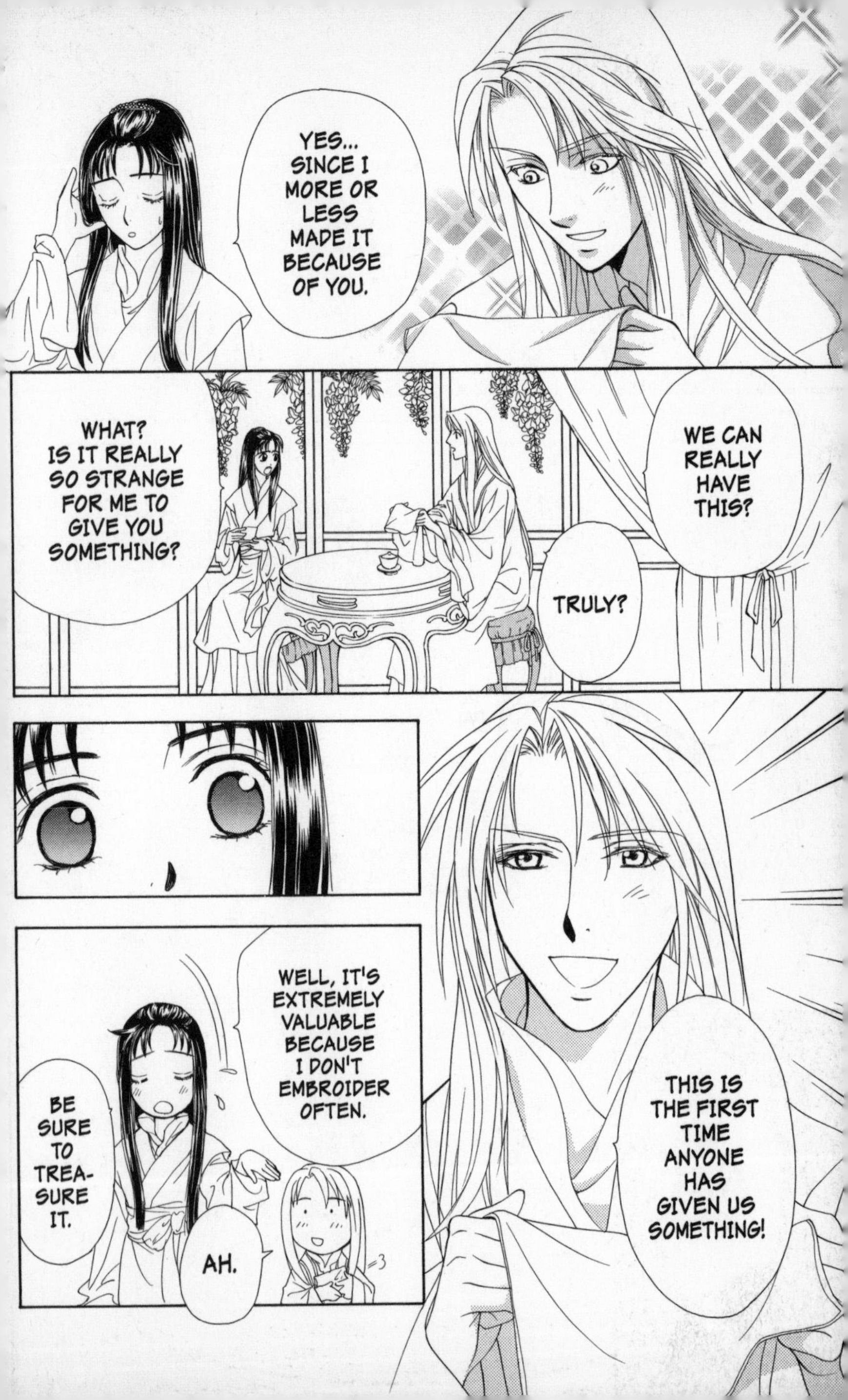
YES... SINCE I MORE OR LESS MADE IT BECAUSE OF YOU.
WE CAN REALLY HAVE THIS?
TRULY?
WHAT? IS IT REALLY SO STRANGE FOR ME TO GIVE YOU SOMETHING?
THIS IS THE FIRST TIME ANYONE HAS GIVEN US SOMETHING!
WELL, IT'S EXTREMELY VALUABLE BECAUSE I DON'T EMBROIDER OFTEN.
BE SURE TO TREA-SURE IT.
AH.

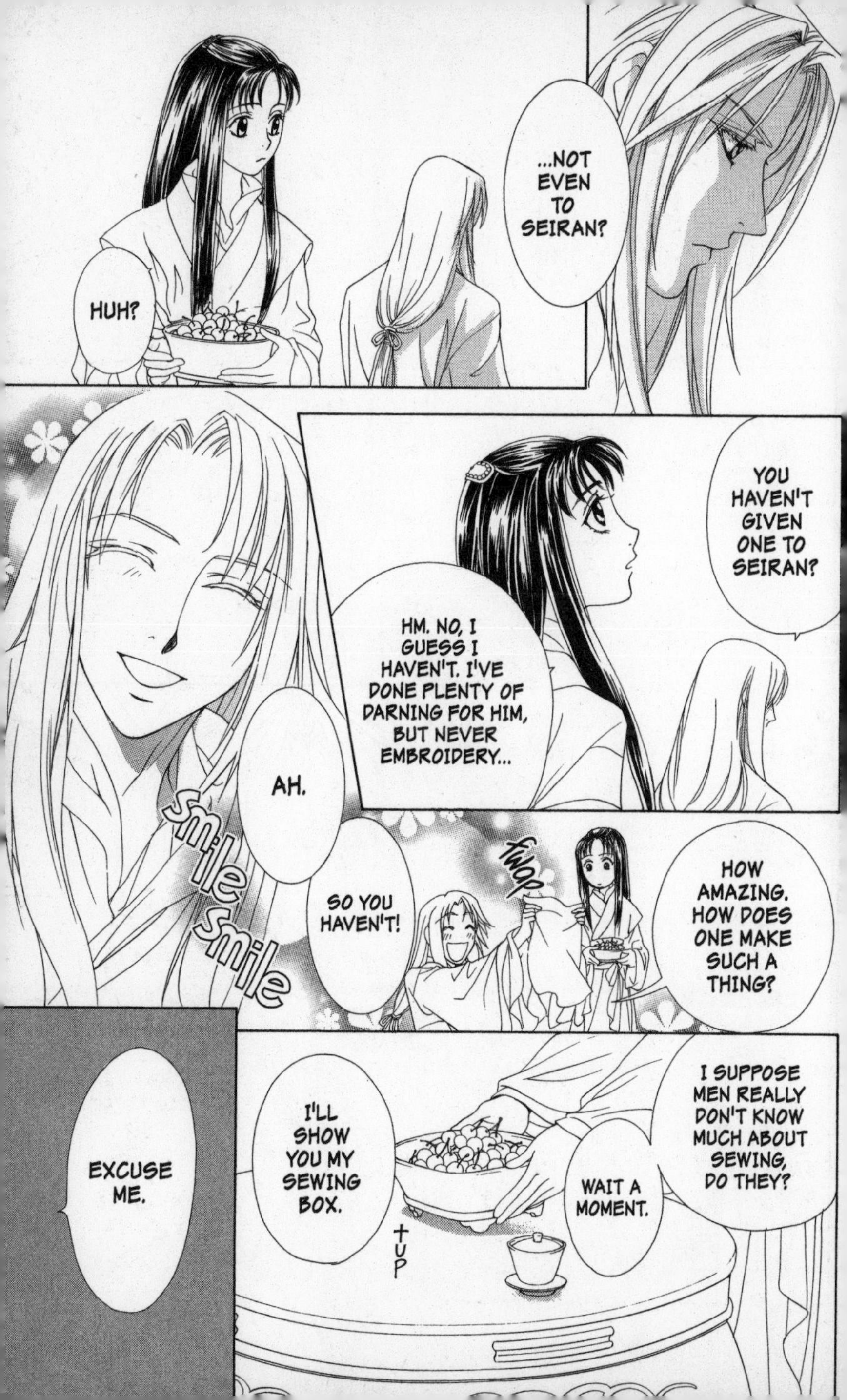
...NOT EVEN TO SEIRAN?
HUH?
YOU HAVEN'T GIVEN ONE TO SEIRAN?
HM. NO, I GUESS I HAVEN'T. I'VE DONE PLENTY OF DARNING FOR HIM, BUT NEVER EMBROIDERY...
AH.
SO YOU HAVEN'T!
smile smile
HOW AMAZING. HOW DOES ONE MAKE SUCH A THING?
fwap
I SUPPOSE MEN REALLY DON'T KNOW MUCH ABOUT SEWING, DO THEY?
WAIT A MOMENT.
I'LL SHOW YOU MY SEWING BOX.
TUP
EXCUSE ME.

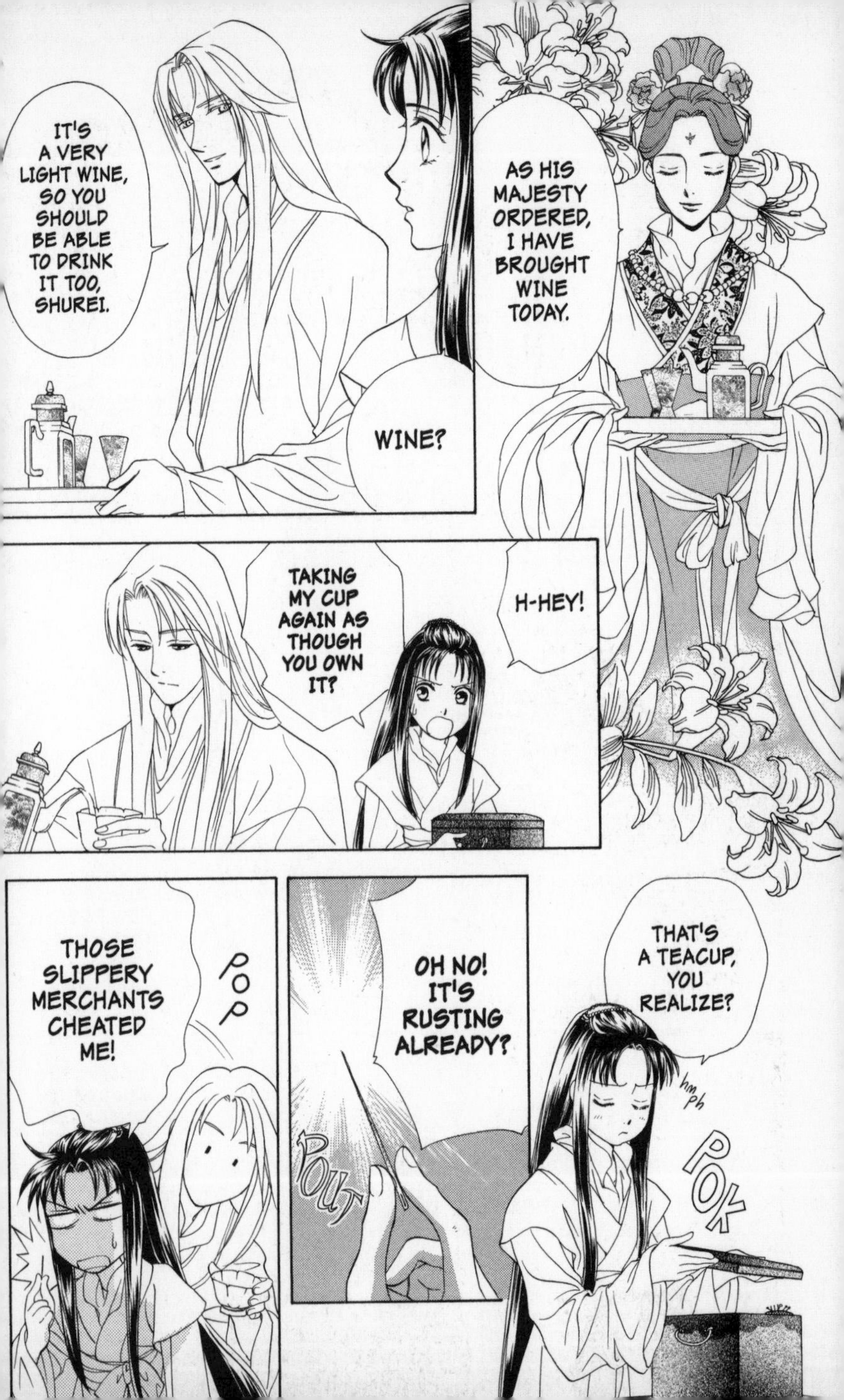
AS HIS MAJESTY ORDERED, I HAVE BROUGHT WINE TODAY.
WINE?
IT'S A VERY LIGHT WINE, SO YOU SHOULD BE ABLE TO DRINK IT TOO, SHUREI.
H-HEY!
TAKING MY CUP AGAIN AS THOUGH YOU OWN IT?
THAT'S A TEACUP, YOU REALIZE?
hmph
POK
OH NO! IT'S RUSTING ALREADY?
POUT
THOSE SLIPPERY MERCHANTS CHEATED ME!
POP

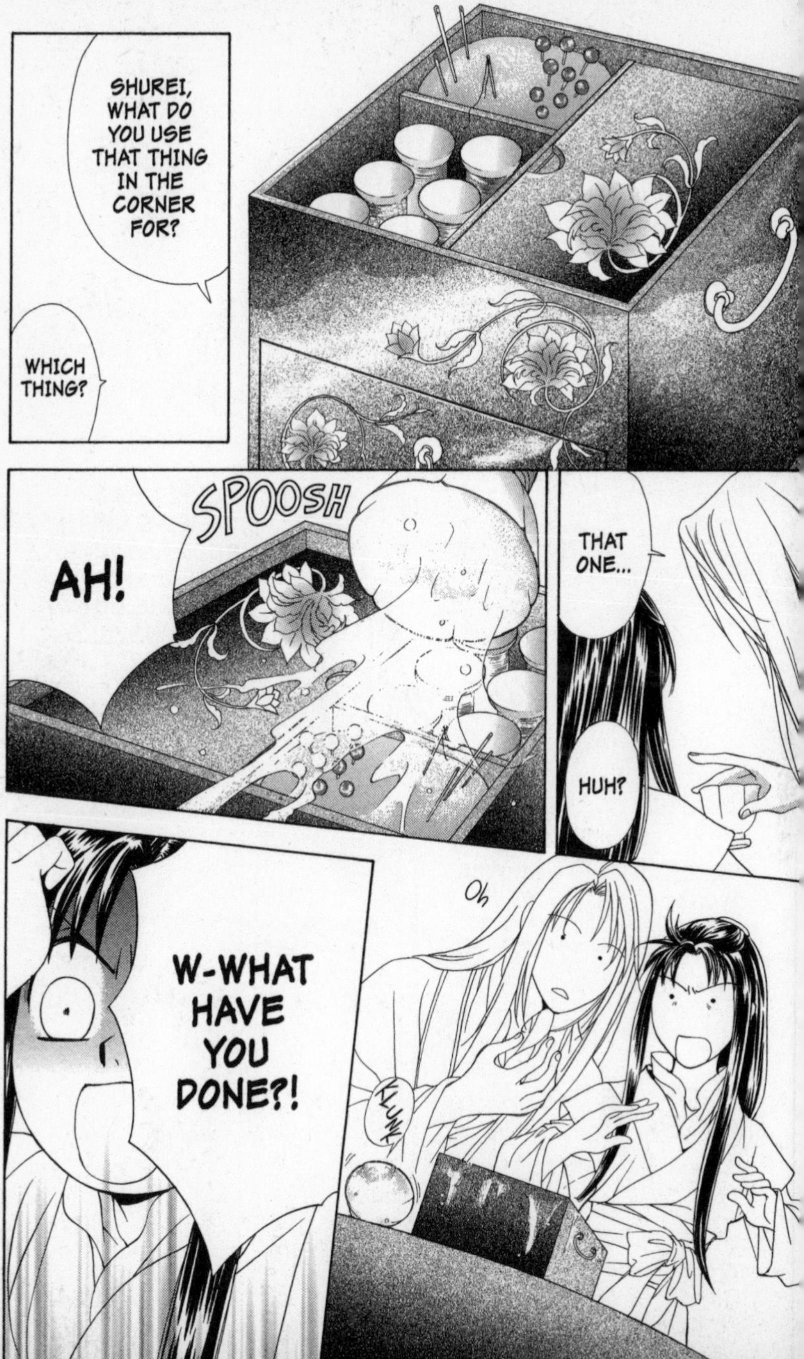
SHUREI, WHAT DO YOU USE THAT THING IN THE CORNER FOR?
WHICH THING?
THAT ONE...
HUH?
SPOOSH
AH!
Oh
KLUNK
W-WHAT HAVE YOU DONE?!

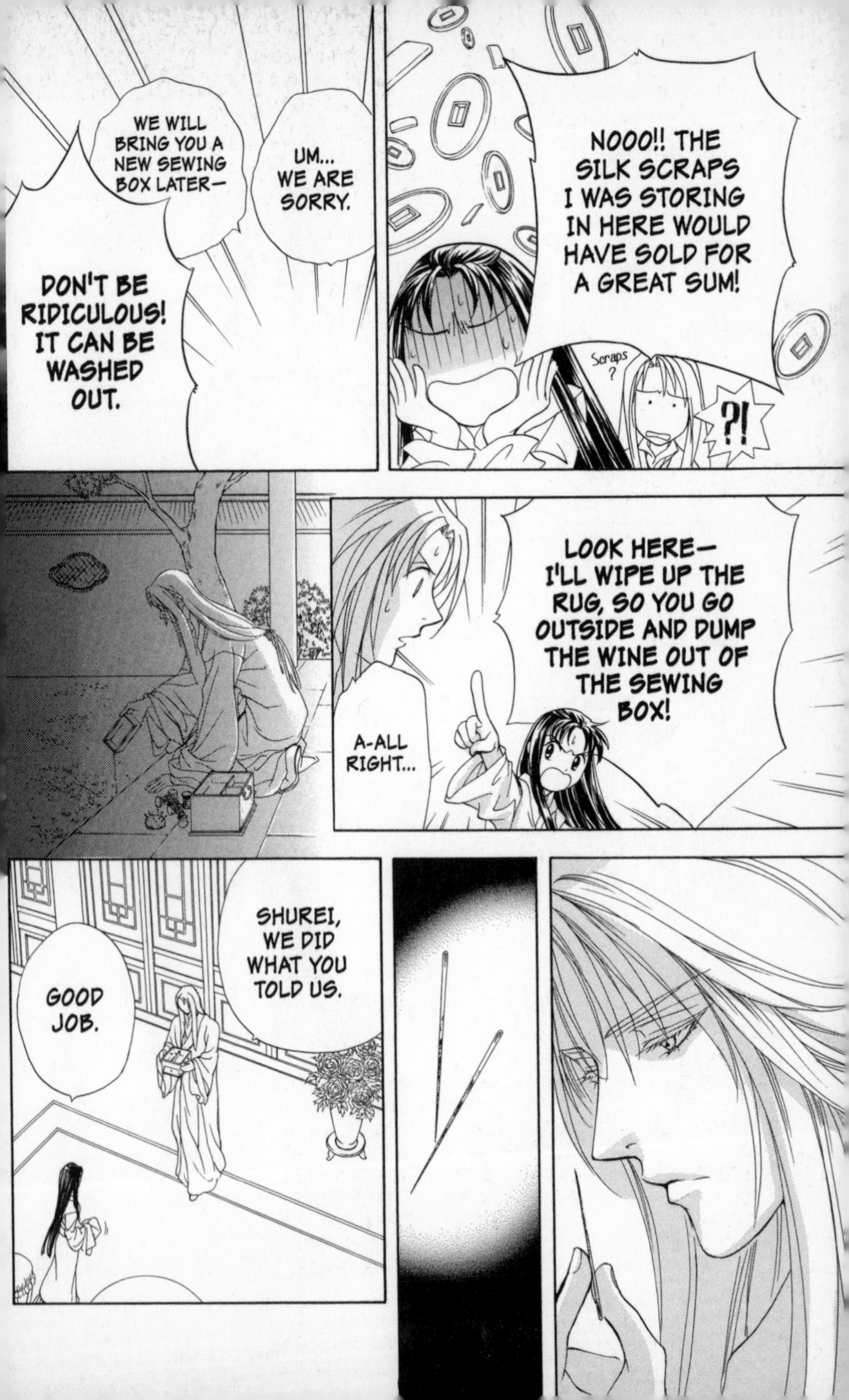
NOOO!! THE SILK SCRAPS I WAS STORING IN HERE WOULD HAVE SOLD FOR A GREAT SUM!
Scraps ?
?!
UM... WE ARE SORRY.
WE WILL BRING YOU A NEW SEWING BOX LATER—
DON'T BE RIDICULOUS! IT CAN BE WASHED OUT.
LOOK HERE— I'LL WIPE UP THE RUG, SO YOU GO OUTSIDE AND DUMP THE WINE OUT OF THE SEWING BOX!
A-ALL RIGHT...
SHUREI, WE DID WHAT YOU TOLD US.
GOOD JOB.

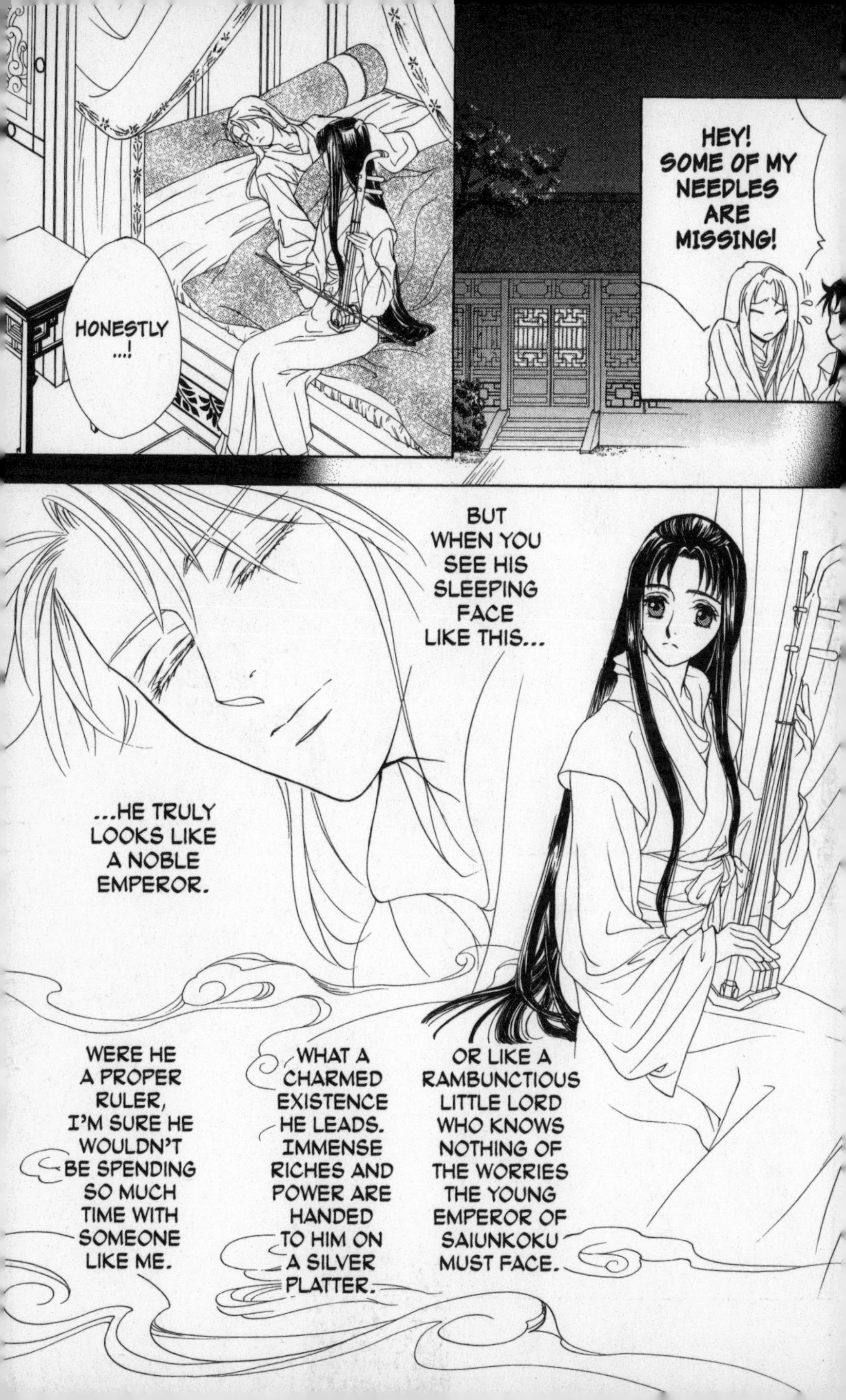
HEY! SOME OF MY NEEDLES ARE MISSING!
HONESTLY ...!
BUT WHEN YOU SEE HIS SLEEPING FACE LIKE THIS...
...HE TRULY LOOKS LIKE A NOBLE EMPEROR.
OR LIKE A RAMBUNCTIOUS LITTLE LORD WHO KNOWS NOTHING OF THE WORRIES THE YOUNG EMPEROR OF SAIUNKOKU MUST FACE.
WHAT A CHARMED EXISTENCE HE LEADS. IMMENSE RICHES AND POWER ARE HANDED TO HIM ON A SILVER PLATTER.
WERE HE A PROPER RULER, I'M SURE HE WOULDN'T BE SPENDING SO MUCH TIME WITH SOMEONE LIKE ME.

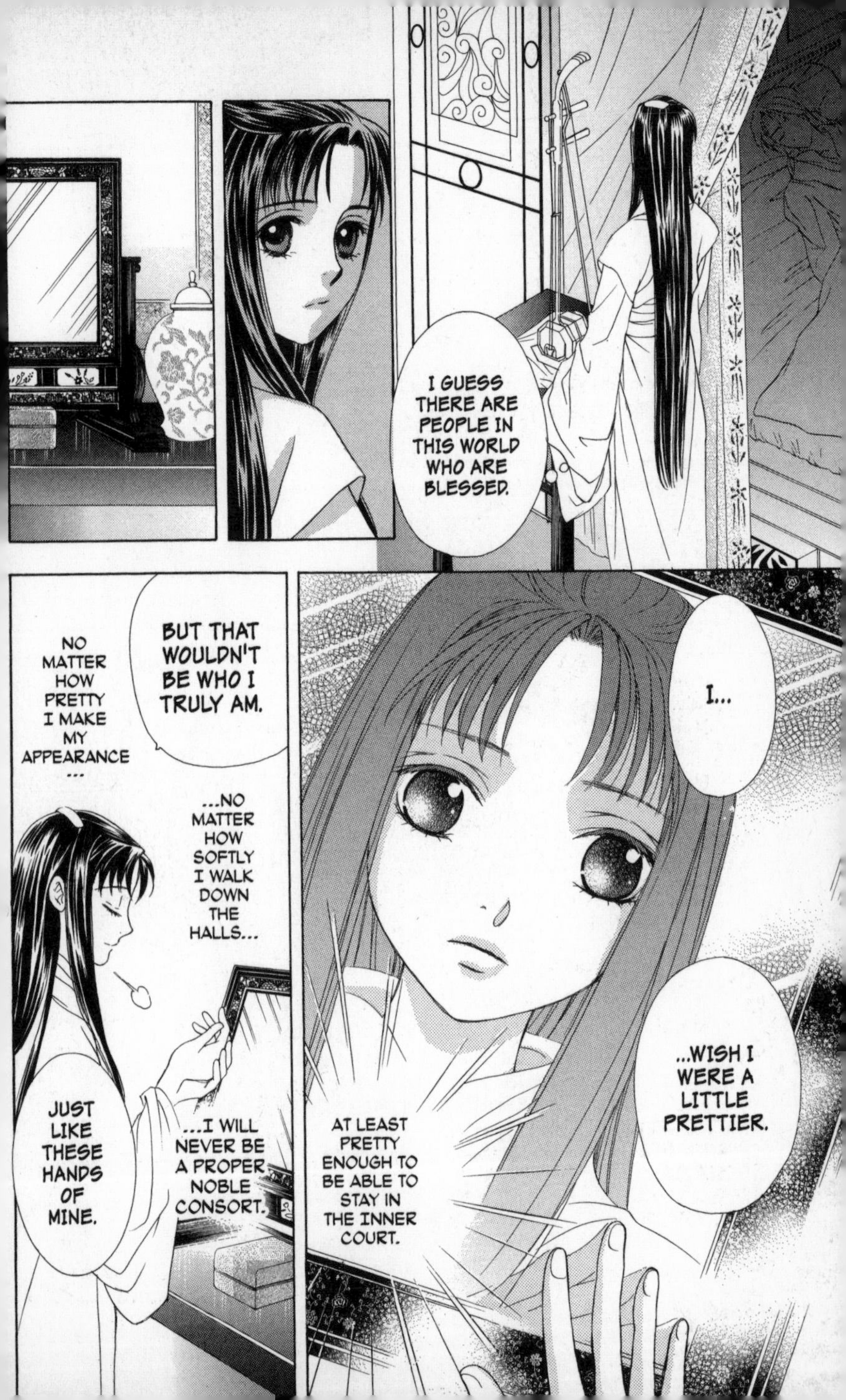
I GUESS THERE ARE PEOPLE IN THIS WORLD WHO ARE BLESSED.
I...
...WISH I WERE A LITTLE PRETTIER.
AT LEAST PRETTY ENOUGH TO BE ABLE TO STAY IN THE INNER COURT.
BUT THAT WOULDN'T BE WHO I TRULY AM.
NO MATTER HOW PRETTY I MAKE MY APPEARANCE...
...NO MATTER HOW SOFTLY I WALK DOWN THE HALLS...
...I WILL NEVER BE A PROPER NOBLE CONSORT.
JUST LIKE THESE HANDS OF MINE.

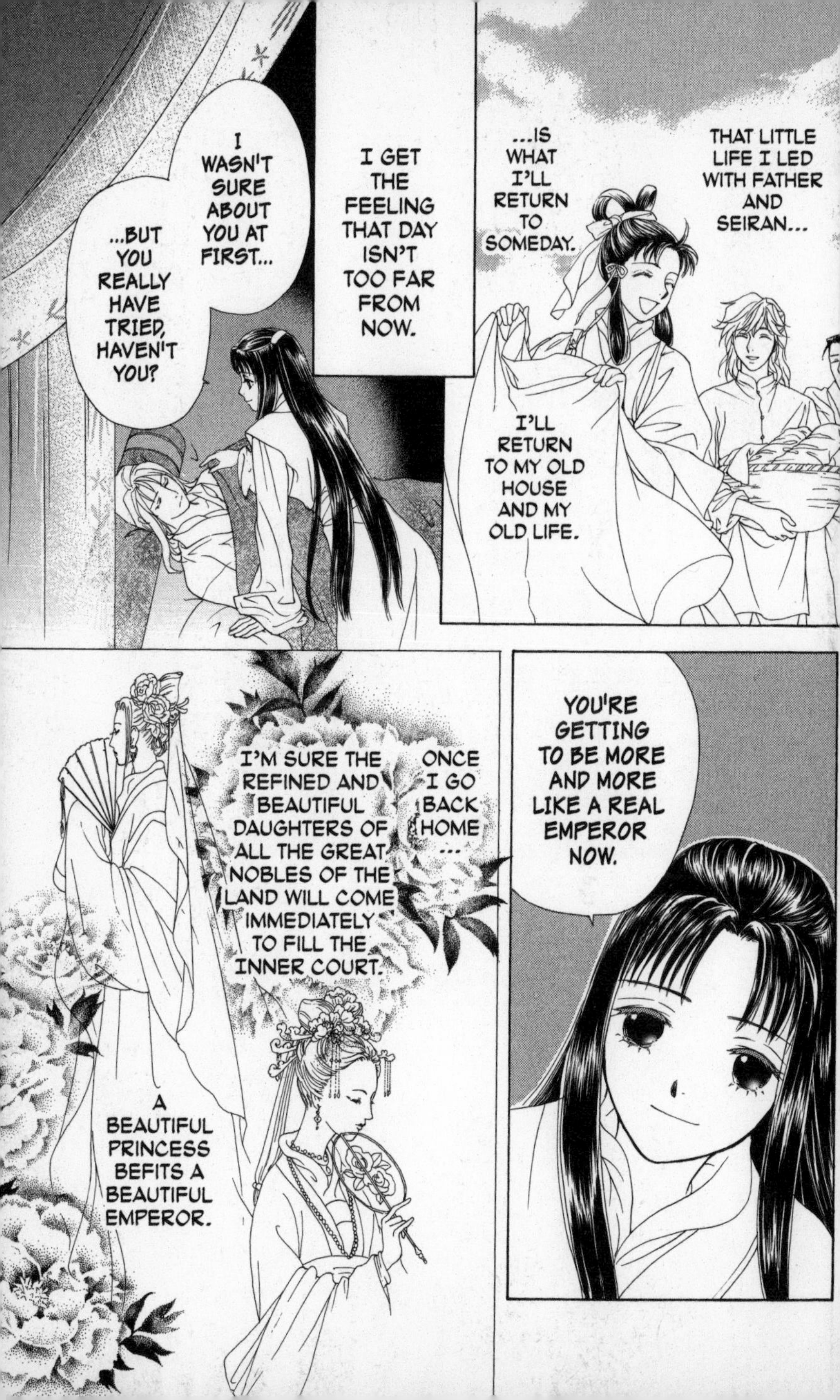
THAT LITTLE LIFE I LED WITH FATHER AND SEIRAN...
...IS WHAT I'LL RETURN TO SOMEDAY.
I'LL RETURN TO MY OLD HOUSE AND MY OLD LIFE.
I GET THE FEELING THAT DAY ISN'T TOO FAR FROM NOW.
I WASN'T SURE ABOUT YOU AT FIRST...
...BUT YOU REALLY HAVE TRIED, HAVEN'T YOU?
YOU'RE GETTING TO BE MORE AND MORE LIKE A REAL EMPEROR NOW.
ONCE I GO BACK HOME...
I'M SURE THE REFINED AND BEAUTIFUL DAUGHTERS OF ALL THE GREAT NOBLES OF THE LAND WILL COME IMMEDIATELY TO FILL THE INNER COURT.
A BEAUTIFUL PRINCESS BEFITS A BEAUTIFUL EMPEROR.

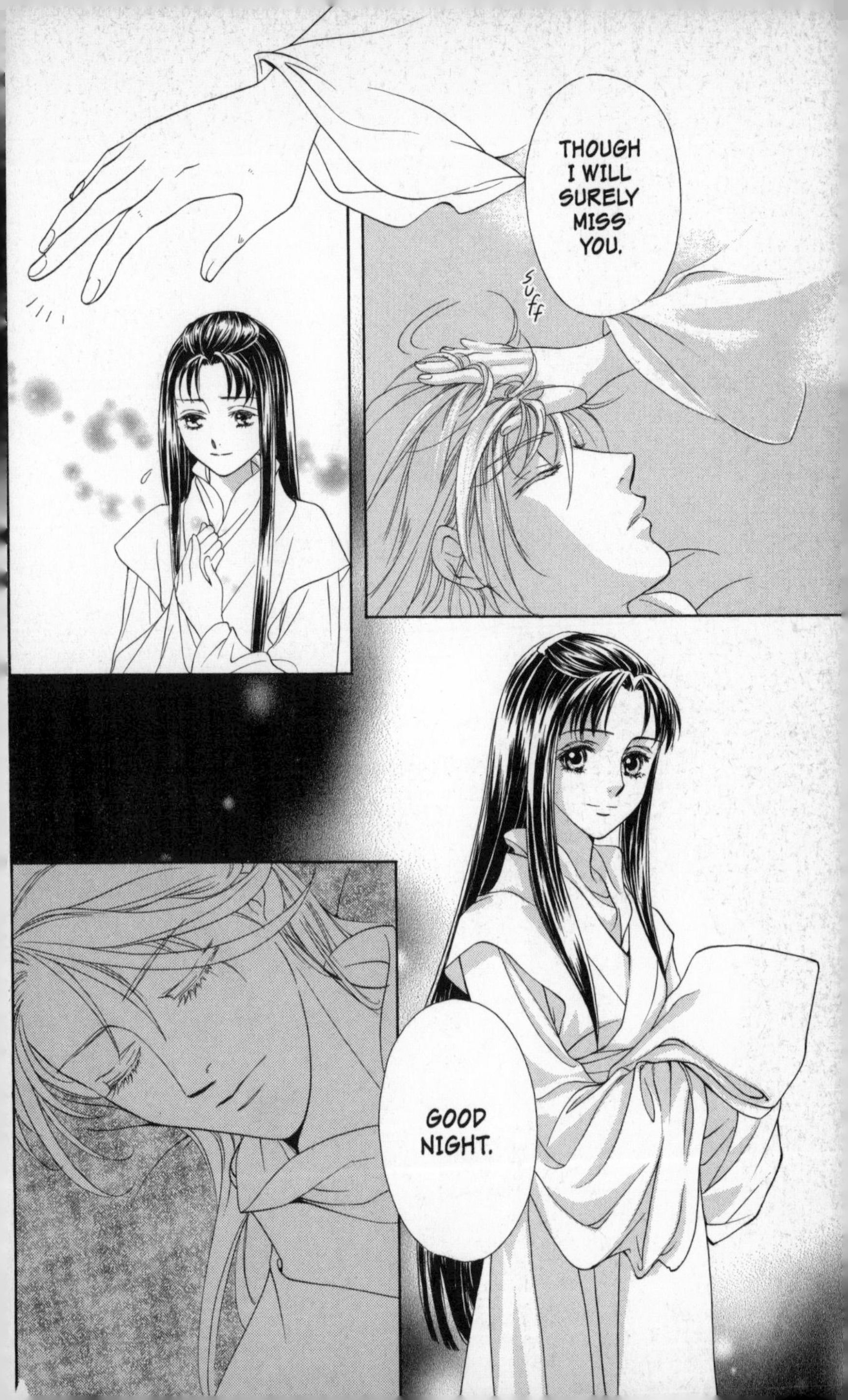

THOUGH I WILL SURELY MISS YOU.
suff
GOOD NIGHT.

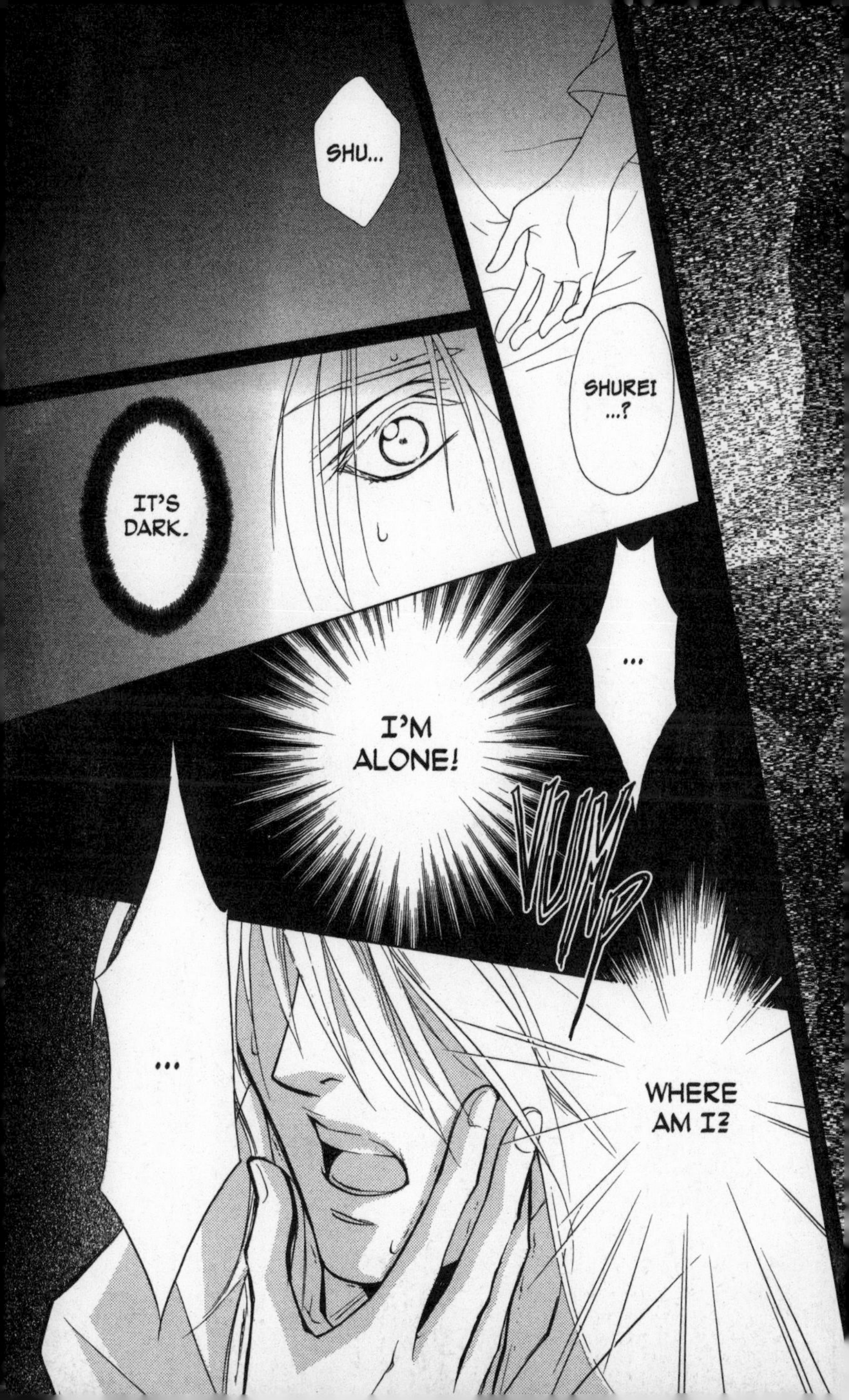
SHUREI ...?
SHU...
IT'S DARK.
...
I'M ALONE!
VUMP
WHERE AM I?
...

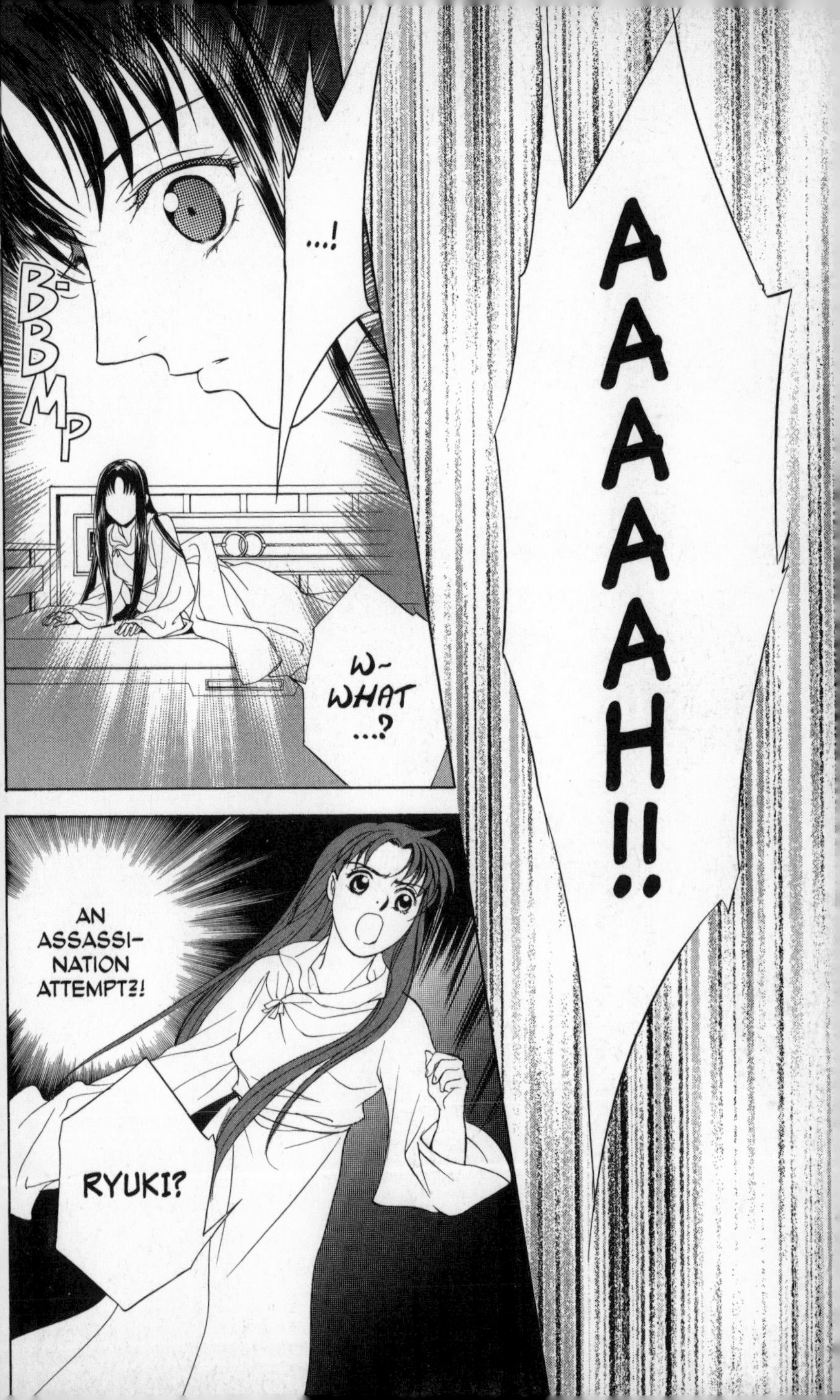
AAAAAH!!
...!
B-BBMP
W-WHAT...?
AN ASSASSI-NATION ATTEMPT?!
RYUKI?

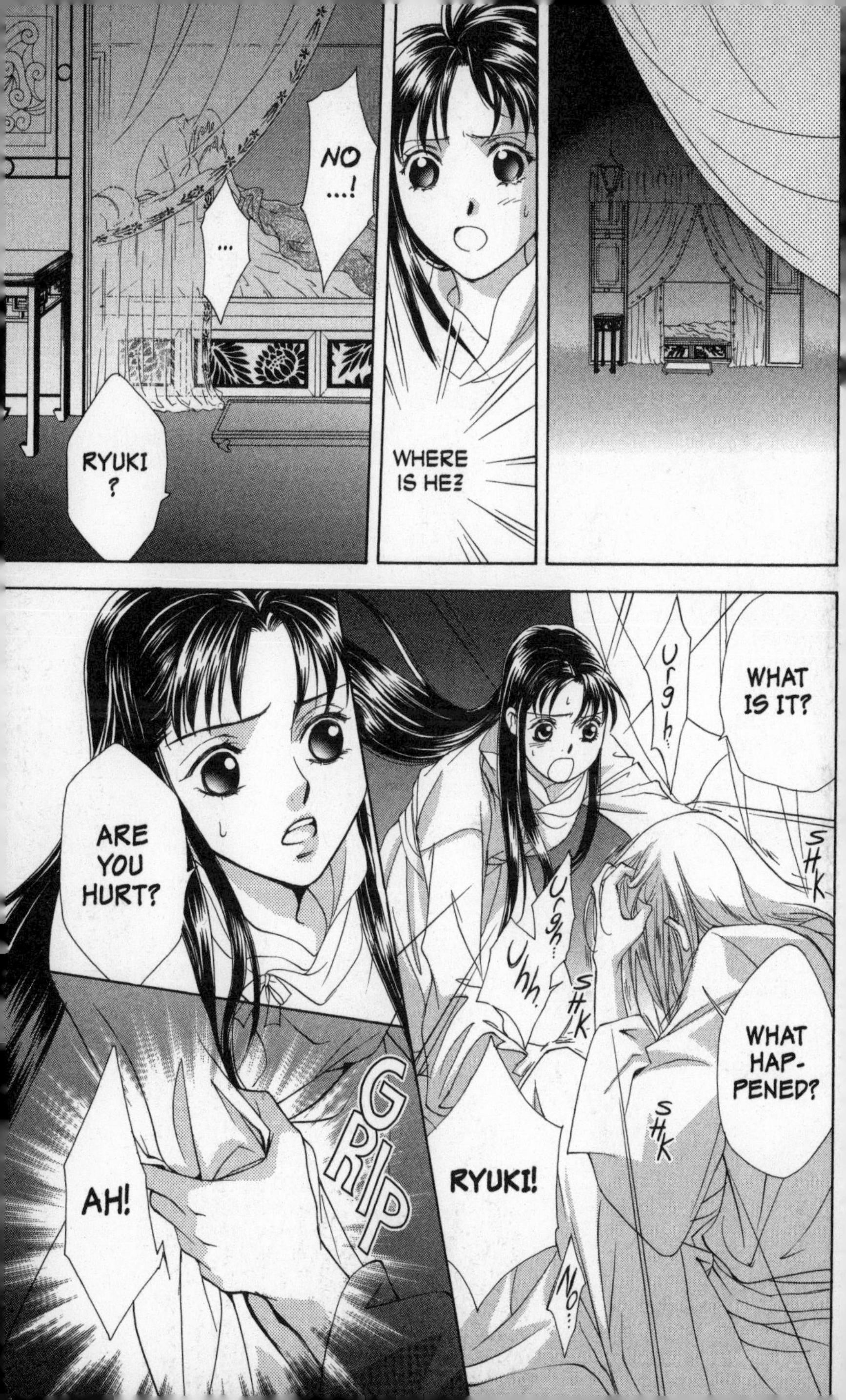
WHERE IS HE?
NO ...!
...
RYUKI ?
WHAT IS IT?
Urgh...
SHK
Urgh...
Uhh.
SHK
WHAT HAP-PENED?
SHK
RYUKI!
No...
ARE YOU HURT?
GRIP
AH!

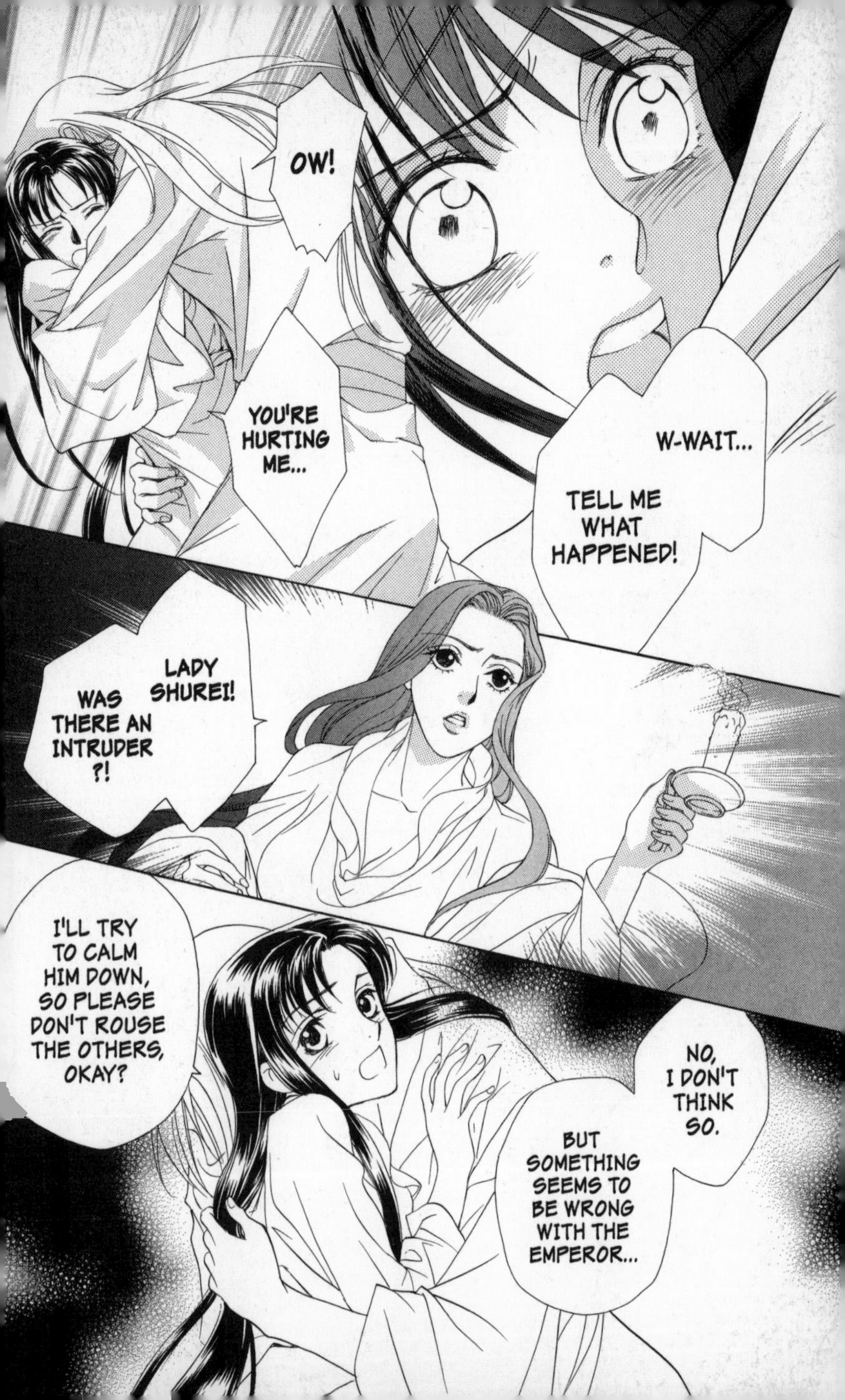
OW!
YOU'RE HURTING ME...
W-WAIT...
TELL ME WHAT HAPPENED!
LADY SHUREI!
WAS THERE AN INTRUDER ?!
NO, I DON'T THINK SO.
BUT SOMETHING SEEMS TO BE WRONG WITH THE EMPEROR...
I'LL TRY TO CALM HIM DOWN, SO PLEASE DON'T ROUSE THE OTHERS, OKAY?

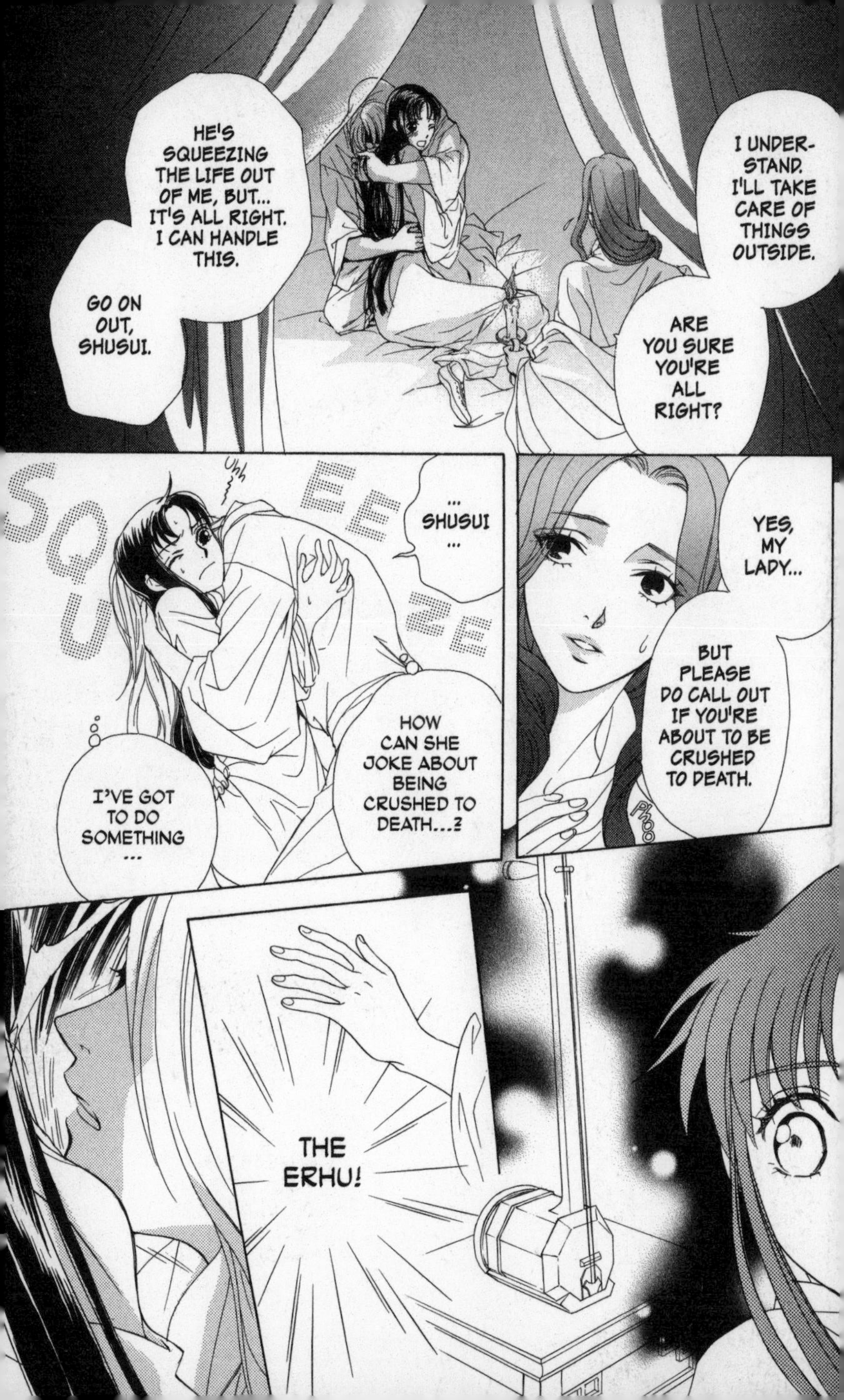
I UNDER-STAND. I'LL TAKE CARE OF THINGS OUTSIDE.
HE'S SQUEEZING THE LIFE OUT OF ME, BUT... IT'S ALL RIGHT. I CAN HANDLE THIS.
ARE YOU SURE YOU'RE ALL RIGHT?
GO ON OUT, SHUSUI.
YES, MY LADY...
BUT PLEASE DO CALL OUT IF YOU'RE ABOUT TO BE CRUSHED TO DEATH.
Phoo
... SHUSUI ...
SQUEEZE
Uhh
HOW CAN SHE JOKE ABOUT BEING CRUSHED TO DEATH...?
I'VE GOT TO DO SOMETHING ...
THE ERHU!

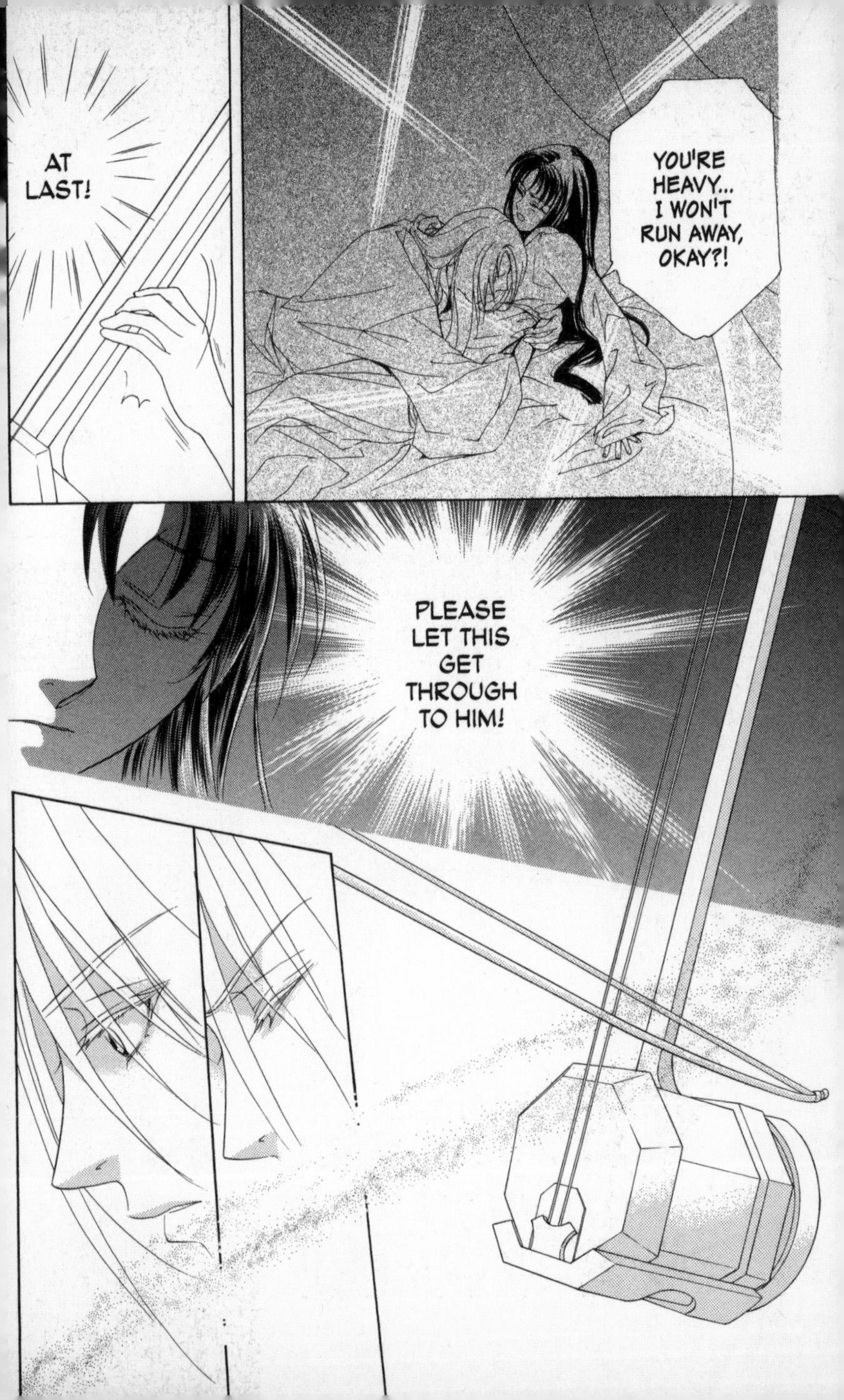
YOU'RE HEAVY... I WON'T RUN AWAY, OKAY?!
AT LAST!
PLEASE LET THIS GET THROUGH TO HIM!

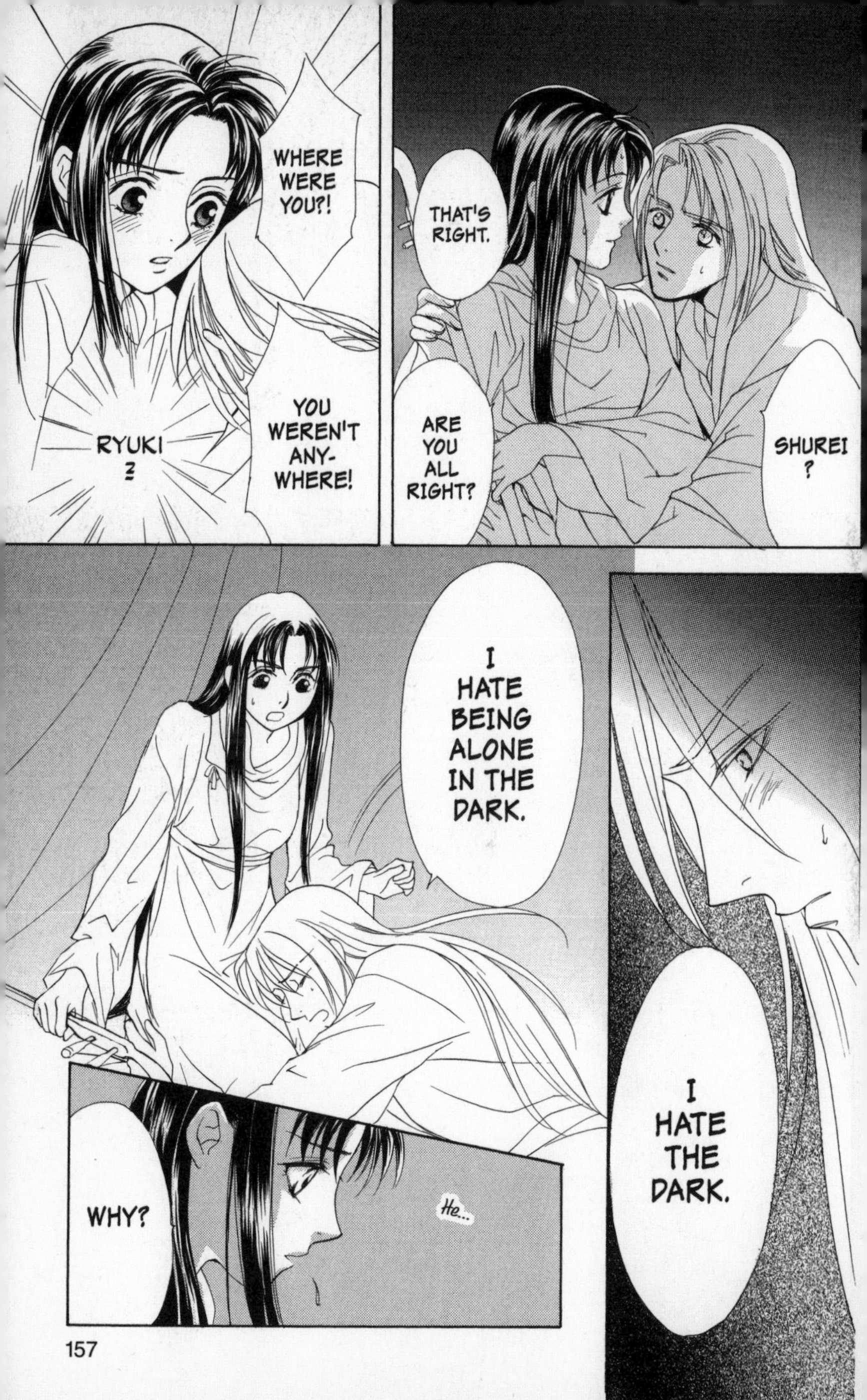
SHUREI?
THAT'S RIGHT.
ARE YOU ALL RIGHT?
WHERE WERE YOU?!
YOU WEREN'T ANYWHERE!
RYUKI?
I HATE THE DARK.
I HATE BEING ALONE IN THE DARK.
He...
WHY?

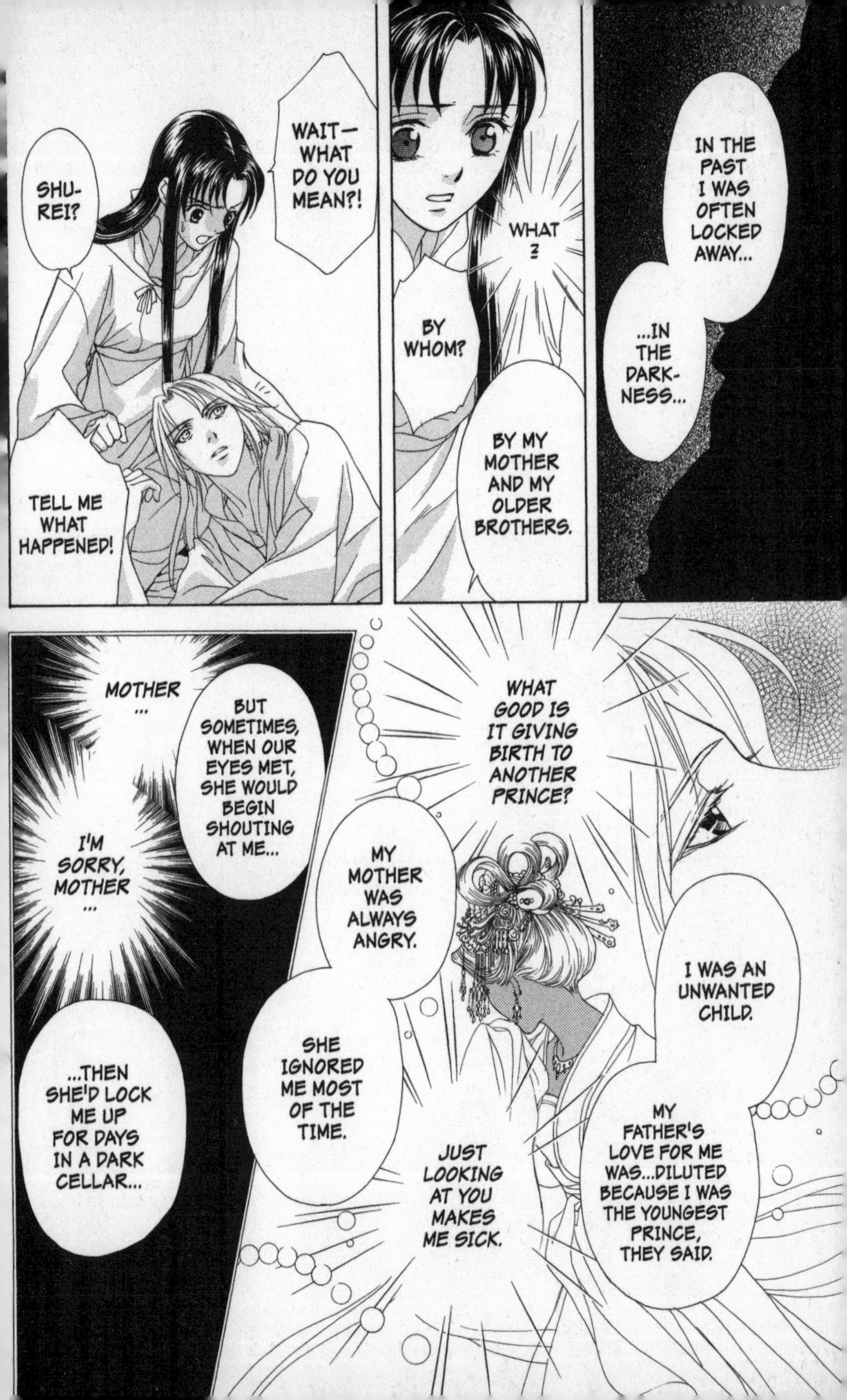
IN THE PAST I WAS OFTEN LOCKED AWAY...
...IN THE DARKNESS...
WHAT?
BY WHOM?
BY MY MOTHER AND MY OLDER BROTHERS.
WAIT—WHAT DO YOU MEAN?!
SHU-REI?
TELL ME WHAT HAPPENED!
WHAT GOOD IS IT GIVING BIRTH TO ANOTHER PRINCE?
I WAS AN UNWANTED CHILD.
MY FATHER'S LOVE FOR ME WAS...DILUTED BECAUSE I WAS THE YOUNGEST PRINCE, THEY SAID.
MY MOTHER WAS ALWAYS ANGRY.
JUST LOOKING AT YOU MAKES ME SICK.
SHE IGNORED ME MOST OF THE TIME.
BUT SOMETIMES, WHEN OUR EYES MET, SHE WOULD BEGIN SHOUTING AT ME...
MOTHER...
I'M SORRY, MOTHER...
...THEN SHE'D LOCK ME UP FOR DAYS IN A DARK CELLAR...

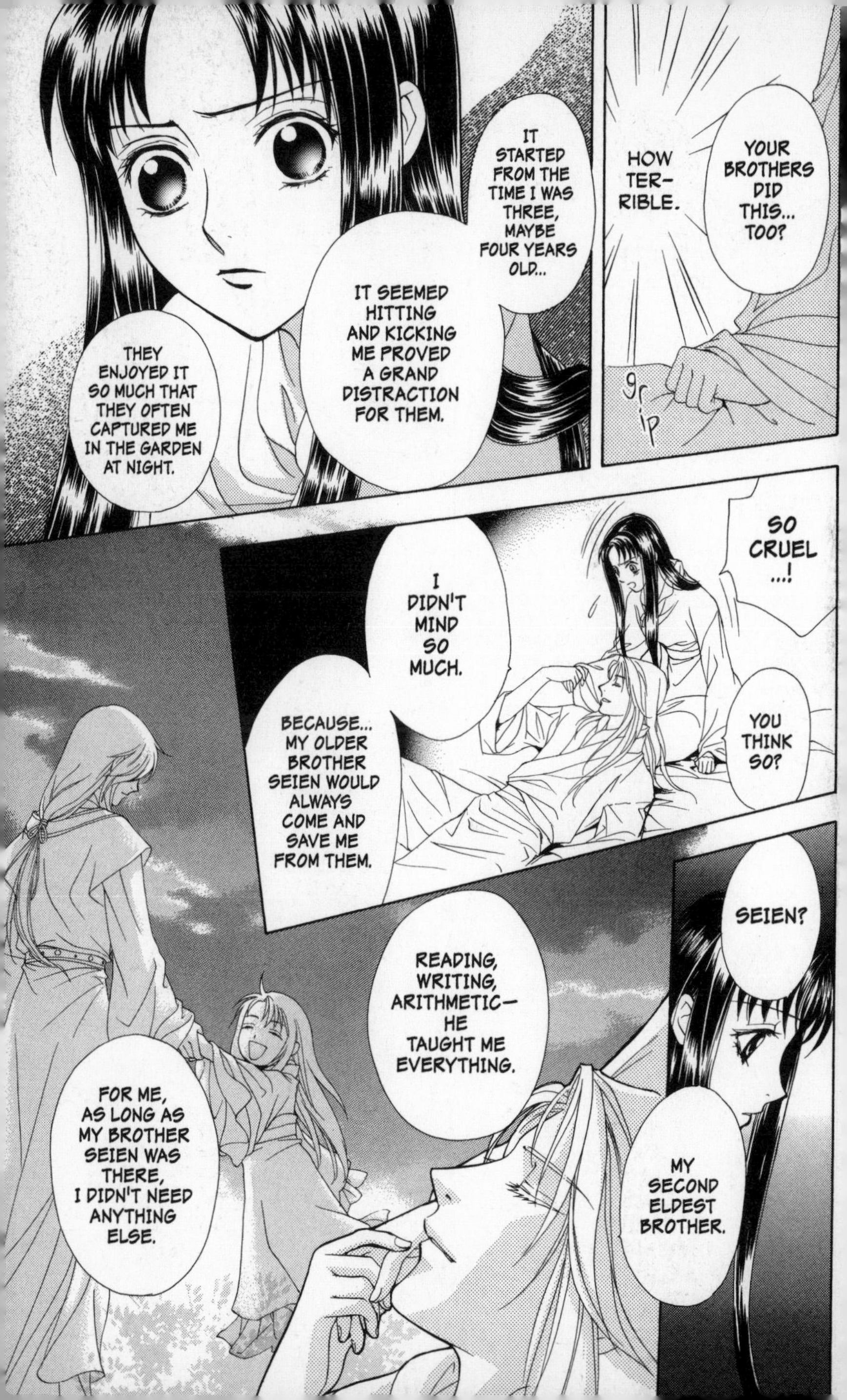
YOUR BROTHERS DID THIS... TOO?
HOW TER-RIBLE.
grip
IT STARTED FROM THE TIME I WAS THREE, MAYBE FOUR YEARS OLD...
IT SEEMED HITTING AND KICKING ME PROVED A GRAND DISTRACTION FOR THEM.
THEY ENJOYED IT SO MUCH THAT THEY OFTEN CAPTURED ME IN THE GARDEN AT NIGHT.
SO CRUEL ...!
I DIDN'T MIND SO MUCH.
YOU THINK SO?
BECAUSE... MY OLDER BROTHER SEIEN WOULD ALWAYS COME AND SAVE ME FROM THEM.
SEIEN?
READING, WRITING, ARITHMETIC— HE TAUGHT ME EVERYTHING.
MY SECOND ELDEST BROTHER.
FOR ME, AS LONG AS MY BROTHER SEIEN WAS THERE, I DIDN'T NEED ANYTHING ELSE.

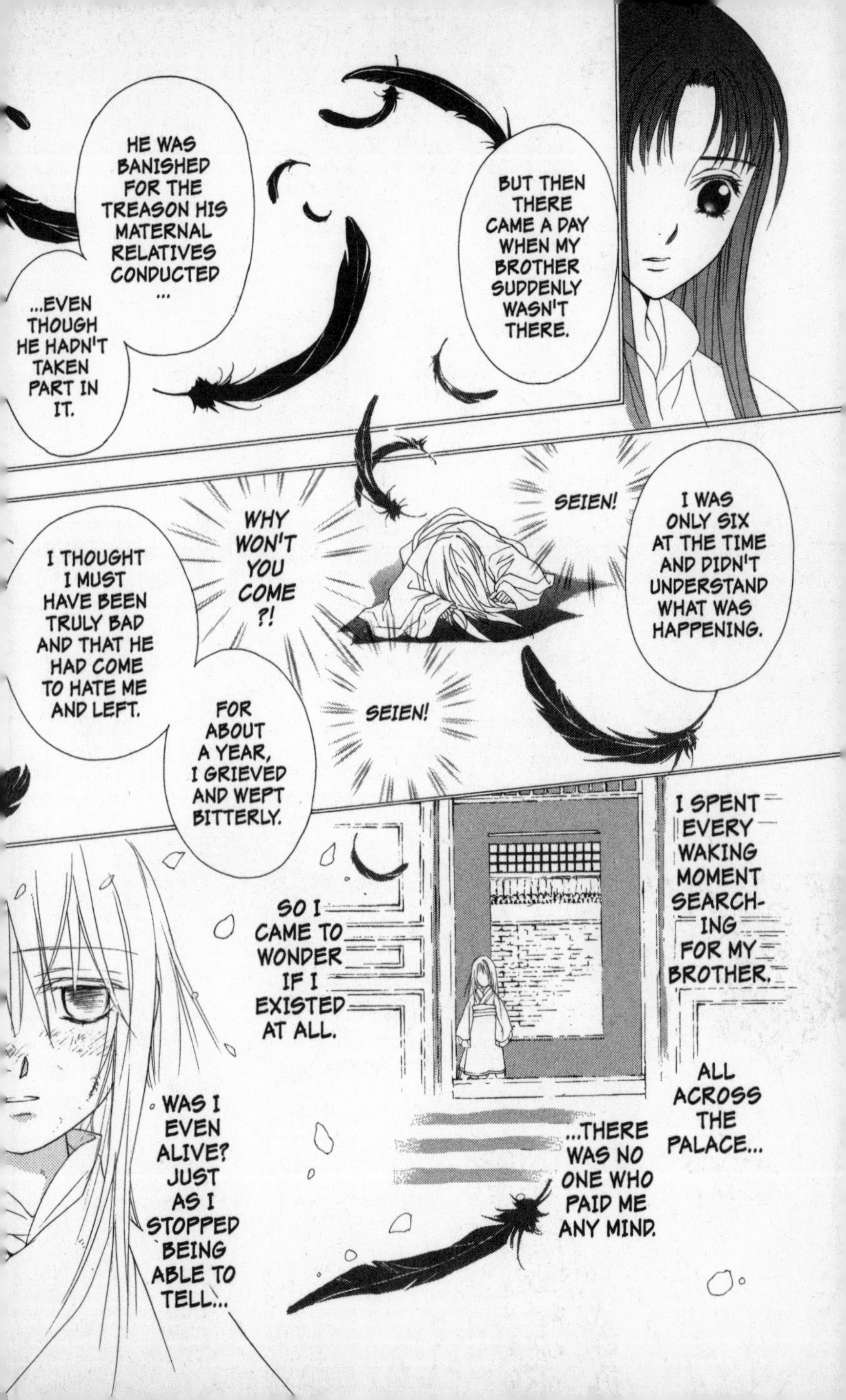
BUT THEN THERE CAME A DAY WHEN MY BROTHER SUDDENLY WASN'T THERE.
HE WAS BANISHED FOR THE TREASON HIS MATERNAL RELATIVES CONDUCTED...
...EVEN THOUGH HE HADN'T TAKEN PART IN IT.
I WAS ONLY SIX AT THE TIME AND DIDN'T UNDERSTAND WHAT WAS HAPPENING.
SEIEN!
WHY WON'T YOU COME?!
SEIEN!
FOR ABOUT A YEAR, I GRIEVED AND WEPT BITTERLY.
I THOUGHT I MUST HAVE BEEN TRULY BAD AND THAT HE HAD COME TO HATE ME AND LEFT.
I SPENT EVERY WAKING MOMENT SEARCH-ING FOR MY BROTHER.
ALL ACROSS THE PALACE...
...THERE WAS NO ONE WHO PAID ME ANY MIND.
SO I CAME TO WONDER IF I EXISTED AT ALL.
WAS I EVEN ALIVE? JUST AS I STOPPED BEING ABLE TO TELL...

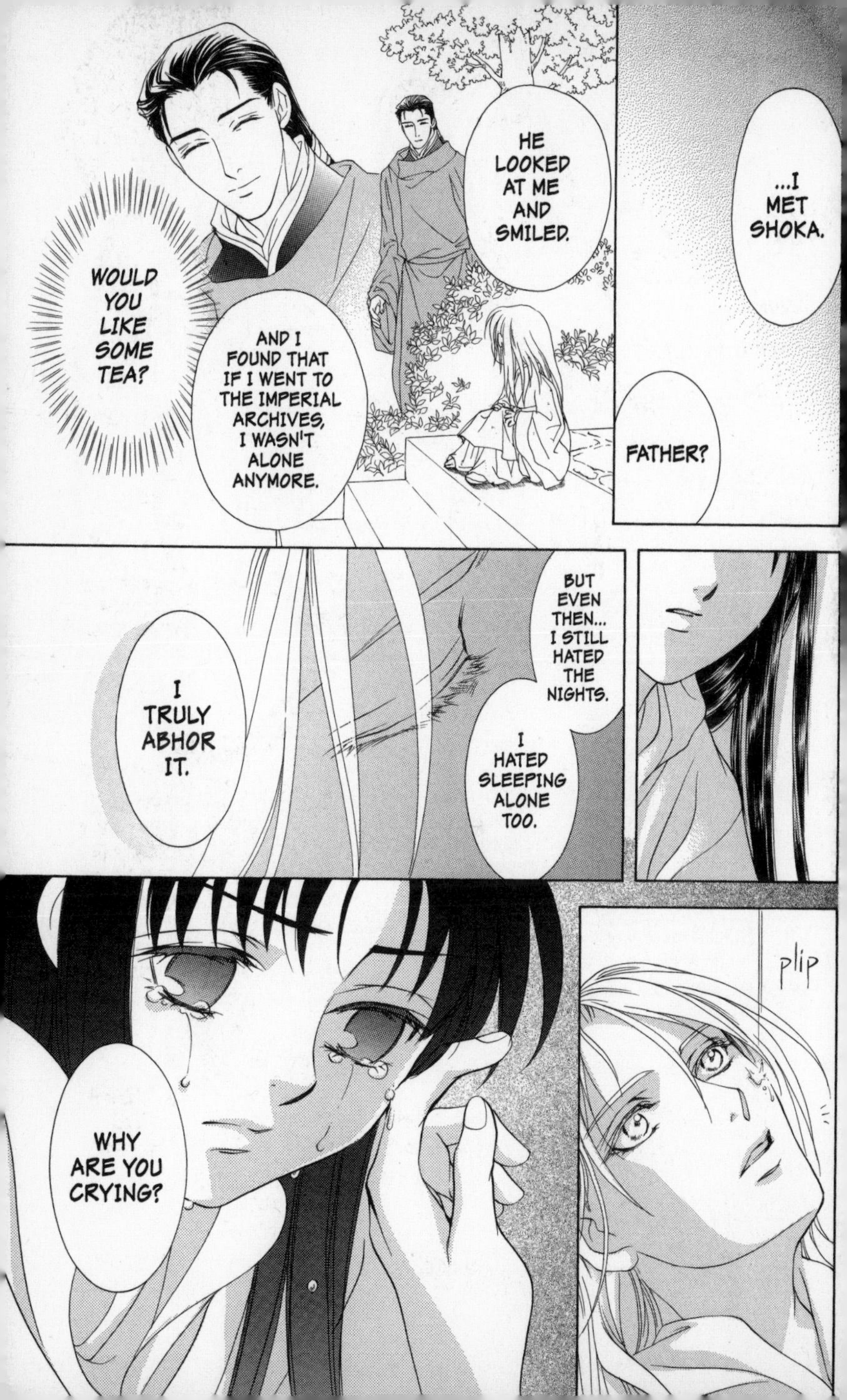
...I MET SHOKA.
FATHER?
HE LOOKED AT ME AND SMILED.
WOULD YOU LIKE SOME TEA?
AND I FOUND THAT IF I WENT TO THE IMPERIAL ARCHIVES, I WASN'T ALONE ANYMORE.
BUT EVEN THEN... I STILL HATED THE NIGHTS.
I HATED SLEEPING ALONE TOO.
I TRULY ABHOR IT.
plip
WHY ARE YOU CRYING?

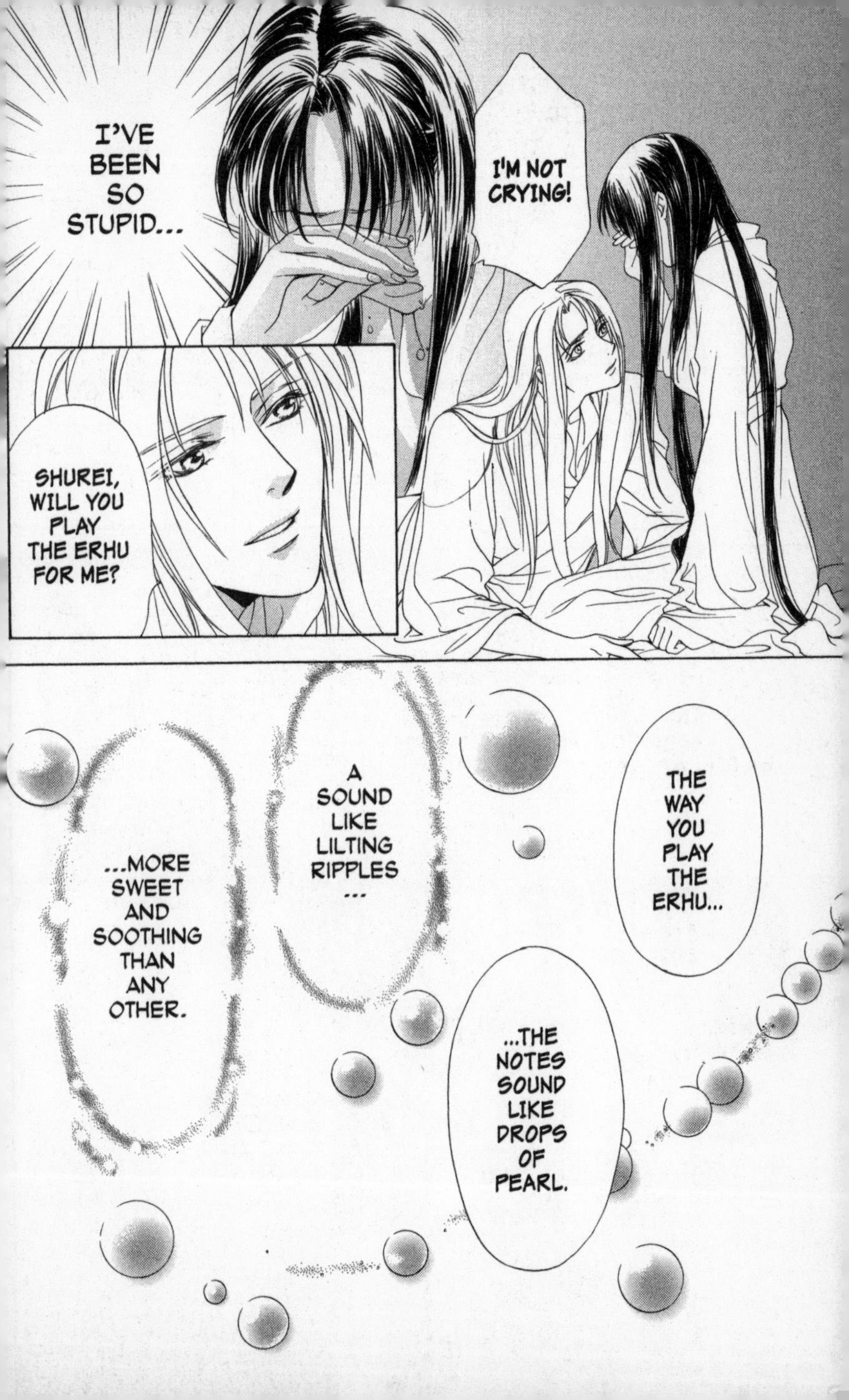
I'M NOT CRYING!
I'VE BEEN SO STUPID...
SHUREI, WILL YOU PLAY THE ERHU FOR ME?
THE WAY YOU PLAY THE ERHU...
...THE NOTES SOUND LIKE DROPS OF PEARL.
A SOUND LIKE LILTING RIPPLES...
...MORE SWEET AND SOOTHING THAN ANY OTHER.

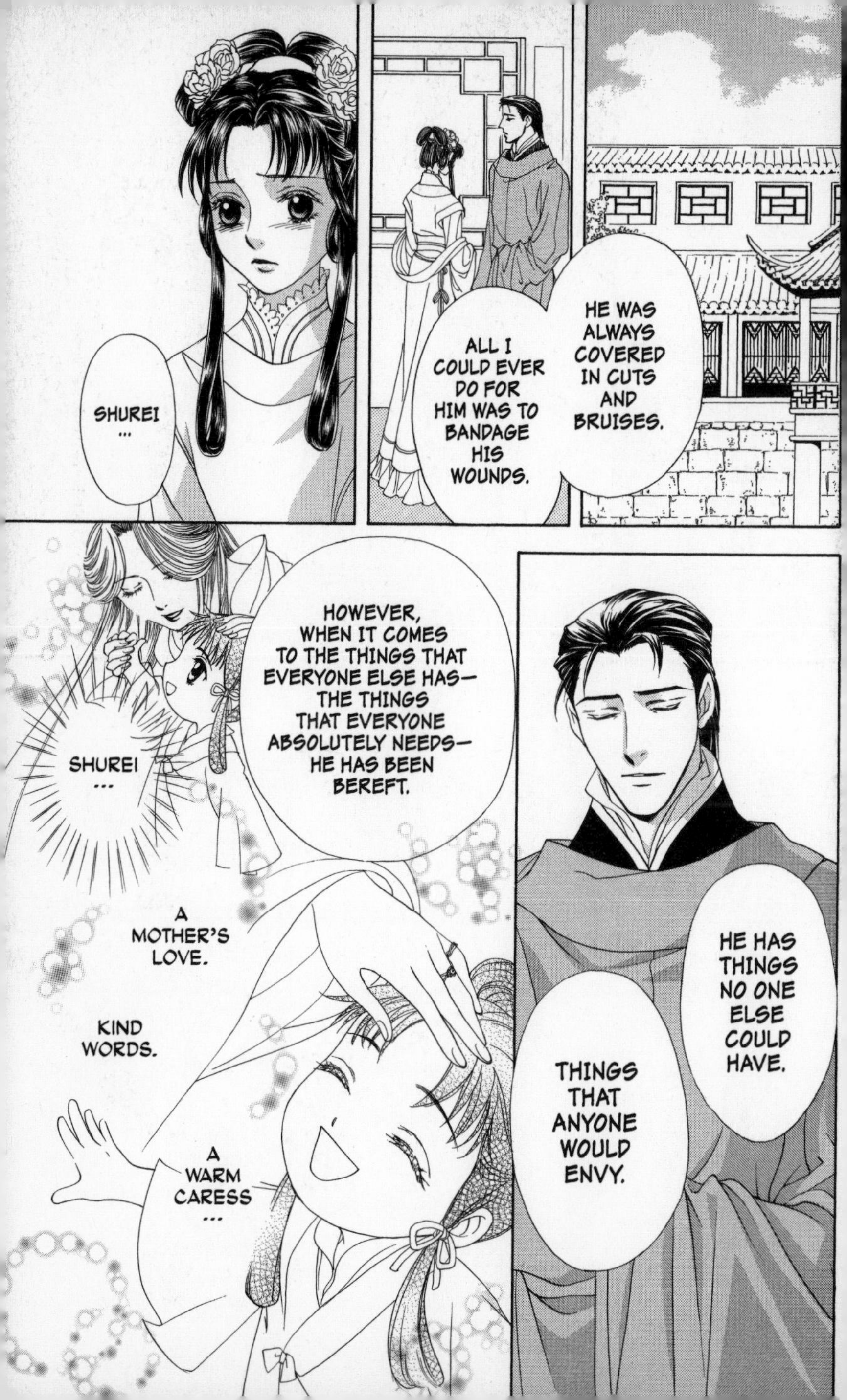
HE WAS ALWAYS COVERED IN CUTS AND BRUISES.
ALL I COULD EVER DO FOR HIM WAS TO BANDAGE HIS WOUNDS.
SHUREI ...
HE HAS THINGS NO ONE ELSE COULD HAVE.
THINGS THAT ANYONE WOULD ENVY.
HOWEVER, WHEN IT COMES TO THE THINGS THAT EVERYONE ELSE HAS—THE THINGS THAT EVERYONE ABSOLUTELY NEEDS—HE HAS BEEN BEREFT.
SHUREI ...
A MOTHER'S LOVE.
KIND WORDS.
A WARM CARESS ...

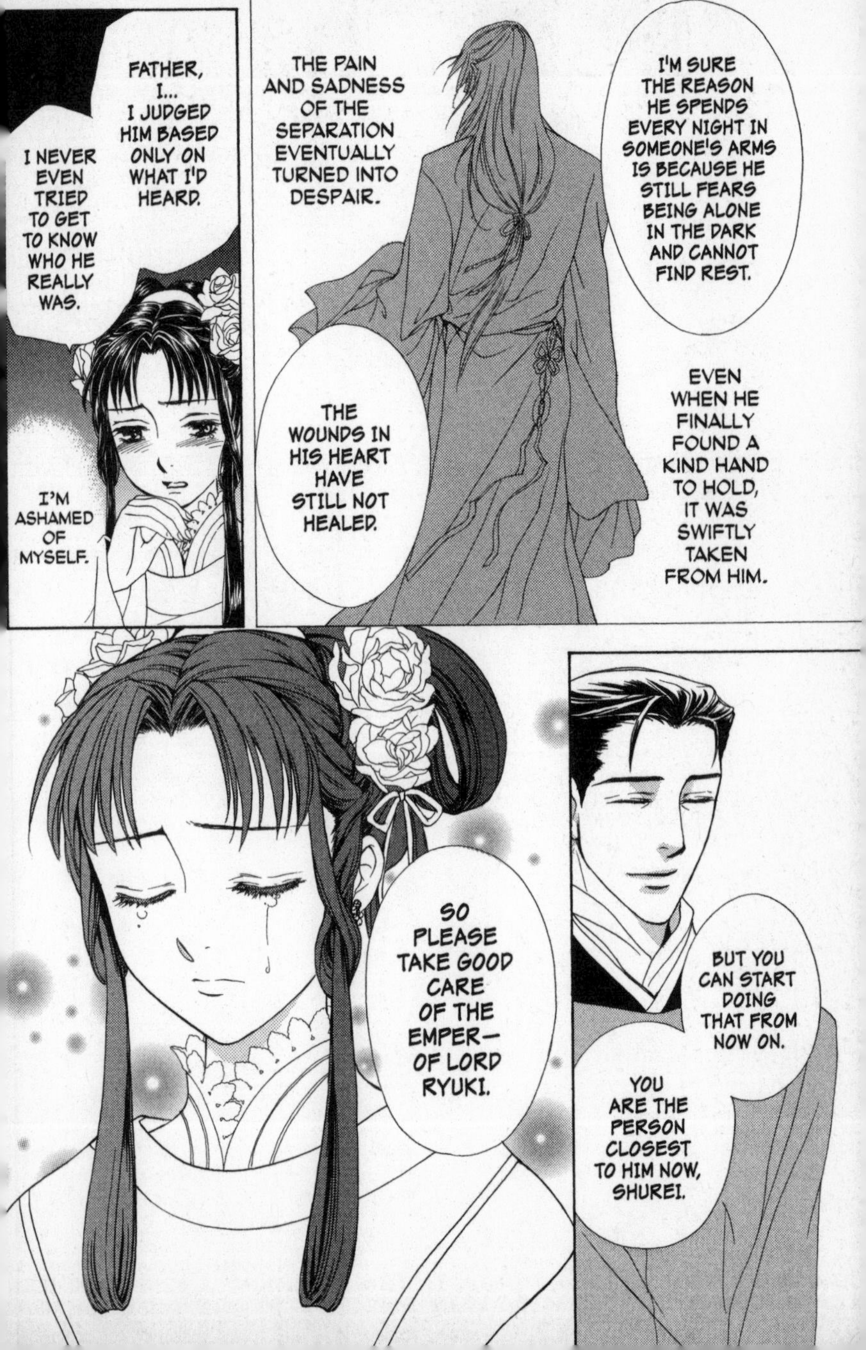
I'M SURE THE REASON HE SPENDS EVERY NIGHT IN SOMEONE'S ARMS IS BECAUSE HE STILL FEARS BEING ALONE IN THE DARK AND CANNOT FIND REST.
THE PAIN AND SADNESS OF THE SEPARATION EVENTUALLY TURNED INTO DESPAIR.
EVEN WHEN HE FINALLY FOUND A KIND HAND TO HOLD, IT WAS SWIFTLY TAKEN FROM HIM.
THE WOUNDS IN HIS HEART HAVE STILL NOT HEALED.
FATHER, I... I JUDGED HIM BASED ONLY ON WHAT I'D HEARD.
I NEVER EVEN TRIED TO GET TO KNOW WHO HE REALLY WAS.
I'M ASHAMED OF MYSELF.
BUT YOU CAN START DOING THAT FROM NOW ON.
YOU ARE THE PERSON CLOSEST TO HIM NOW, SHUREI.
SO PLEASE TAKE GOOD CARE OF THE EMPER— OF LORD RYUKI.

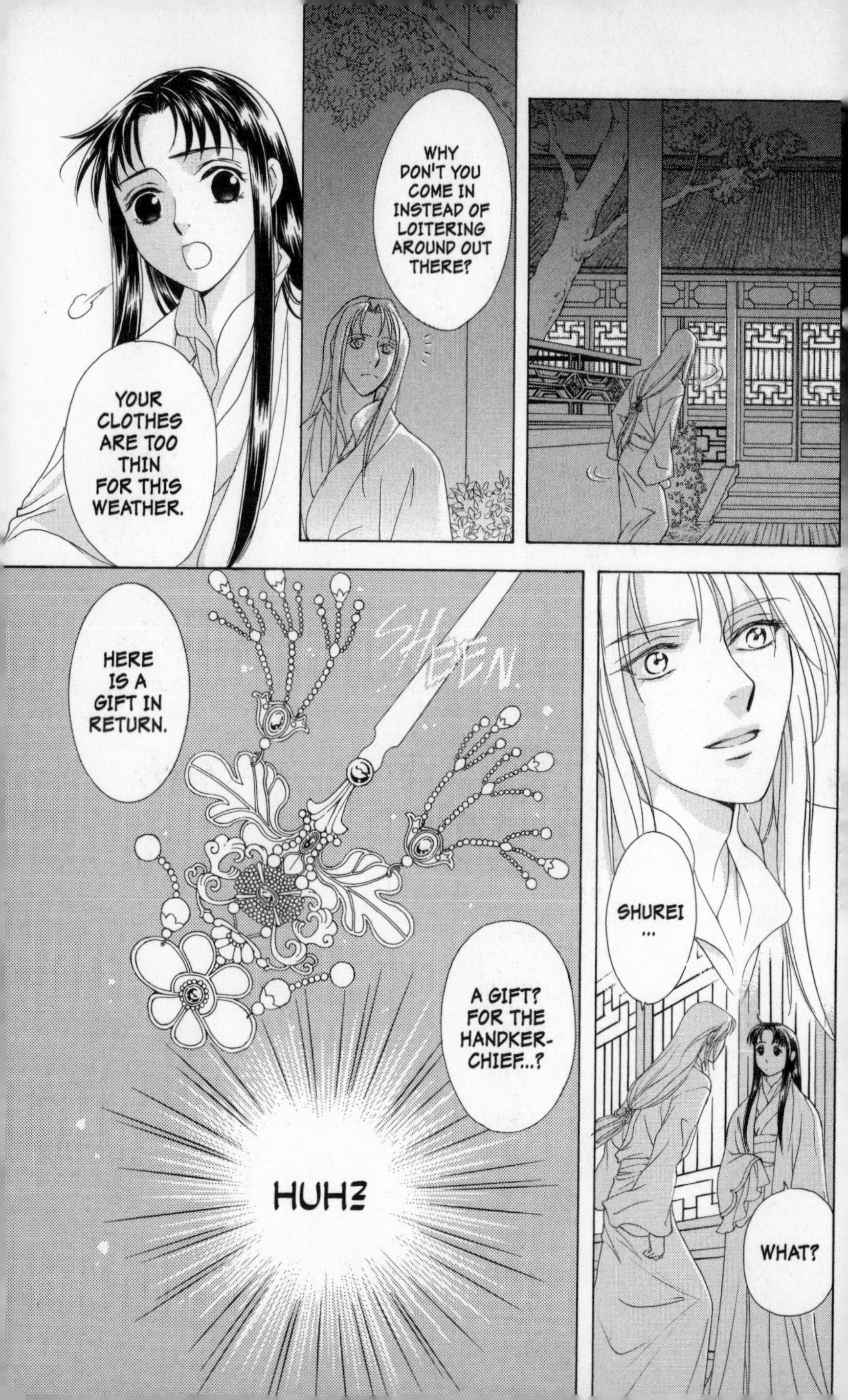
WHY DON'T YOU COME IN INSTEAD OF LOITERING AROUND OUT THERE?
YOUR CLOTHES ARE TOO THIN FOR THIS WEATHER.
SHUREI ...
WHAT?
HERE IS A GIFT IN RETURN.
SHEEN
A GIFT? FOR THE HANDKER-CHIEF...?
HUH?

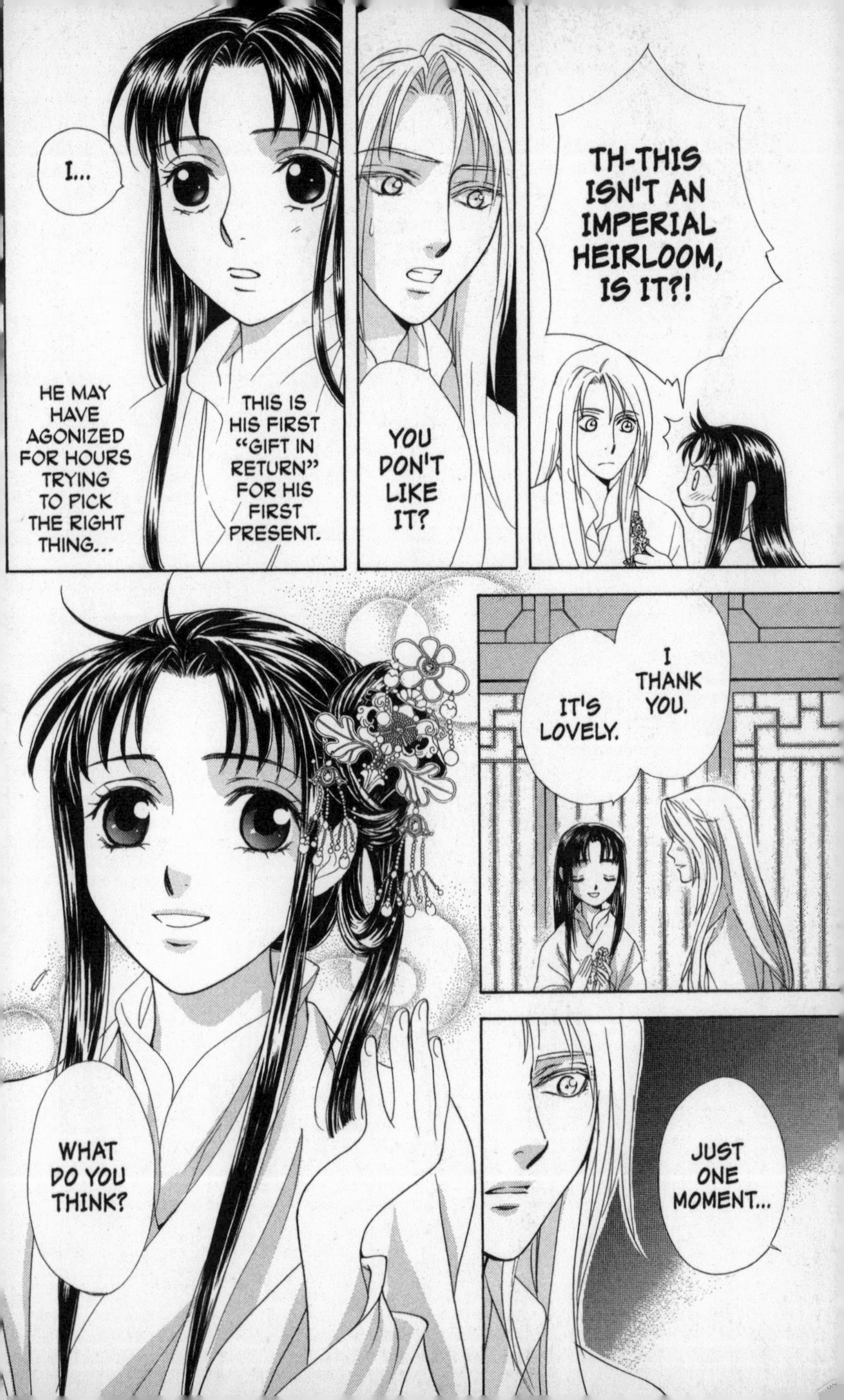
TH-THIS ISN'T AN IMPERIAL HEIRLOOM, IS IT?!
YOU DON'T LIKE IT?
I...
THIS IS HIS FIRST "GIFT IN RETURN" FOR HIS FIRST PRESENT.
HE MAY HAVE AGONIZED FOR HOURS TRYING TO PICK THE RIGHT THING...
I THANK YOU.
IT'S LOVELY.
JUST ONE MOMENT...
WHAT DO YOU THINK?

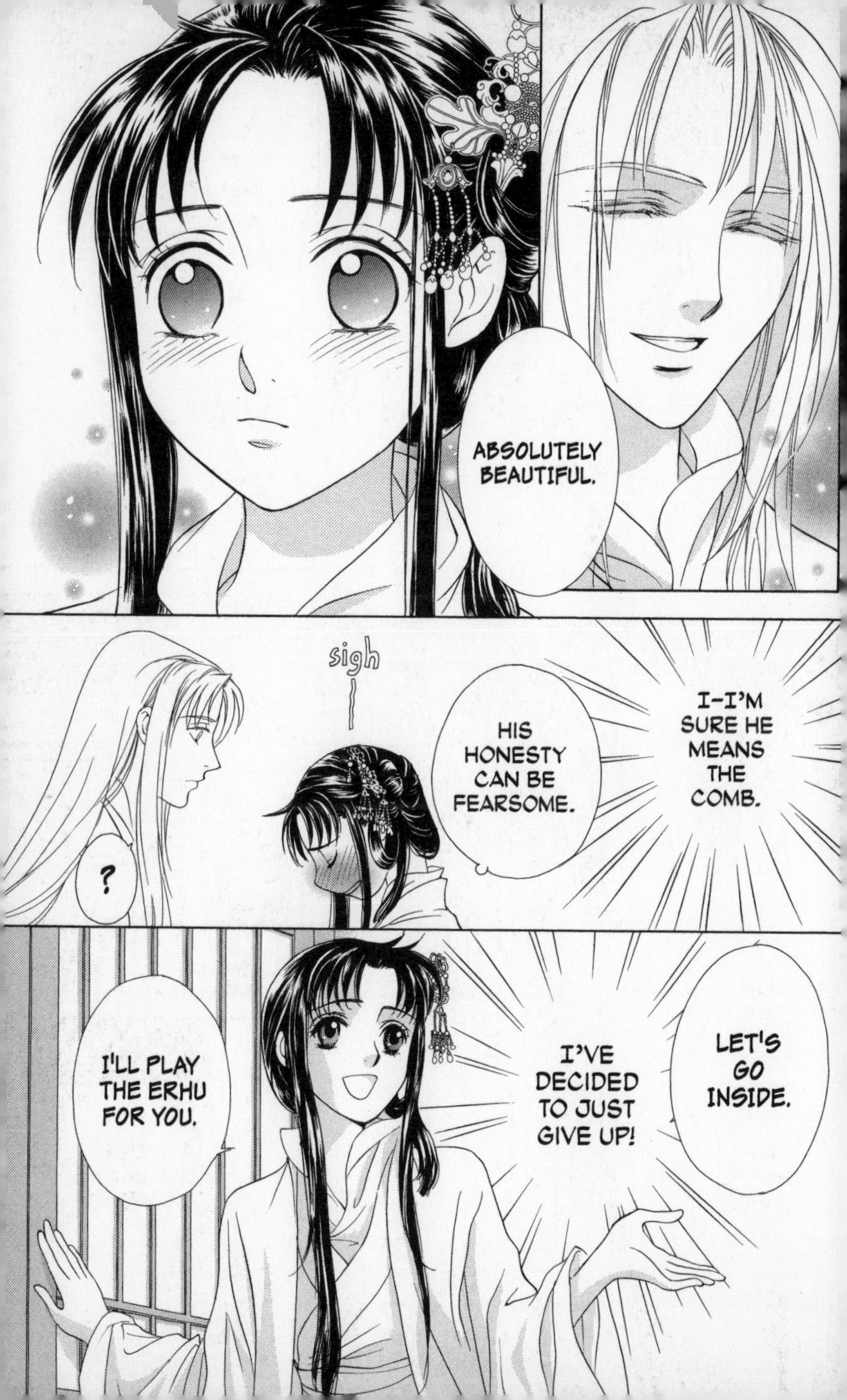
ABSOLUTELY BEAUTIFUL.
I-I'M SURE HE MEANS THE COMB.
HIS HONESTY CAN BE FEARSOME.
sigh
?
LET'S GO INSIDE.
I'VE DECIDED TO JUST GIVE UP!
I'LL PLAY THE ERHU FOR YOU.

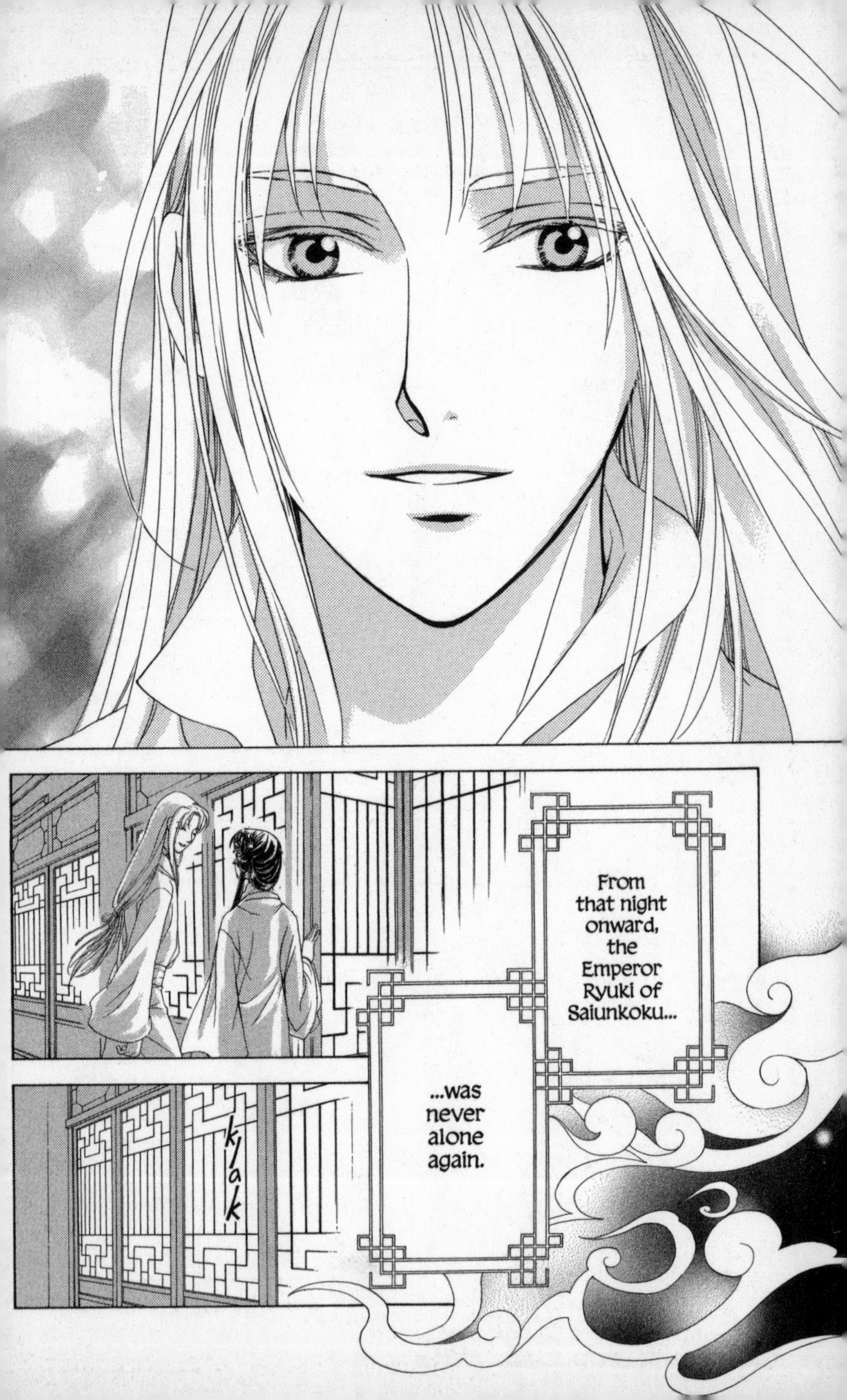
From that night onward, the Emperor Ryuki of Saiunkoku...
...was never alone again.
klak

❖ Illustrator's Note ❖

Kairi Yura

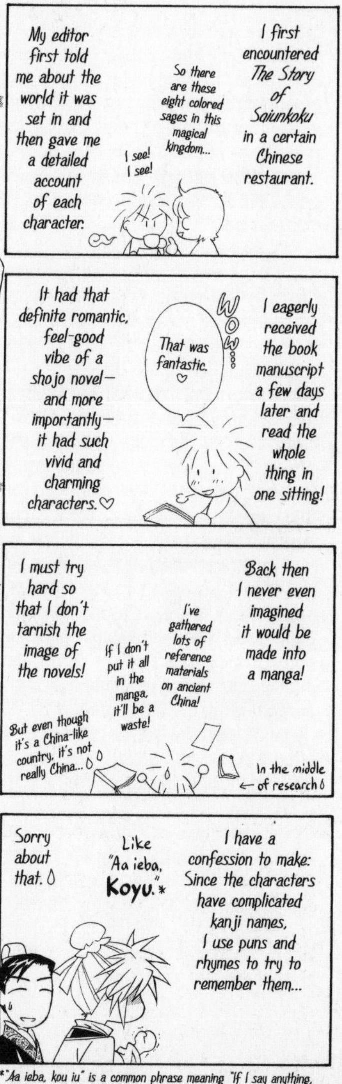
I first encountered *The Story of Saiunkoku* in a certain Chinese restaurant.
So there are these eight colored sages in this magical kingdom...
I see! I see!
My editor first told me about the world it was set in and then gave me a detailed account of each character.
I eagerly received the book manuscript a few days later and read the whole thing in one sitting!
WOW
That was fantastic. ♡
It had that definite romantic, feel-good vibe of a shojo novel—and more importantly—it had such vivid and charming characters. ♡
Back then I never even imagined it would be made into a manga!
In the middle of research
I've gathered lots of reference materials on ancient China!
If I don't put it all in the manga, it'll be a waste!
I must try hard so that I don't tarnish the image of the novels!
But even though it's a China-like country, it's not really China...
I have a confession to make: Since the characters have complicated kanji names, I use puns and rhymes to try to remember them...
Like "Aa ieba, Koyu."*
Sorry about that.

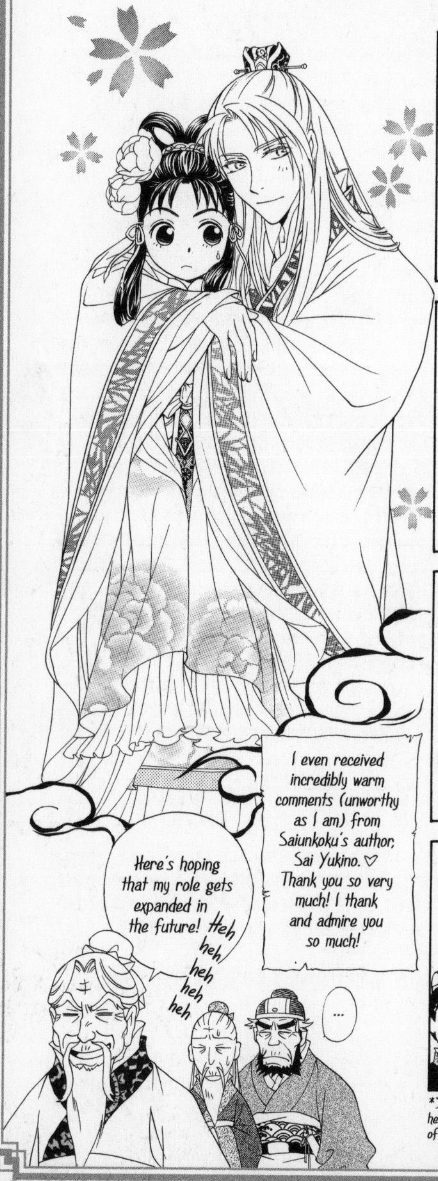
I even received incredibly warm comments (unworthy as I am) from Saiunkoku's author, Sai Yukino. ♡ Thank you so very much! I thank and admire you so much!
Here's hoping that my role gets expanded in the future!
Heh heh heh heh heh
...

*"Aa ieba, kou iu" is a common phrase meaning "If I say anything, he has a comeback." The "comeback" is close to the pronunciation of Koyu's name.

❖ Author's Note ❖

Sai Yukino

It's been about three years since I received Yura Sensei's illustrations for my novels. Despite how busy she was, she kindly humored me as I went on and on with my requests like a wailing baby demon. And now she's even gone so far as to turn the story into a manga! Three years ago I never would have dreamed this could happen. I'm sure poor Yura Sensei must have been thinking, "Oh boy, how did it come to this...[sweatdrop]?" But the way *Saiunkoku* comes to life on every page of this manga through her beautiful artwork is so amazing. Reading it has really been like a dream come true.

You could say the first and greatest happiness that has come out of *The Story of Saiunkoku* for me was being able to meet Yura Sensei. Strictly speaking this manga isn't just a manga adaptation of the novels. I mean, the story may be the same, but there's more to it; it's the way the characters speak and move, the progression of their hearts, each individual phrase and expression, the balance between serious and comical moments, even the few original lines Yura Sensei added in there—every little thing in this manga is just bursting with the essence of *Saiunkoku*. Even the things I couldn't fully describe in the books she somehow expressed perfectly through her drawings. (Without me even telling her about them!) I truly take my hat off to her. In fact, the manga actually got me thinking there wasn't enough sensuality in the novels... I'm sorry, R**ki, Ko**, S**ei... Your author completely forgot that you three are gorgeous men... I guess I just never put you guys in the right atmosphere, etc., the way she did. It's like Yura Sensei and I were both looking at the same tangerine, and while I expressed it by writing about it, she expressed it by drawing it. It's in that sense that I mean this is not merely a manga adaptation—it's another telling of *The Story of Saiunkoku* that is as true as my own. Plus it includes a certain charm that is unique to Yura Sensei's illustrations. This is the sort of book you'd want to read over and over, and even if you already know what's going to happen, your heart will pound each time. That's how good a manga this is in my opinion.

Since I started writing *Saiunkoku* so many blessings have showered down on me. This manga is by far the most amazing blessing of all. I feel such immense gratitude to Yura Sensei that I can't even find words to express it fully. Everything I've written here doesn't even scratch the surface.

So, everyone, I hope you'll truly enjoy Yura Sensei's take on *The Story of Saiunkoku* as much as I have.

雪乃紗衣

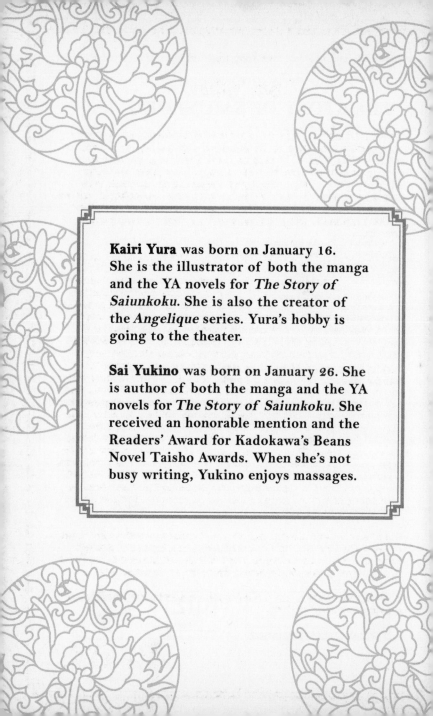

Kairi Yura was born on January 16. She is the illustrator of both the manga and the YA novels for *The Story of Saiunkoku*. She is also the creator of the *Angelique* series. Yura's hobby is going to the theater.

Sai Yukino was born on January 26. She is author of both the manga and the YA novels for *The Story of Saiunkoku*. She received an honorable mention and the Readers' Award for Kadokawa's Beans Novel Taisho Awards. When she's not busy writing, Yukino enjoys massages.

THE STORY OF SAIUNKOKU
Volume 1

Shojo Beat Edition

ART
KAIRI YURA
STORY
SAI YUKINO

Translation & English Adaptation/Su Mon Han
Touch-up Art & Lettering/Sabrina Heep
Design/Yukiko Whitley
Editor/Nancy Thistlethwaite

Saiunkoku Monogatari Volume 1
© Kairi YURA 2006
© Sai YUKINO 2006
First published in Japan in 2006 by KADOKAWA SHOTEN Publishing Co., Ltd.,
Tokyo. English translation rights arranged with KADOKAWA SHOTEN Publishing
Co., Ltd., Tokyo.

Printed in the U.S.A.

Published by VIZ Media, LLC
P.O. Box 77010
San Francisco, CA 94107

10 9 8 7 6 5 4 3 2 1
First printing, November 2010

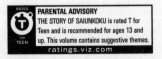